BEING
experiencing
a numinous
reality

ANDY GREEN

LITTLEFOX PRESS

BEING: Experiencing a numinous reality
Andy Green

Published by Littlefox Press
PO Box 816
Kyneton VIC 3144

ISBN: 978-0-646-80886-4 (paperback)

Notes: Includes endnotes

First published 2021
Copyright © Andy Green 2021

No part of this book may be resold, hired out, reproduced, stored in a retrieval system or transmitted in any form or by any electronic, mechanical or other means without the prior written consent of the author or the publisher.

Thank you to my wife Kavisha Mazzella for the original cover photo taken in Tuscany Italy (and Valdo the 'philosopher' in the image) to Joe Malignaggi at joemal.com for creative work with the original image and cover design, and to Sharon Dunn at Greengraphics for the beautiful design layout of the book.

Copy editing by Kerin Zable-Brown

BEING

experiencing
a numinous
reality

PHILOSOPHY

Philosophy is intrinsic to human beings, regardless of era, nationality or education. Wondering about the nature of existence, and how to live, is basic to us *Sapiens*, the wise hominid. It's what makes us sapient.

Curiosity is the driver of philosophy; but curiosity can be stunted by cultural and ideological conditioning - programming. Philosophy can also be stymied when it narrows to dogmatic or purely academic pursuits: when it turns away from its real purpose as a love of wisdom. A turning away that ignores our multi-dimensional nature.

The philosopher's home can be the university, but in truth it is the universe at large. We're philosophers when we question existing structures, conventions or beliefs to discover not only conceptual truths but lived ones.

If you're steady in this philosophical journey, you discover the marvels of our intellectual prowess. And further, that intellect and language point to the reality that *intelligence* is also not constrained by human sensibilities, as *it* informs nothing less than everything. Experiencing inner stillness brings this understanding.

Knowing and experiencing that *intelligence* is the subject matter of this book.

CONTENTS

ACKNOWLEDGMENTS   [i]

INTRODUCTION   [iii]

PART 1: AWARENESS IS OUR EXPERIENCE OF CONSCIOUSNESS   [3]

1. BEGINNINGS OF AWAKENING   [5]

    In the middle of a new era in self-knowing   [8]
    Awareness is our primary intimacy   [10]
    Is the 'self' real?   [14]
    Awareness and identity   [16]
    The body *is* desire   [18]
    The Truth of Being   [20]

2. KNOWING OUR IDENTITY CHANGES EVERYTHING   [23]

    Awakening from the collective 'waking-dream' of individualism   [26]
    Self-absorbed mind is a resistance to Being   [28]
    Understanding 'no-self' is experiential   [31]
    Resting in awareness transforms the fragmentation of self   [33]
    Transcendence – the illusion of 'self' striving for ideals   [34]
    When the 'self' breaks down   [35]
    Navigating the 'dark night'   [39]
    Without 'self' comes true co-operation   [40]

3. 'SEEING' WITHOUT BELIEVING   [43]

    'Seeing' is beyond believing   [43]
    'Seeing' without filter   [45]
    What is believing?   [47]
    Belief is the illusion of certainty   [50]
    A reflection on believing in God   [54]
    'God', a metaphor for separation   [57]

4. EMBRACING IMPERMANENCE AND UNCERTAINTY [61]

    The certainty that awareness provides is the truth of Being [63]
    Welcoming impermanence by resting in awareness [65]
    Let go, and rejoice! [67]
    Finding our true nature [68]

5. NO-MIND AND NON-DUALITY [70]

    Individuating from tribal group-think [73]
    Silence is everywhere if we are good at listening [75]
    Different kinds of laziness [77]
    Meditation and no-mind [80]
    Attachment – not thought – is the problem [83]
    No-mind and spirituality [86]

6. FREEDOM BEYOND THE KNOWN [90]

    Accepting 'what is', is to rest in reality [93]
    Freedom is much more than an ability to choose [97]
    Mistakes and consequences [99]
    Freedom brings responsibility [101]
    Choice-less awareness [106]
    Separation is suffering [108]

PART 2: OUR EPISTEMIC WINDOWS: THE PHENOMENAL AND THE NOUMENAL [113]

7. 'BEING' IN WESTERN PHILOSOPHY [115]

    The mystical in Western philosophy [117]
    A rationalist experiences the mystical [119]
    Mysticism: experiencing the expansion of consciousness [122]
    The noumenal in Western philosophy [124]
    Metaphysics of Being in Ancient Greece [126]
    Baruch Spinoza's 'infinite substance' [129]
    Noumenal and phenomenal resolve experientially in one reality [132]
    The split in Western philosophy – analytic and continental [135]
    Continental philosophy [137]
    The 'subjective' and 'objective' are different modes of thought [140]
    Process oriented philosophy [144]
    No-thingness is 'knowing consciousness' [148]
    For the philosopher, Being is the elephant in the room [151]

8. OBJECTIVE KNOWING AND DIRECT PERCEPTION [155]

    The meaning of knowing [156]
    Knowing in science [158]
    Rationality: its uses and abuses [160]
    Epistemology: two types of knowing [162]
    All human knowledge is completely subjective [166]
    The rise of 'objectivist' knowledge [169]
    Conceptual reality is real, but there is infinitely more to reality [173]

9. THE METHOD OF THE PHENOMENAL AND 'THE WAY' OF THE NOUMENAL [175]

    The primary assumption: separating the 'knower' from the 'known' [176]
    The scientific method/noumenal experience [181]
        A question is formulated based on observations [181]
        A testable hypothesis is formed – 'falsifiability' [182]
        An experiment must be repeatable [184]
        The force must be known [185]
        A scientific theory must make predictions [186]
        The analysis of results and peer review [187]
    The role of anomalies [188]
    The method is the 'ideal' but the reality is a little different [190]
    The authority science assumes is not absolute [192]
    Science is a unique narrative [194]

PART 3: THE ADVENTURE OF SCIENCE AND PHILOSOPHY [199]

10. AN INTELLIGENT UNIVERSE? [201]

    The great error: 'a mechanical universe' [202]
    Is the universe a random event? [205]
    Randomness is pivotal to a materialistic view [208]
    Chaos theory [211]
    The ordering and patterning intelligence of nature [212]
    Chaos: finding equilibrium in living [214]
    Fear of disorder drives the desire to control [217]
    Living creatively [219]

11. THE METAPHYSICS OF PHYSICS [221]

    Quantum granularity [223]
    Life in the quantum world [224]
    Wrestling with the 'double-slit' experiment [226]

Non-locality: Bell's theorem   [229]
Fundamental physics: 'an interpretive science'   [231]
Pilot wave theory   [236]
Super-determinism: destiny among 'hidden variables'   [239]
Quantum faddism   [242]
What is the fuss about Schrödinger's cat?   [243]

12. ONTOLOGY OF AN INTELLIGENT UNIVERSE   [247]

Physics encounters consciousness   [248]
Quantum theory and experiential knowing   [253]
Quantum theorists find parallels in Eastern philosophy   [257]
Bohm's universe of hidden order   [263]
The holographic universe and the 'holomovement'   [269]
An informed universe: consciousness interpenetrating matter   [272]

13. PROBLEMS IN PHYSICS AND PHILOSOPHY   [278]

Why is there something rather than nothing?   [279]
What is reality?   [287]
What is consciousness? Is there a 'consciousness' problem?   [291]
Materialism   [293]
Dualism   [297]
Idealism   [301]
Experiential non-duality   [307]
Science and the nature of time   [309]
The anthropic principle: is our universe special? Are we special?   [319]

PART 4: SPIRITUALITY – THE PATHLESS WAY   [327]

14. THE PARADOX OF TIME   [329]

Time, personal history and identity   [331]
Does time heal all wounds? Why it can be difficult to live in the now   [333]
Resolving the past: the body is a reservoir of consciousness   [338]
Living for the moment   [342]
The danger of 'short-cuts' to the now   [343]
Destiny   [347]
Freedom from time is a conduit to 'free energy'   [350]

15. SYNCHRONICITY AND OUR PERCEPTION OF REALITY [353]
    Collective unconscious [355]
    The archetypes [358]
    Collaboration between the physicist and the psychoanalyst [360]
    Synchronicity and non-locality [362]
    No-mind is the matrix of synchronicity [364]
    Jung and alchemy [366]
    Awakening consciousness: the kundalini [370]
    Experiencing kundalini [373]

16. HOW LANGUAGE AND CULTURE INFLUENCE OUR PERCEPTION OF REALITY [379]
    Collectivist and individualist cultures [382]
    Cultural views of 'matter' [384]
    Animate languages [386]
    Verb-based languages: events and processes rather than entities [388]
    Language and time [392]
    Language and space [395]
    The 'rheomode': David Bohm's new language system [398]
    Parallels between Indigenous people's world views and new physics [401]
    Perception beyond the influence of language [402]

17. TRADITIONS OF NON-DUALITY [406]
    Spontaneous insight: the 'Jnanis' of Advaita [409]
    The 'effortless way' of Taoist philosophers [414]
    No-mind of Gautama and Zen [419]
    Does a monastic culture exemplify a 'middle way'? [424]
    Stoicism: the individuating sage in harmony with Being [426]

PART 5: PILGRIMAGE WITHOUT A DESTINATION [433]

18. A NEW AGE BESET BY OLD PATTERNS [435]
    Fool's gold: the New Age spiritual marketplace [437]
    Fast tracking to nowhere [439]
    The vacuum of individualism [441]
    Appropriation of ancient practices [443]
    Gurus: the 'god-man/woman' complex and its 'shadow' [446]
    The shadow is ignorance [449]
    Can we be masters of Being? [452]
    Is a guru necessary? [453]

19. FREED FROM ILLUSIONS [459]

    Is spirituality an evolutionary process? [460]
    Spirituality: 'a way without a path' [462]
    'Non-doing' with practices [464]
    Residing in awareness: 'presence' – the only spiritual practice [467]
    The myth of enlightenment [468]
    Signatures of spirituality [473]

20. ABIDING IN THE REAL [475]

    Living authentically [479]
    Deep listening [483]
    Strengthening the 'awareness muscle' [486]
    Living harmoniously is the ending of stress [489]
    A life of meaning [491]
    The absolute and relative resolve in experiential knowing [494]

REFERENCES [500]

ACKNOWLEDGMENTS

I am grateful to a number of people: my lovely daughters who encouraged me in the process of preparing this manuscript; Alex Sturmer who provided initial advice and corrections in the earliest phase of the manuscript; Linda Joy who gave valuable advice and grammatical correction; Melvyn Cann my philosophy lecturer at University for suggestions on an early draft of the manuscript; and Louisa Dent Pearce, who edited earlier versions of this book and whose patience and insight have proved invaluable. The selection of final editor was indeed a fortuitous one. Kerin Zable-Brown's thorough reading, correction and questions have been marvellous, ensuring the book was readable and accessible, maintaining a coherence throughout.

I am grateful to John Macgregor for his rigorous critical assessment and patience with my linguistic foibles, which has proved invaluable and for sharing in our morning 'philosophy corner'. My appreciation also goes to Christine Mathieu who gave salient advice, corrections and encouragement and subsequently publishing the book with 'Littlefox Press'. A special thank you is due to my darling wife Kavisha for her perseverance, love, wisdom and valuable feedback.

Most of this book has been written in, inspired and informed by Dja Dja Wurrung country. Writing in this sacred area of its original custodians, the Dja Dja Wurrung people, has been a privilege, and I pay homage to their elders past and present.

INTRODUCTION

'The unexamined life is not worth living.'
—Socrates, during his trial for heresy in Athens (399 BC)

Socrates was in trouble. By encouraging the youth of Athens to be curious and to question those in authority, he was challenging the political and religious status quo. Socrates was in trouble not for teaching people *what* to think, but for teaching them *how* to think. The price for such philosophical mischief was the choice between exile and a fatal dose of hemlock. He defended himself at his trial, but to no avail, in the end accepting the hemlock.

Socrates symbolises the great spirit of enquiry: a search for truth and authenticity, as well as a resolute defiance in the face of state-sanctioned bullying and forces that keep people shackled in unquestioned, limiting beliefs. He championed the 'examined life' as an antidote to living in a state of semi-conscious slumber, as if on 'auto-pilot'. As with most states and political milieus since ancient Greece, the agenda, with some modification, continues to be the teaching of 'what to think' and 'what to believe', the tenets of which, if accepted, invariably lead to a perilous form of collective sleep that is corrosive to a consciously civic culture.

I have always been curious about the meaning of Socrates' 'examined life', and I have used this as a recurrent theme throughout this book. The philosophical expansion, sometimes referred to as the 'Greek miracle', occurred with the pre-Socratics, most notably Parmenides, Heraclitus, and later with Socrates, Plato, Diogenes and the Cynics, Zeno of Citium and the Stoics, and Plato's student Aristotle. And, simultaneously with the pre-Socratics, in different parts of the globe around 500 BCE, Lao Tzu and Gautama Buddha were engaged in a similar examination of living, but with a more spiritual bent.

Yet if we only examine life through intellectual enquiry and analysis, as has been the way in the modern era of Western philosophy, we reduce ourselves to a particular thinking function of mind – rationality – thereby making our examining only partial. Important as our ability to think and to be rational may be, there is a profoundly deeper kind of knowing in the core of consciousness that does not involve thought at all. There is infinitely more to us, and our capacity to know, than just our ability to think and be rational.

At the heart of this 'examining' is the knowing of who we are, because it is in this knowing, that we come to understand how we can be limited by our attachment to the mind itself. This wisdom is exemplified to some degree in the teachings of Socrates, more so in the Stoics, but particularly in their two Eastern philosopher-colleagues Lau Tzu and Gautama Buddha.

In Western culture post-Plato and Aristotle, the mind and its capacity for rational thinking had 'transcendental' status as evidence of the divine, and hence was commonly regarded as an idealised source of human identity. Later, Neo-Platonism was used in developing the transcendentalist religious culture of Christianity, with its emphasis on deifying Jesus, the projection of a transcendent God, and the supreme authority of the church.

Fierce religious attachments ensured that the truth in Plato's and Plotonis' spiritual philosophy, and the depth of the human being remained largely undiscovered. The dictum was to follow and believe, as an enslavement to the developing religious culture of Christianity. To the curious, the questioning of this believing culture, or the finding of other ways of knowing that did not involve the authority of the church, could place your life in peril. But curiosity in humans is irrepressible.

Curiosity given free reign will uncover that if we are seeking our identity through the mind by looking at how it attaches to our thoughts, to an ideology, to beliefs and to self-images, our investigation will be superficial. Superficial, because we have conflated two things, thought and consciousness (although these are not really things). This leads to the assumption that thought *is* consciousness, a common error throughout Western cognitive history. Thought arises from consciousness, and attachment is the process of thought attaching to itself. Thought as an instrument of consciousness is not its ontological genesis.

This book explores the nature of consciousness and how it is not reducible to thought. The result of this misunderstanding, arising from attachment, has led people to seek their identity in their thoughts, their beliefs, and their stories. It has led to a toxic form of dualism which has its origins in the mistaken identity of the ego or self, and is what places us in peril separating us from each other and the living systems of the planet. The natural duality of our phenomenal experience and the emergence of science are not part of this toxicity.

The habitual belief that the mind (consciousness) and body (matter) are separate, emerges from dualism, possibly originating from the Aryan invaders of Greece, that was to find its primary voice in Plato's transcendentalist philosophy. Yet the Platonic universe was still a oneness with a universal organising intelligence, the Logos. With the advent of early Christianity Plato's oneness went missing. A transcendental God was separate, humans were tainted with original sin, seeing themselves as both separate from and had dominion over nature. Salvation lay in the unquestioned following of the church and its doctrines. These dualisms were toxic resulting in great suffering to life across the globe.

Dualism holds the belief that equates consciousness and thought, with consciousness being of a different substance from matter; matter being a *separate dead substance*, foundational to the physical universe. Yet there is a true jewel of dualism: science. Science is the primary epistemic instrument of thought and is an essential way of knowing for us, and for our survival. Our phenomenal experience is founded in the fundamental duality of subject and its object of study. The beginnings of science can be traced to Aristotle, Plato's student. And science has been, and continues to be, a remarkable human endeavour. Duality used specifically in the sphere of science is its true area of genius, but when fuelled with irrational beliefs, it is *the* source of problems.

However, to only perceive duality is a limitation. To the incurious, dualism is akin to being satisfied that the ripples and the surface area of a pool of water are all there is to know. To the curious, the ripples on the surface signify something more, pointing to hidden depths beyond the empirical reach of the mind and senses. Curiosity reveals that there is no separation: that the surface and the depth are one body of water. This is a metaphor for our true nature, and the true nature of the universe itself. Adopting a dualistic mindset is a path to relative truth in the form of science, but is in error when it comes to human identity, our relationship with each other, with nature, and ultimately with life itself. This is because ultimately there is no separation of different substances as consciousness and matter. There is only *one* reality – that of non-duality. That is, only *consciousness*, with 'mind' and 'matter' as conditioned interpretive concepts of the one reality, consciousness.

When one rests in the real beyond the conceptual, there is no 'mind' that is separate from the 'body', and there is no separation from nature: we are nature. Thought is just one aspect of consciousness. Mind and body are different manifestations of the *one* consciousness, as a *living* universe. Nature, the universe and all that it is, is consciousness.

This book explores how the universal error of mistaken identity, arising from our habitual process of 'attaching', results in our experience of division. The belief that this separation is real is the source of our troubles.

There are five sections in this book: identity beyond the narrative of the 'self', the nature of awareness, freedom, Being and nothingness; epistemology – how we know what we know and the different types of knowing; the adventure of science and philosophy, and perennial mysteries such as time, consciousness and the nature of spirituality found in certain traditions of 'non-duality'; and, in the final section, some patterns of discord in the New Age, on authenticity, presence, and ending with further reflections on nothingness, Being and spirituality.

The genesis of this book lies in two experiences: the first is meditation, which I began to practise at the age of 20, and which inspired an examination of my life at a level much deeper than is possible by intellectual enquiry alone. The second is a natural curiosity, which led me to ask lots of questions, and eventually to take a break of several years from my undergraduate studies of philosophy. For by the time I had reached the second year of an Arts degree, I could see where this academic road was leading. I had developed a certain level of skill in clever argument, and a surface knowledge of certain theoretical positions, but I surmised that this knowledge was quite superficial, only encouraging dexterity in thinking. Where was the wisdom?

I sought an examination of life that was *experiential*, that would engage me at the very core of Being. I came to understand that the kind of philosophy offered at university – particularly the form of semantic gymnastics of the 'analytic approach' – was only addressing a tiny part of life. The convolutions of thought and impenetrable language spoke more of sophistry than wisdom. Only a temporary halt to my academic studies could enable me to satisfy this quest. I was after a philosophy that could not be assessed academically as pass or fail, nor a structure of belief, but rather as a way of living. I sought a philosophy that offered some form of salvation from what I perceived as the intellectual dryness and confusion on offer at university. I yearned for the deeper meaning and significance in living. I soon discovered there is 'a way' that brings each moment of existence into sharp relief, revealing a numinous experience of reality and the true nature of spirituality.

My relationship to thought, to emotions, to my personal history and to what I thought my identity was, changed completely. My break from academic studies, coupled with meditative practice, created space for a kind of 'inner revolution'. A couple of years into travelling and meditating, I was experiencing life in a profoundly different way, as though I had emerged from a trance. Everything I was experiencing seemed to be vibrating with life connected in seamless Being. And some forty-three years later, this experience continues.

This state of being was not 'subjective' or arising from mental speculation, belief or imagining. While thinking was there as needed, I was largely experiencing living directly, without thought. I was discovering a new epistemic, one of knowing directly without the mediation of thought. This in itself was revolutionary. With it came a deep non-intellectual understanding of life. To my amazement, my mind was mostly *still* and exceptionally lucid. And, importantly, this experience was found without drugs, despite them being readily available (even though I did try a couple of plant-based substances, but only very spasmodically).

I have been living this way for most of my adult life and now, in my sixties, I have realised that there is no big 'arrival', there is nothing to attain. Living is, instead, a moment to moment proposition. The restlessness felt in the search for transcendental experience, whether it is for enlightenment, or God, is characterised by duality: the restless search of the ego to attain something, such as an idealised state like enlightenment. Instead, when we directly experience Being, this 'here now-ness' is *immanent*. And, in the words of Lao Tzu, one of my favourite philosophers: 'If you want to awaken all of humanity, awaken all of yourself'.

There are many things in the way we live that signify that our relationship with the mind is clearly out of balance. This is seen in our restless search for identity, for love, for happiness, for experience and for owning stuff. 'Out of balance' is when thought runs away with itself. Our relationship with the mind is like 'the tail wagging the dog', because we have become so completely identified with the mind, and also with the body. This is heightened in a digital age especially, when people's minds seem increasingly hyperactive and in a general state of distraction, over-stimulation and hyper-function. Can the mind solve this?

The following pages challenge the cherished notion that our beliefs and ideologies (whether religious, scientific, philosophical or political) are the answer to our ills. But we cannot solve our problems by using the very thing that created them. We cannot just 'think our way out' of our predicaments. However, to realise that thought is only an aspect or manifestation of consciousness, and to know that by not attaching to thought, a different level of understanding does reveal itself. We can then experience *a way of harmony*, wherein we have discovered a 'knowing source' in us beyond thought. We will understand that thought can be utilised differently, 'in service' of consciousness. Most of us experience thought differently, in the form of the 'thinker' or 'ego' holding sovereignty, as ruler.

The great 'seers' of the ages encourage us to look for the solution beyond our mental conditioning, beyond belief, and beyond thought altogether. This reveals the essential innocence in the heart of every human being, showing us a way that is not ideological, and how to live harmoniously. If we listen to the advice of the seers, and do not blindly follow nor believe, to discover the truth of Being for ourselves, we will know our identity, and our life on Earth will radically change. The solution to our ills is spiritual, rather than religious, scientific or secular. This solution would lead to a transformation in political, social, economic and environmental states of affairs, because all social and environmental policy would be informed by love. Radical indeed.

The specific type of knowing which is the basis of a non-dual experience of living is sometimes called the 'original mind', the 'natural mind' or 'no-mind'. This is available to everyone regardless of education because 'no-mind' is not conceptual knowing and is only to known experientially. In 'no-mind' we perceive or know directly. That is, knowing with the lens of perception clear of conditioned assumptions and beliefs.

So much about our living these days is complex, and if we do not experience a deep inner quiet we can become terribly lost. Through 'seeing things as they are', and deep listening, we cut through complexity. Complexity dissolves in the spontaneous experience of inner silence, which becomes the source of an ever-present elixir of renewal. What is new is an abiding experience of presence in all the activities one is engaged in.

Living consciously in this way reveals a paradox. For while we are embodied and have a specifically human experience with our relationships, families, work or study, we are also connected to the vastness of Being that is an infinity beyond measure. This boundless awareness understands the relative (phenomenal) and the absolute (noumenal) as one.

The ultimate nature of our existence is not one of duality – of self and other. Life cannot be fully understood by objectivism as found in scientific descriptions, explanations or theories, nor by the subjectivism offered in religious belief or imaginative speculation. Both of these are different forms of thought; both are inadequate to the task of apprehending reality at the deepest level. Experiencing reality as numinous is neither subjective nor objective, because it is not a product of thought, and it is not something attained by the ego entity. Rather, we experience the numinous only as our 'lens' is unconditioned.

This book is a call for a different epistemic than the one we are conditioned to as subject and object. It is a call for *direct experience* rather than knowing through the filter of thought, with its theories, ideologies and beliefs. Experiencing the numinous involves decluttering the mind of all its assumptions and prejudices, to reveal the absolute.

A note on terms used

'**Awareness**' is our experience of consciousness. It is prior to thought and the only certainty we have. In our awareness appears the ephemeral: thoughts, emotions, sensations and perceptions.

'**Being**' refers to the all-inclusive, alive universe that can only be known experientially, beyond the mind. Being includes the animate and inanimate, the formed and the formless. Rather than being subjective, which implies that it is a 'thing' concocted by one's thinking, it is beyond thinking.

'**Consciousness**' is Being, as the universe itself is consciousness. What are referred to as matter and mind are different manifestations of the one consciousness. This may seem outlandish to a materialist or a dualist, and to religious orthodoxies. A more complete discussion occurs in Chapter 10.

'**Duality**' is the belief that there are separate realities – of mind and body, spirit and matter, and the separation of phenomenal existence into things and beings.

'**Epistemology**' is the theory of knowledge: what we know and how we know and the different types of knowing available to human beings.

'**Immanent**' means existing, operating or remaining within; of, or relating to, the pantheistic conception of God as being present throughout the universe, compared with transcendence (see below).

'**Metaphysics**' is specifically investigating the nature of reality, and this can include how the universe came into being.

'**Mind**' usually refers to the thinking aspect of consciousness; however there are occasions where I use this in the broader Western philosophical sense. The context should make this clear.

'Non-duality' is the experiential apprehension of undivided reality.

'Numinous' comes from the Latin word 'numen', much employed by Roman authors, meaning divine will or power, or divinity. This word stems from its cognate verb 'nuere', meaning 'to nod': that by which a god's will is achieved. *Numen* is the divine mystery arousing awe. Noumenal was conceived as the opposite to phenomenal, being that which is beyond sensual experience. It signifies a profundity that is beyond thought and rationality, giving us insight into the hidden order of Being.

'Ontological' is sometimes used in exchange for 'metaphysical' because both primarily deal with the origins of things or existence.

'Panpsychism' is the view that consciousness is a universal and primordial feature of all things ('pan' – all; 'psyche' – mind/soul).

'Pantheism' is the view that all existence is divine – that the universe or nature is a manifestation of an all-encompassing immanent god.

'Presence' is experiential undivided attentiveness in the now. Also, presence-awareness.

'Transcendence' refers to a climbing or going beyond to a world of otherness: to a divine realm (Platonic) or to a supernatural God (Christian).

Acronyms
CI – Copenhagen Interpretation
MWI – Many Worlds Interpretation
PWT – Pilot Wave Theory

A note on 'self': In Advaita circles 'self' is used in lower case to indicate the individual ego, and in upper case to indicate the absolute 'Self' as one's true identity - *universal consciousness*. In Buddhist circles 'self' is used solely to indicate the thinker or ego.

Generally I have opted for the Buddhist way to use 'self' as only pointing to ego, but this is not always possible because 'Self' is used differently in Greek and Advaita to convey a different dimension of human experience. Knowing the Self is an intimate experience of our identity as Being.

PART ONE

AWARENESS IS OUR EXPERIENCE OF CONSCIOUSNESS

Our experiencing or capacity for awareness is the true and direct source of our knowing, prior to thought. We can be aware of being aware, which instantly takes us to the source of Being itself.

CHAPTER 1

BEGINNINGS OF AWAKENING

Awareness is our experience of consciousness. Without awareness there is no curiosity. Curiosity drives us to find our identity, but sometimes in the process of this investigation we can experience unanticipated challenges to our sense of who we are, and what is real. This is when our curiosity pushes us beyond what we have known, and what we have come to believe is real; where our awareness has expanded beyond parameters that we know. Here, habitual modes of thinking and beliefs must be left behind, in order to apprehend the new.

As a sixteen-year-old, I experienced this in a significant and unprecedented way. It was like a crack opening in my apparently stable universe. As a regular teenager, I was rebellious and shared the troubles, the 'blues' and excitements of my friends. One day, while lying in the sun after being in the wild surf at an Australian beach, I experienced a profound sense of awe as I looked up at the sky. I suddenly felt no separation from the sky, from the clouds and everything around me. There was no time. There was no 'me'. I was just this mysterious 'awareness'. Beneath the sounds of pounding surf, I was engulfed in a unique silence.

Everything seemed to be touched with a kind of luminosity. I felt an elevated lucidity and I noticed that my mind, normally busy and filled with hormonally driven urges, was now completely quiet. I had no sense of time so it may have been for just a few minutes or half an hour that I lay there. I was eventually drawn back into ordinary reality when a friend came over to speak to me. Afterwards I felt unsettled, for I had no frame of reference for what I had experienced. I knew only that it was a glimpse of something of a different order of reality, something unconditioned and unknown. This glimpse of another reality was to remain dormant for a few years.

In my formative years, nothing was mentioned of awareness, the importance of being present, or the possibility of experiencing some universal truth. In my earlier school years as a Catholic Christian, I was taught that I had to believe in God, follow certain religious rituals and adopt a whole ideology without question. But there was nothing in this to feed a natural curiosity, or a knowing of an experiential nature.

Curiosity, in fact, was discouraged. Later, at university, I learnt the clear demarcations of duality: the mind was separate from the body. This was exemplified in learning of age-old intellectual dilemmas: the mind versus the body, free will versus determinism, theism versus atheistic materialism, empiricism versus rationalism. In 'Ethics' we explored rule-based ethics versus rationalist utilitarianism, while in politics we argued about socialism versus democracy. But there was nothing about awareness or experiential knowing.

A notable exception to this was an inspiring philosophy lecturer teaching 'the philosophy of music' in my undergraduate degree in philosophy. He had to surreptitiously introduce experiential exercises in his tutorials in order to convey insights that were outside the domains of rational argument. As students we were invited to collaborate secretly as his methods were hidden from the watchful gaze of his departmental seniors. Word of his 'experiential endeavours' had got out previously, and he had already been warned against committing these transgressions against academic teaching protocols.

The lecturer engaged us in experiential exercises that pointed towards another dimension of healing through sound, that expressed a fundamental unity beyond the duality of rationalism and empiricism. In other classes generally there was little encouragement to question the dualisms that were part of the programmed mindset in Western philosophy. We could question within certain parameters, but basically we had to fit in and play the academic game, which to my mind was an obstacle to curiosity.

In fact, everything I learned seemed to be contra-awareness.

The culture of religious belief, and the intellectually clever culture on offer at university, seemed stultifying in their different ways. Some of the analytical philosophy I studied amounted to a complicated form of 'semantic mental hygiene' that, in a very sophisticated way, seemed to say very little. On reading it I very quickly developed a feeling of being mentally 'boxed in'. Philosophy was no longer the love of wisdom or a path to freedom, but the love of semantics.

Curiosity drove me to seek knowledge outside these constrictions. I soon found my way to the new voices that were arriving from distant shores. They spoke of a different order of understanding and experience of living. These 'teachings' articulated insights about 'awareness', 'consciousness' and 'experiential knowing'. And in doing so, they addressed what my native culture had failed to address. The truth in these teachings resonated with me. This was in the mid-1970s, an era of self-knowing was on the horizon and, with a rush of enthusiasm mixed with starry-eyed idealism, I felt I was breaking new ground.

In the middle of a new era in self-knowing

Historically, the prospect of 'self-knowing' in European culture was seen as an endeavour solely for the religious or intellectual elite. By the 20th century this was changing; it was considered less elitist to enquire at least intellectually, as it became possible for poorer people to study at a tertiary level. There was broader access to education for the emerging middle classes. And for the first time, importantly, women were included. There was more sophisticated, philosophically informed intellectual enquiry, and also an increased willingness to challenge authoritarian structures of knowledge and traditional belief.

Nonetheless, enquiry into the nature of identity was generally not viewed as a pathway to happiness, and was still largely considered an intellectual exercise, exclusively involving thought. 'Knowing' was generally interpreted as knowing through the mind, with the assumption that consciousness equals the act of thinking. Knowledge was gained from reading books, attending university and becoming sophisticated in theories, debating, thinking and analysing, and all in a rational manner. To me, the teaching of philosophy seemed arid and irrelevant and so I planned my escape route.

I left university for a few years and discovered a different kind of knowing – that of 'direct perception', as expressed in the wisdom teachings from the East. This way of knowing was also familiar to some mystics of the West and the Middle East, but often there was great risk associated with their expressing this.

Teachings of this ilk, such as the Tibetan wisdom teachings, ancient Buddhist and Taoist texts, meditation techniques, ancient Hindu philosophy and Yogic practices had now become freely available in Western culture. Translations of Middle Eastern poets and philosophers were also available. In the past many of these traditional wisdom teachings were only for a chosen few initiates. However, now they were accessible for the first time to an audience completely unfamiliar with these traditions.

Tibetan lamas and Indian gurus journeyed to the West and so we became familiar with Jetsun Milarepa. We read *The Tibetan Book of the Dead*, Lao Tzu's *Tao Te Ching*, Chuang Tzu's playful wisdom, and the compelling *Secret of The Golden Flower*. We learnt of the Zen patriarchs and the Dzogchen teachings in Buddhism. We avidly read Krishnamurti, Nisaggadhata and Ramana Maharshi, along with the *Autobiography of a Yogi*, Patanjali's *Yoga Sutras*, Nagarjuna's *Fundamental Verses of the Middle Way*, and the Buddhist scripture *The Heart Sutra*. We read the poetry of Kabir, Rumi and Hafiz. We explored and were in awe of the confabulated teachings of Carlos Castaneda's Don Juan.

In the teachings from these diverse sources there were consistent messages: that suffering lies in attachment or clinging to the mind; that true happiness arises from experiencing liberation from attachment; that we must cultivate a harmonious and balanced life; that the deeper knowing of who we are lies in the non-conceptual experience of Being; and that the experience of 'non-duality' is the foundation of spirituality.

But after a few years of reading this material, I'd had enough because, regardless of their merit, I felt I had become colonised by all these teachings. I realised that it was still all 'second-hand information'. I did not want to be just another believer following blindly in others' footsteps. I realised that without having a genuine experience of the 'other dimensional' for myself, for all I knew, it was just a fabrication.

This insight was liberating. I let go of any beliefs in anything, simultaneously giving my curiosity complete free reign. I continued practising daily meditation of sitting in pure observation. That is: no mantras, visualisation, or specific techniques. Observation, in essence, is not a technique because all techniques involve thought. All meditation 'techniques' involve some kind of manipulation of consciousness, whether it is watching the breath, practising mantras, et cetera. I avoided reading any spiritual teaching. My curiosity burned with the pressing need to remain true to experiencing my own ignorance, as it was, and to be with what is. I read nothing for about two years.

Awareness is our primal intimacy

What is awareness? Awareness, in a useful analogy commonly used by Advaita teachers such as Rupert Spira, can be likened to a screen on which a movie is shown. The screen itself is at once removed from being affected by the characters, the thoughts, action and emotion and all the drama of the film, here representing the 'contents' of consciousness. Awareness (the screen) remains the same from birth to death. It does not age, for it is only the contents of consciousness that age: the body, memory, sensation, thinking, and so on. The screen, as awareness, remains unmoved or unscathed by the 'drama' of our living as it appears on it. We develop skilful ways in turning away from the screen of awareness as we identify with what appears on it: with repetitive habitual behaviours, through compulsive thinking, through addictions such as gambling, or the many substance addictions. Despite all the abuse of the 'self', awareness itself remains untouched, pristine.

Awareness is no-thing; it is not an 'it'. Everything that we know, that we think we know, that we feel and that we sense, happens *in* our awareness. Awareness is always there, even if subliminally. When we are in a deep sleep, we are aware that we have been in deep sleep, or that we have been dreaming.

Does awareness have a location? Is it in the body or, more specifically, in the brain (which is the standard view amongst those in the field of neuroscience)? If we look carefully, without any assumptions, awareness has no specific location. It is more immediately experienced in the head and throughout the body. But, equally, it is located in the world at large. It is in the apprehension of the apple on the table, in the table it is sitting on, in the grass of the lawn outside, in the distant hills and in the clouds above. Awareness, as our experience of consciousness, is both local and non-local. Awareness as consciousness is ubiquitous throughout nature.

Awareness is our immediate experience of consciousness. Our personal experience of awareness, once we investigate it, is really completely impersonal and universal. It is not your awareness and my awareness, because ultimately there is no demarcation separating consciousness and, as such, awareness.

Awareness gives us a knowing that is prior to thought and prior to language. Awareness gives us a primal knowing that we are one with the world around us, and that we are most fundamentally here and now. Awareness gives only the one, but the cognition of thought gives duality and the many. Being aware of awareness is not our thinking of it, but is our unique intimacy of Being, and this is only possible in humans. In a sense one cannot be aware of awareness, one can only *be* awareness.

Awareness is the light of Being. This means that awareness, as our experience of consciousness, is suffused throughout nature as a field of attention. We are only aware of this when we 'look' without thought or preconceptions of any kind; when our lens of perception is clear.

For example, when I am looking at the *being* sitting next to me that is my wife, and the *being* that is my cat sitting on the chair in the kitchen, and then as I move into the backyard and look at the *being* that is the massive tree in the center of it, and the birds – *beings* that are feeding in the bird-bath, I experience that this awareness or consciousness, is present in 'all' in varying degrees. When I am looking from this naked awareness I see beings that are ultimately not separate from Being, as the One Consciousness. I am using language and concepts now to point to a perception that is beyond both language and thought.

This naked awareness has no anthropomorphic conditioning, and it is not personal. Its origins are pre-cognitive and pre-linguistic. It does not deny the importance of our cognition and languages, nor the particular relationships that I have with each of the beings mentioned above (particularly my wife). In fact, all these relationships are enhanced in this experience of non-duality with Love.

It is the 'original mind' that precedes cognitive and linguistic development, that yields the noumenal. This is the 'Truth of Being'. It is our birthright. It is a oneness that we can experience while simultaneously enfolding the relative: the particular special relationships with unique people, animals, plants, things and places, and with the impersonal absolute – *Truth of Being*

Awareness, or the original mind, can be enhanced by meditative practices, and temporarily with certain drugs. Awareness in this way can be modulated just as a dimmer switch modulates light intensity, thereby illuminating the contents of what is perceived.

Awareness can be more globally experienced in the body, and at a very subtle level, particularly seen in Taoist Gong Fu masters, Qigong masters, and Tibetan yogis. Their special knowledge of extending normally unconscious domains of body experience is demonstrated in such practices as Tibetan 'tummo' breathing, that radically transforms the body's ability to withstand cold (important if one sits for long periods in the Himalayas).

Awareness, when not diminished by injury, addictions or an excessively busy mind, brings a perception of the nature of awareness itself. When there is awareness of awareness a shift in intensity follows because there is no separation: one is 'looking into infinity' without a separate you as the observer. Characteristically, this has a profound influence on our thinking, reflected in an experience of connectedness, and informing a global and holistic outlook. You become wise.

When we become aware of the 'world' as we generally know it, this 'world' is constructed by our thoughts and language, as we describe, label and explain things. The original mind or pure awareness becomes overlaid with a new epistemic as we learn cognitive processing, and a particular language. We can soon become completely distracted by the noise of this 'thought-language constructed world'. When we attach to this 'mindscape', we lose touch with a level of *unconstructed reality* that is not separate from, but metaphorically 'beneath' this. This world-cum-reality simply exists, as the silence of Being. But this 'silence' is always in peril of being obscured by the noise of many identities as we attach to the restless activity of 'self'-driven thinking and believing. The silence of Being, however, is always inescapably with us, just as the sun exists even when it is obscured by clouds. But is the 'self' real?

Is the 'self' real?

If asked who we *are*, we will usually respond with a narrative that may include some of the following: a nationality, an ethnicity, a gender, an occupation, a political or philosophical belief, a sexual orientation, a skin colour, a religion, core values, ancestral lines and stories, and a unique personal history. Our conditioning is to adopt these 'tags' for the purpose of constructing an individual notion of 'self'. This self can also include a particular knowing of how we respond to certain people, a particular moral code, how to behave in certain situations, and the like or dislike of certain things.

These constructs, as a definition of who we are, indicate what our preferences will be and how we will respond to certain things, people or situations. The 'self' is also central to our effort to control our environment, and the desire to create some ever-increasing level of certainty. But our construction of a constellation of thought patterns, beliefs and behaviours that we know as a 'self' is a form of mental rigidity, an unnecessary limitation, and it is an error.

The 'self' is a continuing narrative constructed by thought and memory. But does it capture the deeper truth of our identity? The fact is that we are infinitely more than a thought-constructed narrative. The idea of a 'self' limits who we are. And it is not that these tags are completely untrue, it is that they are superficial. When any one of them is seen as primary to our identity, we have moved into a form of delusion. For example, when we see the colour of our skin as being central to us, we have separated from all those without the same colour. It is this process of *identifying* with something (and it could be anything – skin colour, tribe, philosophy, religion, clothing) that brings problems. What drives this need to identify? Why identify with anything? Why attach to anything? To all these restless questions 'Being' is the answer, because we are habitually encouraged from childhood in a direction away from our spiritual source.

The belief in our constructed identity is the genesis of our separation from and conflict with each other. The constructed self is objectified: we *become* a description and a series of images – a 'story'. This narrative in our own minds is one that we also encourage in the minds of others, as the particular image we project for them to believe about us. This is how we so easily become disconnected from each other, because we inhabit these thought-constructed islands that are rooted in narratives built on the past and projected into the world. In doing this we are not directly present, now. The casualties of this narrative of self are intimacy, openness, honesty, authenticity and experiencing the universality of Love.

Our belief that we have a self as a continuum of the past, becomes an obstacle in the way we do everything and how we interact with others. We may feel anxious before an event or a meeting, but what is it that feels anxious? What is it that lacks confidence? If we examine this carefully it is this self-image that we want to protect: a 'self' who is frightened, insecure, arrogant, timid, or intimidating. On examination the self is only a construct; it is, ultimately, not real.

Letting go of the past and this idea of 'me' means meeting and connecting with people, situations and events without the veil of mind (as the memories and images of the past) between you and the other. This brings freshness, openness, spontaneity and authenticity. Understanding that there is no self brings a new level of creativity and an intimacy with everything. We develop a quiet inner confidence that comes from having nothing to prove or defend. We have become a numinous *no-body* released from the restless pressure to cultivate the dream-sleep of an individual some-body.

Awareness and identity

Awareness is inclusive of thought and reveals that one's identity is beyond thought altogether. Thought is part of the activity that appears on the 'screen' of awareness, but it is transitory. Only awareness has permanence, and hence is the primary anchor for our identity. Awareness of Being is both the pathway and the source of our true identity. This statement may give the impression that awareness and Being are separate – that 'you can be aware of something separate called Being'. However awareness and

Being are ultimately the same. Being, as consciousness, generates awareness in us. Awareness, as the 'light' of Being, is our experience of consciousness.

Entitlements are invariably negative but awareness is our unspoken, unrecognised, and true entitlement. Awareness is without complexity. It is immediate and all encompassing, but commonly there is great difficulty in realising both the scope and importance of awareness. We become so consumed with what we are aware of – as the contents of consciousness appearing on the screen as thoughts, feelings and sensations – that we ignore what contains all this. Because it is not the contents of consciousness that are the primary source of our identity; rather it is awareness itself. And rather than understanding what is fundamental as the ground of Being, we believe in the veracity of the thought-structure.

We maintain our troubles by habitually ignoring awareness and our true nature, instead seeking the answers to our existence in the mind. This ignoring is our fundamental ignorance. We tend to live on automatic pilot with so much of our beliefs and attitudes unexamined and unquestioned because we are unaware. In this unawareness we allow our lives to be scripted by our conditioning, which affects our authenticity and our freedom. Too easily we become fearful of challenging our own status quo as we continue on in a form of relentless doing, fearful of silence, of being idle, of being empty, of simply being aware. We maintain our slumber by relentlessly pursuing the inessential, the falsities, the inauthentic, and by constructing all manner of self-images.

Curiosity can rouse us from this slumber to face the nagging fear of emptiness, that drives the restlessness of 'self'. To let go and rest in our awareness is to be with what is and whatever arises in our living. This liberates us to 'the way of non-doing'; that is, doing without self.

The body *is* desire

Generally, in religious cultures (Hinduism, Buddhism, Christianity, Islam, Judaism) the body is regarded as something defiled, a source of pollution, and something to be transcended. For the religious the struggle against desire is a form of tyranny. In secular culture the body is more often seen as a vehicle of pleasure (hedonia). But if we rest in awareness, there is no sense of separation from the body, nor is there the struggle with desire. Rather, desire then becomes healthy, proportioned, because it is neither repressed nor indulged and hence distorted. The instinctual, expressed as urges, functions proportionally in the light of awareness.

The body *is* desire – to eat, to breathe, to be in sexual relationship, to continue living.

Desire, signifying our instinctual life, manifests both consciously and unconsciously. Desire to continue living also manifests unconsciously with the most fundamental functioning of the body to continue its healthy existence as a self-organising entity. We see this in the form of immuno-surveillance, immuno-responsiveness (white blood cell activity), cell-replication, cell-apoptosis; all the parasympathetic functioning: blood and lymph circulation, digestion and peristalsis, endocrine functioning, circadian rhythms, micro-pulsations of the nervous system – and the exquisitely intricate interfacing of all these systems into a functioning whole. When this instinctive level of intelligence of the body – to continue living – is disrupted (for example, with auto-immune diseases where certain cells/systems of the body turn against themselves) attitudinal healing and meditation may enable the sufferer to achieve marked results through co-opting a deeper harmonic response from the 'body's intelligence' where there has been disorder.

Desire, as the instinct to look after the body so that it continues living, is present when we jump out of the way of an oncoming car; or when defending ourselves from an impending assault; or as an extension, to protect our family from injury. If this basic desire/instinct is interrupted, it is usually from acquired, or inherited, injury to the nervous system that would disable this kind of responsive intelligence.

To struggle with desire is to struggle against the body. The struggle is what happens when thought in the form of ego grapples with instincts, and this is the suffering that signifies attachment. It can go either way: in the form of pleasure-seeking indulgences or, particularly in religious circles, in the form of restrictions, vows and taboos as attempts at control. In religious circles from Christianity to Buddhism there is great fear associated with the body, instinct and desire.

To live in the innocence of Being, there is no struggle with desire as the body, it is just not an issue. In the Buddhist ideal 'to be free of desire' there is a struggle with the body, with attachment arising in the form of denial. As such it moves away from a middle path, instead becoming a form of extremism of the mind, as a 'will' to dominate and control the body. This is a separation. The move against desire, to control it and deny it, is religious rather than spiritual. This only strengthens the 'self' as part of its restless strategy to achieve transcendence, as a projected enlightenment. Being in harmony with desire is critical to awakened Being.

By feeling directly – not thinking – into the body's sensations and energy in each moment, our awareness extends infinitely to unbounded Being. What can inhibit our ability to feel, however, can be traumatic experiences held deeper in the conscious field, that make 'feeling' too painful. So, in order to feel, sometimes healing work needs to be done, to enable 'feeling ability'.

Feeling through the body reveals how it is seamlessly embedded in nature. When the body is regarded phenomenally as a separate object it is commonly viewed as stopping at the skin, but our awareness is not bound by phenomenal or conceptual limitations. Rather, it extends throughout the body to the seamless and dynamic continuity of 'Being'. Awareness in this sense is embodied, and it is also unbounded.

The Truth of Being

Understanding the nature of consciousness involves journeying into oneself to unchartered domains that are prelinguistic and precognitive – the 'original mind'. The locus of consciousness is most immediately experienced in the head and body, but it extends infinitely. It intimately embraces the light source from a distant galaxy to the glow of colour in a blade of grass, as an inner glow of consciousness that pervades everything. The locus of consciousness is everywhere. And in experiencing awareness we can directly know the ubiquitous nature of consciousness, because it is everything.

Feeling 'Being' through the body and the senses does not involve thinking, because to 'feel' the mind must be quiet. We tend to be oblivious to the essential role that feeling the energy of the body has to teach us, because the body is nature, and nature is consciousness. Feeling the body like this is to sense constant change, always bringing us into what is happening now. Further, listening deeply to the inner life of the body can reveal dimensions normally hidden to us because our attention is usually captive to a busily thinking mind.

If we become distracted by thinking as we construct our lives in our heads – experienced as an ongoing narrative of a 'self' moving through time from the past, with plans for some kind of future – we miss something fundamental about who we are. We can miss the grounding that awareness of the body and the senses gives us, as we are side-tracked by our ruminating, because this 'grounding' occurs in the newness of each moment. And while our empirical sensing cognises constant change, awareness itself is beyond this, anchoring us in the unchanging. If we are too mentally busy we miss the fundamental nature of the 'here' – body located *now* – in timeless Being.

For while the stories of our families and ancestors are important, locating us meaningfully in a community, they occlude a depth in us that is beyond the narrative. This depth is the source of our spirituality. It is unfathomable because it points to a reality that can never be constructed or remembered – that is not in the form of a narrative. It is a depth that can only be revealed in a continuous now. If we are captive to the activity of the mind, we fail to see the vastness of who we are.

Potentially we are all philosophers. But it is hard to be philosophical if we are fearful for our life, or suffering from malnutrition. And sometimes even when there is enough food on the table and shelter overhead, other factors can come into play to thwart our natural curiosity – trauma, abuse, poverty, war, or dislocation. All these factors can affect the choices we make, even though we may be unaware of our ever-present epistemic power to know our identity.

It takes both courage and curiosity to face the obstacles that our conditioning presents. This conditioning may have given us a false identity – beliefs and prejudices – that are the things that obscure our true nature. But, by becoming aware of them, and leaning gently into the suffering they perpetuate, their traumatic hold over us is released. An identity informed by the unresolved insults of the past becomes transformed into 'memories without charge', giving us a deeper appreciation of living now.

Past insults that are unresolved can become central features of the 'self' (that can develop protective behaviours in order to 'wall-off' painful memories) as we attach to them. In turn we view ourselves as victims of events of the past. With healing, the ongoing reality of these psychic wounds shifts, and thus their resonant activity, that is repeatedly distorting consciousness, dissolves. We can still recall the events with great clarity, but are freed from emotional resonance perhaps displaying as fear, self-loathing or rage.

In the all-seeing light of awareness these ideas and images we have held about ourselves or others (including the belief in an enduring 'self') become untenable. Awareness brings a new and expansive reality as the dissolution of self heralds a profound intimacy in living. We experience the impersonal, universal energy-intelligence of Being, understanding that it has always been, only obscured by the noise generated by the ruminating mind.

CHAPTER 2

KNOWING OUR IDENTITY CHANGES EVERYTHING

People through the ages and across cultures who have experienced an inner transformation have asked the same fundamental questions: *Who am I? Why am I here?* Questions about our identity have been echoed in modern times by quantum theorist Erwin Schrödinger who wrote, in *Science and Humanism* (1953): 'The answer to this question is not only one of the tasks but the task of science'. Knowing who we are, and our place in the vastness of Being, is our birthright. To discover our true identity gives both guidance and purpose to us as sapiens. The consequences of erring in our understanding of who we are, as we are currently doing, is disastrous for the wellbeing of ourselves and the planet, as we are finding out.

When the mind enquires 'who am I' its responses will inevitably only reflect its conditioning and tend to be either scientific, philosophically intellectual, or religious, none of which addresses the primary imperative to know what the Self is.

Addressing the question of identity cannot be done through thought, when thought is held as the essential medium to resolve it. The kind of knowing that involves thought is appropriate for the many creative fields of endeavor and for building a web of conceptual knowledge, but not for the intimacy of knowing our identity.

In science, the objectivism of empirical research furthers a theoretical web built on an agreed set of assumptions. The most fundamental of these involves duality – the separation of the 'knower' (thinker) and the 'object' (the known). For example, in neuroscience, the object of study is the brain's biochemistry, its molecular biology, its electrophysiology, its cognitive and behavioural functioning, brainwave frequencies, et cetera. The authority this knowledge is given is misplaced because it only yields knowledge of the physiology and psychological theory, but fails to address the experiential understanding of who we are, which is only born from our inner experience. The mind – as thought – is not the right medium for us knowing who we are, only the vastness of consciousness itself, which is prior to thought, can do this.

Religions will have their own set of responses with regard to identity built on the authority given to sacred texts, structures of belief, ritual practices and the deification of special people. The dualities religions generate are different, yet the result is the same. *Different*, in that they involve the transcendental – the separation of a soul/atman from God/Brahmin. *The same*, because both science and religion are constructed dualities thought has invented, that overlays a vacuum of ignorance about what our identity actually is.

Both the rational approaches in science and philosophy, and the theological responses of religions, are ever limited because of their conceptual nature. The conceptual and theoretical knowledge of science (objective) or theological beliefs (subjective) are built on different types of knowledge of the past. As such, neither is experiential. But by clearing the lens of perception and looking with eyes afresh, uncontaminated by the past, we can directly address the 'vacuum of ignorance' by knowing experientially. Then knowing 'who am I?' is revealed without recourse to conditioned mindsets.

This kind of honesty brings a resounding silence. And within this silence, arising from a very different kind of knowing, is an understanding that would potentially see the transformation of every human being.

'Seeing directly', unmediated by thought would fundamentally change how we live. It changes our relationship with each other, and with the planet and all of its species, enabling the possibility of a radically different world, free of conflict and disorder. 'Seeing directly' reveals the truth of our identity, because all the problems that beset human beings ultimately stem from not knowing who we are and why we are here. We are living in an unparalleled time when there is a greater impetus for this understanding to happen, and it is more accessible. Yet we continue to show that we can be extremely adept at resisting this understanding.

Our greatest obstacle to 'direct perception' is our attachment to thought. The ego is our resistance to Being. It can be likened to an addiction, and freeing oneself from any addiction naturally causes angst. Who am I then, without the addiction? Being remains inaccessible when we are addicted to the continuously ruminating mind. Experiencing Being directly is trusting in awareness itself, which includes 'feeling' the sensing body. And rather than habitually focusing on our self-ruminations and believing in them, we can apprehend the primordial silence underpinning all existence.

Our resistance stems from the mind's fear of Being. Experiencing Being is the great unknown, it is much easier to keep ourselves busy, thinking, seeking stimulation and endless distractions. The immensity of Being exists beyond the comfort and certainty of thought. Its opposite, non-Being or nothingness, is perhaps regarded as even more terrifying. In Western philosophy, the Existentialists correctly describe this fear as 'existential angst'. But by facing the discomfort – our vacuum of ignorance – which is really our ignorance of Being and Nothingness, this 'angst' transforms. Being present in our ignorance dispells the conditioned trance we inhabit, then we can cognise that we are connected in a living, knowing Universe.

Awakening from the collective 'waking-dream' of individualism

What we call 'being an individual' is not a statement of truth but a form of our 'collective trance'. Individualism is the expression of our belief in the confusion arising from an experience of duality, because we see ourselves as separated individual selves. To awaken from the trance is to realise that the consciousness in the body and throughout nature, *is us*. Essential to living in a trance is the belief in the reality of apparent separateness, with the assumption that we are individual islands of consciousness. This is a form of group-think that is part of our 'dream-sleep', and generally it goes unchallenged.

However, to 'individuate' is an entirely different matter. Individuating is a paradox because when we become aware of the group-think belief of being a separate individual, this automatically has the effect of releasing us from enmeshment in an unhealthy form of collective trance. Individuating is to stand aside from group-thinking by not seeking our identity in it. The paradox is that individuating reveals our connection as Being. Here our experience of awareness is cognizing itself as the true source of our identity: that we are this Consciousness, and this Consciousness is pervasive – *it is all that is*. Individuating is not a mental identification process like individualism (*my* religion, *my* political persuasion, *my* favourite brand, *my* beliefs); it is to understand that you are whole, standing in your own light, at one with all that is.

Being is timeless. Eternity resides in the ever-present moment of now and is the basis of experiencing reality as numinous. *A phenomenal reality is one that is interpreted as material, as thing-like:* different objects (lemons, bodies, pebbles, tigers, conifers) or things that can be measured and located in time and space. It is a conceptual reality based in time. Experiencing a numinous reality is not a vision, flight of fancy, or something to be believed in. It yields experiential truth that is beyond the range of rational thought and can only be known in the 'now'. It is thus not subjective, as a flight of imagination is, nor an objectified conceptual one. It is neither attaching to a belief, or a mystical vision, nor heightened experiences from taking psychoactive substances.

However valid 'peak experiences' may be, they come and go like any experience: they are not the 'natural mind' or 'original mind', which is a resting in awareness. Resting in awareness is pre-cognitive and pre-linguistic, in which we experience everything as part of an unconditioned numinous reality: that everything is consciousness. We see that consciousness in us and as us. This consciousness is the same Intelligence that organises the galaxies and manifests as everything that is, without moral distinction.

Self-absorbed mind is a resistance to Being

'Man is the only creature who refuses to be what he is.'
—Albert Camus

The fears, anxieties and insecurities of a self are the resistance to Being. Our belief in the agency of the self, authoring the continuous stream of thoughts in our heads signifies our fear lest we be overwhelmed by the silence of Being. Fear can well up when confronted by pauses in conversations, or in periods of waiting in queues, or when we are being idle, with nothing to occupy our minds. We may ask, 'Who am I between these thoughts?' or 'Who am I *without* the thought?'

Boredom is only experienced when consciousness is colonised by an 'experiencer' who demands entertainment. Instead of feeling the quiet joy of original mind when we are alone, we experience boredom, restlessness and the specific loneliness that only a self can know. We can feel stuck in the isolated island of 'self', disconnected from people or life in general. The restless search for distraction from our unease can lead to a desire to escape, to alter our inner state with drugs, alcohol or some other habit. It can be seen in the need for continuous noise or stimulation, such as constantly having the TV or radio on, or checking our electronic devices. It is the ruminating self that we want to drown out.

Generally, we may be unaware that the stream of thinking we have is constant. Usually the first thing people report when they start regular meditation, where their awareness of the content of consciousness is amplified, is surprise at how much thinking actually goes on. Figures ranging between 40,000 and 60,000 have been cited as the average number of thoughts people have in a day. If we did an honest stocktake of the different thoughts passing through awareness, we would notice the following: the repetitive nature of thought; being focused on the future (anxious) or the past (regretful); an attachment to fulfilling desires (often sexual or financial); worries about self-esteem, relationships, work or study. Often all these can be negative in character.

Via all of this thinking we play a trick on ourselves: we insert the separate agency of 'self' – the 'thinker' who thinks these thoughts. The gallery of chattering monkeys we harbor will only be silenced with the understanding that our identity is found neither in identifying with them as the mind, nor as the body. Much energy is wasted supporting the unreal.

The 'self' informs, through its interpretive filter, the 'dream-sleep' of duality: of knowing, projecting its desires, preferences and avoidances, and 'it' becomes our connection to everything. It is the experience of embarrassment we feel, or the saving of face when this self is 'exposed'. It is the anxiety about looming events and the feeling of 'butterflies in the stomach'. It is the feeling of self-importance from being praised, or the shame when its hidden behavior is discovered. It is the desire that burns for revenge, the feeling of jealousy, and the desperate grasping for status. It is the seeker of pleasure and the avoider of pain – the seeker of wealth, stuff, and enlightenment.

However, by letting go of a belief in the veracity of this separate agency, we are liberated. Without self, gone is the fear of death that underpins much of our behaviour. This liberation translates as a deeper appreciation and gratitude in living.

Each of us learns a language and is given a mind map so that we can navigate our culture. While language and thought are wonderful gifts, it is the unnecessary complication of 'self', that negatively influences how we use these gifts.

When we inherit the mind maps of our forebears, far too many of us are willing to accept these without question, because sometimes questioning can be dangerous. The early, warm, oceanic feeling of babyhood soon shifts. By the teenage years, the 'complication of self' is entrenched, and our experience of consciousness can be clouded with limiting, distorted or toxic narratives of the surrounding culture. If we passively acquiesce or react in rebellion, each signifies we have become colonised.

The separate self strengthens with cumulative experiences and, when unresolved, can be likened to a form of 'inner baggage'. This exists as emotional/mental noise, congesting the mind-body, often subliminally. When inner baggage is not resolved it can lead to a plethora of problems in relationships, in our sense of meaning, in social connectedness and in mental and emotional health. This inner baggage, if unprocessed, also inexorably accelerates our biological ageing. The burden of self can become so great that it may seek its own elimination.

Suicide is generally not a good resolution. We are simply trying to escape our unfinished business. But there is no escape. The thought structure – self – as an aspect of consciousness, will continue unresolved, even after the death of the body, and will continue into a new (life) with an opportunity to resolve, signifying that consciousness has dimensionality.

Understanding 'no-self' is experiential

Writing on the illusion of self is not offered as a doctrine, for that too would be another burden. The Buddhists created a doctrine out of 'no-self' – but viewing something as doctrine becomes an obstacle to understanding. Finding truth entails checking everything through questioning everything and believing nothing! True understanding is experiential.

Enquiring into the nature of the existence of a self is not unique to Eastern traditions. In Western philosophy the belief in 'self' holds no currency for the Existentialists. David Hume, the empiricist of the 18th century, stated that there was no 'self' with devastating clarity. People at the time found his conclusion shocking. I suspect this was because it erased the distinction between 'self' and 'world', an assumed duality. This is the primary duality that has dominated Western thought since early Christianity, and was famously articulated by Descartes in the 16th century. Hume's 'no-self' assertions were regarded as unbelievable, with people more willing to hold closely to the 'common sense' illusions they were familiar with.

If you become aware that you have spent your life accepting that the world is 'dualistic' – that a separate 'you' and a separate 'other' are the absolute of reality – with a little more curiosity you can embark on a journey that will demonstrate that this reality is only relative. In the immediacy of now, through resting in awareness, beyond notions of self and other, you experience a oneness that knows no other. This is not a form of transcendence but is the immanence of Being.

Curiosity sees the questioning of the very mode of 'belief-making' that only leads us into error, so as to discover the true nature of reality. 'What is real', is based in facticity (such as the absence of 'fear driven' conspiracy theories) of the reality we share, and in going further encompasses the other dimensional nature of our existence. So understanding the meaning and impact of 'no-self' is not achieved through clever argument, it is experiential. It comes from direct inner knowing, without thought as intermediary. This inner knowing usurps the sovereign place of thought as expressed in the self. Or, one could also say, thought is no longer central in our field of attention.

Discontinuing the constructing of identity from thinking or imaging leads to the innocence of non-conceptual knowing. Thought is still used, but not in the ways that a psychological 'self' or ego-identity requires. We are liberated from the 'high maintenance' entity of self-esteem. The natural dissolution of self is the recovery of innocence.

No Water No Moon
This way and that way I tried to keep the pail together,
hoping the weak bamboo would never break.
Suddenly the bottom fell out.
No more water; no more moon in the water –
emptiness in my hand

—Chiyono, Zen Buddhist nun

Resting in awareness transforms the fragmentation of self

By paying attention to our daily living we break unconscious patterns of behaviour and thinking. Transformation does not happen through force of will. When we 'rest in awareness' we are directly challenging the controlling nature of thought, and the sovereignty of the thinker. It is this un-attaching, or resting in awareness, that frees us from the tyranny of conditioned thinking, habits, and addictions. Resting in awareness is utterly simple, yet not necessarily easy when we have spent so much energy in cultivating attachments and developing habits.

Through paying close attention to the whole landscape of consciousness, we realise it is pointless to continue with the 'mind games' that keep us limited in the contraction which is ego. The light of awareness exposes how we really are. We cannot truly love another, for example, without being inwardly loving. If someone says that they 'love' you, for instance, and yet exhibit the opposite in how they are inwardly (being 'self'-negating', being unkind to others) we can legitimately ask whether we can trust their 'love' claim. Love only truly increases with the diminishing of inner conflict and ego.

Paying close attention to our inner dialogue can reveal that there are fragmented aspects of the mind. We may become aware that there are what appear as different inner voices, or aspects of self. Examples of this are: an 'inner critic'; a 'whining complainer'; a 'recalcitrant child'; 'a domineering tyrant', or a 'meek submissive'. While these voices are real, and for healing to occur, need to be heard and accepted, they do not require a belief that they are true. If we believe in them, we are lost. Instead, resting in awareness is to *be* in the ground-bed – consciousness – from which any voices or clamoring of self, arise. Abiding in awareness brings a peace that is beyond the mind.

The fragmentation of self can also manifest in the form of an inner struggle between voices for an imagined ascendency. A projected 'true or higher self', is seen in conflict with an ever unruly 'lower self'. Fragmentation like this keeps us trapped in a cycle of inner conflict which has a reality, but is delusory. It is the common struggle for an idealistic truth found in all religious traditions, much of New Age teachings, and also in the secular world.

Transcendence — the illusion of 'self' striving for ideals

When we strive for ideals such as perfection, being our true self, or enlightenment it necessarily strengthens the opposite, by creating a repressed and unruly 'shadow' fragment of self. The pining for transcendence is generated by a fear of 'shadow material' in the psyche (repressed desires, fantasies, ambitions, et cetera), a duality of its own making. We cannot have striving for transcendence without some form of 'shadow' we want to transcend in the first place. In theistic religions a transcendent God must be in struggle with 'his' shadow — a force of evil — personified in the Devil. In the secular world it is seen in the ideal of the rational self, as it struggles for supremacy from unruly, repressed and irrational emotions and desires.

To sustain this conflicting type of mindset requires ongoing effort. Its energy costs are significant. But there is a way other than this endless inner division of struggling selves and unachievable idealism: *the effortless way of resting in awareness.*

Instead of putting our energy into the mental struggle of competing selves, we use available energy for observing. In this 'non-doing' we are trusting in the power of awareness and we are essentially giving up the struggle. By accepting all inner resistance, it becomes no longer tenable to judge ourselves or others. Neither can we support the struggles and complexities of the constructed images of self, which is a lie that we construct in us and present to others.

Deep acceptance of 'what is', is a welcoming of everything that arises in the form of thoughts, images, fears, anxieties or worries, to be witnessed in the healing light of awareness. And just noticing how there might be a 'pull to jump at shadows', or how we might 'habitually react' to certain people, situations, thoughts or emotions, allows the transformative light of awareness to come in. Because it is the mind's desire to control and manipulate that has kept us chained by the ignorance of habitual modes of resistance to simply being.

Paying close attention to our inner life without judgment naturally reduces the inner mental/emotional noise, revealing the ever-present silence of Being. Left behind is the convoluted psychology of a divided self, itself a symptom of being colonized by the confused voices of the world. This manifests as the 'waking dream' we have been living.

When the 'self' breaks down

Being normal in the world is the state of a living trance, the 'normal neurotic'. It is a state of disturbed equanimity – struggling desires, aspirations, conflicts, wishes, hopes, hidden thoughts, ensuring mental compartments, beliefs and moral dilemmas, all supporting the cultivation of a core self-image as a form of mental artifice. Taken together these are a resistance to Being. This normality is also a form of fragility, prone to reactivity and easily insulted, precisely because its grip on reality is tenuous, with its misplaced search for love and happiness in hedonia rather than eudaimonia.

Central to what makes for this mental and emotional fragility in the first place is a belief in the veracity of its own narrative. The story of self that can be riddled with contradiction, conflict, but the act of self-imaging is essentially the same whether one is Sri Lankan or Irish. Fundamental to this narrative is a belief in its own separation. This is the state of 'normal', and many cling desperately to stay entranced till the end of their days. Unless, life events step in to disturb this 'normality' pressing it to breaking point.

Sometimes the pressure to maintain the façade of self gets too much, which happens when there is a check to the sense of reality it specialises in creating. Because this is what the mind does: it creates its own reality. But breaking the shell of ego can also occur simply with the sustained curiosity to explore what is beyond the limiting prism on our perception that the self imposes. When this illusory sense of reality is fractured, as the self, there is disintegration.

What is a mental breakdown? What is it that breaks down? A friend shared her story with me about her 'breakdown', which had happened some years before. I asked her what she felt it was that 'broke down'. She said, 'I certainly couldn't have articulated this at the time, because I was so overwhelmed and felt shattered. What broke down was who I thought I was. And also, what I thought my life was… and what I thought I should be doing. Along with this was the sense of certainty about where I was going.'

This 'breakdown' is poignant yet it is also unremarkable because commonly self's do break down due to their inherent fragility. It can be precipitated by events such as the breaking of a relationship, experiencing abandonment, an acute experience of loss or failure, experiencing abuse, drug use, or a range of other events that are experienced as traumatic. How these events are interpreted can present a fundamental challenge to the basic idea of 'who we think we are', and what we think is 'real'. In short, a challenge to the kind of 'waking dream' that we have been living.

Breakdowns are the experience of being overwhelmed, where it is all too much. They can be minor or major, depending on the level of mental/emotional investment in believing the particular psychological narrative we have created, and the fall-out experienced when it is shown to be an illusion. When we are brought to face truth. Breakdowns like this are 'spiritual emergencies', as articulated by Stanislav Groff, because while there is suffering, they also present an opportunity: to expand into a greater reality of Being, and potentially to discover the truth of one's identity, beyond the illusions of self.

How a breakdown is managed and the kind of support both sought and given, is relevant to whether it becomes a desperate search for a new normal, or a pathway further down the 'rabbit hole' of mental illness. However, it can also be an opportunity for a deeper spiritual understanding. Over the short term, those who experience potentially dangerous symptoms such as self-harming, suicidal tendencies, psychosis, and severe panic, may need to be managed with medications and even temporary hospitalization. But if this is all that is offered, the opportunity for a more profound 'recalibration' to a deeper more expansive experience of reality can be lost.

It is worth considering Eckhart Tolle's story. He became famous for his book *The Power of Now* after appearing on the Oprah Winfrey show as a spiritual teacher. His story of breakdown included years of experiencing what would be diagnosed as clinical depression. After some years of this he had a spontaneous dissolution of this mental state, transforming through a dis-identification with his mind. He no longer identified that 'he' was depressed and stuck in 'his' situation, but through resting deeper into awareness, he could see that thoughts like, 'I am depressed' and his particular mood state were phenomena, appearing and disappearing on the 'screen of awareness'. Rather than identifying with his thoughts, and believing that there was a separate 'him' having them, *'he was the awareness in which they occurred'*.

Thoughts of self-loathing, such as 'life is not worth living', or any continuing 'self' thoughts, he regarded as the same: all aspects of fragmented mind passing through, appearing, and disappearing, in awareness. He realised that all these passing thoughts and mood states had no bearing on who he really was. He was the blank screen of awareness and, characteristic of awareness, it remains uninfluenced by whatever emotions, dramas, sensations, moods or thoughts appear on it.

He no longer believed in the self that was stuck in the mire of its mis-identity. The two central illusions were shattered: the illusion of believing that his identity was in the stream of thoughts; and the illusion that there was a separate self, thinking these thoughts. Released from these illusions he understood that he was Being.

Navigating the 'dark night'

When the breakdown of the ego shell occurs as a result of spiritual exploration, it can be profoundly unsettling, and we can feel as though we are dissolving. Experiencing this disintegration occurs as the lies the ego has constructed, and how much these lies were believed in, are exposed in the light of awareness. For some, sailing through these waters can be fairly smooth, but for others with particularly strong ego shells, it can be an emotional roller coaster, vacillating between ecstasy and despair. But either way, smooth or turbulent, there is a sense of disorientation because the truth is that you are losing your 'self'. You are losing the habitual moorings of your mind with all its attachments.

For some this loss can result in an extended period of depression. All the motivations that were used and believed in are discovered to be based in ego illusion, and this is what leads to a collapse. We are left facing a void, which can be bewildering and frightening. And for those suffering turbulence and deep melancholy from this loss, they are experiencing 'the dark night of the soul', a term specifically coined by Christian mystic, St John of the Cross. This, however, is not unique to Christian contemplatives, but is an experience commonly shared in all contemplative traditions where the usual attachments of mind, including to itself, are profoundly challenged. Passing through this 'dark night' is a necessary process as one moves from bewilderment to be-wonderment.

The 'dark night' is really 'resistance' to the transformation of consciousness in the process of awakening. Even dwelling on it as substantial and identifying with it as a 'process' is giving 'it' more reality than it actually has, thus feeding a phase which may itself become problematic, and further obscuring the freedom already at hand. The 'dark night' is another stage in the dissolution of 'the illusory self', so is it all really real anyway, or just a further part of the illusory 'waking dream'?

'Letting go in whatever is arising' is central to us safely navigating through breakdowns, whether they occur by happenstance or through spiritual enquiry. It is also essential for passing through what seems like the 'dark night'. But regardless, breakdowns and dark nights occur as manifestations of the trances we live, and our destiny. Yet mysteriously, as we step towards understanding ourselves as Being, as we surrender to the immensity of life, assistance comes in many, and often surprising forms.

Letting go or resting in awareness is really the foundation of true sanity. This is because in witnessing we are anchoring in the domain of consciousness from whence mind arises, rather than the restless search engaged in by the ego in order to maintain its illusions and, specifically, its own substantiality. Ultimately there is no-one navigating anything. Resting in awareness is both a form of trust, unattachment, and surrender, to an all-encompassing reality: one that is not created and sustained by the ego. It is a surrender to the truth of Being: an abiding in the real.

Without 'self' comes true co-operation

Over thousands of years we have honed our ability to think by assiduously using the magnificent creative tool that thought is. We have produced great feats of art, music, mathematics, science, medicine, languages, and engineering. On a more sobering note, through social conditioning, propaganda and advertising, we have also programmed children and even whole populations to think and behave in ways that are tribal, brutal and destructive. Countries have waged war and committed atrocities arising from clashing ideologies. We have proved that we are skilled at spreading and indoctrinating prejudice in the spheres of politics and religion.

But, as Stephen Pinker has carefully outlined in his book, *Enlightenment Now*, after having extensively researched different markers in global population studies, it is apparent that on many measures there is clear indication that advances in civilization are occurring, from improved health, reduction in murder rates, improved sanitation, increased democracy and increased education. These markers indicate that, collectively, we are becoming more cooperative, and peaceful. And we are now called to reach new levels of cooperation in order to resolve continuing conflicts and barbarities and, most alarmingly, the looming threat that human-induced climate change is rapidly forcing upon us.

Cooperation is the key to how we have survived and thrived as a species. We are the *Cooperative Hominid*. To cooperate is to act harmoniously; to be in unison. The primary resistance to our ability to cooperate is belief in a separate psychological self. This is because there is only a partial cooperation through many selves rallying around a given ideology. But, it is because we cling to ideologies whether they are religious, national, political or philosophical, for its identity, that we are challenged to expand further than tribal identification affords. Functioning under the banner of different beliefs or ideologies only provides limited cooperation within the tribe. With our challenges now pressingly global (now with the COVID 19 pandemic), each of us must find a deeper cooperation, not limited by belief and ideology, but grounded in the actuality of Being. Our challenge is to function as 'global citizens'.

The Taoist philosophers of ancient China, using the imagery of water, suggested that we 'flow like a great river'. They remind us, 'don't push the river', and to 'follow the water-course way'. In *accepting* resistance, we navigate differently, no longer pushed and pulled by the content of consciousness. We experience the wisdom of the heart, and a kindness spontaneously arises that naturally extends to everything.

Resting in awareness brings a transformation that is real not just when we are sitting on a cushion alone at home, but when it is manifest throughout our daily living. It involves a transformation from believing that the duality of self and other is real, to an experiential understanding of our identity as *ever-present awareness*. This is the direct way of non-duality, where the destination and the path are one.

> *Then, Bahiya, you should train yourself thus: In reference to the seen, there will be only the seen. In reference to the heard, only the heard. In reference to the sensed, only the sensed. In reference to the cognised, only the cognized. That is how you should train yourself.*
>
> *When for you there will be only the seen in reference to the seen, only the heard in reference to the heard, only the sensed in reference to the sensed, only the cognized in reference to the cognised, then, Bahiya, there is no you in terms of that.*
>
> *When there is no you in terms of that, there is no you there. When there is no you there, you are neither here nor yonder nor between the two. Thus, just this, is the end of stress.*
>
> —The Buddha

CHAPTER 3

'SEEING' WITHOUT BELIEVING

'Seeing' is beyond believing

Is it possible to 'see' – to understand through perception – without the interpretation of mind or thinking? And, what is it that 'sees'?

Our minds are conditioned from an early age with beliefs, opinions, attitudes and prejudices. This conditioning is neither necessary nor useful for us to function in the world; in fact it impairs good and harmonious functioning. On the other hand knowledge in the form of language, science, mathematics, music and art, are essential for our functioning and connecting into the world of human beings. Yet all this conditioning, both the useful and not useful, becomes the filter through which we perceive. If there were a way of seeing without this filter, what would we see?

When we look with the 'original mind', it is ever-present, and is prior to our cognitive and linguistic development. Looking deeply like this at a tree, at the stars or at another human being, brings an experience that is not just phenomenal. When you do this, at first you may just see the phenomenal 'object', as part of your cognition, through an acquired knowledge of categories such as tree, stellar object or person. When we say tree, on seeing a tree the use of the word is an idealisation. What we actually see is a shape, and we only see this shape from a particular perspective, not the whole – stereoscopic – thing. In the cognition of 'tree' there is other embedded empirical knowledge.

To continue this process of pure observation, un-attaching to the word or other knowledge, we may 'see' trees freshly as Being, as if for the first time. In this we are beginning to observe beyond the constrictive prism of accumulated knowledge, to experience something 'other'. If we 'look' with total attention, without the mind interceding with its labels and stored knowledge or memories, you step into a fresh, unknown world – the numinous. The numinous is a pre-cognitive, pre-linguistic world. The constructed world of language and mind is simply overlaid on this deeper and 'hidden' order, given that it is an unexplored reality.

In looking deeply, our minds become spontaneously quiet, enabling the direct perception of a deeper experiencing of reality. In our daily living, if our minds are generally quiet, this experience is amplified and becomes our moment-to-moment mode of perception. Then we abide in a reality that is beyond the constructs of mind, and yet those constructs and memories are always available. We can still recognise the shape of being as a tree, and the different shape of being as the person who is sitting opposite us, and is our dear friend of many years.

This quietness of mind, without preconceptions, called 'original mind' or 'no-mind', is a mode of perception, where we experience the infinity of Being. Perceiving in this way signifies that we have moved from the *phenomenal*, with its labels and all the intellectual knowledge and memory we have accumulated, to the *noumenal*. This term was used by German philosopher Immanuel Kant (1724–1804) to describe a different order of experiential knowing, although Kant believed that this was forever inaccessible to humans. He was wrong about this, and central to this book, it is an essential feature of our epistemic repertoire.

Experiencing the *numinous* indicates a deeper level of perception than the 'phenomenal world of appearances' which is associated with our conditioned information, both cognitive and linguistic. Importantly, though, the phenomenal is not an illusion, as is held by some in mystical traditions and spiritual circles. Maintaining that the phenomenal is an illusion is to deny the 'truth-value' it obviously has, but it is one that is 'relative' rather absolute. Perceiving the numinous, however, occurs when the mind is naturally silent, allowing a kind of knowing that is non-rational, but not irrational.

'Seeing' without filter

When thinking and labeling occur, we begin a process of mapping: the brain cells activate, sending messages within the neural circuitry as we name and categorise. As we develop this cognitive process of mapping, we reinforce the map's stability with memory, in order for things to become familiar. In this way, mental or thought activity and the function of memory are tightly correlated with brain mapping, but not completely.

The mapping of reality that we do through language and thought becomes our knowledge of the world and, subsequently, the filter through which we see. We start in childhood by calling a particular shape a 'tree'; henceforth, all similar shapes that we see are filtered through this mental/language construct, and are also called 'trees'. I do this with my grandson as I walk with him and he touches things or points to them, and I provide the language for each thing, naming, objectifying and mapping his world. And this is also how the past becomes the filter for our present experience. All our maps of what we consider reality, including elaborate theories of mathematics, physics, philosophy, botany and biology, are creations of the mind, drawn from accumulated knowledge of the past. Knowledge of the phenomenal is not an illusion. But in a very real sense all knowledge, because it is based in thought, is of the past. *However, it is an illusion to think that this is the only kind of knowledge with truth-value that humans can have.*

We tend to use these maps mostly in a manner that is unconscious as part of our living trance. They become the world of the known, like a groove in which we function, and as we navigate through this meticulously constructed reality, we are in turn creating the kind of world that we see. When this reality, or some aspect of it, is challenged, there is often a passionate 'holding on', signifying emotional attachment as belief. This then becomes a measure of how this particular map has become cherished. Beliefs always carry this strong emotional charge. Yet this act of attaching and believing is completely irrational. Many who champion rationality seem to be unaware that they too have become victim to this very basic error of attachment. When they protest loudly if their cherished map of reality is challenged, it is an act of desperation to make it more real than it is.

Maps are not absolute; they are conceptual representations. They are real, but they are just one kind of reality. They are no more real than what the mind has created. However non-conceptual knowing is perceiving a connected reality that really has no maps. It is the order of Being hidden from the conceptual mind, and is a dimension of reality that thought can only point to, but cannot know.

What is believing?

The Oxford Dictionary defines 'belief' as: 'an unquestioned acceptance of something in the absence of reason; acceptance of an alleged fact without positive knowledge or proof.'

Although we may become invested in our beliefs, is the act of believing a sound basis for knowing reality? And can believing something be anchored in truth-value, as the basis of who we are? If the mind is already laden with beliefs, and beliefs are always a part of our conditioning, how is it possible for one to see anything other than the mind's own projections?

Our programming constructs our reality unconsciously and we are complicit in our acceptance of this. In this way, we are truly living in a trance. Awakening occurs when we become aware of this conditioning, which then loses its grip on informing our perception. Awareness, curiosity, and non-attachment break the spell that this conditioned colonisation of the self, holds over us. William Blake referred to this as 'the cleansing of the doors of perception'.

> *If the doors of perception were cleansed, everything would appear to man as it is, infinite. For man has closed himself up, till he sees all things thro' narrow chinks of his cavern.*
> —William Blake, *The Marriage of Heaven and Hell* (1790)

When we become acutely aware of our conditioning, we start to differentiate what is useful and important from what is unnecessary and false. It is easy for us to accept the conditioning of language, because it empowers our communication and cognitive functioning and, while not being strictly deterministic, it can also influence us negatively. Because unless we are aware of the way in which a given language is used, with the kind of structure and the meaning it conveys, it may have a powerfully constrictive influence on our perception, and how we live.

Certain cultural conditionings we may find limiting; for example, many men have been conditioned to think that showing their feelings is a sign of weakness, and that being nurturing or affectionate towards others is not 'manly' behaviour. Beliefs like this are purely cultural, with self-limiting and negative consequences; awakening for a man in this situation is to become aware that this conditioned belief has no basis in truth, and only leads to a distorted experience of reality. Not caring for children and not demonstrating affection for friends and family has negative consequences. Examples of positive conditioning might be: men being demonstrably kind and nurturing; children encouraged to practice good hygiene, such as hand washing after using the toilet to prevent the spread of disease; or in role modelling boys being encouraged to listen and show respect for females, or girls being encouraged to articulate their ideas and contribute equally with males in the classroom, and in the world.

Cultural and religious beliefs can serve to modulate behaviour and control, and are all too frequently used to oppress. For example, the belief that there is a giant, grey-bearded super-man called 'God' in the sky, who watches over us, and who might get angry and condemn us to an afterlife of eternal damnation in 'hell', if we neglect 'his' rules. This is a belief based in fear, explicitly designed to subjugate and control. It perpetuates a myth of dualism found in all transcendentalist cultures: a 'self' or an immortal 'soul' tainted in 'sin', praying for a good place in the afterlife, separated from its punishing God. And there are specifically appointed priestly representatives to oversee the correct proceedings of these affairs.

This structure of belief, like all beliefs, is not something that arises from any form of direct perception. Rather, at some point it is originally invented, but then becomes 'second-hand', reinforced by religious authorities and writings elevated as sacred. And for various reasons, often to do with the manipulation of power, people invest authority in themselves continuing the practice of inventing stories.

The very act of believing only serves to maintain a status quo, acting as a form of self-deception overlaying the vacuum of ignorance. We cling to beliefs as the cornerstones of a 'self'; they can become the 'clothing' of our identity. The self's dualistic nature functions to separate what is interpreted as inner/outer, objective/subjective, good/bad. However, 'seeing' without the interference of thought as held beliefs, collapses any sense of separateness, along with the artificial notions of objective/subjective and self and other. This 'collapse' brings an experience of the 'non-dual' nature of existence. Experiencing 'non-duality' then informs one's ethical compass beyond culturally conditioned narratives of morality that are based in judgment and separation.

With understanding, we can no longer function in a mode of believing, because beliefs are seen for what they are: constructed attachments of the mind. As such, they are without truth-value. Exposing beliefs to the light of awareness evaporates the energy charge around these beliefs. This is because we feel beliefs emotionally; we hold them passionately. But even after beliefs are gone, their residue patterns may continue for some time because of their habitual nature. However, eventually they do naturally wither, just as a plant will die when it is not watered.

Freed from belief, we experience a profoundly new level of spaciousness and liberation. The 'seeing' that arises from the spontaneously quiet mind is referred to as *non-conceptual awareness* – a term used in the Dzogchen tradition of Buddhism – meaning that it is beyond thought, and hence unconditioned. What 'sees', is pure awareness suffused with intelligence. This is what sees, but it is not an 'it', or a 'something'; it is the one consciousness that is universal.

Belief is the illusion of certainty

Believing is irrational because it is a fear-driven leap of emotional attachment to an idea, used to overlay the vacuum of ignorance. For example, 'if I believe in God I will be looked after and won't go to hell', or 'if I believe in Buddha and follow the precepts and attend the rituals I will have good karma and move further on the path to enlightenment'. Believing that the world is a certain way, or that it should be a certain way, leads to a wilful bending of a particular reality. And rather than living in the truth of what is, we live in a self-created illusion.

Believing is a clinging to an illusion of certainty. This certainty is the self's protection from directly facing its ignorance. When we believe, we live in a state of contraction because we are frightened of our own ignorance. This fear begins to dissolve the moment we admit that 'I do not know', and stand nakedly in the truth of this ignorance. Living without fear is to embrace 'unknowing', where there is no longer a need for belief. By being unwaveringly present in our ignorance, a transformation can happen, which sees ignorance transforming into an experiential understanding of Consciousness itself.

Religious beliefs provide many examples of irrationalities: in Christianity, we are invited (perhaps by St Paul the 'spin-doctor' of the ideology of Christianity) to suspend our intelligence and 'believe' in the notion of the 'virgin birth' of Jesus, and his resurrection from the dead. These patently irrational kinds of things are demeaning to the 'intelligence' that moves us and the man called Jesus. He was a mystic and a Sapien. We are at times much too adept at making things up.

While science is not irrational, at times even extremely clever scientists, can be. For example, the notion of bi-location is where a person or an object is believed to be physically in two places at once (not to be confused with 'out of body experiences', such as remote viewing, or astral travelling, which are skills that humans can develop, and which I have experienced 'involuntarily' on a few occasions as a young man). This is a superstition found in some religious circles, and yet it is also central to the standard interpretation of quantum theory. Known as the Copenhagen interpretation, it invites just this: that a sub-atomic particle is bi-located – labelled as being in a state of 'superposition' (this is more fully discussed in the chapter on quantum theory) – and is simultaneously spread out over an unknown area. Much of what is regarded as the weirdness associated with quantum theory, hinges on this irrational idea.

Science invites us to 'believe' in various models of reality, such as the Standard Model of quantum particles, or the Big Bang birthing of the universe. Yet these models are relative and undergo constant modification in accord with the progressive nature of scientific knowledge. And, importantly, scientific knowledge can never provide absolute certainty. Scientific knowledge deserves our interest, respect and admiration but, as with all knowledge, it should not be believed in.

I suspect that it is this inability of science to provide certainty in knowledge, that is the driver behind the 'flat Earth' and 'conspiracy theorists' (such as 'climate change deniers', and the 'hollow moon' believers) with their sometimes bizarre and irrational claims. Conspiracy theorists driven by fear engendered from their own ignorance, hook on to this uncertainty- which is essential to the progressive nature of scientific knowledge, which they assume gives them licence to indulge in flights of ludicrous fancy with self-appointed authority. 'True believers' also exist in other sectors of society, such as in the militant forms of atheism. Take, for example, the political doctrines of Marxism, complete with its own catechism as a structure of belief, maintaining in its central theory that human society moves through different stages, from capitalism toward a final communist system. Perhaps when Marx stated that 'religion is the opiate of the masses', he did not realise that his theory would also become a 'doctrine' and could be included as part of this form of 'collective opiate taking'. Belief, as the emotional attachment to ideas, is equally seen in people with religious, as well as materialist ideologies, from the mosque and the temple to the Humanist Society.

Holding any ideas with emotional attachment is both unnecessary and irrational. It is irrational to hold the idea that 'reason and rationality' have some kind of elevated or 'divine-like' status. Our capacity to reason is a gift, but it can never be more than the arbiter of *relative truth*, within an existing conceptual framework. Rationality and reason are relevant for assessing the inconsistencies that politicians specialise in, or for evaluating an objectivist model of phenomenal reality. But reason and rationality as forms of thinking cannot apprehend what is beyond 'mind-constructed' knowledge, as the Truth of Being.

Sapiens show remarkable tenacity in holding onto beliefs. And, regardless of having been shown clear evidence to the contrary, some people's beliefs are thoroughly rusted on, even in the face of overwhelming evidence to the contrary. This is known as 'cognitive dissonance'. A US President exploiting this fact, once said something to the effect that he could shoot someone, and people would still believe in, and vote for him. Sometimes people will die or commit horrific acts for their beliefs. Yet the 'self' and its beliefs stand as a fundamental discord with reality. Ever needy it wants to belong, to have certainty, to feel validated, to be safe, to impose itself and be important. Believing is the very basis of tribal behaviour. We believe in ideas, ideologies, religions, philosophies, social movements or political parties. But believing is a form of blindness, and a distortion of intelligence.

The 'self' with its projected identity overlaying a vacuum of ignorance is unaware that its existence and the knowledge it clings to is just not based in reality. But sometimes there is an opening in the ego-centre, exposing the chasm of ignorance as a glimpse into nothingness. Glimpsing this 'nothingness' can generate tremendous fear. Adopting beliefs acts as a shield from this fear, and from facing ignorance, because, by living in this manner, we can remain unaware that the ego-centre is the particular trance we are living in. The breakdown of self reveals a chasm of nothingness.

Yet nothingness is the basis of everything, as Being. Nothingness is a certainty that thought can neither know nor cling to. With beliefs only serving as a resistance to experiencing the immensity of Being, inner silence takes you beyond beliefs to experience a vibrant, wondrous universe ending thought's search for certainty.

A reflection on believing in God

Apparently, there are more people on the planet (approximately 3.5 billion) who believe in God or a Supreme Being, than those who do not. For those who do, there is often a strong sense that there is something 'up there' or 'out there' – something external to the person, and larger and more knowing than the human mind.

Could 3.5 billion people be completely deluded, merely engaging in some form of collective opiate, as Karl Marx suggested? And, considering the diversity of religions, how could one be true and not another? If we grow up in America, it is more likely we will be a Christian than a Buddhist. If we grow up in Iran it is more likely we will be a Shiite muslim than a Shia muslim, or a Buddhist. Each religion sees itself as the unique harbinger of truth. Each religion has different forms of belief inculcation, and each requires the unchallenged adoption of its set beliefs. With some religions, it is made clear that it is very dangerous to our well-being if we question proscribed beliefs.

When great natural disasters happen on the planet, such as the tsunami that hit Southeast Asia in 2004, people's belief in God is either intensified, or called into question. Physically, the whole planet was affected by that tsunami and the earth shifted measurably on its axis. Tragedies like this challenge the belief that we live in a physically stable, unchanging universe. Also challenged is the belief that we are separate, because people across the globe are affected by such events, given the immediacy of modern-day media reporting. Commonly, we hear of believers questioning whether a benevolent God could exist and cause such destruction, or whether God is punishing humans for being so sinful.

People's beliefs about how a Supreme Being should or should not act, are irrelevant to the cosmic forces behind events such as these. Such beliefs are really projections of our own mental and emotional frailties, arising from fear and ignorance, underpinned by the belief that we are separate from the universe itself. And it is a universe that can act with tremendous destructive violence, so we require a God to protect and oversee us, but sometimes, brutally, it does not.

What is real is that the universe does not function according to the fear-informed narratives and projections of the human mind. Projections such as; 'God is punishing us', 'we are more important than any other species', that 'the universe is specially designed for us', or that 'we, in particular, are the 'chosen ones' because we belong to the one true faith'. These notions are fabrications of the mind indicating a form of addiction to an anthropocentric view. This is a kind of measure of our self-importance and frames how we perceive. However, if we have no belief in a self-centre, nor in the collective importance of ourselves as a species, this precludes an anthropocentric view. Even though humans have a unique place on the planet, we are *unique like everything else*, but no more important than anything else.

Direct experiential knowing has an immediacy that signifies a different order of knowing from the empirical, which is dependent on sensual evidence, or rational argument, or a passionate belief in an idea. Apprehending the noumenal is a different order of truth, one subject to a different kind of knowing than the kind of truth that is phenomenal reality. The process of induction and deduction and the use of empirical evidence is relevant in objectivist knowledge, but in regard to the noumenal, it is indicative of an epistemic limitation, because to know Being requires experiencing without the filter of mind.

The famous psychologist Carl Gustav Jung, when asked if he believed in God, paused for a moment before replying that he did not believe in a projection in the sky. Instead, he said he knew 'God' directly, experientially. The 'God' that Jung is referring to is certainly not the religious, partisan God so frequently used to invoke a brutal war, moral outrage, or to validate a certain group as 'chosen', therefore creating division amongst human beings. The 'God' Jung was referring to is metaphysical and impersonal. It is more a formless universal consciousness or a cosmic intelligence that is experientially known. Rather than relying on belief, we can know totality experientially.

However, for religious beliefs to maintain stability, they must ensure a culture of reinforcement. Followers must attend the church, temple, synagogue or mosque, spend time with other believers, read scripture and pray or chant. All this is necessary in order to affirm the religious ideology, which also serves to expunge any doubt. It requires tremendous energy to maintain the constancy of a particular 'belief system'. By these means, the belief achieves a relative stability in order to maintain the illusion of certainty.

But this hard-fought-for certainty is ever precarious. Sometimes all it takes to dismantle the belief is for an inquisitive, curious mind to ask a 'difficult' question. Or, it might be a major life event, something catastrophic and unexpected, shaking beliefs and exposing them as the frail grasping of the mind – overlaying ignorance – which is all they really are.

> *Sitting quietly, doing nothing,*
> *Spring comes, and the grass grows by itself.*
> —Zen poem

'God', a metaphor for separation

At some stage, long ago perhaps, the term 'God' may have meant 'all-inclusive universe' before it became corrupted. Generally speaking, 'God' has now come to mean something 'partisan' supporting a particular group of people, and invoked to justify all manner of exclusions, injustices, prejudices, brutalities and war. Hence, given the historical baggage associated with how the term 'God' is commonly used, it does not refer to the 'totality' or Being. Given this, I cannot use it here.

Religions have developed strict codes of conduct, enforced through fear of punishment and reward, in order to control people's thoughts, bodies and behaviour. For example, it is universally common in religions for women to be treated unequally. They are deemed, by the self-appointed authority of men, as unclean, not worthy of holding the same office, or incapable of understanding and, in religious matters, to be segregated from the men. The only thing this really indicates is a fairly widespread fear of women. And it occurs from the monasteries and temples of the East, to the mosques of the Middle East, and the churches of the West. All of these are cultural and religious beliefs; none of them is spiritually informed. What is clear is that, at some point, people – most men – have got together and decided this inequality is part of the divine nature of things. But people make things up all the time; whether it is in the religious sphere, how things are made up in the world of politics, or how, in many countries, there is the scurrilous rewriting of history.

Moreover, believing in a separate transcendental God, and to reinforce the trance, engaging in the many rituals that support this, actually removes its followers from directly experiencing the non-separate, universal nature of Being. *Experiencing Being is one of immanence rather than transcendence.* Religious hierarchies have generally been fearful when members of their own flock have a 'direct experience', or something mystical outside the proscribed program. Direct experience is intimately available to everyone, because we are *all* chosen by virtue of being here. Experiencing Being requires no permission from any religious intermediaries.

The cosmologist and physicist Steven Hawking once stated that it was completely unnecessary to invoke God as the initiator of the beginning of the universe, as modern physics accepts the fact that something can come from nothing. This is in contrast to Hawking's earlier position, when he stated that God was an open possibility for getting the universe going, contrary to previously-held views on the laws of physics. The problem here lies in Hawking's conception of God. It is no different from that of traditional, theistic religions that see 'God' as a transcendental Supreme Being, separated from 'man', and who constructed phenomenal existence.

The Buddhists, Taoists, Advaita Vedantists, Yogi's and some of the classical Greek philosophers were wiser in this matter. They realised the inherent error in beliefs that arise from 'duality'. Instead they speak of an impersonal, universal consciousness – a consciousness that begins the universe, and experiences it through us – we are not separate from it. In the case of Buddhism and Taoism the 'emptiness' or 'void' can only be truly understood experientially, because 'non-Being' is the basis of existence. In this understanding, humans (and all other beings) have no self, or separate essences (soul). There is one consciousness, not individual ones. The 'void' is not a vacuity (as a form of mental vacancy or dullness) as it is sometimes misunderstood to be by Western thinkers and theologians, but rather is alive, suffused as knowing consciousness.

Let us consider what it would be like if the term 'God' were used to signify something akin to 'all of space'. For example, that which enfolds all fields, all matter, including 'dark matter', everything. 'Space' is present at the microcosmic level of quarks and the macrocosmic level of galaxies and their clusters. If we accepted that 'God equals space' then it would not be possible for people to conceive of it personally, or hold on to it emotionally in a partisan way. God/space could neither be considered as 'on our side', nor 'on someone else's side'. It could not be used in promoting a certain ideology of 'chosen people', because space is all-encompassing and all-inclusive.

Rather than believing in the notion of a separate transcendent God, it seems that more people are now becoming conscious of being connected to each other and to a 'living' planet. This is not necessarily being used as a new ideology (although this may well arise) but is part of a generalised awakening to Being. This is a form of spirituality minus religion, and is evident in some of the poetry quoted in this book, where we see the term 'God' being used in an expansive all-inclusive and experiential sense.

CHAPTER 4

EMBRACING IMPERMANENCE AND UNCERTAINTY

Many of the assumptions we employ on a daily basis are unavoidable. They speak to our existence in phenomenal reality. For example, when we plan for tomorrow, we trust that that there will be a tomorrow. We trust in systems of mathematics, language, physics and engineering, with the latter enabling us to build bridges that support our cars to drive safely over them. We agree on notions of set time and a calendar so that we can plan ahead. We trust that the body will do what it does (breathing, blood circulation and cell replication) to keep on living. But, of course, the body needs the right conditions to be healthy (food, air quality, fresh water, sleep, postural alignment, rest, exercise, et cetera). All such concepts necessarily hinge on certain assumptions.

Yet in each of these instances, including the continued functioning of the body, there is an important degree, however small, of uncertainty. And, rather than being problematic, there is a beauty in this uncertainty, because in welcoming the unknown, any attachments we have to the known, or to fear of the uncertain, effortlessly fall away. The process of attachment is our grasping at permanence and control, and it is the prospect of impermanence and being out of control that is the genesis of fear that results in the invention of beliefs such as a separate transcendent God.

The concept 'tomorrow' relies on the underlying concept of linear time, and a further underlying concept of our continued existence through time. Here we encounter uncertainty, for we do not know for sure if we will be here. But it is our unconscious attachment to these concepts that elevates them to something more in our own minds because we ignore the uncertain and ephemeral nature of things. But clinging to the illusions of certainty and permanence only increases our fragility by giving us a false sense of security. And with our perception thus conditioned it is now in a form of 'stasis', entranced.

Instead of being more present, we take things for granted because we are living according to a narrative of time, and a falsely weighted expectation that things will continue. It can happen surreptitiously, because soon we can feel entitled in a reality we have created that is self-focussed, static and objectified. It is a narrative of continued 'self', unconsciously inattentive to what is happening now. We anxiously project into an imagined future, or regretfully ruminate in the past. Both tendencies are created from clinging to ideas, and this clinging to ideas may well be a person's reality, but is it reality based in truth?

We know we are truly living in reality when we accept the impermanence of everything. Accepting impermanence is an antidote to taking things for granted, and the feeling of entitlement. Living is intrinsically uncertain because we never know when the winds will change and turn our lives upside down, through illness, injury, good fortune, or death. The mind can never foresee this, as hard as it may try. Calamity may strike so that the blessed of today become the refugees of tomorrow. The Stoics are particularly sage in how they refer to unexpected events, that is with a wise indifference.

Yet so much of our way of living speaks of our attachment. We go out of our way to insulate ourselves from discomfort and impermanence. We avoid facing the uncertainty of living, and try to protect ourselves from things unknown. Because of the insecurity that this generates, we have relied heavily on the insurance industry and pursued a model of economic growth and a style of living that we feel insulates us from impermanence and uncertainty.

However, the beginning of wisdom is to realise that impermanence and uncertainty are in fact essential, and central to our condition as ephemeral beings. By embracing uncertainty and impermanence we at once dismiss taking our lives, and each other for granted. Also destroyed is the falsity of entitlement, which has spread through much of the world in this current era. In its place is gratitude for living in a universe of beauty and wonder. This is the wisdom embedded in the truth of phenomenal reality.

The certainty that awareness provides is the truth of Being

The only certainty is awareness itself or, we could equally say, Being. Beliefs, as already discussed, require constant reinforcement to maintain. They are a misplaced search for certainty. But naturally the pressure to believe also engenders doubt in the more enquiring mind. The belief commonly held in Western culture is that it is our ability to think which is the primary – if not the only – tool through which we can know about ourselves and the world.

But consider for a moment *that thought cannot truly know anything*. It is rather that only consciousness knows, and thought is not consciousness; it is a manifestation of consciousness. Thought itself has no cognition; it is an expression of cognition. Yet it is this belief in the primacy of thought that has completely obscured the epistemic significance of direct perception and obscured the true nature of consciousness. The upshot from this is manifested in the way we live disconnected from nature.

Confidence comes from seeing things as they are, free of unnecessary assumptions and wishful thinking. In this, we have neither expectation nor entitlement. In this moment pause and experience the immensity of Being, beyond conceptualisation, to a silence where there is no room for beliefs or doubts. This knowing is the only truly certain knowing we can have, as the awareness of Being. Awareness is the only permanence that we can have; not thought, not feeling, not sensation, not experiences.

> *We have to nourish our insight into impermanence every day. If we do, we will live more deeply, suffer less, and enjoy life much more. Living deeply, we will touch the foundation of reality, nirvana, the world of no-birth and no-death. Touching impermanence deeply, we touch the world beyond permanence and impermanence. We touch the ground of being and see that which we have called being and nonbeing are just notions. Nothing is ever lost. Nothing is ever gained.*
>
> —Thic Nhat Hahn, *The Heart of the Buddha's Teaching*

Welcoming impermanence by resting in awareness

Everything changes, nothing remains without change.
—The Buddha

Resting in awareness brings a knowing of being at home anywhere we find ourselves. Gone is the search for any form of external affirmation; rather we abide in Being. With nowhere to go, nothing that we could miss out on, and nothing to achieve in terms of an imaginary 'self-development', there is acceptance of whatever comes our way. The mind cannot grasp the immensity of this. Accepting whatever happens is a state of deep alignment with the universe as it is. This does not mean that we are in any way psychotically insulated from what happens around us. Grief is experienced when a dear friend dies, but not as a loss to 'self'. It is rather the acceptance of what is, that enables us to navigate difficulties and losses, and then see the way ahead. It is a way of travelling lightly but with full gravitas.

In this way being present brings both true stability and, paradoxically, an exquisite vulnerability in greeting the impermanence of existence. In fact, strength lies in realising the essential vulnerability of living, as opposed to any form of grasping entitlement, which reveals, in people who do this, the development of a façade of invulnerability. In reality they are only increasing their fragility.

This embracing of impermanence is encapsulated in the adage, 'This too shall pass'. This saying was advice, given by a wandering Sufi mystic to a Sultan, on the merits of not clinging to, or seeking, experience. The story tells of how the Sultan, a man who owned everything and yet always craved more, was impressed by the youthful vigour and merriment of a Sufi he encountered sitting on a wall of his palace. The Sufi was eating a pear he had taken from the Sultan's tree. The Sultan had the Sufi bought before him, reminding him that he could be executed for this theft. The Sultan could see there was no fear in the Sufi's eyes, but instead a mysterious wild merriment, and asked him why he was not afraid, and what was the source of his happiness. The Sufi replied that, as with all experiences, 'this too shall pass'. Upon hearing this wisdom – that non-attachment to the mind and life events sets us free – the Sultan immediately asked to become his disciple. Here the Sufi represents the difference between Eudamonia (experiencing the joy of the numinous), and the Sultan's failed search for happiness in Hedonia.

Another famous Taoist parable expresses this impermanence just as well, emphasising the wisdom of equanimity and non-attachment:

A farmer and his son had a beloved stallion that helped the family earn a living. One day, the horse ran away and their neighbours exclaimed, 'Your horse ran away, what terrible luck!' The farmer replied, 'Maybe so, maybe not. We'll see.'

A few days later, the horse returned home, leading a few wild mares back to the farm as well. The neighbors shouted out, 'Your horse has returned and brought several horses home with him. What great luck!' The farmer replied, 'Maybe so, maybe not. We'll see.'

Later that week, the farmer's son was trying to break one of the mares and she threw him to the ground, breaking his leg. The villagers cried, 'Your son broke his leg, what terrible luck!' The farmer replied, 'Maybe so, maybe not. We'll see.'

A few weeks later, soldiers from the national army marched through town, recruiting all the able-bodied boys for the army. They did not take the farmer's son, still recovering from his injury. Friends shouted, 'Your boy is spared, what tremendous luck!' To which the farmer replied, 'Maybe so, maybe not. We'll see.'

Let go, and rejoice!

By understanding that nothing is permanent, we are 'grounded' in reality. The attempt to achieve permanence is the way of the world because it is only the mind, with its craving, that seeks to create permanence. Misplaced ideas of permanence manifest in two ways: through transcendental beliefs such as in a separate immortal soul; or in an attachment to phenomenal reality, such as in the desire to own or possess something, or someone, of this world. But both of these beliefs in the transcendental and the phenomenal are delusory.

In relationships, institutionalised marriage has often been used as a way of safeguarding a lifestyle and giving a sense of permanence through the possession and control of another. In objectifying the other as a 'possession', the sense of loving commitment in a relationship is replaced by entitlement, resulting in taking our spouse for granted. In the mind that grasps and wants to control, there is the loss of innocence and with this, love disappears.

Marriage only truly works if we can release the other from our mental projections and expectations. By loosening mental attachments and the craving to be in control, we accept impermanence, experiencing the delight and wonder of living with that other special and ephemeral being. A commitment, as symbolised by a marriage, is a recognition of a connection of special significance; something that cannot be manufactured or imagined, but rather that can be deeply understood and felt and, only then, meaningfully shared in ritual. In this meeting of significant relationship, is a palpable sense of destiny.

Understanding the truth of phenomenal reality is to experience that 'life is change', whether it is in noticing the fall of a leaf in the creative play of nature, the inner landscape of our sensations, or the fleeting joy of family, partners and friends. Understanding impermanence is an antidote to entitlement and as the Upanishads advises 'let go, and rejoice'. An examined life reveals that the content of consciousness is life's impermanence, along with the understanding that only awareness has permanence.

Life is a series of natural and spontaneous changes. Don't resist them—that only creates sorrow. Let reality be reality. Let things flow naturally forward in whatever way they like."

—Lao Tzu

Finding our true nature

Looking at all that is impermanent is discovering what we are not. Essentially it begins the discovery of what we are revealing our true nature beyond self. The Advaita teacher Ramana Maharshi taught this, using his questioning technique to reveal what was ultimately true. The device is a question posed 'who am I? and the response elicited: Neti-Neti in Sanskrit means 'not this, not this' to any identifications with the mind or body.

We can commence this line of investigation with: I am not my thoughts because I am aware of thoughts and they appear and disappear in awareness; I am not my feelings because they too come and go in awareness; I am not my bodily sensations because they too come and go in awareness. I am not the various roles I have in life as teacher, farmer, employee/employer, girlfriend, son and friend et cetera, because these too are all impermanent. These impermanent roles do have a relative truth and they all need to be honoured in good faith, but without understanding the deeper source of our identity, we remain ignorant of the vastness of Being as the inner truth of our identity.

We are that which does not change, as the permanence of awareness/consciousness. This, and only this, has no bounds and is the source of all there is. It has no beginning and has no end: it is neither born nor does it die, yet ultimately it is who we are.

CHAPTER 5

NO-MIND AND NON-DUALITY

Into a soul absolutely free
From thoughts and emotion,
Even the tiger finds no room
To insert its fierce claws.
One and the same breeze passes
Over the pines on the mountain
And the oak trees in the valley;
And why do they give
different notes?
No thinking, no reflecting,
Perfect emptiness;
Yet therein something moves,
Following its own course.
The eye sees it,
But no hands can take
hold of it —

> *The moon in the stream.*
> *Clouds and mists,*
> *They are mid-air*
> *transformations;*
> *Above them eternally shine*
> *the sun and the moon.*
> *Victory is for the one,*
> *Even before the combat,*
> *Who has no thought of himself,*
> *Abiding in no-mind-ness*
> *of Great Origin.*
>
> —A Taoist priest [5]

Originally the term 'no-mind' comes from the Chinese 'wu-hsin', and was introduced by Hui-neng (638-713 AD), the sixth and last patriarch of Chan (Zen) Buddhism in China. We also find, in the Japanese warrior culture connected with Zen, the term 'mishin no shin', meaning 'mind of non-mind', shortened to 'mishin'. This term was used to describe a state of alertness and mental stillness where we are completely present in the moment. This state was essential for going into combat, free of ego-based fear, thought and emotion, but was also used for daily activities. It is a form of *heightened presence*. In this highly developed warrior culture, a warrior no longer saw himself as a fighter but just as a living being, moving through space, responding creatively to the moment, and experiencing a 'mysterious flow'.

I am using the term 'no-mind' to convey two things: first, 'no-mind' is a general, spontaneous quietness of the mind – or 'no-thing-ness'; second, it is unconditioned because there is a 'seeing' without the filter and interpretation of the mind, language, and emotion. In experiencing no-mind comes an understanding that thoughts and thinking are not the primary source of our identity.

Useful thinking, as opposed to 'self' rumination, is relevant for specific types of knowledge, such as practical matters in problem solving, constructing 'models' of reality, communicating ideas, and creative expression. 'Self' absorption is dysfunctional thinking.

No-mind, then, is not the complete cessation of thought, because it remains to be used as a practical and creative tool. Rather, it is the ending of the self-absorbed, incessant internal dialogue that is a symptom of living on auto-pilot, in maintaining the trance of ego, with all the insecurities, fears and neuroses that this entails, which are all forms of unconsciousness.

In different cultural settings it is referred to as 'original mind' or 'natural mind'. It is akin to the child-like state of consciousness that exists before our minds become confused by the world, occupied with 'self-absorption' and habitual patterns of thinking. This deep mental quiet is spoken of, particularly in the spiritual traditions of non-duality, by sages and mystics. For example, amongst the Advaita sages in India, in the Buddhist traditions of Chang, Zen and Dzogchen, in the Taoist tradition of China, in the Shamanic traditions of Indigenous peoples, and also as part of Sufi, and Christian mysticism.

In religious orthodoxies and secular intellectual culture, however, there has been a failure to understand this unconditioned state. This is due to a number of factors: because it is experiential in nature and does not fit into any form of orthodoxy of belief in a religious sense; in secular and scientific culture it is not a part of any systematic form of rational thought or having an intellectual function and is a minus in knowledge building.. No-mind is something unknown, and consequently there has been fear and suspicion of this kind of experiential knowing from the religious and rationalists alike, because it is outside their epistemic norms. Often, in religious cultures, for those having 'direct experience' or experiencing other states of consciousnes, outside of what is authorised as 'sanctioned' experience, it is better to keep quiet about it.

In science, there is a tendency to regard mystical experience with irrational prejudice because it cannot be reconciled with rational thinking. Someone experiencing 'oceanic' states or 'inner silence' is seen as regressive, irrational, and irrelevant, and maybe even suffering from a form of mental instability. However, conclusions like these are unexamined, signifying a lack of experiential insight and informed by a fear of the unknown. Narrow thinking like this, is commonly held in the philosophical ideology of materialism. Philosophers and scientists who hold these views only demonstrate how unaware they are that their lens of perceiving is clouded with conditioned ideas.

Individuating from tribal group-think

No-mind brings an innocence and freshness to moment-to-moment experience, because no-mind is *resting in awareness* or we could call it *presence*. It differs from the innocence of the child who has not yet developed a sense of her individuation. The child is still unaware of the true nature of Being. As she matures, she naturally separates from her parents and becomes aware of being a unique person. In order to individuate as an adult, she will need to separate from the herd mentality with its collective belief systems, to stand in the light of her own awareness to authentically be herself.

If maturation does not fully occur, she will not separate from the herd mentality and will simply adopt the beliefs and attitudes which are her conditioning. She will have become an isolated island of thought, an individual self, and may even hold the misguided belief that she is free and authentic. However, this is a form of immaturity. By identifying with tribal thinking, attaching to collective opinions, ideologies, consumerist behaviour, belief systems and prejudices you have ensured that you are chained. Individualism and tribal group-think go hand in glove, as markers of this immaturity. In contrast, we mature by realising that we are not our thoughts, and by not identifying with our thoughts about others. We individuate by liberating ourselves from all forms of group-think.

This journey in the maturation of consciousness contains a paradox: as we individuate from our society of human beings to stand alone, we come to experience the connectedness of undivided Being, and the sense of ourselves as 'global citizens'. You stand beyond all forms of ideology.

With individualism there is a desire to be different from everybody else, as expressed by superficial acts of choice and will. But these choices are orchestrated by a thought centre which is conditioned, and hence conforms to its own prejudices, as was correctly pointed out by philosopher Baruch Spinoza. There is no free will, but there is freedom of Being, which is entirely different. Individualism is never more than conditioned behaviour seeking markers of identity that give an illusory sense of belonging, whether to the church, to the 'branding' of consumer goods, to a philosophy, a political ideology, or a guru.

In contrast, individuating is something that occurs at a deeper level. It stems from the insight arising from not attaching to thought itself, in the understanding that ego, the individual, is an illusion. Individuating frees us from comparison, envy and imitation, bringing a genuine authenticity – a point well-articulated by the existentialists. Paradoxically, in order to use thought appropriately, practically, and creatively, we need to separate from it. This comes in the letting go process of resting in awareness.

Individuating is a process of liberating from the conditioned mind, and all forms of 'group-think', as we come to know ourselves alone, as 'undivided Being'.

Silence is everywhere if we are good at listening

There is nothing special about experiencing no-mind, because it is natural. We do not have to sit in a cave or live in a monastery to find it. In fact, these activities are not guaranteed to make us less mentally busy at all. The Silence of Being can be apprehended by any person, anywhere, any time, but is only detectable if we are good at listening. It is present even in the most intense and busy cacophony of any of the world's major cities. Indeed, the silence of Being has nothing to do with how well we can hear.

Most of us have had at least some experience of a spontaneous, inner silence; for example, when we witness something truly beautiful such as a sunset or the night sky; when we see a work of art; when we take certain plant hallucinogens, or in moments of sexual ecstasy. The mind in these instants is spontaneously silent. We feel awe in the presence of natural beauty in a moment of intense communion. We experience a moment without time, and can be aware of a sense of the infinite. People sometimes refer to this state as 'God', because it is a brush with the immensity of Being. Joy is a commonly experienced side effect of the cessation of the internal dialogue.

This type of experience cannot be fabricated or manufactured by our thinking; nor can it be willed, because it happens without the control of thought. Often after these 'peak experiences' the mind quickly moves in, grasping for more, wanting to repeat what is already now past and nothing more than a memory. We may then try to look for the next 'peak experience' as the ever-restless self, grasps to recapture what was.

The real source of happiness cannot be found in chasing experiences in *Hedonia*. Rather, it lies in resting in awareness itself, completely ungraspable to the mind - *Eudaimonia*. It is a blessing to discover this natural reservoir of peace, but few of us do. Why is this? The answer is simple: because we are distracted by the internal dialogue that drives us to seek pleasure or happiness in things, people and situations – in fact, everywhere but in the simplicity of Being. We endlessly verbalise this in our minds, thinking, 'I wish I didn't do that', 'I hope this happens', 'What if this happens?', 'I wish this wasn't happening', 'I'm terrified of that happening again', or 'If I do this or that practice or initiation, I will feel better'.

This inner dialogue vacillates with all the choosing, strategising and analysing. In the end it disempowers, fragments and depletes us. It is a restlessness that is unsustainable; we waste a tremendous amount of energy maintaining a momentum of restlessness, perpetuated by an ongoing neediness. We can become befuddled, rigid, scheming, self-concerned, complaining, timid, arrogant or frustrated. Rather than an effort of will, it is resting in awareness that short-circuits ego-authority and breaks the cycle of self-defeating negativity.

We experience authenticity and inner power when we are present; when we are in the reality of 'what is'. By pausing a thought and listening, we notice that the silence of Being is always here: alive as vibrating consciousness, the source of all manifestation. Being cannot be described, measured and known in the empirical sense, like the phenomenal world, it can only be known in silence.

*All of man's troubles come from not knowing how
to sit still, alone in a room.*

—Blaise Pascal, French mathematician (1623–1662)[6]

Different kinds of laziness

There are some common obstacles that prevent us experiencing no-mind, keeping us in a self-limiting kind of trance. It is only human beings who tend to suffer from this unique form of unconsciousness because while we have the ability to amplify our awareness, we also have a remarkable capacity for self-delusion. Directly correlated with this is that we are the only species that has the potential to be conscious of consciousness itself.

We actuate our species name *sapiens* (Latin meaning 'wisdom') when we realise our innate potential in expanding awareness, because awakening consciousness in us, is our evolutionary imperative. At the same time, we are individually and collectively expert at creating obstacles to this, that are primarily psychological in nature.

The Buddha referred to these obstacles as 'forms of laziness'. I venture that there are more than the three he is said to have initially described:

> ***Slothfulness:*** When we suffer from slothfulness, we just cannot be bothered and prefer the dullness that comes with repetition and habituated thinking and behaviours. Anything and everything can seem effortful, and this basic inertia stymies our curiosity. This maintains awareness at the lowest possible so that we are only dimly aware.

Negative 'self'-talk': 'I am always like this', 'I always react in this way', 'I'm stupid', 'I never succeed at anything', 'I'm unlovable', 'What's the use in trying?', or 'I always fail at things'. This kind of 'self-talk' keeps us in isolation, with the nagging belief that we are victims, leading to a downward spiral of self-pitying. Awareness is diminished by identifying with the self and all its limiting beliefs.

Compulsive doing: Where we have identified with doing itself. The workaholic must keep constantly busy. There is a restless need to fill up every moment with excessive activity, excessive thinking, or excessive communication. This can also be in the form of the endless forms of electronic connectivity we currently indulge in. Ironically, this laziness stems from the fear of being idle, yet it is often in great idleness or meditation that we experience the profound – the great unknown – that is truly ourselves as.

Imitation: We remove ourselves from the universal creative intelligence when we try to be like others. This is a form of laziness and is the root of living inauthentically. All religious orders are based in this kind of laziness. Imitation is an important part of learning, with language, with studying music, or learning a Tai Chi form, but it is retrograde in the truth of Being.

Living on auto-pilot—the 'waking dream': This is a generalised laziness of unexamined living, wherein there is no real curiosity to become aware, just a desire to continue in a mode of living that only furthers egoic existence.

Identifying with prevailing systems of belief: By adopting herd mentalities, we are partaking in the 'opiates' that maintain our personal slumber, as a part of the unconscious of society. This is common in all religions, political and philosophical ideologies, and in consumerist and materialistic cultures. It is the laziness of 'group-think' and the following of doctrines, including religious Buddhism, which functions like any other 'ism'. Following group-think and doctrines are an obstacle to perception serving only to diminish our awareness.

These kinds of laziness cannot be defeated by thinking our way through them, such as believing that through a supreme act of will, we can transcend such laziness. This is because it is the unconscious identification with thought and the body that is the source of the laziness. The effort of will, which is thought's attempt to rouse itself, only furthers the fragmenting of mind and strengthens the ego-shell. Rather, it is the power of our awareness which is magnified as we let go and rest in 'it', that dissolves the obstacles. This happens with determination, but not with the effort that will entails. In giving up the 'struggle' to transcend laziness, or to reach an ego-projected end-state to become enlightened, paradoxically, the spell of the trance we have been living is broken. Being is already enlightened, because enlightenment is not a state that the self can ever achieve nor possess.

Meditation and no-mind

Stop all physical activity: sit naturally at ease.
Do not talk or speak: let sound be empty, like an echo.
Do not think about anything: look at experience beyond thought.
Your body has no core, hollow like bamboo.
Your mind goes beyond thought, open like space.
Let go of control and rest right there.
Mind without projection is mahamudra.
Train and develop this and you will come to the deepest awakening.

—From *Ganges Mahamudra* (trans. Ken McLeod)

Meditation is an umbrella term for the formal practice of focusing on our inner life with the express purpose of quelling the unruly nature of ego-based thought. Thought's unruly nature only happens where there is ignorance. Meditation, then, is a potent way of bringing understanding, by challenging the way that thought dominates our attention.

The effect of meditative practices when done well is twofold: first, by not attaching to thought we stop identifying with our thoughts. And second, the quelling of incessant and habitual thinking gives an experience of the greater expanse of consciousness. Taken together these enable us to experience liberation by no longer being colonised by conditioned thinking; empowering us to use thought, rather than to be used by it. The net result from meditation is the cleansing of the lens through which we perceive reality. This is profound because it is through this lens that we understand and experience the nature of our identity.

By shifting the hold our conditioning might have on us, we also experience a reduction in anxiety, the reduction of habitual unconscious thinking patterns, and a new sense of equanimity because we are no longer prey to depressive moods and self-pity. And consequently the persistent belief that we are a hapless victims of circumstance, is exposed, erasing itself from our consciousness. Beneath the conditioned dross of 'self' is a happiness which is unconditioned, as our natural state.

We discover another 'way', which does not involve imposing our will on others and manipulating the environment in pursuit of our goals. Goals may still exist, but in this 'way', we are no longer *driven* by goals; we are not attached to outcome, and we rest more deeply in acceptance of 'what is'. This way is expressed by the Stoic philosophers of ancient Greece, where what is considered primary is our connection to Being in a moment-to-moment basis. Goals can still be pursued, but neither to the detriment of, nor to the exclusion of, our harmony in Being.

The inner quiet from meditation takes us beyond habitual modes of thinking, and from thought's misplaced sense of sovereignty. This facilitates an increase in creativity and an increased capacity for concentration and productivity. This 'way' brings an underlying ease in the way we do everything, rather than the habitual effort (created by thought resistance) where everything we do can feel like a struggle.

Although there are countless ways of meditating, they can be divided into two basic approaches:

> ***Under the agency of thought – concentrating the focus of attention:*** These are meditative practices in which thought provides us with something to focus on, such as a mantra (repetition of a phrase or word, whether in Tibetan, Sanskrit or some other language), mandalas

(contemplative artwork), the subtle energy landscape of the body (chakras), the breath, or prayers. There are specific meditations for forgiveness, compassion, and healing. There are also some body-oriented meditations and movement practices such as yoga, tai chi, qi gong, Zen walking, labyrinth walking.

Being as agency – the pure observation/mindfulness: With this particular approach in meditation there is no object of focus. Pure observation has no known origins except in Being itself. One observes in a relaxed, attentive manner the 'content' of consciousness – thoughts, feelings, moods, urges, sensations as they arise and simultaneously let them go. And it also includes observing consciousness itself. Key to pure observation is 'letting go', or 'resting in awareness'. This is not strictly a 'technique', because the term 'technique' usually refers to practising something repeatable, or a pattern, like chanting, for example. Rather than a doing, *meditation, in essence, is being.*

It is particularly with this second approach that we can experience a radical shift in our relationship with everything including thought, feeling and sensation. Meditation 'practised' in this manner, is like food to awareness. With regular practice, it evolves from a secluded, time-limited experience, to be had while sitting on a cushion in a quiet room, to an ever-expanding awareness through the whole of our living in every moment. In this, the 'meditator' has disappeared and pure observation continues throughout our life, regardless. The only casualty is the sovereign place of the thinker.

Attachment – not thought – is the problem

The Buddha taught that mindfulness meditation – paying attention to the content of the mind in regular sitting practice and observing any attachment to this content – is highly beneficial, if not central, to awakening from the trance of the separate self. Furthermore, as mentioned above, meditation does not stop at the end of sitting practice, but inevitably magnifies to engulf all of one's day-to-day living.

But the term 'mindfulness', relatively recently introduced in English, is not completely accurate, because it conveys the idea of a mind full of thinking. Rather, by resting in awareness we restore all that occurs as the content of consciousness, including thought, into a proper perspective. And as is taught by the Buddha, it is only when our *attachment* to the content of the mind loosens, that thinking itself dissipates. And with this, a profound experience of stillness or emptiness can develop: the experience of 'no-mind'.

It also should be born in mind that *the goal of meditation is not to stop the mind.* Stopping the mind is like trying to silence chattering monkeys or herding cats. Attempting to stop the inner dialogue only gives the monkeys something more to talk about. Or, as we attempt to corral one cat, the others will easily slip through. The mind cannot be stopped! And why should it be stopped, when it is not the enemy. *Attachment is the problem and this is what ego is.* Thought is a friend, but when it is in the form of ego it is truly one's enemy. It is this attachment to mind, body and desire that keeps us in ignorance. In pure observation, the mind ceases its habitual noise by itself, without coercion.

By giving all-inclusive acceptance and attention to the stream of thinking, without judgement, thinking effortlessly dissipates. A good litmus test that your meditation is working is that, if it feels effortful, you are on the wrong track. Many people, as a result of ignorance in the way they approach the unruly nature of mind, discontinue meditation because they are trying to control or stop thinking, *by willing it*. Very soon it can all seem too hard, particularly if a meditation instructor has given a command to sit in mental stillness. It is not surprising that many who are introduced to this approach conclude that it is not natural for them to meditate, or experience inner quiet.

Inner quiet happens because *the mind stops by itself*, and this is a state that can be considered the most natural state of the mind because it is unconditioned. Conversely, a habitually busy mind is not a truly natural state, because constant self-referential thinking is symptomatic of our conditioning. (Of course, at times there may well be a pressing need for us to get busy to solve a problem, with our work or study, or to be creative with our thinking). However, a mind that is in a constant default state of busyness is functioning on an unconsciously conditioned 'auto-pilot'. In neuroscience the house of the ruminating ego is known as the 'default mode network', which is a structure throughout the brain. In studies meditators have been measured to naturally switch off this network as they experience inner silence.

In mindfulness the *mind is viewed as a friend* as we simply witness the stream of thoughts without trying to stop them, equally noticing the spaces between thoughts. This has the effect of reducing the inner struggle and increasing the experience of inner spaciousness. This is the beginning of our separating from thoughts, rather than attaching to them, acting on them, or judging them, and hence, identifying with them. Staying present in this witnessing, particularly in the beginning, requires patience and a compassionate attitude. This will include accepting habits of self-judgment or negative thoughts about our situation, or that of others.

Spontaneously, almost by stealth, a sensation of space emerges and a mental quiet happens without force. The chattering monkeys begin to rest peacefully. Because if meditation is not effortless, then we are engaged in some form of willing and controlling, which only stimulates the chattering monkeys, and further strengthens the 'doing' of the mind, and the notion of 'self as controller'.

All attempts to control the mind are born of division, where one part of the mind is trying to control the runaway part, our errant thinking. Controlling practices are themselves unsustainable because they require effort; we are constantly swimming against the tide, wherein thought is, from the outset, perceived as the enemy. Hence, we become inwardly divided, creating the duality of the 'controller' and the 'controlled', or the 'observer and the observed'. Meditation collapses this duality into pure observation.

Do we have to meditate or practise mindfulness in order to experience awakened consciousness? No, this is not necessary at all. But as someone once said, if awakened consciousness is viewed like having an accident happen to a person, then meditation makes you more accident-prone. Meditation is a process of consciously 'leaving the window of awareness open', and the breeze may or may not blow in. In awareness there are no guarantees, but it is a blessing when the zephyr comes through.

A deep natural quietness allows us to experience the impersonal energy of consciousness. Each of us *is* this consciousness. We are not just a tiny isolated island of thought living a trance, because our clinging to the content of consciousness is learned, and a matter of habit, keeping us in chains. And equally through understanding we can unlearn it and the chains fall away. Unlearning this the way of liberation. In Advaita, the phrase 'I am that' is used to signify the realisation of our identity in awakening to this non-duality of Being: with resting in awareness 'the way'. Meditation is really just being. And being is beyond all methodologies that the mind can invent.

Below, a Tantric Buddhist practitioner, Talopa (988–1069) gives this advice on meditative practice, translated from the Sanskrit, to his student Naropa:

Don't recall. Let go of what has passed.
Don't imagine. Let go of what may come.
Don't think. Let go of what is happening now.
Don't examine. Don't try to figure anything out.
Don't control. Don't try to make anything happen.
Rest. Relax, right now, and rest.
—Talopa, *The Six Words of Advice*

No-mind and spirituality

The term 'spirituality' is often confused with 'religion', but there is an important difference: religions comprise beliefs and constructs of the mind, whereas spirituality is purely experiential, relying on our direct knowing through a lens unclouded with mind and belief. The latter being conceptually-driven realities.

'Spiritual' means 'from spirit', and the word 'spirit' can have several meanings. It can conjure the idea of a non-physical entity; it can imply the notion of a soul or spirit of ourselves, or it can refer to the universe, like the 'Great Spirit' as used by American Indians. Also, there is the 'world soul', indicating a deeper dimension of Being. I am using 'spiritual' to describe direct knowing, as an experience of impersonal consciousness: a singular consciousness that is suffused in all that is. There is no denomination for this, nor any theology, nor even any theoretical arguments to support it. This is because it is not a product of thought, nor is it an intellectual position arrived at through a process of reasoned argument. And because spirituality is purely experiential, it cannot be known through the mind.

Spontaneously experiencing no-mind sees the 'energetic locus' shift from the thought centre in the head, to the 'spiritual heart', which informs our actions and ethical conduct in the world. But *no-mind is not a state of transcendence; it is one of immanence, of presence.* No-mind is not held by conceptual boundaries such as a separate 'higher' and 'lower' self, nor by the culturally conditioned morality of good and evil.

No-mind sees the genesis of an ethical compass aligned in the experiential harmony of a living universe. It produces an ethics that is fundamentally different from the duality of good and evil, which derives from a culture of transcendence. There is a deeper ethical compass of 'ultimate good' as a 'way of harmony'. This is beyond the culturally conditioned morality, and is akin to the ethics as expressed by the Stoics from ancient Greece, and much later by philosopher Barach Spinoza. It is most eloquently expressed by the Taoist philosophers of ancient China, such as Lao Tzu.

In the widest sense of the term, everything that 'spirituality' encompasses, can also be expressed with the word 'consciousness': a knowing-intelligence, even at the most rudimentary, inanimate level. It is essentially present everywhere. What we call 'matter' (a term that has been dramatically revised with the quantum era – see chapter 9) along with the space that matter occupies, is alive and intelligent as consciousness. Each of us can know this consciousness because from top to toe *this is what we are.*

The view that nature is suffused with a creative intelligence is congruent with ancient wisdom from the East, and with certain Western mystics such as William Blake, Meister Eckhart and Giordano Bruno, and philosophers such as Plato, the Stoics, Pythagoras, Parmenides, Heraclitus, Plotinus, Jesus, Leibniz, Swedenborg and Spinoza, and is common among Indigenous cultures.

Consciousness is not born, nor does it die. While birth and death occur for biological organisms, there is no birth and death in consciousness. While organisms die, at a deeper level, consciousness continues, for it is not a thing, rather it is an intelligence-energy. When we die, bacteria and maggots decompose the body so that it becomes food for worms; thus, *everything is the changing shapes of the one consciousness.* At a cosmic level consciousness is transforming through infinite cycles as the universe is eternally birthing and dying (the cyclic universe).

Life is a process of constant transformation just as the 'process philosopher' Alfred North Whitehead proposed in his radical book *Process and Reality: An Essay on Cosmology*[7]; while in death there is an end to an organism as we may define it, there is also a continuous process into something else.

Consciousness is impersonal because the belief in a separate, personal consciousness, as 'my consciousness' or 'your consciousness' is a fallacy. Likewise, spirits, entities and individual souls are not ultimately discrete. Instead, they have a different level of manifestation, yet their reality – while certainly not perceived by everyone, as this is dependent on a particular sensitivity – is of the one consciousness.

Everything that may appear as though it has discreteness, as a 'conscious entity', can be considered to be like the way a whirlpool appears as a discrete 'entity'. But nonetheless it is not separate from the greater body of water in which it occurs. In the same way, all beings are part of the infinite ocean of seamless consciousness. With notions such as matter, body, thoughts, souls, feelings and galaxies are as waves of different magnitudes in the infinite ocean of Being – nothing is self-existent, except Being itself.

> *Moonlight and the sound of pines are things we all know*
> *zen mind and delusion distinguish sage and fool*
> *go back to the place where not one thought appears*
> *how shall I put this into words for you?*
> —Hanshan Deqing (1546-1623)[8]

CHAPTER 6

FREEDOM BEYOND THE KNOWN

Recognise that the apparent is unreal
While the unmanifest is abiding
Through this initiation into truth
You will escape falling into unreality again.
—Ashtavakra and Nalin N. Nyas[9]

What is freedom? Freedom is unlimited expansion in space and time. Can we be free? The self as an individualised, crystallised thought structure is the bound confinement of a primary limiting belief: the belief in itself. If we believe we have a self, we are not free, and yet the freedom of Being, our true nature, is ever-present. If we experientially understand that we are infinite, timeless Being, then we know freedom.

When people think of freedom, they often think of political or social freedom. In many parts of the world we see the antithesis of freedom in cultures of dominance and subjugation, in warfare, political dynasties, tyrannies, systems of social class segregation or caste, along with all the various forms of exploitation. People punish, oppress, conquer, control or manipulate others to satisfy their own imagined needs, in an attempt to ensure that others are not free. But in identifying with these roles, either as the conqueror, or as the conquered, neither is free. For so-called 'freedom fighters' who are intent on achieving their brand of freedom, usually justified through a means that often includes violence to achieve their ideological end which is an end that can never really be justified because the net result is not freedom. This is because inevitably they become the new oppressors, who are in turn limiting the freedom of others. And so the cycle continues, because genuine freedom is not won through these means.

When we truly experience freedom, we cannot impose injustices or inequalities on others, because the true experience of freedom comes from experiencing the fundamental unity of everything. If we have truly understood the fallacy of 'self', we cannot engage in practices that further separation, that would justify exploiting or oppressing another, or in any way 'using' another human being for selfish ends. To do so would necessitate a belief in our own separation, and this only signifies our ignorance.

In countries with open democracies, freedom is championed as an ideal, yet people may still feel confined and oppressed. Some democratic countries have very high rates of depression, anxiety, and suicide, along with the prescribing of psychotropic medication. There may be less political, social or religious persecution and restriction, yet people may may still feel afraid, bullied, stressed, defeated and apathetic. It would seem that political, social and economic freedoms, important as they are, are not necessarily the defining criteria for the true experience of freedom.

This is because we can be politically free yet feel as burdened by the chains of our conditioning as if incarcerated in a prison. But even in prison we can still experience the freedom of Being.

This tyranny is due to mental and emotional conditioning, such as painful experiences from the past that may continue to plague us, as they negatively inform how we function and relate to others, and the world. This 'baggage' is the accoutrement of what constitutes the self, and as long as we carry this within us, we are not free.

Conversely, we may not feel burdened because we may be unaware, as these burdens have been so successfully buried. And instead, we may sincerely believe, and even stridently protest, that we are free. But the strident protesting of freedom is a give-away, indicating that we are not free and, rather, suffering from a form of delusion. Leaving these burdens unexamined only ensures that we never truly experience the liberation that lies in our innermost.

> *The only way to deal with an unfree world is to become so absolutely free that your very existence is an act of rebellion.*
> —Albert Camus

The description of being a 'free thinker', means that our thinking exhibits a certain plasticity and creative flexibility, unconstrained by conventional thinking, enabling 'thinking outside the box'. Yet being a 'free thinker' does not preclude identification with the mind itself, or having a belief in a self. Subtly, 'free-thinkers' may still harbour self-images and engage in comparisons, such as being superior to, or cleverer than, others and, in so doing, they are certainly not free. Freedom truly lies in not creating any images of a self and released from this burden enables us to use thought freely.

In freedom we realise that we are not our thoughts, nor are we confined by our personal narratives, self-images, emotions or the body. This opens unlimited possibilities. We are 'free' regardless of our circumstances. Confusion only arises when we believe otherwise, that our freedom is dependent on our situation. Commonly there is also a confusion between freedom and license, but they mean and lead to different things. Freedom leads to eudaimonia, whereas license leads to hedonia which is an increase in suffering.

Accepting 'what is', is to rest in reality

In our living, we each have an opportunity to fulfil our potential as the wise hominid, to awaken from the slumber of duality, and experience what has always been with us: the freedom that is Being. In order to know this freedom of Being it is useful to ask, 'Am I really listening?' If we have no experience of the all-pervading silence of Being, is it because we are too distracted by the inner noise of thought?

Awareness is the prerequisite for this deep listening, no-mind is the method, and non-doing is the art.

As mentioned above, the noise of our conditioning may be obscuring this silence. And, far from feeling liberated, we feel hemmed in, frustrated or trapped in certain circumstances, or with burdensome memories, such as the traumas of the past – things over which we may feel we have no control. We may struggle against what we perceive as our 'situation'. However, freedom lies in a different direction. It lies in the *deep acceptance of what is*. In this acceptance we begin to let go and loosen the feeling of being stuck. Then we can no longer frame ourselves as 'victims'. Acceptance brings the understanding that we have total responsibility for our response to whatever our situation is. And then by 'leaning-in' to the stored feeling of pain (of being stuck) that our current situation holds, or the trauma of troubling memories, there is the possibility of a healing transformation. Then an unmistakable experiencing of freedom comes as a blessing.

Acceptance is not to be confused with timidity or acquiescence to things that are unjust or unethical. Deep acceptance is being with what is. This automatically shifts our relationship to the past and to our situation; there is a 'letting go' that allows insights to arise along with opportunities that life presents, to resolve persistent problems. This might also manifest as the freedom to assert that we are not a 'doormat', or to be energised to address that nagging injustice.

A story comes to mind of a man I knew who was significantly paralysed by a stroke (cerebrovascular accident – CVA). Despite his physical disability, he told me of the joy he felt regarding his experience of Being. Paradoxically his illness had allowed him to fully participate in his life in a way that he had not experienced before the stroke. He recounted the pleasure of seeing the light early in the morning, the smell of freshly roasted coffee and the beauty of the changing seasons; all things he had taken for granted before his stroke. He was now acutely aware of such beauty and the simple bliss of living. For the first time, he recounted, he was experiencing awe. He said he felt remarkably free of thought in the form of worry and anxiety, from which he had suffered previously. Now he had no complaints, and was enjoying feeling and sensing things as they are, in the fleeting impermanence of each moment.

Situations are what we make of them. They could be viewed as intolerably restrictive or oppressive, or when accepted as is, there is equanimity. The resistance to what is, manifests in the tendency to worry or feel doom and gloom. These projections immediately sink us into the mire of 'self' and we feel 'stuck' in our situation.

This generates thoughts of self-pity or frustrated anger as we feel victimised by our 'terrible circumstances'. 'Why is it happening to me?' As we identify with these thoughts we feel helplessly trapped. However, if you pay careful attention you will notice that it is this *identification* with the thoughts (the mulling over of our circumstances) that is the very source of the feeling of restriction, not the circumstances themselves. Instead, if we stay present in the deeper acceptance of what is, then from the depth of this practice strength and resolve will arise, and the way ahead will open. This might be to break free of an abusive relationship, or to creatively use our 'time' if, for example, we are actually incarcerated in a prison, to deepen in our understanding in Being.

A deeper understanding sees the transformation from being a victim of circumstance to embracing whatever is happening now. Because, regardless of whatever movie (our life situation) is playing on the screen of our awareness, by accepting and letting go, *resting in awareness is the direct way to realising our freedom as Being*.

Being is without confinement; only the mind can be confined. When there is no ruminating about our situation, we are creatively open and freed from worrying. The feeling of being stuck disappears. There is no one to worry about! And far from needing ideal conditions, we can experience the freedom of Being even in the most extreme circumstances. This was the inspiration for Victor Frankl's book, *Man's Search for Meaning*, in which he spoke of his experience as an Austrian Jew in a German concentration camp during the Second World War. In this most horrendous type of incarceration, Frankl contends that:

Everything can be taken from a man or a woman but one thing: the last of human freedoms, the ability to choose one's attitude in any given set of circumstances, to choose one's way.
—Viktor Frankl[10]

How do we gain such freedom? The answer is simple: we already have it. Contrary to some speculation, we do not have to *do* anything; freedom of Being is independent of circumstances. If we do not feel free it is because we have allowed ourselves to be colonised with narratives that say we are not free: that freedom is dependent on particular circumstances. And while it might be marketed to us that we must do certain things in order to be liberated, the truth is that we do not need to *do* anything. We certainly do not need to belong to a special group, perform certain practices or initiations, attend endless workshops, or believe in something in order to gain what we already have. Because it is not a matter of 'doing' and 'believing'; it is rather a matter of 'non-doing' and 'non-believing'. It is from going deeper into the nature of awareness itself, which is choice-less, that gives us the freedom to choose a response, or attitude, within any given context. In this way, we are truly authoring our lives, rather than following conditioned narratives or acting habitually or predictably in a formulaic, or reactionary manner (as a victim, for example) which is patently not free.

There is no greater mystery than this: being Reality ourselves, we seek to gain Reality. Our real nature is liberation. But we imagine we are bound. We thus make strenuous efforts to become free while all the while, we are free. We will be surprised that we were frantically trying to attain something which we have always been and are.
—Ramana Maharshi (1879–1950)[11]

Freedom is much more than an ability to choose

A common misunderstanding about freedom is that it is defined by our ability to choose. Choice is used as the defining criterion for our personal, political, religious, social and economic freedoms as our 'freedom of choice'. But 'choice', if we look closely, is really a play of mind. The nature of choosing in this way is a mental activity, and invariably this is predicated on the existence of the separate self, the 'chooser', who is doing the choosing. The act of choosing is rather like a mirage of what freedom really is. Because if the choice we make is determined by the particular conditioning we have, it is not an expression of freedom at all.

True freedom, however, does not come from the process of mentally choosing, because it is beyond our conditioning, and hence beyond mind. Freedom, instead, comes from experiencing the nature of awareness itself. Awareness is the spaciousness in which different possibilities can be seen. From this awareness, it is not just a matter of 'will I do this, or that' as a process of thinking, reasoning and then deciding; rather, it is a 'listening to the impersonal intelligence' of Being. Only then, do we intuitively know the right way ahead that is not conditioned.

The way we live can ask us to make myriad choices, many of them driven by our conditioning, furthered by the frenetic commercial culture that we are surrounded with. Without an inner stillness, the mind can spin with the busyness of it all, to the point where many people feel overwhelmed and confused, giving rise to a new phenomenon described as 'choice exhaustion'. If freedom were simply reduced to a matter of choice, it would be 'the more, the better'. Instead, the mind becomes over-stimulated, to the point of mental burn-out.

There is a tendency in some parents to pass on their confusion and their own 'choice addiction' to their children. Yet if children are given too much choice at an early age, it does not give them greater insight into the nature of their freedom. Instead it gives them the burden of self-importance, by reinforcing the power of the thought entity as the 'chooser'. Parents, in doing this, are unwittingly feeding a monster, as the thought entity gathers importance, feeding on the power to make choices. Children in wealthier countries with this constant stream of 'choice stimulation' can soon develop a misplaced feeling of entitlement, unconsciously following the patterns of their parents.

The commercial world panders to the choice addiction of both adults and children, furthering a culture of individualism, consumerism, and entitlement. Concomitant with this is a rise in narcissistic attitudes and behaviour.

In traditional American Indian culture, youth are encouraged, at a certain point of maturity, to go into the wilderness and sit for as long as necessary in a state of deep receptivity. There they receive a message from the 'Great Spirit' (consciousness) about what they are meant to be doing with their lives. It is known as a 'vision quest'. They are not asked to 'choose' between a plethora of options, but rather to receive guidance from their 'inner being' as to what their mission in life is. This is a very different process from the more superficial choices and information overload that our youth are currently confronted with. The absence of a culture of inner listening and trust in Being, along with other oppressions and pressures the young are faced with, contributes, to some degree, to the unfortunate rise of mental health problems, addictive behaviours, and youth suicide.

Mistakes and consequences

The notion of mistakes comes from idealised projections of how things 'should be' in a transcendentalist culture, where we are always striving for perfection. The insecure self is often engaged in measuring and comparing itself against others, striving for perfection, or reaching for a transcendent 'higher self', that is forever unreachable because it is an unreachable idealisation.

Then there is the rumination over so-called lost opportunities, incorrect decisions or bad choices. On a movie set there might be different takes of a scene in order to achieve the pre-conceived vision of the director – in this sense, mistakes are 'miss-takes'. But in the reality of living, each moment unfolds as a perfect expression of the Destiny of Being. At this deeper level, it is choice-less, and mistakes are just not possible.

Everything that happens is an expression of an infinitely patterning intelligence in which there are no mistakes. And this includes all events that we may interpret as terrible, including natural disasters. Our attempts to control and idealise become fraught with difficulty because we get so attached to our preconceived goals and outcomes. But I am not suggesting we should not plan or envision, but our problems arise from attaching to what we want to happen. *Attaching* to our plans or outcomes gives rise to a fear of making mistakes, which inevitably creates anxiety, sometimes enough to paralyse one from action.

Awareness that we are Being naturally shifts our behaviour because we are aware that we *are* this impersonal consciousness. And, by fully accepting the reality of 'what is happening', we appreciate what is specific for us in our particular life situation. Each of us receives the lessons that we need from whatever our particular situation presents. And, *by not minding whatever happens, we are in the freedom of accepting whatever does happen*. Making mistakes are just not part of the equation: the concept of mistakes is rather a construct from the constrictive prism of self, because whatever actually is, is perfection.

Fear and self-concern reinforce the mind as the separate 'doer', 'problem maker' and 'resolver', when in fact *attachment to the mind itself is the problem*. Every action *does* have consequences. But all actions are right actions if, and only if, these actions are informed from an awareness of undivided Being. In awakening from the trance of self, there is no attachment to the outcome of our actions. Actions that are born of this understanding, are congruent with the wellbeing of others, harmonious with the totality.

At times, artists and poets in their different media allude to the experience of being inspired and creatively engaged at a level beyond the superficial mentality of choice and mistakes. While an artist might use the accumulated experience of mind as an essential reference for their work, there is also a more important appeal to a level beyond mind that is unconditioned and hence without artifice. The Australian surrealist painter and art critic, James Gleason, offered an insight into his creative process. He spoke of a state of consciousness wherein fear is transcended, and the 'work flows unimpeded', as if the artist is 'channelling energy', like a form of transmitting device. Gleeson expressed that, in this state, the artist no longer thinks about how they are going to do it: 'There are no mistakes because whatever happens won't be a mistake'.

Freedom brings responsibility

Man is condemned to be free; because once thrown into the world, he is responsible for everything he does.
— Jean Paul Sartre

Thoughts pass through our awareness but some get stuck as a specific set of self-images, narratives and beliefs. People who attach to very destructive patterns of thinking may become dangerous to themselves or others. When there is no separation from thought, and instead it is where we seek our identity, any one of us is prone to a degree of mental imbalance. This is a result of the persistent attachment to, and unquestioned belief in, the independent reality and sovereignty of the 'thinker'.

Emotions are also thoughts but with an extra charge of energy that we feel in the body, generally below the neck. Emotions felt in the body are at the interface between the hormonal system, the nervous system and the internal organs. There is merit in the way traditional Chinese medicine provides an experiential landscape of the body, associating the key emotions with the major body organs, and meridians or channels that conduct subtle energy (chi) throughout the body. Emotions are deeply embedded and embodied, but they are still thoughts; it is just that they have different locations and associated energy charges from the general Western model of emotions being located in the head.

When we get worked up emotionally, these thoughts activate the hormonal system, flooding the nervous system with peptides giving us strong bodily sensations. This manifests in butterflies in the stomach when we have pre-performance anxiety; adrenaline-charged fear if we are approached by a dangerous predator that makes us weak at the knees and can even paralyse us; anger rising from the solar plexus to the head; intense sorrow experienced as a pain in the heart; grief that makes us sob uncontrollably, connected with the lungs; or joy and excitement that increase the heart rate and charge the whole body with tingling pleasure. Even cowardice is expressed as a lack of 'intestinal fortitude'… or in the saying that 'he or she does not have the stomach for it'.

Just as all emotions are coupled with an energetic charge, they are also preceded by thought, even if this occurs without much awareness. For instance, if we harbour stubborn thoughts about how things 'should' be, and then things do not happen that way, we may feel an emotion on the anger spectrum, anywhere from irritation to building frustration, anger, and eventually to full blown rage. Through being inattentive to this build-up we can 'blow a fuse' and explode with violence that is harmful to both ourselves, and to others. But so long as we have a functioning conscience it may later fill us with regret. With anger and rage there is also the cost of the adrenalin load in the body as an aftershock, and it can take some time to re-establish equanimity after this kind of emotional discharge.

Only sustained pure observation (rather than analysing or judging) will short-circuit the attachment to thought, and short-circuit the 'body-based thoughts' of emotions. 'In situ', we become aware of building attachments. And in noticing this process of attaching, the momentum of what was previously an unconscious process of building emotion to an eventual tipping point, is dissipated. And just as thoughts do, emotions will pass, vanishing like clouds moving across the eternally clear sky of our awareness.

Some emotions and moods, which might be labelled negative, can get stuck. These can be held in the body-mind for years, even a lifetime, as an underlying mood or attitude, often creating various forms of mental illness, and, if left unresolved, can affect physical health. Memories of incidents interpreted as traumatic, if unprocessed, can also haunt people inter-generationally as they pass through ancestral lines, as is verified by studies in epigenetics. In this way, we can truly carry the 'sins of our ancestors'. For each of us, our lives can be viewed as an opportunity to heal and release these burdens or issues that we may carry from our particular ancestral heritage.

But we have no ownership of thoughts and emotions. They are neither yours nor mine. And this is because there is no separate entity that is the genuine author of thinking, feeling and sensation. While there is an important level of reality in our narrative and history, we are universally seduced into believing in this 'phantom self', and that it is even the arbiter of what is real. Hence, we define who we are from this history. At a profoundly deeper level, though, we are neither our personal history, nor our ancestors' histories.

But what of responsibility? We are totally responsible for how we respond to everything of our inner life (thoughts emotions, et cetera) and for our actions. We are in error when we blame others for how we feel or behave, because no one can make us 'feel' angry, or influence our behaviour, without our total complicity. 'Reacting' with anger is an act in unconsciousness. Responding with anger may well, in a given situation, be the appropriate response, but only when – in the light of awareness – it is used for effect. It is more an issue of how conscious we are. If we have unconscious baggage and experience our 'buttons' pressed by the behaviour of someone else, it is, rather, an opportunity to get in touch with the conditioning that we still undeniably carry … and let it go.

We are responsible precisely because we are free. Freedom as the de-conditioning of self, necessarily brings increased responsibility, because then we can feel how to respond appropriately to everything, rather than being in a state of unconscious reactivity. Even when we behave as an automaton as a result of being so thoroughly conditioned, we are still responsible. This holds true when we may be only dimly aware, and function in the misguided belief that we have no responsibility at all, blaming the other with 'it's their fault'.

Each of us enfolds the collective consciousness of humanity which connects us intimately with the journey of all human being. Consciousness enfolds 'all' because it is 'all' and this occurs in the timeless present. Thus, all human thought – from the most horrendous to the most sublime – is enfolded. Understanding this is experiential and it brings a liberating connectedness and compassion. And concomitant with this is a sense of responsibility.

> *What problems can there be which the mind did not create? Life and death do not create problems; pains and pleasures come and go, experienced and forgotten. It is memory and anticipation that create problems of attainment or avoidance, coloured by like and dislike. Truth and love are man's real nature and mind and heart are the means of its expression.*
> —Nisargadatta Maharaj (1897–1981)[12]

During relaxation and meditative practices and if we are particularly attentive in our daily living, we can experience the body in a numinous way: as a 'field' comprised of levels of subtle energy/intelligence that cannot be accurately portrayed phenomenally as 'physical'. We may previously have been unaware of this energetic level and, on first experience, it is a revelation of a previously hidden dimension of Being. Everything in the body, when experienced as consciousness, is completely interconnected as a seamless whole. And energetically this extends infinitely.

The question arises: is there anyone *doing* this? Is there an independent 'you' exercising control over these bodily and energetic processes whether they be of a phenomenal or noumenal kind? Even when intentionality is involved, such as the intention to soften and relax the breath, is there anyone doing this? It does not mean that there is a separate self, as 'you' doing this. It just means there is 'intending' as a thought command taking place, plain and simple, not a separate you!

Generally, breathing takes place by itself whether or not there has been a thought to pay attention to it, or regulate it. As with other functions of the body, there is no 'you' that is beating your heart right now, or replicating your cells, or creating peristalsis in the gut. It is clear that the biology of the body is a marvellous form of intelligence running itself. In the same way, there is no 'you' who thinks 'your' thoughts, or feels 'your' emotions. The sovereignty of the 'thinker' is a myth.

In a similar way, there is no separate transcendent God running the universe, because the universe is alive and, as consciousness, running itself. Experiencing this is a revelation that brings inner peace and joy. When you apprehend the one impersonal intelligence orchestrating and manifesting as everything: the body, passing thoughts, the surging ocean, the motion of the planets and stars, in sum the Totality, you experience a freedom without measure.

Choice-less awareness

Desire and anger are objects of the mind,
But the mind is not yours,
Nor ever has been.
You are choiceless awareness itself,
Unchanging – so live happily.
— Ashtavakra and Nalin N. Nyas[13]

In this verse, 'choiceless awareness' is expressed in the Ashtavakra Gita, a 2,500-year-old philosophical dialogue between Ashtavakra and his student Janaka. Later, philosopher Juddi Krishnamurti (1895-1986) expressed the same when he said:

*Freedom is found in the choiceless awareness
of our daily existence and activity.*
—Jiddu Krishnamurti

It was through Krishnamurti's writing that I first encountered the term 'choice-less awareness'. It was a recurring theme in his talks and writings for two reasons: first, because 'choosing' is not the defining signature of liberation as is often assumed. Second, because we do not choose to be aware as a function of thought, the opposite is true – awareness is prior to thought.

Awareness *is* there already, prior to mental choice. If we say, 'I am going to be aware', it has no real meaning because awareness just is, regardless of thought and thinker. Awareness is a non-exclusive birthright. It is not under the direction of our thinking, nor is it subject to our choosing; it is universal.

Choice-less awareness is natural and abiding. If we find ourselves in the path of an oncoming car, intelligence in the form of our instincts will naturally move our body towards safety. This is not a result of thought, because we do not have to think to do this. In fact, thinking will slow us down. We do not need an ideology, a belief, a self, or reasoning power. The intelligence acting through the body reacts automatically, because consciousness associated with the body simply looks after itself. There is no 'you' involved. It is impersonal, choice-less and effortless.

The Taoist philosophers of ancient China refer to *wu wei*, or 'non-action in action'. That is, action without resistance, without attachment to the outcome, without self. This is a *way of living in presence*. With this emptying of mind, the body becomes a conduit for a 'subtle energy' (*chi* in Chinese, or *prana* in Indian yoga) to energise our body, unimpeded. In experiencing a freedom deeper than choice, nothing is experienced as personal, and we are invigorated with this 'free-energy'. We can no longer take what others say or do to heart, whether it is deemed as complimentary or derogatory. Rather, we become more sensitive to the thoughts and energies of others, but without a precious sense of self that would take offense, feel hurt, or seek adulation.

The Way is perfect like vast space
Where nothing is lacking and nothing in excess.
Indeed, it is due to our choosing to accept or reject
That we do not see the true nature of things.
—Third Patriach of Zen[14]

Separation is suffering

Why are you unhappy?
Because 99.9% of everything you think,
And everything you do,
Is for yourself,
And there isn't one.
—Wei Wu Wei

We use the mind incorrectly in creating the 'self' identity, because we do not understand the truth of undivided Being. The resulting separation we experience is the primary cause of our suffering. However, thought cannot know undivided Being; rather, it is through surrendering thought that this non-duality is revealed. Thought can only know separation because it is the architect of our phenomenal reality. Yet when our identity is built on thought, fear inhibits our curiosity, which is why we tend to stay in the known. To find out what is beyond thought and the experience of the phenomenal, is a step into a new level of intimacy with life.

Whether we are scientists, nationalists or religionists, we can feel offended if our preciously held tribal beliefs are attacked. But *what* exactly is offended? After all, it is not as if we are being attacked by a real tiger. Rather, it is the mind-constructed shell of self that is identified with certain ideas and, in perceiving a threat, is offended. Attachment to the mind is the perpetrator of separation, but thought is clearly not the enemy, and neither is it the remedy. And this is precisely why intellectual understanding and analysis cannot set us free, just as it cannot give us our identity.

Some tribal groups are harmful and engage in toxic and hateful ideologies, while others serve a particular good purpose. For example, when there has been great injury, injustice or discrimination done to a group of people, forming a collective can be necessary to bring attention to this. This is usually essential in order to communicate an important story that has been either neglected or wilfully denied. The expression of these narratives brings about justice and effects collective healing. All of humanity is raised up with every injustice that is addressed, just as all of humanity is diminished by injustices. But in Being the just and the unjust are not separate.

By engaging with a group, the potential is always there for us to completely identify with the ideology of the group. If this identification process happens, we can soon see yourselves as being in ideological conflict with another group, doctrinally, territorially or even physically. In this way, the simple experience of what connects us all as Being has become eclipsed altogether by the mind. Abiding awareness that we are Being ensures that even if engaging in a group protest we are not in separation.

We can be so attached to the ideology of the nation that we lose touch with the fact that 'nation' is an abstract artefact, when the reality is that we are all equally hominids in Being. And even if we have bought a property, it is not really ours, like some permanent trophy. This is misplaced entitlement. Commercial ownership is part of the 'trance'. Awakening is to discover that simultaneously we have everything, as much as we have nothing. Ownership of anything is a truth that is relative.

With thousands of years of conditioning, we can come to passionately think that nationality and religion are inviolably valid and real. We feel a sense of belonging to these particular sub-tribes, and some of us will even kill to protect and justify that tribe.

But there is really only 'one tribe' – regardless of the many different ancestral groups – *Homo sapiens*. The fact that we are all members of this one tribe is still not universally recognised, let alone understood. In our innermost we are all 'global citizens.

Freed of attachment to the conceptual mind and other conditioning, you experience a different order of energy/ intelligence. This connects each of us as global citizens beyond separating ideologies and nationalities, as Being. We no longer believe in the separation that is the cause of our suffering. Realising that we are all citizens of the world in the manner that I am communicating, is not something of the imagination, nor an ideal. It is a reality available to each of us not a moment away from now.

As a flower blown out by the wind
Goes to rest and cannot be defined
So the wise man freed from individuality
Goes to rest and cannot be defined.
Gone beyond all images –
Gone beyond the power of words

—Sutta Nipata[15]

PART TWO

OUR EPISTEMIC WINDOWS: THE PHENOMENAL AND THE NOUMENAL

In which we explore the role of different ways of knowing: objectivist and 'direct perception'.

This, then, is the ultimate paradox of thought: to want to discover something that thought itself cannot think.
—Soren Kierkegaard[16]

CHAPTER 7

'BEING' IN WESTERN PHILOSOPHY

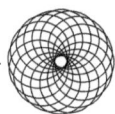

Generally, Western culture has expressed a dualistic tension. On the one hand, it has been enamored with the phenomenal world, shown in its drive to develop an objectified reality through science and technological advancement. Philosophy generally was rationalistic, with an emphasis on substance. On the other hand, there has been a culture of transcendence, an idealism that separates the phenomenal (seen as only appearance and illusory) from the more perfect world of This idealism coming originally from Plato and centuries later the Neoplatonists, was used by early Christianity with the added myth of defiled matter, creating a dualistic morality of good and evil (the pollution of the sensual), along with a culture of punishment.

Early Christianity was central in furthering a dualistic culture and through colonisation this was spread across the globe. The repercussions of dualism have been dramatic, far reaching and long lasting. Through the last two thousand years it has served to poison Anglo–European attitudes to the body and to nature, and skewing what is regarded as civilised, to the point that whenever we think of nature, 'we' are not included; we are tragically separate. This is achieved by the objectification of everything, seen as the most rational 'ideal' mode of our functioning, but in doing this we lose an intimacy expressed in a love for nature, the body, our fellow humans, and deeper still as non-dualistic Being.

'Being' was recognised in the work of the philosophical heavyweights such as Plato and Aristotle, who have been the prime influences on Western culture, but perhaps not understood. In academic philosophical circles, the spirituality of the Greek philosophers as pointed out by Pierre Grimes, is missing. Their universe was fundamentally spiritual, and knowing the 'Self' was the process of connecting to the organising intelligence in everything, the Logos. They were also captivated by rationality and with Aristotle we see the development of empirical science, which stands as a positive crowning feature of duality.

Plato began elevating the use of rational thought as the pinnacle of human capacity, in what he saw as our ultimate calling – to transcend to an abstract realm of perfection, of ideal forms. The senses and nature were regarded by Plato as polluted and a mere illusion, with only the realm of perfect ideas held as real. Plato's universe was a single divine Being, but within it was a duality that was used by Christian culture (without the over-arching oneness of the Logos -that we could experience) which has conditioned the Western world and now much of the Globe ever since.

The spiritual philosophy expressed by the Pre-Socratics, Plato, the Cynics, the Stoics and later with the Neoplatonists (not the Epicureans or the Atomists, for as materialists they were pursuing

Hedonia) was one of transformation, not just information, which is known and gathered by the intellect using reason. Much of the commentary from academic philosophers of the present era misses this 'way of philosophy' as practiced by the ancients. I think this missing can only happen because there is no direct experience of the transformational nature of enquiry which moves one beyond the intellect to a noumenal dimension of Being. Gnosis of the Logos (the universal intelligence throughout nature) cannot be achieved through just intellectual enquiry, rather it is more meditative through experiencing divine illumination. The sage who follows this transformational way, experiences Eudaimonia and the true nature of the Self. In this 'way of philosophy' there are clear parallels with the Rishis of Vedanta, Buddhism and Taoism. . .

The mystical in Western philosophy

Rational thought was to take a primary position in Western culture from the time of ancient Greece, while the transformational mysticism of the Greeks and Neoplatonists was not, and is still not, understood. The irrational, in the form of religious belief, also thrived, as a counterpoint to the rational. But the mystical always surfaces, despite constraining attempts from orthodoxies in religious, scientific, or philosophical culture, because as the wise 'sapiens' we have always had another epistemic window of perception that is direct and experiential, unmediated by thought and not constrained by the conceptual.

But where does this lead? Because once we step outside the confines of rational thought, or conditioned belief, fear of the unknown arises. And soon we are heading into what people of reason regard as the nebulous world of mysticism. This fear of the mystical is what prompted Sigmund Freud, the founder of psychoanalysis, to give stern advice to his student Carl Jung to avoid the 'black tide of mud', referring to Jung's interest in parapsychology and mysticism. Jung proceeded undeterred.

Mystical experiences are universally expansive even when they occur to the religious. They are 'knowing' of a numinous kind, as an intuitive knowing (in the sense of immediate knowledge, not as a hunch or instinct) of a different order of reality from the phenomenal. However, suspicion of mysticism grew from the time of the Enlightenment in 18th century Europe. During this period those in learned circles increasingly trusted in the empirical evidence of science, exemplified by the trio of English empirical philosophers, Bishop Berkeley, John Locke and David Hume.

With an increasing emphasis on rational thought, and the corresponding emerging scientific culture of empirical research and a scientific method, this addressed the central aim of rationality as it struggled against religion and superstition: to be in control. Non-rational states, like the expansiveness of mysticism, were regarded as uncontrolled, contra-rational and a threat to an established order of knowledge. And, with the rise of psychiatry, and the development of mechanistic models of brain function, anyone experiencing mystical states became increasingly pathologised. Mystical experience was seen as a symptom of mental illness, perhaps needing treatment or, at best, ignored. Yet, curiously, the therapeutic use of hallucinogens, a universal pathway to induce mystical experience as attested globally by the many different shamanic cultures, is now being seriously researched as potent way to 'reset' the nervous system in those suffering chronic mental health ailments.

This fear and suspicion of mystical experience shared by religious, scientific, medical and philosophical authority, continues and is more indicative of ignorance than anything else. This is borne out by the difficulty in hallucinogen trials getting approvals from regulatory authorities. However, as illustrated in the story below, numinous experiences can sometimes happen spontaneously, to extremely rational people with no history of leanings in this direction. But what mystical experiences universally tend to do, is to change a person's life and outlook forever. And such experiences can have a magnified and positive effect on the world of human beings.

A rationalist experiences the mystical

Both the relevance and the significance of having a noumenal experience are demonstrated in the story of Bertrand Russell (1872-1970) one of the leading rationalist philosophers of the 20th century. He was a founder of the Analytical School of Philosophy that became popular in English-speaking countries. As a 29-year-old, he described himself as an 'imperialist', believing that Britain, as a 'bastion of civilisation', had a right to colonise and subjugate other peoples as part of the march of a superior civilisation.

On a particular occasion Russell was visiting his friend and colleague, Alfred North Whitehead, whose wife was suffering an acute angina attack. He described having a 'mystic illumination', filling him with mystical feelings about beauty, and a profound desire to help humanity by developing a critical philosophy, to dispel illusions that people were trapped in. Even though this mystical experience only lasted five minutes, he recalled that 'at the end, I had become a completely different person'.

From this 'illumination', his conditioning as an entitled aristocrat and an unquestioning imperialist, dissolved. In an instant he became acutely aware of the suffering of human beings, and felt a deep sense of love for humanity. This experience of 'mystical connectedness' inspired him to become an advocate for: women's voting rights; he become a pacifist and a key leader in the anti-nuclear proliferation movement; he also became a supporter of free education, a liberal and fair democracy, and to eliminate poverty with a universal basic income.

> *"The mystic emotion if it is freed from unwarranted beliefs and is so overwhelming as to remove a person wholly from the ordinary business of life, may give something of very great value, the same kind of thing though in a heightened form, that is given by contemplation. Breadth and calm and profundity all have their source in this emotion, in which for the moment all self-centered desire is dead, and the mind becomes a mirror for the vastness of the universe.*
>
> *Those who have had this experience believe it to be bound up unavoidably with assertions about the nature of the universe, and naturally cling to these assertions. I believe myself that there is no reason to believe them true. I cannot admit any method of arriving at truth except that of science. But in the realm of emotions I do not deny the value of the experiences that have given rise to religions.*
>
> *Through association with false beliefs they have led to much evil as well as good. Freed from this association it may be hoped that the good alone will remain.*
>
> 'Bertrand Russell on Mysticism', https//www.youtube
> taken from *Mysticism and Logic*, 1917, Allen & Unwin

Russell's experience was to shift his sense of identity along with his priorities and connection to the world. But experiences like this are not unique holding an essential place in bringing deeper connectedness and meaning to human beings, beyond the reaches of reason. It informed what became his significant contribution to creating a safer, more connected world. For a man who championed rationality and logic, it is clear that he also had insight into the nature of his 'mystical' experience. But how could those five minutes have changed his life? And what is the core wisdom that he mentions? And how did his conditioning as an imperialist, which developed over many years, dissolve so readily and completely in just five minutes?

The core wisdom comes from directly experiencing, without reason, a profound connection to everything, to nature and to other human beings. His 'experience' was expansive and global, rather than following the confines of a rational, and logical thought process. And it was precisely because of the form of 'intuitive seeing' he experienced, that it had such a powerful effect on him. 'Seeing' like this, as the writer can attest, is powerful enough to rapidly dissolve even the most deeply embedded cultural conditioning.

Russell, as the imperialist, felt a disconnection from other people, exemplified in his belief in the right for one culture to dominate others. His transformation shows a movement from the head to the heart expressed in a commitment to help all human beings make a better world. The resistance to this experiential connectedness is the conditioning that keeps any of us in an unquestioning island of thought, such as regarding that a natural order of things is one of privileged hierarchy, or that a healthy planet is secondary to economic wealth. And remember that Russell experienced the dissolution of his conditioning in just a few minutes, arising from the immediacy of a deeply experienced intuition, not from the time taken to develop, outline and analyse a reasoned argument.

Mysticism: experiencing the expansiveness of consciousness

The expanded consciousness found in mystical experience is commonly associated with the beliefs and superstitions found in religion. The mystic is not necessarily immune from being culturally conditioned, and may well retain the transcendentalism of their religious culture and symbology, and so it is common to see a mixture of the spiritual and religious.

All mystical experience is spiritual because it does not arise from belief. But it needs to be differentiated from the religious, which is only concerned with belief. If we experience a taste of the mystical, when it is run through our interpretive cultural filter, for example if one is a Hindu, Christian or Buddhist, or whatever the conditioning is, the experience itself can take on the symbology of one's surrounding culture. Generally, a mystical experience brings an expansion to any religious or cultural blinkers, which is global and non-dualistic. A mystical experience is a noumenal one. And whereas the mystical has been associated with religion, the noumenal has not. Russell was already free from religious beliefs as an agnostic/atheist, with his conditioning being more of a secular nature and so his mystical experience was of a numinous kind.

It is obvious that mind needs to be freed from any social or cultural conditioning that would keep us chained obscuring our 'true nature', religious, political or otherwise, and when we are freed from it, only good can come of it. But as Russell points out, if the mind is not cleared of false beliefs, there is a danger that mystical experience, in a person with an already distorted psyche, may amplify negative effects. And too often we do see this in the many religious cults that have emerged across the globe. In a power-hungry sociopath for example, mystical experiences can be enlisted to give some moral, religious or political authority over others, and this is always dangerously negative.

Russell saw that the confidence of the mystic's intuition would be balanced by the restraint of reason in the scientist so as to produce a 'largeness of contemplation'. He defined three different criteria characterising mystical experience:

* a belief in unity;
* a denial of the reality of time;
* that all evil is only appearance.

Following this he outlined four considerations regarding the validity of mysticism:

1. Are there two ways of knowing – reason and intuition? And if so, is either preferred?
2. Is all plurality and division illusory?
3. Is time unreal?
4. What kind of reality belongs to good and evil?

Somewhat remarkably, perhaps because Russell was a leading rationalist thinker of his day, was that he took mysticism seriously. But given the spontaneous unpremeditated nature of his earlier experience, not so surprising. The questions he has outlined are important and are thoroughly examined throughout this book. And of particular interest is the epistemological one (the two ways of knowing) addressed in the next two chapters.

The noumenal in Western philosophy

Whether an atheist, like Bertrand Russell, or a theist, experiencing a numinous reality is a more primal level of perception than the mental filters of any philosophical or religious ideology: it is a deeper intuition of Being. But it is also true that peoples' attachment to a mindset such as materialism for example can be very strong indeed, and so even the possibility of experiencing an expansion in conscious awareness is precluded, by such strong conditioning.

Militant materialists or religious fundamentalists are in a certain way of the same ilk, because they characteristically both have such tight mental binders, rigidly attaching to their particular mindset. Being so thoroughly programmed makes the possibility of expanded experience very remote. It is these filters of ideology that are challenged by the non- phenomenal and non-ideational nature of this kind of experience.

It appears that the numinous is gaining more currency, which attests to shifts in the collective psyche. This was illustrated to me recently when I was speaking with a Christian minister who – although he in particular practises on the fringes of his church orthodoxy – stated that, 'these days I don't do any "God" talk, rather I talk of experiencing the numinous, because it is more open and accessible to people to experience for themselves, without the God-talk and being heavily "belief-laden".

In pagan Europe experiencing the mystical connection with nature was universal, but so was a significant amount of superstition. From around the 6th century BCE in Greece, a new revolution of spirituality and thought emerged with early philosophers articulating a new spiritual way through philosophy for Sapiens to know the true identity of the Self as Being. Generally, there was an explosion in knowledge and thinking complexity: with metaphysics, mathematics, politics, ethics and epistemology. And dominant in this was experiencing the Logos through one's inner work spiritually along with the capacity to think with reason. The Stoics in particular was a fine example of 'philosophy as a way' to know the Self, and elevating human rationality and ethical behaviour was central to their vision. Simultaneously in India, experiencing the dimensional shift of consciousness in experiencing/knowing the Self (Brahmin), was also the primary focus.

In the work of Plato for example experiencing a numinous universe was primary, as it was with the philosophers of the East, in India and China. The Greek philosophers were also discovering and developing the power of thought and new ways of structuring thinking. This took different shape in two philosophical giants: firstly, with Plato, with his central thesis of archetypal non-physical perfect forms, created a metaphysical transcendental idealism that has some modern echoes. Examples of this are: in the archetypes of human personality in the collective unconscious of C.G. Jung; the concept of a mental sphere or 'noosphere' as articulated by Pierre Teilhard de Chardin, and the 'morphic resonance' as fields of information postulated by Rupert Sheldrake. Significantly they all speak of a dimension of mental knowledge as fields of information standing as a dimensional shift in the fabric of reality. Secondly, with Aristotle's nomenclature and classification of nature, paved the way for a new scientific endeavour.

Ancient Greece saw the rise of rational thinking with reason and logic being regarded as the primary criteria of ethical and civilised living. In elevating the role of rational thought, it was specifically a province for the educated elite, while experiencing the noumenal in a living universe did not require a carefully cultivated intellect, but rather requires a different kind of rigour, usually a meditative one.

The metaphysical streams from Ancient Greece, focusing on knowing the Logos in a numinous living universe was accessible to human experience, and encapsulated in the dictum above the entrance of the temple of Apollo in Delphi 'Man know thyself'. To know the Self was the salvation, through experiencing the divine illumination of Being. This philosophy of Being as found in Plato, was also central to Parmenides; in the Stoics founded by Zeno of Citium; and in the 'process philosophy' of Heraclitus briefly outlined below. To the common folk experiencing a living universe also pervaded Greek and Roman times, and is fundamental to a pagan view of the world.

Metaphysics of Being in Ancient Greece

Philosophy as a 'way' to know the truth of human identity as the Self, has been lost to our current era where the voices of our ancestors are now deemed as curious intellectual artefacts but perhaps irrelevant. Philosophy now is regarded as an academic pursuit which leads neither to eudaimonia, sagacity nor to the profound experience of the Self.

Parmenides (515 BCE) was the first philosopher in the Western world to explore ontology and articulate Being as worthy of our consideration. In his poem 'Nature', Parmenides describes two views of reality. In 'his way of truth' he states 'what is, is', with reality being One, wherein change is impossible and beings are illusory. And further, that existence is timeless, uniform, necessary and unchanging. In the second view of reality, 'the way of opinion', Parmenides explains the world of appearances, in which our sensory faculties lead to conceptions which are false and deceitful. Here he articulates what he perceives as an unbridgeable gulf between the noumenal and phenomenal. However, in his explorations he discovered only half the truth of Being. Because if he had gone further in his apprehension of Being, beyond thought, he would have understood that experiencing Being at a deeper level reveals its basis. This can be likened to a transparency as 'non-Being', or nothingness. Wherein no-thing has independent existence; ultimately there are no separate things or essences. This nothingness is knowing consciousness.

Heraclitus of Ephesus (560 BCE) also an explorer of ontology, was the first 'process philosopher' of Ancient Greece. He understood that the universe including everything in it is ever-changing, as with rivers and people, famously stating that, 'a man can't step into the same river twice'. His philosophy articulates a philosophy of 'becoming in nature': nature is alive, ever changing, and reality is truly dynamic. He coined the phrase 'everything flows'. His philosophy was a vitalistic kind of phenomenalism. Fire is seen as an underlying pervasive cosmic factor bringing continuous change and transformation. Heraclitus pre-empted chaos theory, and the dynamic nature of the sub-atomic world, and stands in resonance with the Taoist philosophers of Ancient China.

Stoicism, founded by Zeno of Citium around 300 BCE, is less lofty than the idealism of Plato (perfect idealised forms) and more spiritual than the materialism of the Atomists and Epicureans. It holds that nature is imbued with a universal intelligence or logos as a 'living being'. The logos of the Stoics is immanent and experiential. When 'nature is God' humans are not left out of the equation and are immediately obliged to live in harmony with nature as the divine order of the universe, in accord with their 'true nature'. Stoicism assumes a determinism positing freedom in the human being realised through banishing ignorance, which is done by reigning in the passions with awareness and reason. The Stoics shared the dynamism of Heraclitus, viewing that the active principle in matter is a primordial fire or intelligent *aether*. The Stoics maintained that the world is One (monism), and that a divine reality pervades the whole universe. Their ethics led to an egalitarianism counter to the slave culture of Ancient Greece, holding that slaves were not an expression of some 'natural order of things', but are equals before the divine, and denied the importance of rank, status and wealth. Stoicism was more than a set of philosophical ideas, for to be a Stoic was, and continues to be, a way of living. There is a remarkable parallel with the ethical features of Buddhism and Taoism, including some parallels with the story of Zeno, and that of Gautama.

After the Neoplatonists Being appears to have been disregarded in the West, which rather pursued the realm of ideas in the form of belief in a transcendental God through the Medieval period. From the Renaissance onward materialism and objectivism steadily developed with rationality and empiricism holding centre court. But thought, in the form of rationality, was elevated with the rise of the intellect in Western culture, thus assuming its role as the arbiter and the gatekeeper of all knowledge and truth. Indeed, thinking continues to be erroneously conflated with consciousness by scientists and philosophers alike.

Baruch Spinoza's 'infinite substance'

Baruch Spinoza was principally inspired by Plato, the Stoics and the Neoplatonists, and like these sages before him expressed a philosophy of oneness that restored Being as the true source of identity and ethics. In this he moved beyond the dualists characterised his times with its the division between body and mind, spirit and matter, heaven and earth and a morality of good and evil. His venturing outside the gloominess so typical of dualistic thought, and religious transcendentalism, was not an easy one, inevitably inviting ostracism from his community for his philosophy. But Spinoza in stands apart as a refreshing beacon, offering insight into a numinous living universe.

Inspired by the pantheism of the Stoics, Spinoza postulated 'God' as *infinite substance*. With Spinoza 'God' equals 'existence', 'nature', or 'Being'. This was a revolutionary re-orientation, because Spinoza regarded 'God' as *immanent* and experiential, rather than separate and transcendent. 'God' as nature is completely accessible to human experience because 'we are that', as the Advaita philosophers of India maintain. In the West this is known as pantheism with terms like God and Nature describing the one reality, with hominids being god as much as anything else. Spinoza was always going to fall foul of the prevailing religious orthodoxy for views like this.

Spinoza expresses a non-duality distinct from the dualism of Descartes, and the monistic atheism of the Atomists and Epicureans. He is in alignment with the teachings of the Stoics including their moral philosophy. Spinoza's God is *Being* involving the 'is-ness', 'energy force' or consciousness that makes 'reality' what it is. His 'god' is also not anthropomorphic which is a radical departure from that of his cultural context whether Jewish, or Christian. God as nature is unrelated to any human endeavours, hopes, fears, or prayers. 'God', being in essence experiential, is non-partisan, is impersonal and not the product of religious conditioning, which he viewed as childish superstition.

For Spinoza the universe (God) is perfect as it is from its own nature and power. There is no idealised transcendent perfection; 'what is', 'is perfect'. Things are not more or less perfect, according to how they delight or offend human senses, or by their serviceability or repugnance to humankind. Spinoza's writing on this is a very different understanding of God, exactly the kind that Einstein expressed alignment with.

Spinoza's non-anthropomorphic spirituality disconcerted a lot of people in the 17th and 18th centuries, and was condemned by religious authorities as controversial heresy, and he was subsequently expelled from his Jewish community. Spinoza's universe was governed by the kind of causality, with a determinism that finds its echo in the 'super-determinism' as outlined in the 'hidden variable' interpretation of quantum mechanics by Gerard d'Hooft. For in Spinoza's conception, nothing stands outside of nature or Being. There is no 'transcendent realm' that escapes causality, something that is still found in the most popular interpretations of the quantum world, as with the notion of 'superposition' in the Copenhagen Interpretation (discussed Chapter 10).

Spinoza's term *infinite substance* deliberately presents us with a curious paradox. On the one hand it is the use of the word 'substance' which is the 'stuff' constituting the existence of the natural world, an obsession in Western philosophy since Ancient Greece to find the ultimate building blocks of the universe. On the other hand, this substance is 'infinite', moving us beyond the phenomenal with the 'finite stuff' of separate things, to what is essentially noumenal. The 'infinite substance' is a oneness without boundaries, making the 'God' of Spinoza accessibly immanent for all human beings as fundamental to our existence.

Epistemically the infinite substance is known directly and intuitively beyond both the reasoning of mind and the empirical reach of the senses. The infinite substance is known intuitively when we step outside of time in the eternity of the ever-present now. But Spinoza was also a supreme rationalist, and paid homage to rationality and logic by constructing his writings in an elaborately geometric style.

In Spinoza's metaphysics free will is regarded as an illusion, and he, like Nietzsche after him, regarded the morality of good and evil based in the transcendental idealism of Christianity as an error. As a determinist he saw everything as following necessarily from the essential nature of the universe. It only seems like we have free will because we know what we desire, but these desires are themselves conditioned, and to just blindly follow our desires is not a true expression of freedom. By knowing more about the world and by deconditioning ourselves, we can therefore be 'free' in so far as we now know the 'true cause' of our desires and actions. As 'free' individuals, we will no longer be 'unconsciously' ruled by our passions, but use our insight into the fundamental unity of all that is, and our intellect and reason to live in harmony with one another.

Spinoza encouraged living a life of peace and tranquillity, and seeking to understand the true nature of reality. He maintains that consciousness of a voluntary act is not tantamount to consciousness of our freedom, since volitions themselves have a causal history. Spinoza goes to some lengths to debunk not only the notion of free will, but also to directly confront what he sees as some of the particular errors inherent in the Cartesian (dualistic) view. He suggests that we can arrive at a state of 'blessedness', wherein one is in harmony with Nature just like the *eudaimonia* of the Stoics. The view that human beings have dominion over the earth (a view that is still widely held and which has had such a devastating effect on the Earth) represents the position that Spinoza wants to rebuke, since it labours under a kind of naïve anthropocentrism, central to theistic religions and upheld by many in the world of science and politics.

Personal liberation is achieved through awareness, and a process of clarifying the intellect, understanding the emotions and thereby overcoming the manacles of ignorance. Spinoza's notion of cognitive freedom wherein people could liberate themselves through understanding echoes the Stoics and heralds the development of psychotherapy.

Noumenal and phenomenal resolve experientially in one reality

Both Spinoza's *infinite substance* and Kant's *noumena* refer to the absolute, but they radically differ in how we can know this. Both believed that the noumenal could only be known intuitively. For Spinoza it was through knowing directly without thought, and he thus uses the correct meaning of 'intuition'. Kant also used 'intuition' to describe how we know the numinous, but used the word quite differently, to mean 'a figment of imagination' or 'speculation'. This has the effect of relegating the numinous to the inaccessible and unknowable.

Immanuel Kant's (1724–1804) noumena relates to a transcendent realm, separate from the phenomenal; something that we may pine for but never know. However, for Spinoza, it is immanent, and as such we can know it intimately, because 'we are it'. There is no dualism of separate realms. Kant viewed the pantheism of Spinoza as an 'error' arising from his faulty definition of his 'infinite substance'. However, that it defies rationality or knowing through rational or empirical means, certainly does not make it invalid.

Kant was part of the new way led by Germany, with philosophy becoming established as a professional discipline with an intellectual elite employed by the universities. In his writing Kant was responding to the English Empiricists Locke and Hume, who based all knowledge on sensation, whereas rationalists such as Leibniz and Spinoza based all knowledge on intuitive perception, and the rational use of thought. However, Kant was to further philosophical error (in science it is not an error) of dualism as it had generated from early Christianity and carried through from Descartes, with his philosophy creating two distinct worlds: the phenomenal and the noumenal. The latter being given an imagined transcendental status and unreachable; while Kant regarded that humans, as being confined to the phenomenal and 'illusory world of appearance', which is all that we can know.

Kant's response to the question he poses in *A Critique of Pure Reason*: 'What can we know?' is that our knowledge is constrained by knowing empirically through the senses, and by the *a priori* knowledge of mathematical concepts, along with space and time. These constraints exist because it is the mind itself that constitutes the features of experience to the empirical realm of space and time, in how we delineate features of phenomenal reality. We cannot know the super-sensible realm (the numinous) that Kant separated in his speculative metaphysics. Kant was correct in stating that we are habitually under the illusion that it is a separate and objective world 'out there'. This is because our phenomenal experience is an *interpretive reality* driven by the mind's cognitive and linguistic development (see chapter 15 for a more complete discussion of this).

Kant also maintains that the human is not born with a *tabula rasa* (pure innocent mind) because in the human mind in Kant's view, we are 'hard wired' (a priori knowledge), to be limited to the empirical realm involving our sensual experience of space (body), and time (mind). Kant's epistemology of what we can know is a synthesis of sensory and conceptual forms of objects-as-known, phenomena. Phenomena are what we observe and seek to explain as the starting points in building knowledge in empirical science.

For Kant, because our connection to the numinous is inaccessible, we must therefore have faith in it. Kant's problem was that he never found a way to experience the numinous, because of his attachment to thought and the senses as the only vehicles of human knowing. The numinous is relegated to the transcendent as it is just not possible for humans to 'think their way there'. For Kant, having faith in the transcendent realm of the numinous gives us 'free will', 'individual souls' and a 'transcendent God', hence 'transcendental idealism'. The transcendent becomes the source of a morality that is derived from superstition and idealised perfection, with its dualistic culture of rewards in an afterlife, and the fearful risk of punishment while here.

However, numinous, like Spinoza's infinite substance, can only be intuitively known, independent of the senses and reason. In actuality, *it is accessible to those curious enough to look, and sensitive enough to experience 'it', because we are 'it'*. For Spinoza and the Stoics, a deeper form of ethics arises from this perception because it is not informed by culturally conditioned notions of good and evil. Instead, by experiencing an alignment with universal intelligence (the Logos), all apparent dualities are resolved. The manifesting of what have been described as different realities exists in name only: phenomenal/noumenal, absolute/relative, or good/evil. The key is that one experientially 'rests in the real', beyond all conceived divisions, living from the Source.

The split in Western philosophy – analytic and continental

After the loss of 'philosophy as a way to the Self' from Ancient Greece, the central quest in Western philosophy was an idealised form of truth to be found through the rigorous application of reason, analytical skills and logic, reserved for those in the academy. Truth idealised in this way was characterised as objective and non-partisan, but the philosophical blinkers reflected in this view that were on then in those ancient times, are still present to this day. A group of continental philosophers reacted against this fixation on objectivism, while analytical philosophers continued in the same vein, having moderated more recently.

After Hegel (1770–1831) and Schopenhauer (1788–1860), Western philosophy was particularly concentrated amongst a group of German philosophers, some of whom sought a metaphysics that centred on subjective experience in response to the continuing rise of objective scientific knowledge in the 19th century. Another group championing objective truth went on to found the analytic school. European philosophy bifurcated with these different directions: the analytic way that was to become Anglo-centric in English speaking countries (England and America) with an objectivist metaphysic; and the continental philosophy of the French and Germans who developed insights with a metaphysics focussing on subjective experience producing Husserl's 'phenomenology'.

Analytic philosophy began with analysis of language, notably in the works of Gottlob Frege, Bertrand Russell, and Ludwig Wittgenstein. It was more interested in conceptual questions about the meanings of words and statements and their logical relations, than it was in spiritual or practical issues such as morality or the meaning of life. And because of this focus it tends to be dry and technical, finding its most extreme form in the Logical Positivists. Analytic philosophy relies heavily on the vocabulary, assumptions, and equations of symbolic logic in its arguments. Consequently it is defined more by its *method* than by any particular set of questions, arguments, or viewpoints.

For analytic philosophers, any glimmer of metaphysics (somehow they were blind to the fact that their stance was itself a metaphysical position) was seen as an error, even a poison to be expunged. Hence, among analytic philosophers, it was of painstaking concern to align the use of language with meaning, and a formal logical structure, to ensure 'correctness' perhaps, and is best described as a form of 'semantic hygiene'. Philosophy the 'analytic way' was to be as objectivist as possible. This makes complete sense in the practice of science, but not in philosophy. Perhaps it is no surprise that this approach inspired the forensically shallow Behaviourist school of psychology.

The traditional role of philosophy to discuss the big questions about life and reality and how we are to live, was being hijacked by a new analytical methodology. This involved a sophisticated use of language, subject to stringent criteria of analysis, and could be likened to a form of semantic gymnastics. Analytic philosophy avoids such questions, viewing them as unsolvable and badly framed due to their lack of clear definitions. As a result, the role of philosophy having now completely lost its way, the exclusive province of the professional with its strict methodology, and placing itself subservient to the serious business of objective knowledge in the physical sciences.

Hegel: Mostly, Hegel is remembered for his 'dialectic' – thesis, antithesis and synthesis. His insights into the master/slave relationship and its inevitable dysfunction, influenced Nietzsche, Husserl, existentialism and psychoanalysis. But here I want to draw attention to his oft overlooked ontology.

Hegel's deeper metaphysical view has been haughtily described as 'baffling esotericism' by current philosophical commentators, revealing their own default beliefs in unquestioned materialist assumptions. In his book, *Phenomenology*, Hegel describes reality as comprising a single absolute consciousness. He called it 'Spirit' attempting to understand itself through various developmental stages as reality, with individual consciousness and the objects of consciousness all being non-discrete aspects of the 'One absolute consciousness'. Hegel understood that an individual's journey towards self-certainty and self-realisation as absolute Spirit, ends when the distinction between consciousness and its objects, is dissolved. In this awakening, consciousness recognises that 'it' and the 'other' (objects, people, et cetera) are one.

Continental philosophy

What became known as continental philosophy was a reaction against the rising objectivism in philosophy, and a resurrection of the central role of consciousness in all human affairs, as articulated by Edmund Husserl (1859–1938). A German philosopher, he founded the school of phenomenology, its method being rooted in intentionality, operating under the assumption that reality cannot be grasped directly because it is available only through perceptions of reality arising from existing representations already in the mind. Husserl maintained that consciousness is not 'in' the mind: rather, consciousness is 'conscious of something' other than itself (the intentional object), whether the object is a substance or a figment of imagination. Hence the phenomenological method relies on the description of phenomena as they are given to consciousness in their immediacy.

However, what Husserl did not understand was that in experiencing a noumenal reality the *lens of perception is cleansed*. This involves a casting aside of assumptions and pre-existing knowledge (cognitive and linguistic) and all methodologies as constructions by thought – indeed of all thought.

Continental philosophies tend to have certain values roughly in common that distinguish them from analytic philosophy. They are concerned less about mathematical logic, and are more shaped by 'the humanities' such as philosophy, psychology, sociology, linguistics, history, political science, and literary analysis. Continental philosophy frequently deals with questions like the meaning of life – questions that are inherently interesting but also inherently vague. It attempts to objectively study the subjective: the content of conscious experiences such as judgments, perceptions, and emotions. Phenomenology seeks to be scientific, but without science's reductionist tendencies to focus on the brain and nervous system, or study consciousness from the perspective of clinical psychology. Rather it uses systematic reflection to determine the essential properties and structures of lived experience. It places subjective experience centrally, as the 'science of experience'.

Heidegger (1889–1976), an assistant to Husserl, was important in introducing Being as central to human understanding; something he saw as missing from the times of Ancient Greece. Rationality, the search for substance, and the quest for objective truth, had been the primary considerations of philosophy since Parmenides. Heidegger maintained that it was not thinking that defined our existence, but rather a much larger experience of Being itself; one that has largely escaped Western philosophy.

Heidegger's interest in ontology, or the study of Being, took a turn south from his initial insight, 'that Being was largely absent in the history of Western philosophy', because despite this insight he held the mistaken belief that 'thought' was the correct means of revealing the nature of Being. Later, after a change in his thinking, 'the turn', he believed that it was 'language' instead, that could unfold the nature of Being. However neither language nor thought can do this.

What Heidegger failed to understand is that Being only reveals its nature through direct experience itself. Thought and language as instruments of consciousness cannot understand what is ontologically prior to them, Being. They can only be used as instruments to point to what is essentially beyond them. Because of this primary ignorance his philosophy falls inexorably into finely nuanced complexities, that only obscure Being. His work fails to grasp even the partial level of truth about Being that Parmenides did. Heidegger's philosophy demonstrates the limiting capacity of thought and language as the tools of consciousness but totally inadequate to reveal the ultimate quest of ontology: discovering the truth of Being.

Sartre's existential crisis of Being: A theme drawn out by Sartre in existentialism is that of a person confronting the raw fact of existence wherein things mapped as objects with names, descriptions and explanations are revealed as naked Being. A simple 'object' such as a tree or a seat can serve as a trigger to existential angst. To the experiencer this is unchartered territory, with the meanings assigned to the things of the world invented and imposed. Facing this raw fact of existence or Being is shocking, because with it comes the terrifying reality that human beings are 'condemned to freedom'. Denying this freedom is believing that one is a victim of circumstance, a commitment to living an unconscious life and acting inauthentically, a form of bad faith.

As Sartre states, Being precedes Essence (essence being the cultural meanings assigned to things). So, our challenge is to live authentically rather than on conditioned unconscious auto-pilot, and to invent our own meaning or essence.

There is something refreshing about Sartre's work written after the devastation of the second world war. It is a return to 'philosophy as a way', breaking away from traditional ideas of philosophy and religion, challenging us to realise that *we are already free, as a 'fact' of Being*.

The 'subjective' and the 'objective' are different modes of thought

The phenomenal is our sensual engagement with the world. The phenomenal is driven by thought and language, as we divide the world up through our naming, categorising and measuring. It is how we manufacture our sense of phenomenal objectified reality. It is a conditioned reality because it is learned, but this does not make it unreal. It is not illusory. It is our anthropomorphic metaphysical construct, yet we become unconscious to our participation in this constructing process, as it has become automatic. *It is we who create the appearance of things:* we then assume that because it is 'objectified' (it can be cognised, mapped, checked and measured by others) it carries a confirming order. But the truth-value it does carry is relative rather than absolute.

Mostly we fail to recognise that we are engaging in a habitual construction of a particular reality because it is happening so subtly. We are functioning on automatic pilot experiencing a 'reality' we take as given. We only notice that this reality is not all there is, when we suspend the internal 'reality constructing dialogue'. This happens through a spontaneous silence of the mind that is encouraged through meditative practice (the use of plant psychedelics can give a brief glimpse of this, but it is not sustained, and I am not encouraging anyone to do this). Phenomenal reality *is not an illusion* but there is more to reality that is neither thought nor language driven. If we are curious enough to step beyond the chattering monkey-mind, we discover another dimension of reality revealed only in silence.

But when the phenomenal is all that we see, we believe that even our identity lies in this. The process of objectifying goes further into objectifying oneself, as though this is the way to know who we are. And in doing this we enter into delusion, because we are not objects, even if we think we are, and nor is anything in our living universe. It is only our thinking that makes it so. Yet there is a valid place for objectifying which is in the practice of science. *However, if scientists, in their practice of objectifying, are not informed by an understanding that whatever objects studied (quasars, cells, humans, dust mites, or electrons) are in actuality living, then they will always be cut adrift the true source of an ethical compass.*

Objectifying is a more serious problem when it moves into areas that interfere with intimacy, whether it is intimacy within us, with each other, or intimacy with a living universe. For example, when we objectify others we disconnect from them as people, and in turn we can easily disregard them and exploit them. Objectifying also occurs when women are used as sexual objects for men's gratification (of course this happens with men as well, but the scales are heavily tilted towards the objectification of women). One estimate is that the porn industry is worth 97 billion US dollars annually (which could feed 4.8 billion people). The negative effects of this are staggering on human intimacy, young people's attitudes (particularly males towards females) and relationships.

Objectifying also sees humans, other animals and the resources of the earth used as objects in the financial world of making money – capitalism is built on this. 'Objectivism as a social doctrine' reaches its most ignorant and pernicious form in the sociopathic philosophy of Ayn Rand (1905–1982) unsurprisingly favoured by ultra-conservatives and right-wing libertarians.

Descartes' dichotomy 'Cartesian dualism', is foundational to the subjective versus objective, is a conceptual construct, and because it is not actual, it has no basis in reality. When one perceives directly, with an unfiltered lens, there is neither subjective nor objective. Consciousness is a territory that cannot be charted, and cannot be meaningfully separated into objective and subjective, yours or mine, because Being is unconstructed unified reality.

We experience the phenomenal reality separated into trees, laundry lint, stars, and people, but then, if we suspend attachment to the world of things we may notice there is something deeper, something that is not empirical and apprehended by our senses, nor defined by thought. It is useful to remember here that phenomenal actually means *things as they appear*. This can happen spontaneously as an awakening to another kind of reality, previously hidden because we were 'blinded' by the particular truth of the appearance of things – the phenomenal. We experience a shift to another dimension of perception, the noumenal, that is neither separate nor transcendent. Rather, it illuminates and enfolds all that is. It is suffused in all that is, including the phenomenal. However, while the truth of the phenomenal separates into things with their labels, the truth of the noumenal is one, as consciousness.

As mentioned above, Kant was incorrect when he said that we could not know the noumenal. We can know it. But we cannot know it through thought. Both the subjective and objective are both interpretive modes using thought, so neither yields us the noumenal. Their epistemic depends on being filtered through a conceptual lens of belief and imagination, or rationality. The difference between subjective and objective worlds is that the latter are a consensual construction of thought and language that is progressive; whereas a subjective world is more based in belief, and can be part of a collective imaginative construct, found in religions, cults and ideologies, or it can be individually unique.

Most of us are caught in a mixture of the subjective and the objective, seeing only a phenomenal reality where we objectify, or we engage in a subjective interpretation. The objective sees its most precise development in the extensive web of thought that is the progressive knowledge of science. Seeing reality as phenomenal is natural because language and thought are primary to our functioning to create, and survive. The strength of having a phenomenal reality manifests to varying degrees in all cultures, because it is naturally a central part of our 'doing' in the world, with some cultures more doing-oriented than others. Generally, Western cultures have an addiction to doing and regard 'being' with trepidation.

The noumenal is readily experienced in Indigenous cultures living traditionally, where people engage habitually in a different level of intimacy with nature, where *everything is regarded as living*. But even then there can well be layers of subjectivist interpretation and superstition. Yet for those living amidst nature there is a more palpable connection to Being, than in peoples living far removed from nature in post-industrial, urbanised, digital cultures.

Unless we are curious enough to challenge whether there is anything more to reality than the phenomenal and the duality of objective and subjective, the noumenal remains unreachable. It may only be hinted at, and projected as something transcendental, as exemplified in Kant or, for a 'theory laden' materialist, just a fabrication.

The discovery of the numinous is a revelation for anyone, because it is the basis of our identity and the 'ground of Being'. This deeper ontology beyond language and thought welcomes the truth-value of the phenomenal objectivist reality, with an understanding that there is a hidden order of Being, a nothingness that we can all experience yet which defies any description or mapping.

> *The perceived is conceptual. The perceiver is conceptual.*
> *Only the perceiving is real.*
> —Nisargadatta

Process oriented philosophy

'Substance metaphysics' has been the dominant paradigm in the history of Western philosophy, and the obsession of science, since the Atomists and Aristotle. Substance metaphysicians claim that the primary units of reality are substances (for example atoms) and that they must be static and constant through time. Yet it is something of a paradox that, with all this fixation on substance, in our exploration of the nature of phenomenal reality, we have come up empty-handed, there is no 'stuff' there, only forces and fields. Scientists such as Carlo Rivelli are now championing a 'process-oriented' view of the phenomenal world.

There is no ultimate substance, rather it is through the *process of interacting fields and forces* at the sub-atomic level that gives rise to 'quasi-substance' (as the four fundamental states of matter – 'gas, solid, liquid, plasma' and Bose-Einstein condensates) as emergent properties 'appearing' as substance, rather than being so in actuality. 'Substance' becomes an outmoded theoretical position, as one delves deeper into the quantum domain. And, experientially, substance dissolves in a heightened awareness of Being, where 'thingness' takes on a transparency - that is unknowable to the mind – as nothingness.

Process philosophers focus on *becoming* and what is occurring, as well as *ways of occurring*. Process philosophy is an attempt to understand and portray the dynamic nature of *Being as process*. It challenges belief in the solidity of things in an objectified phenomenal reality, in a universe of separate 'static' things/objects. In process philosophy *change* is fundamental. Nothing is truly independent, with everything being related to everything else in a dynamic state of flux. The universe pivots on 'becoming', where nothing is truly separate.

The bias towards substance in Western philosophy seems to be rooted partly in the nature of Indo-European languages, which are 'object oriented', with their cognitive dispositions towards objects, from the culture of ownership and possession of its speakers. The habits that develop from object orientation give a priority to static entities: from substances to objects, states of affairs and static structures, re-affirming a continuing bias towards substance metaphysics. Process philosophy shows a particular affinity with a number of indigenous languages (for an expanded discussion of this see chapter 15 on language and perception) and also alludes to the rich wisdom traditions found in Eastern philosophy.

Hegel stated that, in 'the history of Western metaphysics is the tendency towards substance'. In pre-Socratic Ancient Greece Heraclitus was the first recorded process oriented philosopher. His writings speak of the dynamic flux of the universe as living Being with his famous statement, 'a man cannot step into the same river twice'. More than two millennia later, Hegel postulated that reality is the self-unfolding of dynamic structures or templates. Elements of process philosophy also exist in Heidegger's work, in which human understanding is seen as a dimension of the process of Being. William James (1842-1910), a founder of modern psychology and an early investigator of consciousness, was also engaged in a process-based metaphysics.

Alfred North Whitehead (1861-1947) stands apart in the analytic tradition, articulating, in his very complex manner, that matter itself was not static, but a sea of dynamic flux, where all phenomena are best thought of as 'process-events' rather than static things, whether trees, rocks, human beings, or atoms. This heralded the understandings of the quantum era with its insights into the morphing changes observed at the sub-atomic level, and the very lack of substance in these 'fundamental units'.

Henri Bergson (1859–1941), an influential French philosopher of the first half of the 20th century, emphasises 'pure mobility', unforeseeable novelty, creativity and freedom - all essential features of process philosophy. In reality, Bergson argued that determinism is impossible, and that free will is an expression of pure mobility, which is what Bergson identified as being the *duration*, or an 'eternal now'. And because it is mobile it cannot be grasped through reason or rationality but only through intuition as immediate perception.

Two key points from Henri Bergson's *An Introduction to Metaphysics* may help us to grasp his use of the term 'intuition', as he uses it correctly, in line with the central epistemic theme of this book: that all concepts, while useful, are limited, and that intuition has the ability to apprehend the *absolute*. This is because intuition brings us directly to the things themselves. The term *duration* or now, as he uses it, is mobile and fluid and cannot be understood through 'immobile' analysis (substance metaphysics), but only through experiential, first-person intuition. The third essential concept in Bergson's philosophy is *élan vital*. He used this idea to explain evolution less mechanistically than science was doing, giving it a vital impetus in a more organic manner, as well as accounting for the creative impulse of humanity.

I wonder what would have happened if the Western world had not fallen down the rabbit-hole of transcendental dualism. And instead followed the Ancient Greeks 'way of philosophy to know the Self', and process philosophy, along with Stoic ethics. Certainly, there would have been a major shift towards a more holistic and integrated culture that was not so injurious to the planet, with a deeper social and spiritual narrative of living harmoniously in Being. There would have been an absence of the cultural, mental and spiritual dissonance created by dualism and beliefs in a transcendental realm and separate God.

But this has not been our destiny. The Western world, being insensitive to the error and destructive nature of these ideas, has followed a toxic form of dualism to our peril. It has been the source of the fragmented experience within us, and with the world. The dualistic hypothesis has created conflict between body and mind, mind and heart, between the sexes, between peoples, social disharmony with its hierarchical and divided view, and has given us a flawed dualistic morality of good and evil based in fear and punishment. It has also given us a dangerous sense of separation from nature and the environmental crises we are faced with. And while objectivism as an expression of duality has brought great benefits in scientific knowledge with its particular kind of understanding of nature, 'attachment' to this way of knowledge and a belief that it is the pinnacle of human knowing, rather than the knowledge itself, has given us many disharmonies.

No-thingness is 'knowing consciousness'

In *Being and Nothingness* Sartre begins by rejecting Kant's notion of noumena (things having unique essences), arguing instead that what we see is all there is. But this is not necessarily true. Firstly, apprehending the noumenal does not mean experiencing separate essences. Secondly, because, as discussed, it is rather a matter of perception as to the depth of reality we do experience. If we are limited by our conditioning – belief, language and attachment to a mindset – we will cognise a world that is readily known, as unconsciously embedded thought constructs. When we suspend the role of thought as the lens through which we view reality, what was obscured by this conditioning becomes apparent. We then discover that there is a lot more to reality than we may have assumed.

Sartre then develops this further with the following notion: that if there is no pre-ordained essence, then humans create their being from nothingness. And with no defining separate essence, we create ourselves by the choices we make, and by how we act. So it is through this process that we individuate. As he states, 'we are condemned to freedom'. He is correct in this, perhaps using 'condemned' for dramatic effect. When we behave as victims or blame others for our misery we enter the realm of 'bad faith', by failing to grasp our responsibility for our own state, and our freedom in Being. Conversely, when we do accept our responsibility, a way ahead with different possibilities emerges, and through this acceptance we can celebrate our freedom.

But Sartre's definition of nothingness relies on absence, on something missing, as a conceptual opposite of Being, which he conceives as fullness. Sartre's understanding of nothingness comes more from his reasoning, so it is abstract and conceptual in nature. However, in the deeper experience of Being, with the cessation of the internal dialogue, no-thingness is revealed in actuality; not as a reasoned speculation which is something that the mind constructs, but as an unfathomable actuality.

There is an important place for speculating about 'nothing' as it occurs in quantum physics and astrophysics, for example, but in actually experiencing nothingness you are connecting to everything. *No-thingness is the deeper ground of Being*. To anyone experiencing this it is revolutionary, although without the experience, this statement will appear meaningless.

The point that there is nothing that is self-existent (objects, souls, essences) is well articulated by Buddhist philosopher Nargajuna. He outlines the absence of any separate self, or separate essence in all things (animate and inanimate) in his writing on emptiness. The emptiness or nothingness that Nargajuna articulates, has an equivalence to the way I have used 'consciousness'. The nothingness that Nargajuna speaks of is 'knowing' as consciousness. In the experience of nothingness is consciousness, everywhere and in everything.

If we pause in our thinking for a moment, we can 'know' experientially that we are intimately, seamlessly in contact with the whole of existence through no-thing-ness. This knowing is local, and non-local. We experience the transparency of things/objects (known), and that transparency of the subject (knower) sees the collapse of the subjective and objective in experiencing the undivided nature of Being. While this is thought-constructed in my communication, it points to a reality that is non-conceptual and only experiential.

Yet there is fear around nothingness, because it is seen as a form of negation, or annihilation. It is misunderstood as a form of nihilism. And whilst the experience of nothingness *is* destructive to the process of attaching to thought, exposing the fallacy of believing in the exclusivity of phenomenal reality, we are profoundly enlivened by a subtle energy of noumenal origin, experiencing a oneness and an unconditional happiness – Eudaimonia. In experiencing nothingness, we are released from the psychological self and the struggle to be somebody, and its belief in a world of separate objects. This liberation brings gratitude and compassion for all life forms.

The key to the noumenal is a spontaneous abeyance of thought. It is the reason why meditation has been central to this dimension of experiential knowing. An insubstantial ontology of Being lends itself to all manner of paradoxical and expansive terms: the 'Logos' of Ancient Greece, Spinoza's 'infinite substance', Bergson's 'elan vitale', the 'tao' of Chinese philosophers, and for Buddhist philosopher, Nagajuna, 'nothingness'.

For the philosopher, Being is the elephant in the room

For the philosopher, Being is ever the 'elephant in the room'. Generally, Western philosophers have done their best to leave the ontology of a living universe unexamined, instead addressing their attention to pre-existing mindsets taking up positions in historical dialogues. In this they carry over pre-existing structures of belief, sometimes adding minor modifications of the old. Do this, rather than apprehending the real (the elephant) and directly experiencing the ever-fresh timeless Being. As we explored above, there have been some notable exceptions to this.

So easily the obvious gets overlooked, with attention being captured by dualities that are inherently what the mind creates. The elephant: a living universe, is all that is in our awareness now. It is the elephant in everyone's room. Dear reader, it is your experience now: experiencing your body sitting, the focus you have following the text; it is the text and the book, and, if you look up, it is all that is before you: the room, its furniture, all that is phenomenal experience; and noumenally it is all that is, as the nameless and, instantly beyond it, the Totality – all connected as one consciousness – Being.

> *First there is a mountain*
> *Then there is no mountain*
> *Then there is.*
> —Donovan, *There is a Mountain* (1967)[17]

In my early twenties, the final essay I designed and wrote in my undergraduate degree for a subject called 'Free Philosophical Studies' was titled something like (this was forty years ago) 'Is Academic Philosophy a Pathway Conducive to the Discovery of Truth?'. I outlined in the essay why it was not and, despite the chagrin of my mentor, he somehow still deemed it worthy of a pass. I did not care about the result, but thanked him anyway.

Once philosophy became professional under the governing academic culture, which is a conformist, hierarchically status-driven, and competitive culture, it lost its connection with its roots. The imperative was to follow in known paths of thought, framing perennial dilemmas, and to position ourselves in some philosophical ideology which, taken together, would see the clipping of a fledgling philosopher's wings.

This all signified to me that philosophy as a profession had drifted from its moorings as the 'love of wisdom'. Philosophy as an academic pursuit seemed only to further constrain the philosopher's epistemic range to the empirical and the rational, with no acknowledgement or understanding of looking through an unfiltered lens. *Philosophy's roots are in the known as well as the unknown, in the finite and the infinite, in the authenticity of being.*

The analytic philosophers completely ignored this ontology (shunned the elephant) and, in so doing, effectively disempowered their endeavours so that their philosophising lacked both gravitas and relevance, as they sought shelter in thought's sophistry. To the continentals like Sartre, the elephant is acknowledged and some headway is made, but then things tend to stall because of repeated attempts to penetrate Being with the mind. This operates under the assumption that Being will reveal itself by treating 'it' as an 'object' of thought's contemplation. Thought as a manifestation of consciousness cannot know the nature of its own origins, for this thinking only creates dualities as subject–object. It is ineffective; it is not the way.

What is the way? The way into Being is through being. It is so disarmingly simple. When meditation is done correctly in this way (not the different techniques created by thought – mantras, visualisations, prayer, energy circulation, specific contemplations, guided, et cetera) we are purely being. This is because in simply being we cease supporting the thought constructs that act as filters on our perception. Therefore, effectiveness in meditation is not a matter of doing: we are just 'being'. *Meditation is being.* Being is resting in awareness, thereby challenging the default 'central agency' assumed by thought. Meditation through being connects us to our 'natural state' and the truth of our identity, as Being.

However, an 'ontology of consciousness' like this as the base of existence, may seem intellectually unsatisfying for a mind reared in duality. This is because its opposite, the prospect of non-duality, or experiencing one consciousness, is incomprehensible and completely lacking in any kind of intellectual sophistication. It is incomprehensible because thought cannot grasp the nature of consciousness, in exactly the same way as it cannot grasp Being, as Being is consciousness. Apprehending the nature of consciousness or Being only comes through being.

CHAPTER 8

OBJECTIVE KNOWING AND DIRECT PERCEPTION

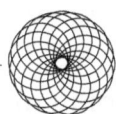

Above the Temple of Delphi in Ancient Greece is written 'Man Know Thyself'. This dictum is given to all as a command to know who we are, with the implication that it is perilous if we do not: to know the Self is to leave the self. To disregard this command is the danger posed by unconscious living. Knowing oneself is the natural unfolding of Being. Being is intelligent and, just like a vine reaching upwards towards the light, this intelligence seeks to know itself. When we are aware of being aware, through us, the universe knows itself. But knowing ourselves is not an obligation; rather it is akin to having the capacity for vision: we do not have an obligation to use our eyes, we simply use them as a birthright.

How we know gives us our perception of reality, informing how we relate to other human beings, animals, the earth and the cosmos. Also, it informs what we regard as important about living. We all answer questions of identity and knowing in some form or other. Many of us do this without any reflection as it is not part of our way, or in ways that can be negative, destructive and self-limiting. Yet if we feed our curiosity in living an examined life, knowing can open new dimensions undreamed of.

In this chapter we explore the different ways of knowing and how each yields different kinds of knowledge and truth. In understanding different ways of knowing, it is essential to consider the role that language can play in the structuring of our perception of reality, and how this informs our relationships with each other and with nature.

The meaning of knowing

The word 'know' is generally used in two different ways. First, it means 'to be aware of'. Knowing, in this sense, is to be aware of the content of consciousness: thoughts, emotions, moods, urges, sensations and perceptions. We can literally be aware of, or conscious of, anything or nothing in particular. We can be aware of awareness itself. That is, awareness without object. We can be aware of things in the phenomenal world, which we have differentiated with names and ascribed meanings and explanations. We are aware of our senses as we cognise clouds, chairs, stars, the sound of a dog barking; or, internally, a passing thought, a feeling, or a mathematical proof. While all of us are aware of the phenomenal because we all know a language, and we all have access to at least some functioning senses, only some of us have awareness of the noumenal. Both are aspects of the kind of reality that we experience, depending on our degree of awareness. Awareness of the noumenal occurs in a naturally quiet mind.

The second meaning of 'know' has to do with thought and memory. To experience the phenomenal world means to recognise, understand and create conceptual maps using factual, concept-building information. Spoken languages and the more symbolic languages like mathematics, chemistry, or music offer different types of linguistic terrain.

This type of knowing frames an 'objectivist' model of reality. We create objects in our process of naming that imbues them with separateness, thing-ness and substance. The English language, for example, is quite noun and possession based. We create a world full of things even when they are as insubstantial as quarks, but also symphonies, formulas and galaxies.

To know something in this way is to be able to contextualise it. We must either be able to recognise it and name it, or add it to our conceptual body of knowledge. In this way, all new ideas – things or theories about things – are built on old ideas as an already existing body of knowledge.

So, knowing has an aspect of pure awareness. That is, awareness with or without reference to specific content. And knowing has an aspect of information and awareness of specific types of information or knowledge, along with the particular structure of this knowledge.

Knowing is essential to survival for both animals and human beings and, really, to all life. But, for human beings, it sets us apart, for we are specialists in knowing. We can know ourselves in a way that a dog or a cat cannot; we can know who we are, which is to know the very source of consciousness in us, as us. With this primary knowing – oneself as Consciousness – that occurs through resting in awareness, we experience the fundamental ground of Being.

Knowing in science

Increasingly, science is now holding the place of authority that traditional religion once had in the collective psyche. We look to science, somewhat mistakenly, to provide answers to many of our problems, even to the point of explaining our identity and our place in the universe. Science has come to fill the void for many in a secular culture, as we seek to derive authority and security from scientific theories and explanations. On the surface these answers appear rational, but frequently they are held with such passionate attachment that they speak instead of fear-driven irrational force. When scientists have this attitude it only limits the progression of scientific knowledge that is essential to its own enterprise. It also reveals a belief that science is the arbiter of truth, and this is an error. Science is, rather, an arbiter of theory and concept-driven reality in the way we model the universe. Science as a precise structure of objectivist thought and a method of investigation can only know within the confines of thought itself: *it can know truth that is relative within phenomenal reality, but it cannot know truth that is absolute.*

Science can never be the arbiter of the truth of Being precisely because it is an inappropriate mode of knowing for this. Only experiential knowing can do this. When science assumes more than what its limitations determine, confusion arises from an elevated and misplaced sense of its own prowess. And this, like any religious belief, is an example of 'tribal thinking'. In this sense scientists are no more immune from tribal thinking and beliefs than anyone else, although they may proclaim that they are by calling themselves 'objective'.

Thus, there are two things that are currently impediments to science:

* First, there is the tendency toward tribal thinking or group-think, seen as group identification and dogmatically held beliefs about theories and concepts. Science as dogma has been referred to as 'scientism'. The Skeptic Society is a good example of those who make proclamations based on a mechanistic and materialistic 'catechism' of beliefs. Yet there is no questioning of their mindset, itself a matter of conditioned thinking. As often happens, the staunchest adherents to a particular theory or position, do not treat their own theories with the rigour that any theory in the spirit of science requires: dispassionate curiosity. Instead they 'over-commit' to a position that is, in essence, temporary, impermanent and relative. This is odd, given that scientific knowledge is by nature a progressive endeavor and constantly changing.

* The second major problem is that science is without an ethical compass to ensure that its applications are at once peaceful, socially and environmentally responsible, and congruent with the integrity of life on our planet. Science frequently partners with big business, government and the military in ways that are non-transparent so that hidden motives, driven by political, or commercially-vested interests, are permitted to influence research and its findings. There are many examples of this, and probably the most widely known occurs in the weapons and surveillance

industries, and the pharmaceutical industry. With the latter, for example, drugs utilised in the field of mental illness are produced to service the proliferation of conditions which, to a considerable degree, are invented by the psychiatric profession which, in turn, has a vested interest in prescribing these drugs.

The lack of moral compass in science means that it is value absent, rather than value embedded. This is a direct result of its materialist ethos, with the object of its study – Nature- seen as 'machine-like', inert and without consciousness. If it were understood, by all those engaged in science, that the universe is completely connected, and that it is living and suffused with consciousness, this would not be the case.

Rationality: its uses and abuses

Rational thought is the ability to use the mind in a logical manner, with thoughts exhibiting a sequential, linear flow. To talk rationally is to talk logical sense. The Ancient Greek philosophers revelled in following lines of argument in logical sequences to a conclusion, thus championing rational thought. Rational thought in modern times holds no less status. Unfortunately, rationality has colonised many areas of life as an ideology and has thus become a problem. For instance, 'economic rationalism' routinely devastates workplaces, as governments and businesses justify the cutting of jobs or pay in the name of balancing ledgers or satisfying shareholders. This 'profit-driven' ideology is destructive to people. The casualties from these rationalistic practices are –

a sense of connectedness, long-term efficiency and the experience of community. Such rationalism is a perversion of its best use. Rational thinking that is appropriately and positively used is indeed essential, for example, in the practice of doing good science.

Rational thinking in modern culture has come to be viewed as the unquestioned pinnacle of intelligence. This assumption holds that there is nothing that will not yield to the probing of human beings' rational thinking capacity. Rationality, particularly in the form of scientific knowledge, is often assumed to be the only legitimate form of knowledge, thus fuelling the elevated status of an objectivist account of nature. As such it has also been used as a reference standard when assessing other cultures and their knowledge, practices, and history.

Indigenous people fare badly in the light of these types of rationalist criteria. If we give a traditional Indigenous man or woman a standard IQ test, they will probably perform badly. If we then judge them as lacking in intelligence, we fail to see that Indigenous people are not skilled in 'rationality' as taught in our Anglo-European–centric culture. However they have developed other ways of knowing that are specifically connected to their way of living, in fact critical to their survival. Nonetheless, their knowledge tends to be viewed as worthless, even irrelevant, by Western standards and so, as a people, they continue to be regarded as backward or primitive. Fortunately, there are positive signs of this changing, but a significant part of the the world's populace would hold this view.

In this way, rationalism is again used as an ideology and becomes just another form of oppression from a colonising group limited by its own tribal thinking and assumptions. No form of tribal thinking, including attachment to rationality, can be used as a universal measuring standard. It is an irony that when the veneration of rationalism results in it being used inappropriately, it becomes a distortion of intelligence.

Rational thinking has its own beauty as a particularly clear use of the mind, and is an expression of intelligence. But it is not the only expression, for like all forms of thinking, it is conditioned, and limited. There are many different expressions of intelligence: social intelligence, emotional intelligence and, more deeply, spiritual intelligence. Thought is not the source of intelligence: rather, intelligence or Consciousness is the source of thought, and the use of rational thinking in human beings is but one aspect of this.

> *All things in their fundamental nature are not nameable or explicable. They cannot be adequately expressed in any form of language.*
> — Aśvaghosa, Indian philosopher and poet (080–150 AD)[18]

Epistemology: two types of knowing

In Western philosophy, the branch of philosophical pursuit that theorises about ways of knowing and different types of knowledge is called epistemology, from the Greek word 'episteme', to know. Epistemology is the study of, and theory of, knowledge. Its primary consideration is how do we know what we know?

I will embark on a different approach from what is standard in academic circles. In discussing epistemology, I propose that there are fundamentally only two ways in which we know anything: indirect knowing and direct knowing.

Indirect knowing is most familiar to us because we live so much in the mind. It is knowledge gained by using our cognitive and linguistic capacities – our use of thought. In fact, to many of us this is all we know. It is our ability to develop and manipulate conceptual thought. It includes all the complex manoeuvrers that thought can achieve: our theories, maps of reality, stored knowledge, hypotheses and assumptions. It is the knowing of reasoned argument and deductive analysis, as well as the passing on of experience, such as when a tribal elder gives instruction to a young woman, a senior physician to a young intern, or an old fisherman to his novice son. It is part of our mind-mapping ability and involves the recourse to memory, essential for our functioning, creativity and survival as a species. It is also the knowing that is embedded in our language and, whatever our language may be, is used to map phenomenal reality. The higher we go in education, the more sophisticated this process of knowledge-building and conceptual dexterity becomes.

Science deals in the relative truth of conceptual thought rather than the timeless, absolute 'truth of Being'. Scientific theories about reality are complex, consensus-driven maps created by thought and modified constantly through time, as they essentially must be. Even the new maps or paradigms that have emerged in scientific thinking, like the move from classical physics to the era of relativity and quantum theory, have seen the development of ideas that are connected as a clear progression from earlier ideas, with the odd leap or two. This is a progressive knowledge, constructed through time because it is subject to constant review and modification.

Direct knowing is experiential rather than conceptual. It is without the filter of the mind and is beyond thought. The simplest example is that you are aware of being alive. You do not have to think that you exist. You 'know' it without the need of thought or memory, although to express it requires language. It is direct and immediate, without recourse to thought. Or you can be aware of being aware, which is not thinking of awareness; thought is not involved. This knowledge is not interpretive nor does it involve explanations or the construction of models about reality.

Direct perception is this direct experiencing prior to thought. It is a knowing that is at once immediate and only possible in the present moment. Memory, conceptual knowledge and language are not involved. In terms of reality, it is the only way we can know the 'is-ness' of reality that is not a construct of mind. However, any person who follows this simplest way of knowing becomes wise, because it is how Consciousness knows itself.

This kind of knowing is potentially a province for everyone. It is not academic, scientific or rational. It cannot be learned as a method, or cultivated the way an intellectual activity can be, or learned as a skill. It requires no scriptures or scientific theories. It carries no status, nor even the need of literacy or education. In fact, identifying with learned status and the sophistication that formalised knowledge brings, could be a hindrance to this knowing. This happens if our mind is burdened with attachments to theories, concepts and any self-importance connected with this knowledge. If so, we may well miss the profound simplicity of pure observation with an unfiltered lens. In this way 'direct seeing' gets completely overlooked, as we busy ourselves mentally with layering over the lens of perception, so that experiencing directly may barely even be possible.

Scientists, like anyone else, are capable of experiencing direct knowing. But, while there are a number of geniuses who exhibit extraordinary levels of insight and creativity with thought, there do not appear to be many scientists whom we would call sages. This is perhaps because scientists make their living from the intensity, creativity and precision of their mental activity. There is the tendency to be intensely identified with their thoughts, their intellectual status, and the status and positioning of their theoretical position in the broader landscape of existing science. But if scientists simultaneously developed a capacity to distance themselves from thought, they could discover that there is a domain beyond thinking, as the source from whence thought arises. Generally, however scientists are more interested in the specific content of the mind than in the 'ground-bed' from whence thinking arises. Those scientists who can achieve some distance from their thinking invariably demonstrate a broader ability to be philosophical and potentially sage-like.

Artists, poets and musicians are less driven by rational thought or a method of enquiry. Some even seem chaotic yet can be totally committed, passionate and brilliant in their art practice. The drive of the artist is to express in their chosen medium their specific intimacy with life. As a result there is a tendency in artists to be more 'open' because they do not have a belief in the supremacy of rational thought, or that things necessarily have to be a certain way to fit a particular view of the world, or model of reality. In this way they can be a creative foil to rationalism, but in a deeper sense this is also complementary. Their creativity is non-rational, often using direct knowing to inform their art practice.

Indirect and direct knowing are not antagonistic; they are complementary aspects of the human potential to know.

All human knowledge is completely subjective

Even if we agree about some fact and it can be proven by various means, it still comes from the consensual, conceptual scheme. This breaks down of course when people in politics invent 'alternative facts', to pass off the palpably false as true. In this arena 'fact checking' is critical. But in a conceptual world in which we identify, interpret, and measure all that we determine as phenomenal, all our labels, theories and descriptions of phenomena are the products of our thinking, sensation and perception. It is a false assumption to think that our conceptual world is in any way truly objective. All thought and phenomenal reality is anthropocentric, because humans think it.

Consider the way science separates reality through a system of labelling. In the quest to find the ultimate building blocks of the universe, labels are given to the infinitesimally small subatomic units which are really vibrations of frequency (quarks and electrons) separated by subatomic forces, rather than substance. They are 'excitations in a field'. This is an objectivist, mind-constructed reality. But all these labels are our creation, and fit – so far fairly well – into the theoretical structure of the 'standard model' of subatomic particles. *However, there is a deeper order of reality that is not apprehended by mind and is not anthropocentric.*

If we look at the objectivist idea of 'table' as an example, we see it is made from wood, which is a natural composite of fibrous cellulose embedded in a matrix of lignin which, in turn, is made from atoms, which are made from electrons, which act like standing waves (waves that appear stationary) located a considerable distance from the nucleus, housing the protons and neutrons made from ever smaller subatomic units called quarks, of which there are different types that are symbolically portrayed as having different colours, and they also have different orientations. These quarks are ultimately more energetic than substance-like (excitations in a field). This all occurs in vast regions of space, relative to the size of these subatomic 'things', wherein they are held together by exquisitely balanced nuclear forces. All of this comes together to give you the very real feeling of 'solidity' when you bump into the table! This is the phenomenal world we can analyse as an objectivist description of reality. But it is a human made world that we describe.

Phew! And yet nothing at this level of reality is truly solid or fixed, for these subtle elements are not permanent and can be seen to transform into different 'things' in a cloud chamber (particle detector). In their quantum energy dance, everything at this sub-microscopic level is really energy, forces, and space. Yet science naturally labels them as 'things' using a language that has difficulty with portraying the real subtlety of this story. And in doing so it creates a myth of solidity and a notion of separation of the solidity of things, in this model of reality. It is a precise, rational story that is both valid and real, within a conceptual context as an objectivist model, but subjective to humans.

The labelling that we do involves tacit assumptions that shape our perception. When we look at a tree, for example, our cerebral cortex interprets impulses from our optic nerve, referring to memories it has accumulated through experience of previous encounters with this shape, which we have learned since childhood and which, in turn, prompt our cerebral cortex to say 'tree!'. The cortex is doing the labelling to create our familiar phenomenal world, as a process of constructing our tangible reality. However, in experiencing a noumenal reality this process of 'thought constructing reality' involving memory does not happen.

I am not questioning the worth of labelling trees or anything else, for indeed it has immense practical worth and is the basis of all our concept building and understanding. Rather, I am pointing out that 'facts' about the tree are conceptual abstractions, created by mind and language. When the mind is in abeyance we experience the one seamless reality that we could call the 'unified universal field'. In suspending the automatic, objectivist interpretations of reality, we experience the numinous reality lying beyond the labels of trees and everything else. This is not imaginary.

Imagination, however, is essential to our modeling of reality, because another tacit assumption that shapes our model of reality, for example, is imaginary numbers. There can be virtually no development of theories such as quantum theory or relativity without the invention of imaginary numbers. An example is the 'Plank constant', a number which links the amount of energy a photon (a light particle) carries with the frequency of its electromagnetic wave, in quantum theory. Imaginary numbers make these theories workable, and any investigation of a map of reality proceeds from these pivotal assumptions. Therefore, no matter how beautifully and painstakingly constructed our scientific knowledge is, the notions of what is 'factual' are built on the shifting sands of conceptual theory and imaginary numbers specifically invented to balance equations to account for continuing phenomenal observations.

In summary, the scientific explanation of the world and phenomena is based on a set of agreed-upon labels, explanations, theories and assumptions. This is a sophisticated form of self-referential knowledge. All human knowledge created by thought is entirely subjective because it is self-referential to the human beings thinking it, and this includes our 'objectivist' account of reality, because it too is anthropocentric. An objectivist account of reality may be perfectly rational but it is completely subjective to us human beings. The basis of subjectivity is that we think it. Objectivity, in this sense, is a myth we have created. The idea that we can stand outside ourselves in some elevated manner to see objectively, is a hangover of Western transcendentalism. We can try to fool ourselves that in the practice of science we are truly objective, but this only reveals our projected self-importance. It is thought intoxicated with itself, an arrogance resulting from ignorance.

A knowing that is independent of self-reference is beyond the mind. Experiencing a numinous reality is not created by thought and, because of this, is neither subjective nor objective.

The rise of 'objectivist' knowledge

Epistemology has powerful implications for the way we live, and is found in the phenomenal world as the relationship between the knower (as the living person) and the known (the world itself). It is an assumed duality that predicates all thought-constructed knowledge. This duality – knower and known – is the basis of objective knowledge. The central model of knowing as taught in all universities across the globe is objectivist, and there are important consequences of this, because it has its own ethical directions and outcomes.

Objectivism is used generally throughout cultures, whether in the East or the West, but has specifically taken root in the West with the rise of science. As a mode of knowing it finds its most sophisticated expression in our universities. It is evident in diverse disciplines from the social sciences to the biological sciences, physics, and engineering. In a university there is a more rigorous attempt to separate the knower from the world, and to prevent knowledge from 'contamination' by subjective prejudice and bias. It divorces knowledge from our intimate experience, and with its main tool – analytical thought – it reshapes the world into an idealised model, necessary for any scientific endeavour. In this way it continues the idealism from the Greek philosophy of Plato and Aristotle, in elevating rational thinking and hence maintaining a pure realm of ideas or theory.

This is not wrong, but there is a cost: in creating a model of a world 'out there', we necessarily become spectators and are thus removed from the world. Everything becomes an object, an object that can be manipulated for our own private, conceptual ends. In this sense, the world is inherently seen as non-living, not alive in its own right with its own intelligence. Objectivism, as taught through our education sytem, trains us in this form of separation, as we look at and create a reality through an ideational lens, disconnecting us by forming a world 'out there' as though the model itself had absolute reality. However, directly experiencing without the mediation of thought and language connects us intimately with everything. There is no separation. There is no separate world out there, and neither is there a separate knower.

It is straightforward to see how this kind of epistemology, with its fragmentary and reductionist nature, develops an ethic of competitive individualism as a natural consequence. If we want to work collaboratively we have to consciously shift our attention from the atomising effects of the objectivist ethos. And, when used blindly, objectivism involves a tendency to exploitation. It is easier to exploit an object, if it is something we have no intimate connection with. The emphasis placed on the abstract and individualistic nature of objectivism discourages a perspective that is holistic, integrative and community-connected. Hence the lack of moral compass in science as it is both taught and practised.

Objectivism is essentially anti-communal because community is centred on, and built by, our direct experience, rather than objectification. The objectivist skill at manipulating thought also means we can fashion a theoretical niche for ourselves independent to what is happening around us because, in this mode of knowing, we have buffered ourselves from seeing things as they are. Hence, we create idealisations and thus tend to live in a world totally mapped by the mind. With this particular conditioning we are perhaps unaware because we have convinced ourselves in the process that we are being increasingly objective – objective simply because we believe that what we are doing makes it so. But this objectivity is really an illusion; instead, it is part of our subjective process.

We learn this objectivist art of disconnecting throughout our education by becoming more skilled at it, and it also becomes a survival strategy for the separate self. As we become cleverer at it, with this kind of knowledge assuming a particular status of authority, we develop a moral compass that is ill-informed because its main basis lies in separation, idealisation, measurement and comparison. Believing in objectivism as the primary way of knowing nourishes competitive individualism, and disconnectedness from reality and nature. However, a world created by mind – an objectivist world – is one essentially without intimacy and vitality. It is a world in which only our analytical head with its conditioned mindset is invited. Of course, it can be shared with other 'like-minded' people, also engaged in this objectivism.

There are certain core fallacies common in our universities that reveal our own epistemic shortcomings: principally, that the individual is seen as the primary agent of knowing. The clever manipulation of thought is seen as the highest, indeed for many, the only form of knowledge. Building knowledge with thought, using rationality, making objectivist models of reality, are an important part of our repertoire of knowing. But this type of knowing, presented to the exclusion of all else, is itself a profound skewing of our true and greater capacity for knowing. This is because it offers a vision of human identity that is not grounded in our essential identity as Being.

The attachment to objectivist knowledge also fosters competition for knowledge, rather than sharing. A competitive ethic sees knowledge being used as a kind of currency. Knowledge used as currency confers status with the hierarchy of knowledge and the rise of the expert. In objectivist knowledge there is a relentless acquisition of potentially everything because knowledge of this type can be commoditised (and theft occurs too, exemplified in the form of cultural imperialism, as Indigenous peoples can attest) and it is used as power in all its guises and abuses.

However, it should be borne in mind that knowing and learning are also communal acts, whether in education or in our parliaments. The continued practice of collaboration, and cycles of open forums of questioning and discussion that embrace disagreement, are essential to checking the excesses that tend to occur in objectivist knowledge. Beyond the models of objectivist knowledge there is relatedness to people, to events in history, to nature, and to the world of ideas. This is theoretically captured by a 'systems approach' but, more profoundly than this, it is most fundamentally captured by intuitively apprehending Being.

A communal way of knowing, aligned with us as co-operative human beings, relies on a capacity for healthy, creative arenas for discussion and debate. The spirit of this kind of open curiosity brings civilised discussion into schools, universities, parliaments or workplaces, having the capacity to release both fear and ignorance as the primary agents causing separation. Curiosity is essential to challenging the authoritarian tendencies inherent in objective knowledge and institutions of learning.

Conceptual reality is real, but there is infinitely more to reality

As discussed in the above section, we often mistake the 'map-of-reality' created by our thinking, as all there is to reality. We believe in this map, becoming attached to things, explanations and theories that we project as permanent or fixed. But facts, even if haloed, are ultimately provable only in as much as they are consistent with the framework of thought that created them. If we accept the limitations of how we create facts, we will not fool ourselves with a fantasised objectivity of thought. If we understand the limitations of mind, thinking, and rationality, we will not be arrogant with our knowledge, but instead be sobered by understanding what thought can, and cannot, know.

It is essential that we distinguish the different orders of knowing and their place in our lives. This is a matter of understanding, care and respect. We all need to balance the important role that objectivist knowledge has to play, while simultaneously engaging in our living with a level of community and intimacy that comes only from 'clearing the lens' so we can know directly.

Yet now is also a time when we are challenged to become more scientifically literate so that we can all participate in making informed decisions about how best to live on this wonderful, revolving, living rock. Even more important is the development of our spiritual understanding, because this is the very essence of our conscious awakening and connecting.

> *Meditate on yourself as motionless awareness,*
> *free from any dualism,*
> *giving up the mistaken idea*
> *that you are just a derivative consciousness;*
> *anything external or internal is false.*
> —Ashtavakra and Nalin N. Nyas[19]

CHAPTER 9

THE METHOD OF THE PHENOMENAL AND 'THE WAY' OF THE NOUMENAL

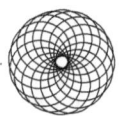

There are assumptions that are essential in practising science and using its method. Exploring these will give an understanding of the scope, the benefits, and the limitations of this kind of knowledge. There is great power and beauty in the careful development of scientific knowledge, but it is not the only form of knowing, and this remains largely unknown to those in the scientific community. This is mainly through an ignorance that has its roots in the cognitive history of Western civilisation stretching back to Ancient Greece, and arises from a specific attachment to a dualistic mindset. Non-rational ways of knowing have at times been disparaged, overlooked or dismissed as 'mumbo-jumbo' because they are mistakenly regarded as confused, irrational and irrelevant. To provide further insight into the different ways of knowing, I will present aspects of the direct perception of Being as a counterpoint, appearing below the features of the idealized 'scientific method'.

The primary assumption: separating the 'knower' from the 'known'

Any practising scientist must accept certain assumptions that are pivotal to furthering their enquiry in order to proceed in building conceptual knowledge, and the most fundamental assumption is about the validity of the very process of enquiry – one that separates the knower and known. This separation, of course, begins much earlier, prior to development of science with thought and language, as we differentiate 'things' and 'phenomena' as the ingredients of our phenomenal experience.

The word 'assumption' comes from the Latin root 'assumptionem', meaning 'a taking or receiving'. In science, its meaning is to take for granted, to take some understanding as 'given'. These are the things that are generally unquestioned and, in a significant way, also tend to function as core beliefs, because it is only when they are challenged, that the emotional attachment to them becomes apparent.

It probably escapes most scientists that the whole practice of science and its method is built on this one core assumption: that of the separation of the subject and the object. But even in challenging it – because it is so fundamentally assumed – it may on the surface seem trivial. However, if we do seriously challenge this, we find ourselves entering an experiential reality of a quite a different order. Our 'assumed' world is turned upside down.

The assumed positing of a dualistic universe: a human knower – separated from the object or phenomena – to be known. This dualism, stemming earlier from Aristotle, and reiterated by Descartes, is posited as the defining epistemic signature of

Western culture, and as the foundation of all scientific enquiry. That there is an external world to investigate, separate from an internal subject that knows, stands as the core assumption of the scientific method.

But consider what occurs when we accept this assumption. In our acceptance of the observer separate from the observed, we move ahead of ourselves, by proposing thought as the *marker of what is real* – that this separation of 'knower' from 'the known' is real. And further, that the *discovery of what is true* lies in gathering empirical evidence, all of which goes to support the validity of that separation. To the thinker this separation is obvious: I am here and the object of study is over there and I can measure its distance in space, and the time it takes for light shining on the object to reach 'me'. This dualism initiates a narrative interrogation of the world that has now become objectified from the knower. But without thought, none of this is true. There is no observer, there is no observed, and there is no time; there is only observing.

Phenomenal reality becomes objectified as we explain and describe phenomena creating a map, as a description or image of what is essentially un-nameable and real. The understanding of this objectified world is a progressive one, a world painstakingly engaged in as part of our knowledge building. But it can never provide absolute truth nor a deeper reality, precisely because it is assumed, and hence subject to the limits of its own epistemic method.

I am not saying that it does not have merit; it certainly does. As a fan of scientific endeavour and knowledge, I enjoy the fruits that this knowledge of duality brings. But just as a shadow of the real is cast, I have preference for experiencing directly a real sunset over an interesting explanation of it, or viewing an image: a preference for the is-ness of Being, unmediated by thought.

With a prior 'calling' to philosophy, I could hardly become a scientist. Because essential to this calling is the questioning of anything assumed, and where nothing is a given, particularly with regard to our conditioning. When our curiosity opens the door to an epistemic that does not involve thought from experiencing no-mind, it makes duality untenable. The non-duality of Being is what the mind cannot possibly figure.

Put another way, by going beyond the assumed dualism underpinning objectivism and subjectivism – that is, 'thought created realities' altogether – one experiences the non-duality of existence. In this more fundamental knowing nothing is assumed, and nothing is believed. Thought is not posited as the arbiter of reality, or of truth. We experience nothingness as the ground of Being itself.

Further assumptions in science that stem from the primary one

* **There are natural causes** (rather than supernatural) for the things around us. Every physical, observable effect has a physical, observable cause. The universe does not have dimensionality. Eventually this assumption will be dropped.

* **Evidence from the natural world can be used to learn about those causes.**

* **There is consistency in the causes that operate in the natural world.** The universe exhibits continuity and uniformity in behaviour: for instance, a hydrogen atom on earth is identical to a hydrogen atom 1 billion light years away (reinforced by observable behaviour such as red shift observations).

* **The universe exhibits order, pattern, structure and regularity,** enabling conceptual investigation and the development of laws. For example, the principle of 'least

action' or 'stationary action' is found in everything from astrophysics to quantum mechanics. That the universe is ordered could be better characterised as an *intuition* rather than an assumption.

* **The laws of nature are invariant** – they are same everywhere in the cosmos.

* **Nothing is self-evident.** Truth claims must be demonstrated objectively – scientific knowledge is essentially public knowledge.

* **The use of rationality (induction and deduction) as well as empiricism is fundamental.** Using the senses directly or indirectly (using telescopes, microscopes, particle accelerators, and Geiger-counters, et cetera, to extend our observations) is the primary and valid mode of thought used. However, essential for its creativity, the non-rational faculties of intuition and imagination are also used.

* **The concept of time is objectified.** The concepts of past, present and future, giving us a historical universe, one in which the laws of nature are constant, is essential.

* **The universe is 'local'.** This means that science is able to perform controlled experiments, shutting out distant instantaneous influences. It is the basis of the phenomenal world, and the basis for relativity, but this, of course, is challenged by the non-locality and entanglement of quantum theory.

These are the base assumptions upon which the scientific method is built. We should be clear that the method built on these assumptions cannot be proved by those same assumptions. Yet it is not uncommon to see some scientists attempting to do just this.

Science is not like mathematics, where there are mathematical proofs that are water-tight in a system that has a rare form of conceptual certainty. Mathematical truths are timeless. But in science, with nature which is constantly changing and evolving as its subject, how can the scientific laws of nature have the timeless quality found in mathematical proofs?

And so just because a given theory works by confirming the predictions it makes, and hence supports the fact that we are justified in using initial assumptions the theory was built on, only proves that our enquiry is on *relatively* secure footing. Rather, the 'proof' of the assumptions, which cannot to be found in the method itself, lies in the practical facts developed in effective enquiry. But while there can be mounting evidence supporting a given hypothesis or theory, there is no water-tight proving in science. However, the disproving of a hypothesis or theory can be definitive.

Assumptions are necessary for this specific type of enquiry to proceed, but they can only ever be a guarantee of a form of truth that is relative rather than absolute. A relative 'truth value' is the case with any system of conceptual mapping. For example, more recently, with the assumption of the absolute constancy of laws of nature over time, it has been suggested that, in actuality, they too must evolve, as the universe itself goes through major evolutionary shifts. Why should 'laws' be immune from evolutionary change that is fundamental to a historical universe? Immutable laws are a form of philosophical idealism, like the Platonic realm of perfect ideas and timeless forms, and the timeless mathematical proofs.

The way science uses assumptions is like a form of 'bootstrapping', to use the Munchausen term, in getting out of a potentially intransigent situation using properties existing in nature (for example, by assuming the 'cosmological constant' as the simplest candidate for 'dark energy'). Dark energy functions as a type of 'anti-gravity' in a continuously expanding universe, leading to the current standard model of cosmology known as the Lambda-CDM model, and hence provides a good fit to many cosmological observations. Assumptions are supported by the reality of scientific achievements, along with self-correcting forms of feedback, as a necessary part of the self-sustaining nature of scientific methodology.

> ** Assumptions are not present in direct perception*, because it is not the kind of knowing that is structured in thought. It is perception of the original mind through an unfiltered lens. There is nothing to underpin. There is nothing taken for granted or as given. There is no need of 'primary' thoughts (i.e. assumptions) and there is no method. Finally, there is no observer separate from what is observed, only 'observing'. The intimacy of this knowing reveals a numinous universe, with an understanding that is experiential rather than gained through the means of thought, rationally or deductively.

The scientific method/noumenal experience

A question is formulated based on observations

The scientific method: A question is asked, such as what are the strange, coloured lights in the sky at the Arctic Circle? Or does a pencil drop from a given height at the same speed as a cannon ball? How is it so, even if one is heavier? And what would happen if all the air was extracted from a space, and we dropped a feather and a cannon ball. Would they fall towards the ground together? Is there some deeper law governing this observation? Asking the right questions then leads to the formulation of a hypothesis.

* ***The direct perception of Being:*** There is no process of formulating questions in a mind that is still. In accepting 'what is', we are observing the essential no-thingness of Being. There is no agenda to discover laws of nature or discover the logical order of things – rather, the 'hidden order' of Being reveals itself. This stillness of thought is not vacuous or a form of mental dullness. Instead, it is a vibrating intelligence that pervades existence. In experiencing no-thingness, the 'things' of the world that we normally describe as our phenomenal world are still there as a reality, but are no longer prominent.

A testable hypothesis is formed – 'falsifiability'

The scientific method: In the practice of good science there is an honesty policy that ensures people cannot just go around making claims about the phenomenal world without providing some way of checking the validity of these claims. The methodology of making hypotheses about phenomena, and then developing testing processes for them to be challenged for falsifiability (as philosopher Karl Popper did), is an important insight into the nature of the specific type of knowledge that is scientific.

Hypotheses that are encouraged are ones that provide a way of researching and then testing specific claims. On the other hand, some claims are not testable and therefore not verifiable. When Galileo looked at the moon through one of his early telescopes, he maintained that the moon was not perfectly spherical; that it was irregular in shape because it appeared dotted with mountains and had an undulating surface. This ran counter to the belief of the day, held by the religious-cum-scientific orthodoxy of the time, that the celestial bodies were perfectly spherical. Galileo's colleague was outraged at such heresy, maintaining that there was an invisible substance that filled these undulations, which he called 'phlogiston'. This 'ad hoc hypothesis' (because it was just an invented explanation) could not be tested, and was incompatible with the spirit of good science.

There can be a tendency for science to be narrow and rigid when examining new hypotheses, because they might be challenging a belief in the precious order of things. Philosopher Imre Lakatos proposed that a new hypothesis should have a 'protective belt' when faced with harsh criticism (as David Bohm's pilot-wave theory did – see chapter 10). That is, the new hypothesis should be given reasonable airing and research before it is dismissed as being without merit. This would ensure that science continued to explore ideas that are at the creative and challenging edge of existing theory, because these ideas might, with further development, provide growth and insight and become central to a deeper understanding in the progress of conceptual knowledge.

* ***The direct perception of Being:*** Is experiencing Being falsifiable? Being is not an object that can be analysed and investigated by thought. Are you, the reader, present as you read this? Do you need to refer to thought to verify this, as Descartes did when he stated, 'I think, therefore I am'? Do you need some form of independent corroboration to validate your existence?

   The mind is expert at manufacturing doubt, but doubt is only relevant when we are engaged in mentally constructing an idea (for example that there is an 'I' that exists) theory or formula. Awareness of Being is prior to thought and is only in the ever-present now. There is no 'prior to' with awareness, and there is no agency that can own it. It is not 'my awareness' or 'your awareness'; nor can there be any external agency that could corroborate the experiential knowing that is awareness. There is no 'I': there is only Being.

Being is intrinsically self-referential, and self-validating, and thus is not falsifiable in terms of standard scientific measurement and verification. Consciousness cannot truly know itself through inference or by deduction, for these are thought-driven, and as such are an indirect form of knowing. When neuroscientists are studying consciousness, they are really studying a form of objectification – magnetic imaging of brain patterns, measuring brain waves, studying the molecular and cellular workings of the central nervous system – not consciousness. Consciousness can know itself directly but this does not involve thought as an interpretive medium. When the Advaita sages say that 'undifferentiated Being is beyond the conceptual mind', in a sense they are proposing a hypothesis, for anyone to verify, not as a logical proposition, but rather through their own direct experience.

An experiment must be repeatable

The scientific method: In science there is a requirement that, if we put forward a hypothesis, we should be able to investigate its veracity by repeatable observations and measurements. For instance, if objects of a given weight and with no air resistance are dropped, the rate of descent depends only on how far the object has fallen, no matter how heavy the object is. The objects will reach the ground at the same time if they are dropped simultaneously from the same height, following the law of conservation of energy. This is measurable, using weight, distance and velocity of the object falling, and all of this is repeatable. Anyone can check the results anywhere on the globe to confirm or deny the veracity of the hypothesis. This is basic to the practice of good science.

* ***The direct perception of Being:*** Nothing is repeatable. Our conceptualisation of time arises from our consensually developed model of phenomenal reality created by thought, rather than an ever-present awareness of Being. No moment that has ever happened can ever be repeated. There is only the eternity of now. Being is beyond the relative, beyond analysis, beyond measurement, and beyond time. And it is in this sense that it is absolute.

The force must be known

The scientific method: A given phenomenon must be explicable within existing theory and known forces (tacit assumptions that explain how things happen within an existing body of theory). The four known forces (at this point in time) in physics are: gravitational, electromagnetic, and the 'strong' and 'weak' nuclear forces that keep atomic structures stable. These forces are like the scaffolding known as quantum mechanics (electromagnetism and the strong and weak nuclear forces), plus relativity (gravity) that supports the current overarching body of theory that explains how matter is held together, how it moves, and how the universe is subject to order and pattern. Because science is progressive, there is already evidence of another force, and no doubt there will be other forces yet to be discovered. Or, more significantly, that all forces emerge from a single underlying force in a single quantumly entangled reality.

* ***The direct perception of Being:*** There are no separate forces, no theories of explanation, no periods of relative stability, no challenging anomalies, no paradigms of knowledge to be challenged, replaced, or held on to. There are not even any concepts to identify with, believe in, or struggle against. Being just 'is'. Being is not anthropocentric because, as with awareness, thought

cannot truly know it. We do not have to seek Being; we already have it, because we are it. In knowing Being we can say that it 'passeth all understanding'. Being includes dimensions unknown to science, exclusive only to experiential knowing.

A scientific theory must make predictions

The scientific method: A theory in science predicts certain phenomena. For example, in the theory of evolution, Darwin predicted that there would be gradual steps between different species' evolutionary transition, that could be found in the fossil record. A number of fossils that bridge some of the big gaps between species have indeed been discovered over the past hundred years or so. The gaps continue to be filled, just as predicted. More recently, in astronomy, Professor Laura Mesini-Houghton, in her particular version of the Multiverse, predicted that an earlier entanglement with another universe would leave a tell-tale signature in a particular place, and that this could actually be detected. A cool spot was found in 2013 exactly where her calculations predicted, in the image of the Cosmic Microwave Background Radiation. (Of course it requires much more than this to firmly establish a particular hypothesis.) Predictions are not all that is demanded of a successful theory, but they are essential to the development of knowledge and future research programs.

* *The direct perception of Being:* There are no hypotheses, no theories and no predictions. Being is noumenal, rather than part of the conceptualising and mapping of the phenomenal world. The noumenal means the essence of everything, but in this there is only one essence, rather than many, as consciousness. And consciousness is everything.

It is only in the manifest phenomenal world that we can measure, analyse or predict anything. Beyond the concept-making mind, in the timeless, there is nothing to predict, nor any intention to predict. There is no need for 'protective belts', there is no need for falsifiability, there is no position to uphold, and no theory to protect.

In the direct perception of Being there is no conflict with any theoretical formulation. Also, there is no philosophical doctrine of Being that could be included and taught in a curriculum, and then argued about and believed in, nor disbelieved. Experiencing Being is fundamental to all our existence; it is not an exercise in intellectual cleverness or sophistry.

The analysis of results and peer review

The scientific method: Analysis and peer review are also essential parts of the process of scientific knowledge. Analysis of results is necessary as a way of discussing the outcome of experiments and observations, understanding what import they have in the current body of theory, and raising questions for future research. The peer review process ensures that a given study or experiment is thoroughly performed and accurately measured, and that the conclusions are rational.

There can be problems with this, as peer reviews can lead to what is called 'incremental science'; that is, scientific endeavour taking place at a snail's pace. It also affects the funding scientists can apply for. A young adventurous scientist with bold and potentially good ideas, yet with no proven peer acceptance, is unlikely to succeed in grant applications. A good example of this difficulty was the Nobel Prize-winning breakthrough in quasi-crystals. Israeli scientist Dan Shechtman was awarded the Nobel Prize in chemistry in 2011 for discovering a new chemical structure, previously thought impossible. He initially faced scepticism and mockery, eventually being expelled from his research team. Eventually his work won widespread acceptance as a fundamental breakthrough. The applications of quasi-crystals lie in the field of thermal-electric energy conversion, where waste heat can be converted into electrical currents or energy, which is significant in the search for renewable energy.

* *The direct perception of Being:* This kind of knowing is intuitive and is not analytical, empirical, or subjective, because it is not based in thought. In direct perception there is no body of experts nor peers to appeal to as a form of authorising or reviewing authority. There is no formality of peer review or of an overseeing body that authenticates anything, or confers status. Neither is there a need for validation in experiential knowing. Only a 'self' seeking its own importance craves for validation, recognition, a 'following', or affirmation. Everyone, as Being, is a peer to everyone else, and potentially an expert and authority in the experience of consciousness itself.

The role of anomalies

Anomalies are irregularities, or observations that cannot be explained by existing theory. For instance, a number of the experiments in quantum theory do not fit neatly into the classical framework of the mechanistic paradigm, based on Newtonian physics. Scientists addressing the challenge posed by anomalies may find themselves at the vanguard of shaping current theory.

Another example is the introduction of the concept 'dark matter', introduced to account for the anomaly of the missing mass of the observable universe. The stars in the outer arms of galaxies were detected as going faster than those towards the galaxy centres. Why is it so, given that gravity would indicate that the opposite would be true. There are, of course, alternative hypotheses to dark matter to explain this.

In a way, anomalies are what really drive science forward in the quest for an ever greater, more comprehensive conceptual understanding. Thomas Khun coined the term 'paradigm shift' for this. Anomalies are at the cutting edge of scientific discovery and new theories must be developed to account for them.

In the practice of science, new theories can go through long periods of instability until they gain confirmation from supporting research and induce another shift in paradigm. In fact, new theories can, as Professor Laura Mesini-Houghton suggests, go through three discernible stages: the first stage is ridicule, then opposition, and finally to be regarded as self-evident.

However, not all anomalies lead to theory changes, let alone paradigm shifts, but they are the necessary fuel that drives change. When enough anomalies occur, or when one that is critical to a particular theory is discovered, there is a period of turbulence as overarching theoretical structures are revised or shifted, in order to encompass the new information.

* ***The direct perception of Being:*** there are no anomalies and there is no body of theory or scaffold of knowledge, and there is no new information that could challenge it. There is neither 'adding to' nor 'taking away' of knowledge, nor a progression, as there is in the structured knowledge of science. Direct perception is not reduced to the world of appearances, or a process of mental filtering or interpretation. But when we deeply

look without mind, at a tree, a landscape or another human being, we will see infinitely more than what could ever be described in any theory, or textbook. If we observe with an uncluttered lens, we apprehend the numinous as undivided Being.

The method is the 'ideal' but the reality is a little different

One of Karl Popper's students was to become a prominent critic of the logical rationale of the scientific method that he had promoted. Paul Feyerabend (1924–1994), a professor of physics and philosophy, in his seminal book *Against Method*, outlined his central thesis – that there is no scientific method. Feyerabend lists a range of mental activities that lie outside the promoted ideal of a rationalistic scientific method. Here, the actuality of science research combines formal techniques with opportunism, intuition, imagination, ad hoc manoeuvres, the use of altered states of consciousness such as dreams, acting on hunches, and leaps of faith. Feyerabend maintained that it is quite wrong to view science as a purely rational endeavour fitting neatly into a rationalised method. He maintained that in practice things are quite different, invariably failing to completely fit the idealised method as described above.

If science is not the hallowed pinnacle of reason, this challenges the special status of scientific knowledge, as well as the authority of its practitioners and institutions. There is a tendency for scientists to idealise their practice as inherently superior because of their specific use of rationality. There is nothing intrinsic to rationality to justify its elevation; rather, it is a cultural belief stemming from the times of Plato and Aristotle. And holding this belief can undermine the ability for critical reflection. As a result, basic assumptions in science will go unquestioned, giving rise to stagnation and dogmatism in its theories and opinions. As well, there is the special status and authority that science and its practitioners confer upon their practice and themselves. But we should bear in mind that anything in the realm of relative knowledge – science being a good example of this - that goes unchallenged, ossifies with time.

Also, there is the danger in giving any thought-based knowledge (such as scientific knowledge) special status, and it behoves us to avoid idealisation, because if we idealise it is because we are not grounded in the source from whence all knowledge comes. It is a direct result of not understanding the truth of Being, and so we look to science (or religion or anything), for example, to lead us because we do not know who we are.

But when the methods of science are used sagely, without them being a dogmatic belief system as seen in the ideological form of 'scientism' (that is, pre-conceived conclusions about what is real, what can be known, and what is possible) the challenge to maintain humility in the face of qualitative knowledge building is positively addressed.

Below Gary Schwartz outlines these points in his comments in relation to the research on consciousness without brain activity in the 'near death experience':

> *Some materialistically inclined scientists and philosophers refuse to acknowledge these phenomena because they are not consistent with their exclusive conception of the world. Rejection of post-materialist investigation of nature or refusal to publish strong science findings supporting a post-*

> materialist framework are antithetical to the true spirit of scientific inquiry, which is that empirical data must always be adequately dealt with. Data which do not fit favored theories and beliefs cannot be dismissed a priori. Such dismissal is the realm of ideology, not science.
>
> —Dr Gary Schwartz[20]

The authority science assumes is not absolute

Science, once portrayed as Western knowledge, is now more accurately considered globalised because virtually all countries engage in its practice. Currently, science has moved steadily to center stage into the increasing vacuum left from the reduced status of traditional religion and mythology. These previously answered our questions on cosmology, our identity and the meaning of human existence, but now science commands an elevated authority, as *the* primary source of knowledge. Yet it is neither capable nor is it the appropriate form of knowing to be this.

The authority science assumes is not absolute; it is, as discussed above, assumed. Commonly now, in science, commentators such as the physicist Brain Cox, in the documentary series 'The Human Universe', offer the argument that the well-articulated description of the universe and our place in it, as offered by physics, medicine, biology, and the other physical and life sciences, is completely enough. Thus, they address our curiosity to know the fundamental questions about living and our identity. But this belief is misplaced.

The philosophising that occurs in popular science shows at times demonstrates a paternalistic and superior attitude, particularly as the commentator refers to the 'outmoded' practices of Indigenous peoples. This implies that the beliefs and ideas held by the uneducated non-scientific mind need to be replaced in the positive development of culture. There is some value in this because sometimes cultural practices of *any* culture need to be replaced, or ceased, but this is not necessarily as a result of science or the lack of it, but because they are destructive to people or the environment.

However, the dictum that 'science knows best' is construed as the triumph of reason. This paternalistic attitude is an example of scientism – science as an ideology – because it is a belief that brings its own form of dogmatism, and its implementation as cultural imperialism. It would appear that because of the elevated status that some scientists assume, (and the public gives) acting like a form of 'high priest' of secular culture, replacing religious priests from a bygone era.

While science does have a unique place in providing essential knowledge for our planetary wellbeing, this does not confer a license, or a legitimacy to pontificate on: the nature of reality other than a conceptual one; that science confers an absolute form of truth; or the meaning and purpose of living.

The danger that we face when we hold a belief in the universal authority of scientific knowledge, is the tendency, through its dominance, to transform all other perspectives or indeed cultures into its own image. This is how science can become a form of cultural imperialism, leading to other cultures becoming colonised by science as a philosophical ideology, rather than by the real benefits of science itself. This only occurs because it operates under two presumptions: that there is only one way of knowing that yields living in reality and truth for us all; and that there is just one type of knowledge – objectivist – that has currency in truth.

In an interview on ABC TV's 'Matter of Fact', 15 May 2018, the gist of what Richard Dawkins (author of the Selfish Gene) said was that religion is always on shaky ground because it is based in faith with beliefs that can never be substantiated with evidence. He went on to declare that all we really have is the evidence-based truth of science, as 'the objective study of facts.'

The first part of his contention is true, but like so many scientists (apparently in a recent survey of scientists' opinions in the UK the respondents freely stated that they thought Dawkins' militant views on atheism and science were not helpful in furthering science) he does not understand that, while science may not be based on beliefs, placing it ahead of religion, it is based on certain core assumptions. And these are articles of faith (the knower is separate from the known), and without making them, scientific practice and knowledge making, cannot proceed. It is uncertain knowledge, but it is certainly not all that we have, for we can know with absolute certainty the Truth of Being, a knowing that is infinite.

When we proceed without making the assumption of the separation of knower and known, we enter non-duality. This is neither belief-based (like religion) nor assumption-based (like science), and the kind of truth it yields is absolute.

Science is a unique narrative

Science is a unique form of narrative that is progressive, and its concepts, knowledge building, and theories are subject to ongoing modification. It is not equivalent to other types of human story- telling such as myths, cultural stories, astrology and religions that are not part of this rational discourse. Relativist or a post-modernist science is regarded as a narrative like the other narratives mentioned above. But these theoretical movements fail to capture science's role as being globally unique. And in this era of rapid climate change the special kind of narrative science provides is of particular importance for Sapien survival and planetary well-being.

Science has a particular kind of truth-telling that comes from its specific form of accountability, where any given claim or hypothesis is in the public domain and can be interrogated in a way that other types of narrative cannot. Art is a narrative; history, music, and mythology are examples of other forms of narratives, but none of these has at its core the ongoing questioning – essential to good science practice – of the contents of its own story. This is seen in the form of falsification, repeatability of studies, and peer review. What science has captured, essential to the kind of narrative that it is, is that it is a dynamic and progressive form of enquiry.

Science holds a unique place in our human story with its special form of narrative, but narrative it is, because it is based in thought. How could it be other than a narrative? Only a zealot of 'scientism' blinded by clinging to an ideology of science, would not see this (for an excellent article on scientism see 'The folly of scientism' by Austin L. Hughes). Science, as a particular kind of conversation/interrogation with nature, and while based on core assumptions, is nevertheless an open-ended enquiry within the confines of thought.

> *I have approximate answers and possible beliefs in different degrees of certainty about different things, but I'm not absolutely sure of anything.*
> —Richard Feynman

The epistemic that science offers is relative, uncertain, and progressive. But this does not mean that it is the most critical thing for our living. The polemics offered by relativists and post-modernists demonstrate a failure to understand why we need science and rationality. And, while they are quite justified in their concern about the status science has assumed and is given, they fail to offer an explanation of why this is.

The elevated status given to objective knowledge is misguided. This has only happened because we have never had, collectively, the kind of understanding of nature and ourselves, that comes with the intimacy of direct knowing. We have become intoxicated with thought, particularly with rationalism and empirical knowledge being regarded as the pinnacle of intelligence. Unquestioned, this results in a form of conformity. However, we are sage when we give primary status where it is due – to direct knowing.

If direct perception is understood and valued it brings us enormous riches: the most important being a new way of living harmoniously together, and peace on earth. Non-duality is a profound peace, whereas living under a belief in duality as the foundation of living only breeds separation and conflict. Yet duality has its place. It is fundamental to science, and essential to its good practice, and now, for our survival.

Experiential knowing serves as an antidote to the attitude seen in professional scientists, philosophers and commentators – that only they, with their specialised knowledge and credentials are qualified to interpret reality for the rest of us. Yet we do need interpreters to translate for us the complex models of reality, the meaning of data and research outcomes, that science is progressively developing. Only 'direct seeing' can ever give us non-conceptual reality, and for this we do not need any one else, or a body of theory, to interpret for us.

So how can we be immunised against being 'mentally colonised'? What protects us from anything like this (religion, cults, superstitions, commercialism, scientism, political or philosophical ideologies) is experiencing in our daily living the profound deconditioning of everything, by resting in awareness in the silence of Being. This intimacy of Being is our most fundamental ally, because it is utterly beyond the reaches of thought.

Song of Myself
It is time to explain myself – let us stand up.
What is known I strip away,
I launch all men and women forward
with me into the Unknown.
The clock indicates the moment – but
what does eternity indicate?
We have thus far exhausted trillions of
winters and summers and summers,
There are trillions ahead, and trillions ahead of them.
Births have brought us richness and variety.
I do not call one greater and smaller,
That which fills its period and place is equal to any.
—Walt Whitman (1819–1892)[21]

PART THREE

THE ADVENTURE OF SCIENCE AND PHILOSOPHY

In which we explore – cosmic order, the quantum world, consciousness, reality and time: and the particular type of knowing in science, which assumes the knower is separate from the known. The 'objectivist' narrative that results from this has become global, and we explore its benefits and limitations. Scientific knowledge is a marvellously inventive, carefully constructed model of reality, subject to continuous modification, but ultimately as with all conceptual forms of knowing, it is ever a shadow of the real.

BEING: EXPERIENCING A NUMINOUS REALITY

CHAPTER 10

AN INTELLIGENT UNIVERSE

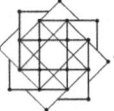

In the next four chapters I will discuss some major scientific theories and problems: chaos theory, quantum theory, Bohmian mechanics, and some of the ongoing philosophical issues that only appear intransigent.

Scientific knowledge, as a form of global knowledge, crosses all borders, using the universal language of mathematics, with specific branches of terminology and scientific formulation. It constitutes a highly specialised and ever more precise use of thought. Scientific knowledge and culture are powerful, pervading every aspect of our outward existence in our digital age, with its pinnacle seen in an objectivist mapping of phenomenal reality. The scientist now has a kind of status that used to be afforded to religious figures, as secular high priests, but they can also be mocked by conspiracy theorists and religious fundamentalists, as misguided hoaxers. Neither really addresses the significance they hold in our social fabric or the human epistemic landscape.

The great error: 'a mechanical universe'

The still-powerful relic of science's mechanistic model of the universe continues to cast its shadow across all of the sciences and the way we treat nature. Its roots, stemming from Platonic idealism, Aristotelean empiricism, the duality of mind and matter, and the atomists' inert units of matter are the informing threads winding through Western culture. The mechanistic idea resulted in a debased view of nature. It is the belief that life is mechanistic or 'machine-like', that matter's constituents – the particles – are dead and without intelligence and further that biological carbon-based life arose randomly. It was just the right fortuitous mix of chemicals occurring in the right proportions at the right moment in earth's history, outlining a mechanistic fantasy. In this 'non-living' universe with the accidental emergence of biological life, consciousness (to a hard-line materialist consciousness does not exist) or mind arrives as an 'emergent' property only found in the higher life forms, such as mammals and especially humans. Likening the universe to a non-living, grand, clock-like mechanism, still holds sway for many practising scientists and philosophers.

The mechanistic view in particular gained popularity following the publication of *Principia*, the seminal work of Sir Isaac Newton, written in the 16th century, where he outlined his theory of celestial mechanics. His ideas built on those before him: the dualistic philosophy of French mathematician Rene Descartes, and even further back with the atomists of Ancient Greece in the fifth century BCE (concurrently there were also philosophers in India in the sixth century BCE who held an atomistic view).

The Newtonian model of the universe was couched in absolute idealism. These atoms, which constituted everything in the universe, had been set in motion by a transcendent creator 'God'. The invisible force of gravity and the mysterious, hypothetical, mass-less elementary particles called 'gravitons', responsible for this force (yet to be detected) moved everything in a precisely knowable and predictable manner.

It was a strictly determined universe that could be rationally explained, giving both reliable and almost exact predictions, such as the timing and locality of planetary motion in the solar system. It was even idealistically proposed that we could predict everything if we accurately knew the space and time coordinates of every atom. We could then predict with perfect precision what would happen next in the chain of determined causation. This clockwork universe had absolute notions of time, with its regularity stretching evenly from the past to the present and to the future, in a continuous steady flow; and space that was also spread out evenly, uniformly and infinitely, and was made up of impenetrably hard units of matter – atoms in an idealised universe.

The mechanistic model of nature informed a materialist ideology of the 19th and 20th centuries. And 'God' as the primary transcendent and creative force behind the universe was eventually seen as unnecessary, and was to disappear as an irrelevance to serious rational and scientific investigation, with the advent of gene-splicing, organ and limb transplants, and artificial fertilization. All was made possible by the belief that matter could yield its mechanistic secrets to our relentless rationalist probing. Yet matter continues to be regarded without intelligence and non-living – just like a machine – and with replaceable parts. Nonetheless this crude mechanistic idea has had some significant pay-offs in the field of biology, and you may have experienced these if you have had the opportunity to visit the emergency ward in a hospital.

However, during the 20th century cracks appeared in the mechanistic model. The mechanistic fantasy was challenged by Einstein's deeper intuition regarding the fabric of space/time (that space and time were not absolute) relative to the matter it contains. But more potently the mechanistic fantasy was 'busted' in two other theories: one that had developed from the 1920s in quantum theory (that atoms were in fact not solid and impenetrable) and another 50 years later with chaos theory (the contextual relatedness of everything exhibiting deeper patterns of organisation) which emerged in the 60s and 70s.

With regard to the idealisation of matter, Paul Davies and John Gribben explain in their book, *The Matter Myth:*

> *Then came our quantum theory, which totally transformed our image of matter. The old assumption that the microscopic world of atoms was simply a scaled-down version of the everyday world had to be abandoned. Newton's deterministic machine was replaced by a shadowy and paradoxical conjunction of waves and particles, governed by the laws of chance, rather than the rigid rules of causality. An extension of the quantum theory goes beyond even this; it paints a picture in which solid matter dissolves away, to be replaced by weird excitations and vibrations of invisible field energy. Quantum physics undermines materialism because it reveals that matter has far less 'substance' than we might believe. But another development goes even further by demolishing Newton's image of matter as inert lumps. This development is the theory of chaos, which has recently gained widespread attention.*
>
> —Paul Davies and John Gribben, *The Matter Myth*[22]

In the 20th century the belief in a randomly emerging universe had taken hold as an essential part of the materialistic thesis. During the 1970s the hypothesis of a universe with a defined starting point – itself a random occurrence – known as the Big Bang, became increasingly popular. The theory of the Big Bang was supported by the majority of scientists and became part of a catechism of ideas that seemed unassailable by the 1980s. Basically, the philosophy of materialism holds that the universe is random, and is governed by both fixed and unchanging laws, with fixed and unchanging universal constants. Yet these laws and constants are in contradistinction to a universe that is clearly evolving – one where change is the only constant. And, rather than being closer to an idealised Platonic vision of the universe, it is much closer to Heraclitus' dynamic 'process oriented' view.

Is the universe a random event?

The *Oxford Dictionary* defines 'random' as: 'made, done, happening or chosen without method or conscious decision'. 'Random' describes events or phenomena that occur haphazardly and without order, meaning, purpose or connectedness – in other words, without guiding intelligence. 'Random' as the Greek Atomists and Epicureans conceived it, was the manner in which the atoms constituting matter interacted. However, the use of random as fundamental to the existence of the universe, the evolution of life and the interactions between subatomic particles is only an assumption, and can be seen instead as more an indicator of our ignorance than anything else.

In the 15th century in Europe the French word 'randon' was used to indicate natural systems such as water rushing without apparent guidance in a haphazard fashion. 'Random' developed as a term from the mechanistic scientific milieu after the late 19th century. Randomness in science is involved in theories about the likelihood of events that are derived from mathematical axioms as propositions of probability, based on ideas which originated in Ancient Greek philosophy.

Using the language of statistics, the axioms of probability describe and predict the likelihood of certain phenomena. They are the same axioms that are used in the gambling and insurance industries. In the mechanistic theory of the beginning of life, randomness describes the probability that the right combination of building blocks is present to create life; building blocks such as carbon, oxygen and nitrogen, as well as the right bandwidth of temperature; that is, distance of the planet from its neighbouring star (the 'Goldilocks Zone'). This belief maintains that it all happened by chance, and without any apparent order or intelligence.

Brownian motion was a phenomenon first noted by botanist Robert Brown in the 19th century when he was studying pollen particles. He postulated that microscopic particles move in a random motion, without any apparent order – colliding haphazardly with each other. His idea became a signpost for nature's inherent disorder, which was conceptualised as a random, disordered 'white noise' occurring as a background to life.

Brownian motion, at the subatomic level, is viewed as the discontinuous motion of the chaotic or unpredictable movement of subatomic particles, as they are 'kicked around' by atoms and molecules that attain velocities approaching the speed of light. It has been speculated that the particles involved in Brownian motion cannot carry a signal because a signal requires an ordered modulation, such as a radio wave. A TV set, for example, receives a waveform signal that does not get mixed up in transmission because the information is received in an ordered fashion – and we watch the result.

Brownian motion was conventionally thought of by the majority of scientists as being random, discontinuous and disordered. However, Quantum theorist David Bohm suggested the contrary. Bohm postulated that Brownian motion has a very high degree of order, and this order has escaped us because we have not paid it closer attention.

The notion of random permeates the biological sciences as well, functioning as a belief. While evolutionary natural selection as a theory is a clearly established narrative, progressively accumulating supporting evidence, this is not the case for the added hypothesis of neo-Darwinists: that the genetic mutations at the root of the evolutionary process are random, or without ordered intelligence. Randomness in nature is rather a matter of belief, and is couched in an underlying assumption of a universe functioning without an organising intelligence. Rather than being blind, nature is, in ways that are not fully understood in science, purposeful and intelligent.

However, there is a growing understanding that the universe does not function according to idealised mechanistic and materialistic notions. Rather, it is an evolving universe developing with enormous complexity, and instead of being likened to a mechanism – with inert separate bits of unintelligent matter – it can be understood as an infinite, totally interconnected organism. But this view, of course, is not a matter that can ever be resolved intellectually, or with science at this point. It can be resolved however, in our direct experience.

Randomness is pivotal to a materialistic view

This notion of randomness is pivotal in the materialistic view, but when one experiences the universe as a deeper manifestation of order and intelligence, by resting in reality, it makes no sense at all. Currently, the most popular interpretations of quantum theory (the 'Copenhagen' and 'Many Worlds interpretations') are often enlisted to support an essentially 'blind' random universe, seen at the most miniscule subatomic level.

However, there is another, more sage interpretation offered by the de-Broglie/Bohm Pilot Wave Theory (PWT). PWT maintains that, rather than an electron being magically 'super-positioned' everywhere in space, popping up fantastically in a specific location when we attempt to measure it. Instead, with the pilot wave it has a defined, non-random, non-probabilistic determined path, guided by a (pilot) wave 'non-locally' connecting to the entire universe. The particle is a historic entity without the absurdity of superposition.

And PWT is not the only theory that suggests a deeper order in the universe, indicating that there are hidden variables that the standard interpretations of quantum mechanics fail to recognise. Super-determinism is a theory that maintains there is absolutely nothing random in the universe, and that every single particle's life is completely pre-determined. It is a universe of unalterable organising intelligence, with our notion of free will being an illusion.

Simply assuming that things are random does not make it so. With the advent of chaos theory, we have come to appreciate that there are deeper emergent patterns in natural systems, which had initially escaped our attention. The advent of chaos theory and the invention of computers has enabled us to model deeper levels of complexity indicating previously hidden levels of order in nature, expressing an immanent intelligence in all that is.

In nature, randomness does not exist. As quantum theorist David Bohm has suggested, the randomness we may assume to be present in nature, is alternatively measuring what we don't know. And at some stage in the future, what was considered to be random will be recognised as exhibiting unmistakable order, intelligence and pattern. Yet Bohm's ideas continue as a challenge within the scientific community, because they point towards developing a conceptual model of the universe featuring connectedness, non-locality and determinism, all features of an 'organising intelligence'.

Einstein, when thinking about randomness and the stochastic (probability) interpretations in the quantum world, considered that:

> *Quantum randomness is ... the product of deeper goings on. The dancing of a dust mote in a shaft of sunlight betrays the complex motions of unseen air molecules, and the emission of a photon or radioactive decay of a nucleus is analogous, Einstein figured. In his estimation, quantum mechanics is a broad-brush stroke theory that expresses the overall behaviour of nature's building blocks but lacks the resolution to capture individual cases. A deeper, more complete theory would explain the motion in full without any mysterious jumps.*
>
> —George Musser[23]

A crucial factor in the notion of randomness is the assumption that all events are independent. In nature, however, nothing is truly independent. The idea that anything is truly independent or separate is an idealisation itself resulting from the central tendency in science to think in a reductive manner. That these isolated bits – particles – are not deeply connected, is an idea embedded in the myth of a mechanistic universe. As David Bohm once stated, 'quantum mechanics, should really be called *quantum organics*'. This is because our conceptualising bears little real resemblance to reality. This factor is well recognised in Buddhist philosophy, which maintains that *everything in the phenomenal world is mutually dependent.*

In science this has been shown to be the case by both chaos theory and quantum theory. Ultimately, everything is connected to everything, as expressed in the both the 'determinism' and the 'non-locality' of the quantum world wherein, by definition, connectedness excludes randomness. On an experiential level we can know this connectedness directly, not through reason, but by perceiving intuitively.

Holding a belief in randomness is indicative of the fragmented state of our experience of living. When a physicist experiences life through the perceptual prism constructed by their conceptual map of a disconnected, mechanistic and probabilistic reality, then experientially there is a disconnect with the actual universe itself. When we are 'living through' our mental map of the world – a model of a disconnected random universe is clouding our lens – things appear to happen in a likewise, random and disconnected fashion. Randomness is not a fact: rather it is an assumption, that becomes a pivotal belief, in the doctrines of materialist philosophy.

Max Tegmark, a leading mathematical physicist from Massachusetts Institute of Technology, sums up:

> *There is no true randomness in the cosmos, but things can appear random in the eye of the beholder. The randomness reflects your inability to self-locate.*
>
> —Max Tegmark[24]

Chaos theory

And now chaos theory proves that unpredictability is built into our daily lives. It is as mundane as the rainstorm we cannot predict. And so the grand vision of science, hundreds of years old – the dream of total control – has died, in our century. And with it much of the justification, and the rationale for science to do what it does, and for us to listen to it. Science has always said that it may not know everything now but it will know, eventually. But now we see that isn't true. It is an idle boast. As foolish, and as misguided, as the child who jumps off a building because he believes he can fly.

—Michael Crichton, *Jurassic Park*[25]

Historically, the majority of cultures in the world have considered nature as being 'female' in quality. In English we say 'mother nature', and the very word 'matter' is derived from 'mutter', a German word, meaning 'mother'. Perhaps this is in recognition that nature, 'she', does not behave according to the overtly rational, 'masculine' sensibility with its particularly linear type of logic and rules.

Chaos theory emerged as an attempt to expand and change the rules of how science had been functioning in an idealised mechanistic mode, by mapping dynamic systems. This was achieved by broadening the standard scope of how nature was idealised, analysed and understood. In both rationalist and theological circles (which were almost completely male) in the West, there is a historical fear of nature in the collective mind. As mentioned, it is associated with being characteristically feminine – in poetry, religion and art it is depicted as wild, disordered and unpredictable, thus defying the linear analysis characteristic of rational (masculine) enquiry.

The word 'chaos' can be defined as complete confusion or disorder, or as being wholly without organisation or order. 'Chaos' also has a mythic connotation, being regarded as the infinity of space or formless matter that is conjectured to have preceded the existence of the ordered universe. 'Chaos' in this sense is a realm of disorder, a chasm or abyss. It is a metaphor for darkness and disorder in nature – a darkness that will not yield to the bright, reductive and investigative rationality of science with its brash and enthusiastic intellect.

Yet the 'chaos' in 'chaos theory' is something of a misnomer because, paradoxically, it represents an important recognition of the deeper ordering and patterning properties of nature. Such properties were previously little understood, because they were thought of as some kind of marginal and random disorder – part of the 'chaotic noise' of nature.

The ordering and patterning intelligence of nature

Things derive their being and nature by mutual dependence and are nothing in themselves.

—Nagarjuna[26]

Self-organised systems have four main features:
1. *They are open* (rather than 'closed') systems which have a strictly controlled energy input and output to an artificial system (such as a machine) and thus they are part of their living environment. At the same time, they are seen to exhibit structure, that can be maintained in turbulent conditions.

2. *Self-organised systems are inherently creative*, as outlined by Ilya Prigognine. The flow of energy in self-organised systems in turbulent conditions brings spontaneity, as new modes of behaviour create novel structures. The galaxies and the universe itself are self-organising structures.

3. *Self-organised systems are inherently extremely complex.* The entire universe can be viewed as an infinite, self-organised system with a network of feedback loops that interconnect its constituents, none of which is independent.

4. *Any given system will naturally display oscillations over periods of time.* That system will show phases of equilibrium to disequilibrium back to equilibrium, as it is in dynamic interaction with its environment. And this intelligent patterning is influenced by the poetic term 'strange attractor' as it moves creatively to higher levels of order. Computer modelling has shown that the current stability of our solar system belies a very dynamic and turbulent early history. And there are movements taking place at unimaginable scales. For instance, it has been detected that, about 150 million light years away, there is a colossal mass in a specific region of space pulling thousands of nearby galaxies, including our own, at 20 million kilometers per hour. The universe is ever a dynamic place, a place captured amongst the process philosophers from Lao Tse to Heraclitus.

The principles and modelling ushered in with chaos theory are readily applicable in all facets of life, from relationships to habitats, climates, the human body, financial market activity and the whole planet. In relation to the planet, the principles of chaos were fundamental in developing the Gaia hypothesis – the idea that the earth is a self-organised and evolving life-form. However, today much of the hype that first surrounded chaos theory has disappeared. It is now understood not as a separate body of theory or research, but rather as a deeper understanding of the complex dynamics of systems throughout nature. Chaos is now an insight and approach integrated and used by all fields of science, from astrophysics to biology.

Chaos: finding equilibrium in living

How do the principles of chaos manifest in the human mind, relationships and society? If disorder is a natural process of any system searching for a higher level of equilibrium – which is more energy-efficient – why are human beings resistant to this on a psychological level? And what is the significance of this resistance?

Our attempt to impose control and maintain some predictability, psychologically and emotionally, is seen in the cunning strategising of the self when faced with a particular set of circumstances. When the mind resists and is unable to face a situation or a person saying, 'I don't like what is happening now', 'I wish I wasn't here', or 'this should not be happening to me', each of these thoughts is a resistance to reality. This is experienced at an emotional level and invariably expressed in the body, with various sensations and constrictions (palpitations, tightness in the stomach, sharp pain in the heart, shortness of breath, constriction in the throat, et cetera) – as a generalised feeling of 'chaos' or being out of control. This can even be to the point of potentially paralysing a person with fear or loss of control over bodily functions. These chaotic inner responses, however, are filled with information as charged energy (psychologically and emotionally) – and if greeted (rather than being suppressed or making attempts to stifle and control) – with the right attitude and inner listening, they can reveal hidden information. So, instead of controlling, we trust our intelligence and welcome all thoughts and feelings that are uncomfortable, because they are the specific issues we have to learn, and in so doing we deepen in our understanding. In going through this disequilibrium there is healing that brings us to a new level of balance and inner harmony. We now exist in a new level of order, and what engendered fear as an emotional trigger previously, is now empty of compelling force. Rumi's poem expresses this with:

The Guest House

This being human is a guest house.
Every morning a new arrival.

A joy, a depression, a meanness,
some momentary awareness comes
As an unexpected visitor.

Welcome and entertain them all!
Even if they're a crowd of sorrows,
who violently sweep your house
empty of its furniture,
still treat each guest honourably.
He may be clearing you out
for some new delight.
The dark thought, the shame, the malice,
meet them at the door laughing,
and invite them in.
Be grateful for whoever comes,
because each has been sent
as a guide from beyond.

—Jalaluddin Rumi[27]

The self may strategise to get its desired outcomes, to prove it has some semblance of control. This is precisely why 'self-improvement' programs and books that promote ways to manifest your deepest desires are so popular. But just getting what you want is a disaster for revealing the true nature of happiness. This is because one of the primary fears of the self is not getting what it wants, and one of its primary beliefs is that by fulfilling these wants, it will achieve happiness and success. It is ironic that in much New Age philosophy, manifesting your desires is portrayed as a hallmark of getting further along the spiritual path. In fact it is by non-attaching to desires that happiness is revealed as *the natural state*, because we have let go of the restlessness of wanting.

In the struggle to keep the status quo – that is, to maintain a strong and stable self – we interpret events to fit our belief systems and try to orchestrate circumstances to suit these ego projections. For example, we may ensure that we meet the right people to enact forms of co-dependent relationships, or relationships filled with dramas and power plays to maintain limiting self-beliefs ('I am not loveable', 'I am not worthy') or attitudes about others ('men can't be trusted', 'women are out to get me', or 'I can't have a close relationship – I'm scarred of intimacy'). These beliefs generate disorder, in the sense that we may engage in rigid modes of behaviour (for example, avoiding women, or trying to dominate them, or selecting the 'bad guy' in the belief that we can change them, or being emotionally unavailable through fear of intimacy) in order to further fulfil these inner dictums, and maintain a 'status quo' to perpetuate this imbalance. But it is a status quo that is always fragile and ever subject to instability.

Disorder naturally arises in a relationship when some unresolved issue between friends or a couple is brought to the surface. It occurs when something hidden – perhaps a 'naughty' secret – is revealed and suddenly the energy between the people shifts dramatically.

There may be sensations of fear felt in the body, a rise in blood pressure, sweating, an increase in heart rate. The mind may switch into overdrive and thoughts may become erratic, moving quickly in different directions, projecting different possible scenarios for the self, including catastrophising. There may be a feeling of losing control because the status quo has been disturbed. In chaos theory language, this would be seen as a period of increased instability or disequilibrium in the process of finding a higher level of order or stability. If the challenge of the disorder is met and allowed to fully unfold, then a new level of order and harmony will emerge between the friends or lovers. There may be less grasping or hiding, with the flow of energy between them being less encumbered by thought resistance, which was being used to suppress what was hidden (keeping the secret has a tremendous energy cost). In this sense a relationship has gone through something like a 'healing crisis' as a period of disequilibrium, and moves on to a 'higher order' or harmony. On the other hand, a 'disease crisis' might occur when the issue stays buried; or, upon uncovering, the issue 'kills the patient' – in this case, the relationship ends.

Fear of disorder drives the desire to control

This is a pervasive fear in societies across the globe. This fear of disorder arises because of the primary disorder people experience in themselves. Belief in the reality of a separate self and all its conflicts and imagined insecurities is the ontology of this fear. It manifests in the 'micromanaging' that occurs in workplaces, in the pervasive 'risk-averse' nature of modern parenting, increasing quantities of bureaucratic red tape (the bane of modern existence), the tendency toward ever-increasing surveillance. In society, we can see this manifesting in the insurance industry, as we strive to protect ourselves from things breaking down or events that will cause disruption to our lives. We try to micromanage ourselves, to keep relentlessly busy, doing things, being task-oriented, ever fearful of being out of control and doing nothing. In relationships with others, the self develops various power games in the attempt to exert control over other people in order to have a certain level of stability and security of self.

The 'self' is a form of power play, and exists solely as an attempt to control thoughts, feelings, manipulate others and the environment. The statement 'I hope that things turn out the way that I want them to', reveals the fear of losing control. The psychological entity is both the seed and the perpetrator of disorder because its very basis – being one of mistaken identity – throws all relationships with others and the environment on to a false footing. In this way the self is a form of fragility and its ending is more than just resilience: it is one of 'antifragility'.

At a societal level, the imposition of order and control is seen politically, economically and religiously. Some regimes act ruthlessly in the face of protest and will quickly act to quell this perceived threat of disorder (which may be an attempt to reach a higher level of order, by addressing justice issues that create disharmony) and will harshly punish such attempts. However, this 'crisis of instability' is necessary in order to achieve a higher level of equilibrium in any society where justice and freedom can be seen as markers of societal harmony.

Control is maintained through misinformation, propaganda and communication restrictions as a lack of transparency. The form of order such societies hold is brittle and requires painstaking vigilance, even ruthless suppression, to hold the populace in check with a tightly controlled flow of information. No one could have predicted the thawing of the Cold War, and that by 1986 the rapid breakup of the Soviet Union into twelve independent states would be completed by December 1991. The societal stress and foment (disequilibrium) cascaded to a tipping point, from whence a new form of equilibrium was established.

Living creatively

Being congruent with 'what is' frees us from 'attaching to outcomes' – a primary feature of the ego's grasping to control – because what is, is reality, and it is folly to be at odds with the real, or to pine for what is not. Freed from idealising and strategising, and without a view to control, we connect to a deeper source of creativity. It is experienced as a state of surrender, but it is a state in which we are energised from a source that is not egoic. And rather than restlessly striving to manifest desires, to manipulate the environment to deliver our wants, we are aligned with the 'will of life' as the expansiveness of consciousness. Resting in reality like this we are more like an 'open vessel', in harmony with the Universal Intelligence as the endless source of creativity.

We may have well laid plans, meetings, tasks at hand and things to do, or a job, but the creative edge in living is the experiential understanding that each moment expresses the unknown, the ever-fresh, allowing for spontaneity. For this the mind as ego has to get out of the way. This understanding brings great flexibility, and the readiness to embrace possibilities as they arise. In the Taoist philosophy of Ancient China, this is known as 'following the way'.

It is not an armchair analytical philosophy constructed by rational thinking, but rather a dynamic way of experiential knowing and being in harmonious flow with all that is.

We can all directly experience this deeper alignment, if we pause our thinking. In this we become aware that we are not blind automatons pushed and pulled by instincts and conditionings that in the main are unconscious. Rather, there is a freedom to respond creatively in each moment, and yet there is, paradoxically, a destiny in unfolding reality. This simple shift in understanding, this highly subtle change in sensitivity – like the delicate flap of a butterfly's wing – can open to a radical transformation of our consciousness. This changes our life forever. It is the fear of disorder which feeds a relentless desire to impose a superficial order as a form of control engineered by thought. In the absence of this fear there is space for a deeper harmony to manifest that is beyond any engineering by mind. It is the art of non-doing. And in this way, all the things that need to be done will get done, without the struggle and effort born of a 'doer'.

CHAPTER 11

THE METAPHYSICS OF PHYSICS

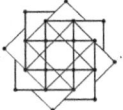

What is today known as physics was called 'natural philosophy' in Ancient Greece. In those times there was no clearly defined boundary between the physical and the metaphysical, and the scientific method was yet to be developed. 'Metaphysic' comes from the Greek 'meta physika', meaning 'after things of nature', and is an umbrella term referring to the nature of reality, including ontology, cosmology and, often, epistemology. It can also refer to that which is viewed as beyond material reality and ordinary human sense perception. Science has been rediscovering over the last forty years that all ontological thinking and epistemology is metaphysical in nature. Physicists either knowingly, or unknowingly, in their practice of science, are engaging in metaphysics by exploring the nature of existence, the fundamental substance of objects, space and time, cause and effect.

But there has been continued resistance to this, to which philosopher Alfred North Whitehead responded with:

Every scientific man in order to preserve his reputation has to say he dislikes metaphysics. What he means is he dislikes having his metaphysics criticised.
—Alfred North Whitehead[28]

Scientists may live in denial, or are simply unaware of the metaphysical nature of the assumptions underpinning their theories and models of how the universe works. This occurs simply because these assumptions are unexamined and unquestioned. For example, in the field of quantum mechanics the construction of the standard model of fundamental units of matter assumes 'concreteness'. This assumed materiality has been the agenda of 'substance philosophy' beginning with the Greek philosophers, when what they are really describing are dynamic processes. This assumption became part of a coterie of beliefs, along with the idea that universe is a random event made of inert units of dead matter, which, in actuality, is an abstraction and an error.

Quantum events, rather, point to a feature of process oriented philosophy, which is a universe of dynamic ever-changing patterns. But in our substance oriented culture we identify a universe of separate 'things', as part of science's objectification. These fundamental units are described as quarks, photons and electrons, but labelling and measuring 'things', does not demonstrate that they are either inert, material, or that they are non-living, or even that they are truly separate. It may be more accurate to regard them in a more contextual sense as *organic processes* than the usual mechanistic. This process oriented view was outlined by A.N. Whitehead, and then much later developed by quantum theorist David Bohm, with his 'undivided wholeness'.

Quantum granularity

Richard Feynman nominated the atom as the single most powerful idea in the history of scientific ideas. The 'atom' idea commenced with Lucretius and Democritus from Ancient Greece. The Atomists conceived that nature was 'granular', with all things being composed of tiny invisible, inert units called 'atoms'. The idea that nature was quantised was a remarkable one ahead of its time. At the beginning of the 20th century, as we experimentally confirmed the existence of atoms, we next delved inside them. This immediately revealed a further granulisation of a 'subatomic' world, which led to the task of identifying further constituents that make up the inside of the atom. But new theories of quantum holism (where all parts make up a unique non-separate whole) like 'quantum monism', have reintegrated the (entangled) granulisation of everything into one single entity, that of an undivided universe.

On a practical level, quantum physics pervades modern living. It is the basis of our use of all semiconductors, and was key in the development of the transistor, eventually resulting in computers. Laser fibre-optics are now primary to communications; light-emitting diodes of modern flashlights, and all the screens we look at far too much. Photoelectric cells are used for solar power, in our digital cameras, and in all the electronics we use, including smart phones and remote controls. All of these developments grew originally from our understanding of the quantum world.

Over the last forty years there has been a growing move to introduce physics to the broader public domain. A quick look in any bookshop will attest that scientists and commentators alike are writing metaphysical books with titles such as *The God Particle*,

What Is Real? The End of Time, God and the New Physics, to name a few – along with the many TV series exploring the mysteries of quantum physics and the cosmos. Some of the content is highly speculative and philosophical in nature. Einstein, himself inspired by the particular type of mysticism of Spinoza, was very encouraging of physicists to engage philosophically in this way.

The birth of quantum theory early last century stimulated great metaphysical musings, rocking classical physics' mechanistic world-view of the Newtonian era, ushering in a paradigm shift. It would lead one of the founders of quantum mechanics, Neils Bohr, to state that 'Anyone who is not shocked by quantum theory has not understood it'. A number of these founding theorists discovered a sympathetic resonance in the mysticism of Eastern philosophy, because nature at this level could not be grasped by a classically informed mindset, nor by analytic philosophy.

Life in the quantum world

Relatively speaking, the regions of space inside the atom are vast. If the atom were the size of a football stadium, the nucleus in the middle would be the size of a grain of sand, with flecks of dust-sized electrons circling the nucleus at the outer edge of the stadium. Our bodies, for instance, contain trillions of atoms and yet amidst all this space (both inside the atom and between atoms), it is the electrostatic forces that give us (as well as individual atoms) a sense of solidity and shape. These forces hold the form of things. And even though as a culture we are somewhat obsessed with stuff, with the objects and physicality of our phenomenal perception, there is no actual 'stuff' in subatomic particles.

As reported in Nov. 23 *Physical Review Letters*, only 9% of the proton's mass comes from the mass of constituent quarks conveyed by the Higgs boson (there are 6 quarks in a proton, creatively divided into flavours and up or down) with 32% going into how the quarks zip around inside the proton (remember that E=mc², so energy has mass). Other occupants of the proton, massless particles called gluons that help hold quarks together, contribute another 36% via their energy. The remaining 23% arises due to quantum effects that occur when quarks and gluons interact in complicated ways within the proton. Where is the 'stuff'? The 'stuff' is in the binding forces, the fields, and the energy in motion. In this sense, the solidity of matter can be likened to a myth.

Max Plank first coined the term 'quanta' in physics to denote his hypothesis that the radiation of heat from a body was indicative of light being emitted in tiny, discrete packets of energy, which was referred to as 'black body radiation'. For this work, Plank was awarded a Nobel Prize in 1918. His work on discrete units, or quanta of energy, anticipated Einstein's proof that light itself was quantised as 'particles' called photons, and not just as 'waves', as light had been regarded since Thomas Young's experiments in 1803.

Quantum mechanics progressed in identifying the 'quanta' of an ever-expanding zoo of subatomic particles; the charge-less neutrons were added in 1932, alongside the protons that form the nucleus in the centre of an atom. Later, the protons and neutrons were found to have different coloured sub-particles called quarks, and these were creatively described as different 'flavours', and orientation; and then there were also gluons and mesons, et cetera. This description of the subatomic world has become known as the 'Standard Model' and continues as the cornerstone of the quantum particle world to this day.

These subatomic 'particles' are not truly solid, but are more like condensed vibrations of energy appearing in, but not separate from, a field (a field being spread out over space). All subatomic particles (*fermions* – electrons, quarks, leptons, and *bosons* – photons, gluons, Higgs bosons) – are *excitations in a field*. Remember also that 'matter' is equivalent to 'energy', as Einstein's famous equation $e=mc2$ demonstrated. So it is in this sense, that everything in the quantum world is less thing-like, and more energetic and field-like and, hence, more supportive of a 'process oriented' view, than the predominant 'substance' view held since the Atomists of Ancient Greece.

Wrestling with the 'double-slit experiment'

In 2002 the 'double-slit experiment' was voted by physicists, in a poll by *Physics World*, as the number one experiment in the top ten scientific experiments of all time. It was first performed by Thomas Young in 1801, but it was not until later in the 20th century that single electrons could be used in the experiment. It was the double-slit experiment that defined the difference between how matter behaved in a significantly different way at the subatomic level, and the way objects do in our regular phenomenal world. What it showed, was something very curious about how subatomic particles acted in their transit though the double-slit apparatus, and on their journey of arrival to the electronic detector screen stationed behind. What is really going on in this fairly simple experiment remains a mystery, and this gap in knowledge is the subject of continuing interpretation. The most popular of interpretations (Copenhagen interpretation), has assumed that the quantum world is subject to unique rules governing its microscopic domain, making it definitively different from that of the macroscopic world.

Photons (particles of light) in the Copenhagen Interpretation (CI) in the double-slit experiment are regarded as 'particle-like', and simultaneously 'wave-like', in how they transit through the slits and are recorded. This is because, just as with all waves, that are capable of causing a pattern of interference with other waveforms, the photons display an interference pattern on the recording screen after they have passed through the slit apparatus. Yet the photons are also seen to be particle-like, confined to a particular place and time (having a substance-like property) and having a specific locality as they are recorded individually hitting the photoelectric screen. When the particle goes through one of the slits in the double-slit experiment, it hits the photoelectric screen behind the slits and registers as a click, enabling the observer to notice the interaction and make a measurement. This 'measurement making' in the quantum orthodoxy of the Copenhagen Interpretation, is referred to as the 'collapse of the wave-packet'.

In a feat of 'magical thinking', it has been generally assumed in the CI, that the particle has no 'historical trajectory', and is smeared out magically in space with an infinite array of routes on its way through the slits to the screen behind. It 'collapses' down to an actual location only when it is observed/measured, giving the observer, and the act of observation, special status known as the 'observer effect'.

The photon is 'magically' described as being in a 'transcendent state' where it is in all possible states simultaneously in infinite positions; that is, both wave-like, and particle-like. This is known as wave-particle duality, with the particle smeared out over space, and yet upon observation it exhibits a specific location (depending on which experiment is performed) at the same time. This is known as 'superposition' and is the cornerstone of the CI, which became an orthodoxy led by Niels Bohr and Werner Heisenberg, from the conference in Solvay in 1927. It is an orthodoxy which holds currency to this day, and with varying minor modifications, is taught in university undergraduate physics courses and textbooks across the planet.

The kind of 'mathematical transcendent realm' known as 'superposition' has its roots in the atomism conceived of by the Atomists and Epicureans: atoms are regarded as subject to chance and randomness, echoing the abstract mathematical transcendence of Platonic philosophy. With the 'superposition' of this interpretation, particles magically escaping a deterministic world, are instead governed by laws of probability in a mathematically abstract transcendent realm, a modern echo of the Platonic idealised mathematical realm. It is a realm only accessible to the trained mathematical physicist. This appears to suggest that the abstruse and complicated nature of the maths is used as a hiding place for the ontologically unreal nature of this interpretation.

In this way the maths was used as a retreat from actuality in the double-slit experiment. Any student straying into questioning the merits of the interpretive orthodoxy raised the prospect of meeting a career road block. Questioning the veracity of the CI, would often be met with the attitude of their physics elders, to 'shut up and calculate'.

Anyone studying or investigating quantum physics is faced with the situation of choice, because choose we must, between the dozen or so interpretations at this fundamental level. However, before going further into the prospect of choosing interpretations and what 'choosing' actually means, we need to explore what makes the quantum world fundamentally unique to the physics of Newton and Einstein. This feature is 'non-locality' standing as the primary signature of quantum mechanics.

Non-locality: Bell's theorem

Non-locality represents a radical break from a classical worldview, and remains a keynote feature (along with granularity) of what is considered 'weird' about the quantum world. In 1935, Einstein and two colleagues, Podolsky and Rosen, published a paper in the *Physical Review* titled 'Can a Quantum Mechanical Description of Physical Reality be Considered Complete?' The EPR (Einstein, Podolsky, Rosen) paradox was a thought experiment which contended that the fastest known, measurable form of communication between particles or worlds is the speed of light. Their paper was presented in an attempt to support the classical physics notions of space and time, as opposed to the weirdly connected, action at a distance (non-local effects) and 'spooky' quantum world. But the EPR paradox was shown to be demonstrably false.

As often happens in physics, it can take some time for experimenters to come up with the technical knowhow to research the 'thought experiments' of the theorists. Almost 30 years after the EPR thought experiment was proposed, in 1964, physicist John Bell, inspired by the physics of David Bohm, developed 'Bell's theorem'. This theorem maintains that there is a clear distinction between the descriptions of classical physics, and the feature of 'non-locality', an aspect unique to the quantum world. By the early 1970s, John Clauser and colleagues at Berkeley University improved on Bell's work, showing that the connection between particles in the experiment was truly instantaneous. The communication between distant particles was measured as much faster than light. In fact, there was no time gap at all. Furthermore, it did not matter how far apart the particles were, whether ten metres apart or potentially a galaxy apart. It signifies a dimensional shift, and, the connection was real!

The particles were seen to be picking up changes in spin state faster than any form of communication travelling at light speed could do. This instantaneous communication at a distance is called 'non-local' connectedness, which means that it does not depend on the location of the particles, nor the time for a signal to be carried. Einstein called it 'spooky', because he was deeply troubled by it because of its challenge to the basic assumption in science of the universe being 'local'. Bohm questioned further as to whether particles are ultimately separate at all and, if not, this suggested to him a hidden, but much deeper unity and order in our model of reality. This feature of non-locality became central to Bohm's interpretation known as the Pilot Wave Theory (PWT).

The drive to discover the primary nature of existence via the feature of non-local connectedness, as demonstrated in Bell's theorem, led some theorists to factor in some fundamental quality of intelligence, or consciousness, at the subatomic level. It was Bell's theorem in particular that pointed to a connectedness at the quantum level, beyond the conventional notions of space and time, and causality. Non-locality indicated, in some physicists' minds, that a kind of knowing property or intelligence is at the very core of matter/energy. While providing no definitive proof that some kind of consciousness was interpenetrating all matter, these experiments enthused a number of physicists and commentators who postulated a kind of 'proto-intelligence' at the particulate level suggesting, in theory, a universe of consciousness.

Quantum entanglement: It is conjectured that entanglement occurred at the birth of the current universe, so it is fundamentally embedded as a constant feature of all matter. The simultaneous, non-local, knowing property of particles that are great distances apart, is known as 'entanglement'. The phenomenon of entanglement occurs when pairs or groups of particles interact in ways such that the quantum state of each particle cannot be described independently of the state of the other(s). This is so even when the particles are separated by a large distance, and instead, a quantum state must be described for the system as a whole. A number of theorists have been quick to point out that this 'entanglement' only takes place at the quantum level in the sub-microscopic world, and that it is incorrect to extrapolate that there is entanglement in the macroscopic world of organisms like us. But this is assuming a strict division between the quantum and the macroscopic world, which is inherent in the 'dualistic' gulf between worlds found amongst Copenhagenists.

In the theory of 'Quantum Monism' all particles in the universe are deeply entangled with each other from the very beginning of the universe. This makes for a single underlying reality of 'quantum holism': the universe is one inseparable entity with infinitesimal entangled parts.

Fundamental physics: 'an interpretative science'

Physicist Sean Carroll described the ongoing debates in quantum physics as 'embarrassing', because they rest on a choice between the different interpretations. Embarrassing, because even after more than 90 years since the Copenhagen meeting was held to settle the matter once and for all, it continues to remain a matter of *interpretation* of the experimental results. At the very core of sciences' attempt to conceptually understand nature, it still comes down to being one of considered opinion.

As a philosopher I can, in good faith, explore the ideas in fundamental physics and question its theories (not the maths) and conclusions. And this includes interrogating both the truth value of adopting any interpretation at all, as well as the nature of the interpretations postulated. The truth value of the phenomenal is plainly obvious as our cognition and senses attest, but when we get to the very small, even our most sophisticated instruments cannot 'see' exactly what is going on, so establishing truth value is extremely difficult.

This absence of clear knowledge results from our inability to see exactly what is going on in the quantum world, and hence we do not know. *With a serious epistemic gap at the core of our phenomenal map, physicists have been forced to use their imagination.* So, from the dozen or so interpretations that all fit the mathematical and observed experimental outcomes, it becomes a matter of choice. The reality is that none of them have real 'truth value'. Any one of them could be true. They might all be completely wrong, but as yet, we cannot say. All of them are possible; some may argue passionately that any one of them is more likely than the others, but in the absence of known reality, what does this amount to? How many dancing fairies can fit on a pin-head?

An imagined reality is real in that it exists in someone's consciousness, but in the same way that a hallucination is lacking in reality, it is not actually real. Imagination is an important human faculty, essential to human creativity and inventiveness, including the process of doing science, but with regard to epistemic truth, it is not a means of 'truth discovery'. So, whether it is to know the truth of Being, or the truth of phenomenal reality, imagination is inappropriate. And as a philosopher – which is to be a lover of wisdom – wisdom arises from one's alignment with truth.

Being fond of the surrealist art movement I initially liked the craziness of the Copenhagen Interpretation because of 'superposition', with its wave–particle duality: the weirdness of its infinite physical 'bilocation' of the particle, until it is observed and then 'located'. But I came to realise that this is equivalent to tales that always troubled me, usually part of religious stories where 'divine' people supposedly bi-locate. It is explained that there are different rules for the quantum world and for the world of walruses, but this is also an assumption held by the CI but not by pilot wave theory.

Bilocation is not to be confused with experiences of out-of-body, remote viewing, non-local knowing, or near-death experiences. These all signify that consciousness is multi-dimensional: that there are subtle dimensions that can be experienced but are not physical. But this does not support the physical bilocation – as expressed in the notion of 'superposition' – with particles, bodies, or anything else. These noumenal type experiences (near-death and out-of-body) indicate that consciousness is non-local, and yet it is also local as experienced in a body that only has one location. Bodies and particles are explicitly local, but they can be non-locally connected.

So, to play the game of choosing an interpretation describing what is actually going on in the quantum world with the double-slit experiment, which one to choose? For the author, PWT is aligned more experientially (this is discussed later) than the others, and because it segues into its founder's (David Bohm) metaphysics which also has merit. But I am not set in concrete about this, I offer it in a more playful sense, because after all, *each interpretation is based in ignorance – in what is imagined – not in truth*. I support PWT in the stoic sense as one of 'preferred indifference', so I have no belief around it and would not be disappointed if it turned out to be false; I would rather celebrate the truth of what actually is.

Remember, all quantum interpretations must fulfil the observational and mathematical requirements, and PWT being on the same footing with all the others, does this. But to approach this as a matter of belief and attach concrete truth value to what is just an 'imagined double-slit scenario', is to mistakenly believe that the one chosen is truly real, and this is only indicative of confusion.

Two books were published in 2018 exploring the interpretive features of fundamental physics: *What is Real*, by Adam Becker, and *Beyond Weird*, by Phillip Ball, both offering interesting insights and a similar pattern. While both are critical of the serious flaws of the Copenhagen Interpretation, they still use it as their default position, even though its epistemic and ontological merit is queried. Significantly, however, both books champion the rationality of PWT.

The Copenhagen interpretation (CI) is anti-realist because it considers the particle–wave function in purely probabilistic terms. Yet of course something does travel along different paths in the double-slit experiment, registering interference and giving a 'localised' recording on the detector screen. But this interpretation is not self-consistent due to the measurement problem, which resolves only by granting real physical existence to the particle. In contradistinction this is a feature that does occur in pilot wave theory (PWT).

The CI continues as one of the most popular amongst physicists, becoming known as the 'standard interpretation' as initially developed by Bohr and Heisenberg. De Broglie's earlier version of Pilot Wave Theory (1930) was taken up and reshaped in 1952 by David Bohm. Bohm's revised version embraced *non-locality* as an essential feature of the quantum world, placing it at the core of the revised PWT. PWT continues as a significant alternative and more coherent explanation, encompassing 'non-locality', and meeting the requirements of the double-slit experimental results. (For a refreshingly clear overview of the interpretations see Jean Bricmont's *Quantum Sense and Nonsense.*)

The 'many worlds interpretation' assumes that each possible state lives in its own universe rather than Copenhagen's blurred possibility of all states (superposition). The elevation of the special status of observer dependence creates a confusion of potential infinite probable universes, each with its own deterministic history. This concept is, in a very real way, a denial of the authenticity and veracity of the historical universe that we collectively inhabit, one that is clearly not constructed by imagination.

Physicists who believe in the MWI do so because it offers a model that is independent of any notion of observers or observation, as championed by Copenhagen. And, because it is deterministic (also unlike Copenhagen), it further ascribes reality in a clearly definitive way within a relativistic local model, but with an added degree of the bizarre, by explicitly lending itself to the imaginative possibility of infinite realities. This is a possibility that, neither in principle, nor in actuality, could ever be verified, because, in the imaginative leap of many worlds theory, these realities are without any real ontological or epistemic merit since they are fantasies. But the elevation of fantasy in MWI is great material for the imaginative genre of sci fi movies and fiction.

Pilot wave theory

PWT was initially viewed by Bohm's colleagues as merely a philosophical bias. Bohm saw the willingness to stifle alternative interpretations like the one he was offering, as being against the 'spirit of science', something he held most dearly. With the predominant interpretation entrenched, curiosity to investigate its own foundations and give weight to any intuitions of real particle trajectory, was damped down. Bohm, ever curious, could not just 'shut up and calculate'. In fact, he was suspicious of the way maths seemed to be used, as demonstrated in the Copenhagen camp, to hijack physics' attempt to develop a deeper understanding of nature.

> *Acclimating to the weirdness of quantum mechanics has become a physicists' rite of passage. The old, deterministic alternative is not mentioned in most textbooks; most people in the field haven't heard of it. Sheldon Goldstein, a professor of mathematics, physics and philosophy at Rutgers University and a supporter of pilot-wave theory, blames the 'preposterous' neglect of the theory on 'decades of indoctrination'. At this stage, Goldstein and several others noted, researchers risk their careers by questioning quantum orthodoxy.*
>
> —Natalie Wolchover[30]

One of the probable reasons that PWT was side-lined was the historical dominance of the Copenhagen school, which saw itself as beyond question. And I think the reason for this is that the CI satisfies a Platonic imperative: having a transcendental mathematical realm of abstraction in the form of superposition, with an idealised and inaccessible particle located everywhere at once and then magically appearing, in abstract and inaccessible transcendent mathematical probability – just like Platonic idealism. Particles magically escape a deterministic world of locality and, instead, are subject to chance and randomness, as conceived by the Atomists and Epicureans. The majority of physicists adhering to this interpretation are following a well-worn groove in the Western psyche stretching back to Ancient Greece.

Another reason possibly lies in the way PWT portrays the guiding wave of the particle as being non-locality connected to the entire universe, at the core of the theory. The implication of this level of non-locality was that every experiment can only be understood in the context of the entire universe. A pilot wave brings information instantaneously, infinitely faster than the speed of light, from the entire universe. To a phenomenally embedded mind, this is mind-boggling in itself. This remains in contradistinction to the view, held by the broader physics community, that nothing can move faster than light, and that non-locality is regarded more as a side-issue of the quantum world. But clearly, with non-locality there is no movement, there is no 'faster than'; it signifies a connectedness beyond the phenomenological. While quantum theory had clearly broken with classical Newtonian physics, in the Copenhagen interpretation it was still being informed by a materialistic ethos.

In his 1976 Nobel Prize lecture, Murray Gell-Mann declared that Niels Bohr, the chief exponent of the Copenhagen interpretation, 'brainwashed an entire generation of physicists into believing that the problem had been solved.' John Bell, the Irish physicist whose famous theorem is often mistakenly taken to repudiate all 'hidden-variable' accounts of quantum mechanics, was, in fact, himself a proponent of pilot-wave theory. 'It is a great mystery to me that it was so soundly ignored', he said.

—Larry Hardesty[31]

The non-locality that was a central feature of Bohm's theory inspired Bell to consider that 'quantum reality' really is non-local. Bell managed to lift the problem from the level of metaphysics into practicality, by deriving an 'inequality'. Bell's Inequality Theorem postulates emphatically that theories that support the idea that there must be some other 'hidden variable' to account for the non-local effects in quantum experiments, are demonstrably incorrect. Bell also remained a firm proponent of Bohm's version of PWT because, while it was a 'hidden variable interpretation', its central feature was that its pilot-wave, the wave that guides the particle, was in fact non-local.

However, Bell also had misgivings about Bohm's ideas describing PWT as 'hideously' non-local. But whatever quantum scenario turns out to be true I suspect it will have non-locality as a central feature, and this will be beautifully aligned with the knowing potential of human experience as it already is. Yet Bell was still a supporter of Bohmian physics as was the maverick of physicists, Richard Feynman, who agreed that there was something to Bohm's physics which he said 'may lead to something new'. Yet, he himself was not willing to work on it because he 'could not see a problem in it'.

Super-determinism: destiny among 'hidden variables'

Bell also suggested there was one other hidden variable hypothesis (perhaps this was offered more in jest) and in a 1985 BBC Radio interview stated that a radical alternative interpretation was also theoretically possible:

> *There is a way to escape the inference of superluminal speeds and spooky action at a distance. But it involves absolute determinism in the universe, the complete absence of free will. Suppose the world is super-deterministic, with not just inanimate nature running on behind-the-scenes clockwork, but with our behavior, including our belief that we are free to choose to do one experiment rather than another, absolutely predetermined, including the 'decision' by the experimenter to carry out one set of measurements rather than another, the difficulty disappears. There is no need for a faster-than-light signal to tell particle A what measurement has been carried out on particle B, because the universe, including particle A, already 'knows' what that measurement, and its outcome, will be.*
>
> Wikipedia: Adaptation from the edited transcript – radio interview with John Bell in 1985

Hidden variables theories like super-determinism and pilot wave maintain that quantum physics is only an approximation of some deeper, more fundamental level of theory that we as yet do not understand – that there are *hidden levels of order*.

Bell's theorem relies on the assumption of free will, wherein the experimenter can freely choose the detector settings in a quantum experiment. But in the theory proposed by Gerard 't Hooft (who won the Nobel Prize for developing the *Standard Model* which outlines the elemental particle zoo that constitutes the visible universe, and is regarded as the crowning achievement of the quantum world) and theorist Sabine Hossenfelder (who proposed a method of testing super-deterministic hidden variables theories in 2013) hypothesise that every movement of a subatomic particle has been known since the beginning of the universe. This is in alignment with the philosophy of Spinoza, that the belief in free will is an illusion.

In contrast to Bohm's theory, super-determinism does not allow for the 'spooky action at a distance' of non-locality, maintaining that all particles have acted according to 'script' since the very beginning of the universe, including how they navigate the double-slit experiment by knowing precisely where their position will be.

The hidden variable in super-determinism is a universal knowing property in all matter that has been there since the pre-particle plasma beginnings of the universe. It is a universe where absolutely nothing is random, and everything is subject to fulfilling its deterministic destiny. This theory raises the notion of determinism – the basic chain of cause and effect – to new levels, hence its name *super-determinism*.

It is not surprising that this has been regarded by many scientists as a 'conspiracy theory' and even 'anti-science', which is perhaps more indicative of having provoked some residual fear in a number of physicists' psyches imprinted with dualism, and inert matter without consciousness. It has been labelled an ultimate conspiracy theory. *The Oxford English Dictionary* defines *conspiracy theory* as 'the theory that an event or phenomenon occurs as a result of a conspiracy between interested parties; a belief that some covert but influential agency is responsible for an unexplained event'. This is clearly used as a derogatory reference implying a religious idea of a separate transcendental supernatural conspiratorial agency – God – that is meddling with absolutely everything.

However, if super-determinism is framed without the paranoia, as a 'universal organising intelligence' immanent in all there is, it has a very different meaning from conspiracy, because everything and everyone, is part of – and with agency – within this Totality. It is an intelligence that does not organise from a transcendence above, as conceived in the dualistic form that has prevailed in Anglo-European culture since the early Christian era. But rather it is an intelligence from everywhere and within, as both immanent and experiential as understood by the Ancient Greeks as the logos in the journey to 'now the Self'.

Yet the knowing of this level of congruence with universal intelligence really begins and ends with our direct perception. Understandably, it presents as mind-boggling to those holding an orthodoxy of interpretation, who have a fixation on inert materiality that is random and without organising intelligence. But it is a mind-set informed by a duality, where consciousness is regarded as a rare epiphenomenon found only in some species on a tiny rocky planet, in a random non-living universe. Yet note this curious saying from Democritus, the father of atomism, below:

To a wise man, the whole earth is open, because
the true country of a virtuous soul is the entire universe.
—Democritus (c. 460 – c. 370 BCE)[32]

Quantum faddism

There is a continuing fascination with things quantum: quantum healing, quantum jumping, quantum consciousness, quantum mind, quantum society; and all this contributes to quantum faddism – quantum whatever is fashionable: it's even used to advertise shampoo. This popularising results in a shallowness, that fails to appreciate the significance and implications of what quantum theory is. We need to be mindful when 'things quantum' are used, particularly as a part of a gimmicky sales pitch, with its mystery, weirdness and excitement. Quantum now is also used as a means of confering legitimacy to things 'spiritual', and we can be assured that when this happens it is built more on the fanciful, than on a genuine appreciation of what quantum physics is, and a cognition of its epistemic gaps, or indeed any deeper inner knowing. Authenticity comes from our direct unfiltered experience, and this requires no legitimacy from any modelling constructed by thought, whether it is quantum or otherwise.

> *Legendary King Midas never knew the feel of silk or a human hand after everything he touched turned to gold. Humans are stuck in a similar Midas-like predicament: we can't directly experience the true texture of reality because everything we touch turns to matter.*
>
> —Nick Herbert[33]

Nick Herbert points to an important truth here, because in the very thinking of things we commence a process of objectification, as the knower and the known. But this fails to grasp that it is through the suspension of thought that we can have a direct experience of the 'non-phenomenological texture of reality', the noumenal. Here we are neither interpreting through the mind nor theorising, because our lens is undistorted. And as Schrödinger so aptly conveyed, we can then discover an intimate 'communion with nature', to which the mind is not invited.

Some of the quantum hype has centered on confusions unique to the Copenhagen Interpretation (superposition, the special role of the observer, and randomness, and indeterminacy). And, perhaps to a lesser extent, the Many Worlds Interpretation (all possible universes are realised simultaneously). Those particularly excited by this confusion are looking for a way to boost their 'spiritual ideology', to give it some form of scientific credence, be it Phenomenological Subjectivism, New Age spirituality, or faith in a set of religious doctrines. Yet if they were to look more carefully it could be seen that a deeper consideration of Bohm's theories does offer a coherence, specifically with regard to consciousness, that is missing in other interpretations.

What is the fuss about Schrödinger's cat?

Multiplicity is only apparent, in truth, there is only one mind ... The plurality that we perceive is only an appearance; it is not real.
—Erwin Schrödinger (1887–1961)[34]

The special role of the observer given in the Copenhagen Interpretation, known as the 'observer effect', inspired a thought experiment by Erwin Schrödinger, referred to as 'Schrödinger's cat'. It has become famous, adding to the perceived weirdness of quantum mechanics and it stimulated much confusion amongst quantum theorists as they pondered its meaning, with the observer assumed to be central in affecting what is observed.

The thought experiment goes like this: imagine a cat is placed in a sealed box with a glass pellet containing cyanide gas. When a certain amount of radioactive decay registers (we don't know when enough decay will occur) thereby activating a small hammer to smash the glass pellet, the gas is realeased The cat will die at the release of the gas, but we do not know exactly when this will happen. After half an hour, it is imagined that when we open the box we will find either a live cat or a dead one. But during this half hour, believers in the CI claim that the cat is both alive *and* dead in a state of *superposition*. Both possible realities (in one, the cat is alive and in the other, it is dead) are existing in parallel universes, with the status of the cat only being determined when the scientist opens the box and sees which reality presents itself (there is a collapsing of the 'wave-function' that, in the particulate world, describes its properties, energy momentum and position existing as a function of probability until the observation/measurement is made). In the Many Worlds Interpretation, rather than two, there are multiple possibilities that are held in suspension as possible realities.

Schrödinger disagreed with the Copenhagen interpretation and its fundamental assumption of randomness expressed in probabilities, and he sought to restore determinism in quantum mechanics by exposing the implausible claim of superposition, with his famous 'cat thought experiment'.

Can we know, in an entangled universe, whether the cat is alive or dead without opening the box? Is there a real splitting of worlds? Are there real parallel universes, where the cat is alive in one world and dead in another, simultaneously existing in potentially infinite possible realities? Is the observer truly separate from the unobserved cat? Because while it is separate in a phenomenal reality, in the noumenal it is not.

Common sense informs us that cats are not in states of 'superposition', and the standard confused thinking which, as with all confused thinking, is dualistic by nature, holds that only subatomic elements are supposed to experience this. But it makes no sense to think that particles are any different. In PWT there is no apparent confusion here because there is no superposition. And even though there is a drastic discrepancy of scale between the macroscopic world of everyday objects, and the microscopic quantum worlds of particles, PWT (Bohm's version) consistently addresses this question.

The many worlds interpretation (MWI) states that, when the box is opened, there is one world with an observer and the dead cat, with another world with an observer and the alive cat, having split into two universes amongst a series of infinite possible universes. In one reality the observer sees a dead cat, and in the other an alive one. The very idea that there may be other universes simultaneously existing in parallel to our own is something we can understand only by using imagination. The creation of an endlessly occurring infinite series of universes is simply magical thinking, but when it is portrayed as something other than magical, and to be seriously considered, no.

Bohm's PWT suggest that the 'quantum potential' is a means of instantly conveying information about a primary property of consciousness at all levels, including the quantum level. So, consciousness is in the human brain, in the box, in the cat, and in the space between, in a conscious universe seamlessly and instantly connected via Bohm's 'quantum potential'. A property of consciousness in all levels of matter is known as *panpsychism*. The implication is that we can 'know' the status of the cat without even opening the box, as a form of non-local knowing accessible to humans, signifying that the observer and the observed are 'one'.

What is essential though, is the sensitivity of any observer. Realistically, not everyone may be sensitive enough to 'know' the status of the cat, and instead may rely only on empirical verification, by opening the box and viewing it. Experientially, it can be done only if one 'tunes in' to having *a non-local connection* to the cat. This is not only possible theoretically, but in fact, actually. If there is a deep understanding that everything is in intimate connection with everything else, we can have a 'noumenal knowing' of the cat.

CHAPTER 12

ONTOLOGY OF AN INTELLIGENT UNIVERSE

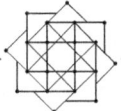

> *Bohm was unusual among scientists in questioning the primary epistemological engine for all scientific inquiry: human thought itself. He stressed that thought creates structures and then pretends they are objective realities independent of thought. Thus our 'objective reality' is largely a construct of thought, and not recognising this leads us to endless circles of self-deception — in science as well as in life in general. Indeed, Bohm felt that much personal and collective suffering has its roots in human thought.*
>
> —Will Keepin, *Lifework of David Bohm – River of Truth*[35]

With David Bohm (1917–1982), physicist and philosopher, the place and scope of consciousness is perhaps more thoroughly developed than by any other quantum theorist. In his quest to develop a conceptual theory of reality, he combined his experiential insights, creating a unique kind of metaphysics. Bohm considered that the connecting core feature of what he called 'undivided wholeness', was found in the two major theories of modern physics: relativity and quantum theory. He considered them as pointers to a deeper cosmological order. Despite the ongoing contradictions between the theories, Bohm developed his own cosmological-quantum model, termed the 'holomovement' and the 'implicate order'. His ideas were unorthodox, even within the conventional weirdness of quantum theory.

Bohm's doubts about the merits of the 'standard interpretation' were fuelled by a discussion with Einstein. From these discussions Bohm began looking for a causal explanation of the subatomic world, but one which would also embrace the essential feature unique to the quantum world, *non-locality*. He understood that consciousness was a primary feature of a universe that exhibited a hidden level of order, and that the universe was in a fundamental sense, alive. Aside from Bohm, how has consciousness generally fared in the world of fundamental physics?

Physics encounters consciousness

The theory that 'matter' as a universal, inert, non-living substance throughout the universe, is a conceptual fiction – a materialistic interpretation and a belief, rather than actuality. Its presentation as truth has informed practices and behaviours that show complete disregard for nature, whether it is animal, vegetable, or mineral (non-breathing) yet nonetheless all living. If we perceive the universe as living we feel connected to and caring about everything.

Eugene Wigner first postulated that quantum mechanics had something to do with consciousness, and by using the CI he surmised that the wave function collapses (in an experiment denoting the position of a particle) in the very act of observation from an observer (consciousness). In this way consciousness enters the system.

> *The emergence of the reality of consciousness, lying at the core of physics' quest to understand reality, has been met with considerable resistance. Materialistic assumptions are held quite strongly as core beliefs by a large majority of scientists. This perhaps partly explains why quantum physics has been so disturbing within the scientific community, and why it is of such interest to the lay public.*
>
> *It may be premature to believe that the present philosophy of quantum mechanics will remain a permanent feature of future physical theories; it will remain remarkable, in whatever way our future concepts may develop, that the very study of the external world led to the conclusion that the content of the consciousness is an ultimate reality.*
>
> —Eugene Wigner[36]

The Copenhagen orthodoxy suddenly ushered in the role of the observer, who became an essential part of the experiment in laboratories investigating the quantum world. Previously the observer was not relevant, in fact in the assumed objectivity of science, the 'observer' (scientist) was idealistically separated from the 'observed', behind a glass screen, with no possibility of interacting with and hence affecting experimental results.

In talking of consciousness and quantum theory probably no-one raises the hackles of physicists more than Deepak Chopra. But remember if you point a finger there are always three pointing back at you: in an essential way, physicists only have themselves to blame. Chopra is just expressing some of the inherent confusion that exists in fundamental physics. At the core of fundamental physics is a crucial ignorance, glossed over with various imagined quantum scenarios, and the most popular ones (CI and MWI) offer unbridled licence for the fantastical, but not with dimensionality which is expressed in non-locality.

Chopra is also speaking to a generation of physicists that have had their curiosity and investigative wings clipped by the dictum of 'shut up and calculate'. To an outsider it seems as though fundamental physics has stalled and is perhaps more concerned to preserve a hegemony of unquestioned belief in the status quo, which is one of ignorance, than actually to face the knowledge gap that exists, and resolve it. So rather than follow in the folly of their physics elders' admonition to shut up and calculate, the new generation of physicists should, in the spirit of good science, 'question and investigate'.

It is also not so surprising that Chopra raises their ire because physicists are so fiercely attached to their conditioned belief in inert matter, that they fail to recognise that he uses quantum mechanics in an analogous way, rather than as statements of hard science; Schrödinger specifically encouraged people to use analogy with the findings in the quantum world. This would seem to indicate that physicists' epistemic repertoire is limited. Physicists universally have analytical skills, mathematical knowledge, and a dexterity with deductive and rational thinking, but how many would have insight into the way of 'direct perception'?

Yet it would perhaps be wiser if everyone were to be mindful that, when using any quantum interpretations, even analogously, they do not have any truth-value. And with using them in analogous sense with Eastern wisdom teachings, when these interpretations exist in the very absence of knowledge (as imagined quantum scenarios), does have value as a philosophical contribution.

In Adam Becker's book on fundamental physics, *What is Real?*, he suggests that, regarding 'the consciousness issue in quantum physics', the fault lies in the CI itself: for its vagueness, its focus on the 'observer effect', and a 'bevy of internal contradictions' that it lends itself to a 'river of New Age non-sense' and 'junk pseudo-science'. Yet, in contrast to CI, Bohm's theories bring consciousness into the picture, in a way that is not vague, minus an 'observer effect'. Although it is not hard science, and has no internal contradictions, it does have a direct appeal to our experience.

If we rest in awareness we are automatically connecting to the ubiquity of consciousness as Being. In this understanding, knowing at a distance is a completely ordinary feature of our experience of living, *because there is no distance and time.* Only the phenomenal world of thought and the empirical-based senses give an epistemic located in space and time. Non-locality is regarded as a 'weird' side feature in the orthodox interpretations of quantum theory, but when it is held as the centerpiece of David Bohm's PWT, the 'guiding wave' (quantum potential) is instantaneously connecting us to the entire universe. The central place given to non-locality in PWT finds correspondence with experiential non-duality, as an experience of instantaneous connectedness with everything.

Outside of science, human beings have long been intuitively aware of 'non-local knowing', with no concern about it fitting any kinds of rational criteria or a particular conceptual modelling of reality. When people are particularly connected through family, tribal or friendship bonds, they commonly experience this knowing at a distance; for example, in Australian Aboriginal culture, knowing that a relative is on the way to meet them, or knowing the exact moment that a beloved relative has died in an accident albeit the person lives on the other side of the globe, or when someone is about to contact or arrive with no previous indication that this was happening, or the knowing of a dear friend's specific trouble that has not been communicated through regular electronic contact.

But let us be clear, quantum theory does not teach us anything about our experience of non-local knowing, for instance, or our capacity to experience it, or its range. Our only source for this lies not in theory, but in the direct experience of consciousness itself. And when the conceptual knowledge of science is used to do this, it is an error. This is because quantum theory (or any other scientific concept) can be nothing more than an analogy or a metaphor; it is clearly not demonstrable. While the quantum potential of PWT is used in connection with consciousness, it is seen analogously, and it is a particularly good analogy, but remember, the quantum potential only has imagined status.

In science there are differing views of what consciousness is, as offered by physicists, neuroscientists, and psychologists. But without exception they are all operating under a natural dualistic premise because they are scientists, which sees the separation of the observer from the observed. Inevitably consciousness is seen as some, as yet unknown, 'emergent' substance, separate from another substance, called matter.

While it might be suggestive to some that quantum physics points to there being some form of consciousness interpenetrating matter, it is not an explicit feature proved by quantum mechanics, nor is it at all a mainstream view in the physics community. As Bohm was fully aware PWT, as an imagined quantum scenario, does offer this, and it was probably this factor that was central to his formulating it. Bohm held a panpsychist view – that 'consciousness interpenetrates all matter' – which is a significant step apart from my own view that 'everything is consciousness' and that there is no such thing as dead matter, but the physicality of the phenomenal aspect of consciousness is location-specific.

Quantum theory and experiential knowing

With relativity as the other major body of theory in physics, it has been an easy process for people at large to embrace its gist at an experiential level. Relativity, as a deeper mapping of the phenomenal universe, and an important development from the Newtonian framework of idealised measurements (time and space), enabled people to embrace something of the extra dimension of flexibility afforded in Einstein's theory. It maps what is most easily accessible, a sense that there are different frames of space and time relative to the space/time frame of other observers moving at different velocities. It is empirically comprehensible. Relativity has become part of common parlance, used by a lay public, having caused no fuss at all to the scientific community.

But not so in the quantum world. Theorists have taken great umbrage at the slightest philosophical musings on the meaning of quantum theory, or even using it analogously. In doing so they maintain there is a straying from the strict mathematical and ideological underpinnings, particularly in relation to 'acceptable interpretations', as decreed by an authoritative body of theorists.

Speaking generally, scientists have an instinctive view that downplays consciousness and experience as a secondary phenomena: theory takes precedence. It is the same instinct that sets them apart as non-participatory observers, separate from what is observed. This setting apart is the idealism of objectivism, yet in all human reality, consciousness in the form of experience is ever primary. And this is regardless of whatever endeavour we engage in, including quantum mechanics.

What has made quantum theory uniquely different in the history of science is that at its core – despite the epistemic gap of knowing what is actually going on with subatomic particles – we are pointed to a different order of understanding than what empirical knowing or mathematical information, can provide. The central concept in quantum theory is 'non-locality', and this is a radical shift from the body of theory that is relativity, which is explicitly phenomenal. But the conceptual map of reality that quantum theory offers, particularly in the interpretation favoured here (PWT), points to experiencing a *numinous living universe*.

While quantum mechanics and direct experiential knowing both require intense curiosity, they both emerge from completely different ways of knowing. On the one hand, with thought in analysing experimental data, questioning and constructing a model; on the other, directly experiencing reality with an unfiltered lens.

In physics this has involved inventing an idea of 'non-locality', to describe what is phenomenologically unexplainable (Einstein called it 'spooky'), with the instantaneous connectedness of particles beyond space and time. These particles, of course, are not regarded as separate, but entangled in 'quantum wholeness'. Direct experience, as a form of enquiry with the conceptually uncluttered lens of *original mind*, is a domain of silence beyond thought, yielding an experience of connectedness that is also of a different order from the empirical. The first is concerned with a constantly changing, evolving model of reality as is the way of progressive conceptual knowledge, and the second with a direct experiencing the 'Is-ness' of reality, a way that is timeless and is ever-now.

In the CI emphasis is placed on the bizarre properties of the particle, being simultaneously wave-like, and localised as particles. Experientially we can have no knowledge of this. We cannot be in two places at once in a state of physical bilocation. But we do experience the phenomenal world and the causal chain as explicitly outlined in the 'historical trajectory of the particle' in PWT, and this is essential to our phenomenal perception. Further, there is the denial of the deterministic nature of the phenomenal reality, a causal chain that we all share in our experience of living. Those holding the notion of 'superposition' will argue that experience at the phenomenal level is not congruent with the quantum world, as a separate world in which only the bizarre can occur. It is a divide which can only be accessed with complex mathematics, but it is an assumed divide, and it is unreal. And it is increasingly untenable now, as reported in Physics.org, *'Probing quantum physics on a macroscopic scale'*, November 30, 2018. Here, experimentalists at Delft University of Technology, have discovered that non-local quantum correlations happen with massive clusters (10 billion) of atoms.

So too with the MWI – there is no experiential access to infinite possible worlds. Importantly, we can only know one, which is not to be confused with knowing different dimensional or parallel realities, but this is a very different thing, because it involves different dimensions of one world. We share in experiencing the one deterministic world, with over 7 billion perspectives, replete with all its consequences, that we all also share. We can imagine other worlds, and we can imagine superposition, but we can never experience either of these, beyond what is imaginary.

Non-locality, central to Bohm's PWT in the form of the guiding wave - the 'quantum potential' - links us to a different order of knowing, and is essential to our experiencing an undivided universe – one that, in non-duality, one does experience.

The particular type of epistemic interpretation found in CI is one that is rooted in information and complex maths, whereas the ontological interpretation of PWT is more rooted in a numinous experience of reality. We can know non-locality *directly* as an essential feature of a numinous experience of Being, but it is impossible to describe using language that is explicitly designed for phenomenal experience. But while this is accessible to everyone, even a birthright, not everyone is willing or curious enough to take this journey.

Of course, the 'quantum potential' is hypothetical, as it has not been measured or scientifically verified. In this sense it is in the same place as 'superposition' or 'many worlds'. But there is an important difference: the two latter interpretations do not even have the potential to match human experience, whereas the first one does. The latter two only meet the definition of the imagined (although MWI is deterministic and agrees with PWT regarding the historical trajectory of the particle) while PWT is experiential. It is experiential on two counts: first, as being congruent with our experience of phenomenal reality, with the determined historical trajectory of the particle. And second, the non-local nature of the *quantum potential* in PWT is analogous to the way any of us can connect instantaneously with the Totality. This is fundamental to experiencing the universe in a numinous way rather than in a phenomenal one.

Quantum theorists find parallels in Eastern philosophy

Given the paradoxical nature of the quantum world, it is not surprising that the founding quantum theorists delved into mysticism, seeking poetic and philosophical parallels, because the classical Newtonian world of physics was being turned upside down. A number of them found resonance in the wisdom teachings of the East: particularly in Buddhist literature, and in the writings from the Vedas and Upanishads from Ancient India, as well as in the Taoist philosophy of Ancient China. In different ways these particular traditions speak of a domain of Being that is beyond the conceptual linear space/time, and the phenomenal universe. These traditions maintain there is a formless consciousness that interpenetrates all existence, where everything is connected in a deeper reality. It is a reality that is not constructed through reason, and can only be apprehended intuitively.

Those quantum theorists who gave birth to quantum mechanics in the 1920s associated it with ancient wisdom. They have been referred to as the fathers of quantum theory: Heisenberg, Bohr and Schrödinger. Each of them read and greatly respected the Vedas of Ancient India, because they saw, in these texts, parallels between the spiritual teachings they contained and the new quantum theory they were founding.

In Renee Weber's interview with Fritjof Capra (author of *The Tao Of Physics*, which popularised quantum physics, linking it with Eastern mysticism, and was soon to be followed by Gary Zukav's *The Dancing Wu Li Masters*) he spoke of how Schrödinger relayed a story about Werner Heisenberg, who revealed that his physics was influenced by Hindu philosophy:

I had several discussions with Heisenberg. I lived in England then [circa 1972], and I visited him several times in Munich and showed him the whole manuscript chapter by chapter. He was very interested and very open, and he told me something that I think is not known publicly because he never published it. He said that he was well aware of these parallels. While he was working on quantum theory he went to India to lecture and was a guest of Tagore. He talked a lot with Tagore about Indian philosophy. Heisenberg told me that these talks had helped him a lot with his work in physics, because they showed him that all these new ideas in quantum physics were in fact not all that crazy. He realised there was, in fact, a whole culture that subscribed to very similar ideas. Heisenberg said that this was a great help for him.

—Renee Weber[37]

Nobel Prize winner Niels Bohr said, 'I go into the Upanishads to ask questions'. Both Bohr and Schrödinger, as avid readers of the Vedic texts, observed that their experiments in quantum physics were in fact consistent with what they had read in the Vedas. For example, Schrödinger, in speaking of a universe in which particles are represented by wave functions, said:

The unity and continuity of Vedanta are reflected in the unity and continuity of wave mechanics. This is entirely consistent with the Vedanta concept of All in One.

—Erwin Schrödinger[38]

Schrödinger considered that it was not possible to demonstrate the unity of consciousness by rational arguments. Rather, he thought that this could only be done experientially, by communion with nature, and by using the persuasion of analogies. He understood that in Vedic terminology the eternal nature of the conscious self (Atman) was ultimately inseparable from the Supreme Being (Brahmin).

This theme of exploring parallels between quantum theory and Eastern philosophy has been an ongoing dialogue in popular culture. And while it has generally been regarded with disdain in in the physics community, at a conference on November 2015 at the Jawaharial Nehru University, Delhi, in India, titled: 'Quantum Physics and Madhyamika Philosophical View', Buddhist teachers including the 14th Dalai Lama, and quantum theorists, presented on the parallels between core Buddhist Madhyamika teachings, and quantum theory. Prominent among the Buddhist teachings are the insights of Nargajuna (c.150 – c. 250 BCE).

Nargajuna was a key Buddhist philosopher and a founder of the Madhyamika school of Mahāyāna Buddhism. Central to this school of Buddhism is a philosophy of emptiness/nothingness in all things. This applies to people, planets, oranges, rocks, and atoms. Emptiness is inclusive of animate and inanimate things, as well as the analytic categories that are used to describe them, for they too are viewed as lacking any inherent essence, or existence. This 'emptiness' holds that all phenomena lack their own inherent existence, because their very existence is dependent on the conditions that gave rise to them. That is, nothing has a fixed and permanent nature in itself. But importantly this emptiness is *knowing* as Consciousness.

Nargajuna's philosophical treatise was the result of his experiential contemplative endeavour. His insight was not offered as a matter of speculation or belief, but rather was an articulation of his experiential knowing of 'non-Being', at the heart of Being. Nargajuna's insight was offered with the essential caveat that, anyone seeking to understand this truth, could only do so through the same process: the contemplation of Being. However, as always happens in religious traditions, insights become doctrines, and doctrines become core tenets of belief. And it is the ossifying process of following doctrines that maintains the lived trance of its followers.

> *In order to clarify this, Nagarjuna posited two truths: a conventional truth and an ultimate truth. In so doing, he recognised that it is possible to simultaneously perceive things as actually existing out there in the world (the conventional truth) as well as recognising that they lack any inherent existence (the ultimate truth). Holding these two seemingly contradictory positions is only possible by recognising that 'reality' is an experiential phenomenon, not one that has an objective existence independent of our experience of it.*
> —Daniel Oberhaus[39]

Nargajuna's philosophy directs us to one of the problems at the heart of both quantum theory and science itself. Is there an objective, independent reality that is capable of being quantified? Or, are all such measurements subjective, by virtue of the fact that they are always dependent on a separate observer to make these measurements, to separate the object of measurement, to hold the conceptual body of theory the scientist is working in, and is thus merely reflecting the observer's knowledge, thereby reinforcing their conceptually driven conditioning? This all underpins the primary assumption of separation – observer and observed – which is at the core of all science, as already discussed.

There is a way to resolve this, as the physicists at the conference pointed out. This is by understanding that these seemingly contradictory pathways to reality (direct intuition and reason) only make sense if you take them both together, while at the same time realising that they represent 'two truths'. This is encapsulated in the principle of the 'middle way', much like the 'middle path' that is central to the Madhyamika philosophy, and is a point alluded to by Bertrand Russell. In this middle way, we have the conceptual objectivist model on the one hand, as constructed by thought, and on the other, a non-conceptual apprehension of the real. Both are true, and their apparent separation (as phenomenal and noumenal) only appears conceptually. It is not real and is *subsumed experientially in a unitary vision of reality*.

Like Nargajuna's philosophy, quantum theory also exhibits two levels of truth: a conventional truth, analogous to the determinate particulate world, as the reality brought about through observation, and a deeper truth, which is an indeterminate reality expressed in 'non-locality'. And I suspect that the founding fathers of Quantum theory would have been in resonance and well pleased with the conference' proceedings. But maybe not some of their modern counterparts who may regard their theoretical field as a safe bastion of materialism, and to be defended from being sullied by things philosophical.

Yet there are truths of quantum mechanics which do mirror Madhyamika philosophy insofar as the latter professes that things do actually exist out there in the world, yet have no intrinsic, objective, separate essence. They only derive their 'thingness' (quarks, strawberries, crustaceans and neutrinos) from our subjective interpretations, because we create the process of objectification and phenomenal experience using thought and language (or mathematics). Nargajuna's Two Truths find a more obvious resonance with Bohmian metaphysics with the 'implicate' and 'explicate' order as discussed below.

In the case of entanglement in quantum mechanics, we can also regard it as a quantifiable expression analogous to Nagarjuna's notion of 'dependent origination' wherein the state of a particular quantum particle cannot be expressed because it is dependent on the quantum system as a whole. The analogy here is that much like Nagarjuna's insight with objects, things, people (or particles in this case) things do not have their own inherent or independent essences, because their existence is dependent on the conditions that brought them forth.

The connection between Eastern philosophy (like that of Madhyamika) and quantum theory is of course only analogous, with one being a conceptual world-map of the infinitely small, the other an experiential contemplation of Being. And because each signifies a different epistemic order, the correspondence is no more than this. From experiential knowing of Being we can recognise and validate patterns of correspondence occurring in a conceptual scheme, such as in ideas about the quantum world. But conceptual knowing, by virtue of its limited nature, cannot validate what is beyond itself – the infinite.

When quantum theorist Nick Herbert was asked about whether quantum theory was similar to Eastern philosophy, he responded:

> *Oh, in some sense, but not in particulars. There's a vague similarity to Eastern philosophy, more than to Western philosophy, that's true … Eastern philosophy talks about connectedness, everything being connected. It talks about the Tao, that's unspeakable, wholeness that envelops everything, and the flavour of that is like quantum theory. There's no doubt about that. More so than a mechanistic clock-work*

universe. But the details – no one ever anticipated that kind of universe. So, my guess is that, when we get a fuller picture of the world, it will be equally un-guessable. It would not have been anticipated, and quantum mechanics was just a kindergarten lesson for how we're going to have to change our minds to make the next step.
—Nick Herbert [40]

Bohm's universe of hidden order

Bohm maintained that the causal interpretation revealed the operation of creative, underlying, subtler levels of reality. For example, Bohm views electrons as highly complex, dynamic entities. He rejected the view that their motion is fundamentally uncertain or ambiguous. Instead he maintained that they follow a precise path determined not only by *conventional physical forces*, but by a subtler force which he calls the 'quantum potential'. It is this 'quantum potential' guiding the particle, capturing a new level of clarity with regard to non-locality, central in PWT, that in itself is challenging to many physicists. The quantum potential 'guides' the motion of particles by providing 'active information' about the whole environment, like a ship being guided by radar signals.

The 'quantum potential' pervades all space and provides direct connections between all quantum systems. Mathematically, the 'quantum potential' corresponds to the 'wave-function' of conventional quantum mechanics, and evolves according to the Schrödinger equation, with the positions of the particles not affecting the wave function.

In 1959, Bohm and his young research student, Yakir Aharonov, re-discovered an important example of quantum interconnectedness. They found that, in certain circumstances, electrons are able to 'feel' the presence of a nearby magnetic field, even though the electrons are traveling in regions of space where the magnetic field strength is zero (which in classical terms would be assumed as separate, and hence 'they' should not 'feel anything'). Bohm attributed this to the 'hidden variable' of the 'quantum potential'. This became known as the 'Aharonov–Bohm (AB) effect' and was listed by *New Scientist* magazine as one of the 'Seven Wonders of the Quantum World'.[41]

Bohm postulated a further radical idea that raised the stakes of the idea of non-locality. He proposed that subatomic particles remain in contact with each other, not because of some mysterious subluminal signalling, but rather because *their apparent separation, is an illusion.* That is, the deeper ground of physical reality is not a collection of separate objects. Rather, it is an undivided whole that is in perpetual, dynamic flux. Here Bohm is echoing the process philosophers, from Lao Tse and Heraclitus to Whitehead.

For Bohm, the insights of quantum mechanics and relativity theory point to a universe that is undivided, and in which all parts merge and unite in one totality. It is an order that is 'implied', which he termed the *implicate order*. Bohm had this to say:

> *Younger physicists usually appreciate the implicate order because it makes quantum mechanics easier to grasp. By the time they're through graduate school, they've become dubious about it because they've heard that hidden variables are of no use because they've been refuted. Of course, nobody has really refuted them.*
>
> —David Bohm[42]

During the 1960s, as Bohm was exploring the nature of order, he saw an experiment on a television program. It consisted of two concentric glass cylinders with the space between them filled with glycerine, a highly viscous fluid, and a droplet of ink was placed in this fluid. As the outer cylinder was turned, the droplet was drawn into a thread that eventually became so thin that it disappeared from view. The ink particles appeared to have been randomly distributed in the glycerine, making for an opaque colour. However, when the cylinder was then turned in the opposite direction, the thread reappeared to eventually re-form a droplet. Bohm realised that when the ink was diffused through the glycerine it was not in a state of disorder, but in fact possessed a hidden, or non-manifest, order.

The 'quantum potential' postulated in his causal interpretation of PWT corresponds to the 'implicate order'. Bohm maintained that the quantum potential reveals an implicate level of order, one that is 'implied', or 'hidden' to thought, embracing the universe at large. What we see, what we can measure, what we can describe, is an unfolding from this order. This manifest order, the phenomenal, he called the *'explicate order'*. In each passing moment the explicate order – the universe we experience with our senses – is revealed from a deeper, infinite, timeless field that is in continuous communication with all of itself at once, as the 'implicate order'.

Bohm's described 'sub-totalities' as being all of the seemingly separate manifest forms, from subatomic particles and multicellular organisms to planets, galaxies and galaxy clusters. These forms are relatively stable yet temporary. Indeed, some seem eternal but in reality they are not. As humans we are one of these forms and we are derived, like everything else, from an implicate order of unbroken wholeness. And he proposed that there may well be an infinite series of implicate (or 'generative') orders, some of which form relatively closed loops, and some that do not.

Bohm believed that the implicate order has to be extended into a multidimensional reality. In other words, what he coined as the 'holomovement' was a term to describe how reality endlessly enfolds, and unfolds into infinite dimensionality. Within this milieu there are independent sub-totalities (such as physical elements and human entities) with relative autonomy. The layers of the implicate order can go deeper and deeper to the ultimately unknown. These higher implicate orders would feed back to the original explicate order, which could produce complex dynamics over time, allowing creativity and novelty to unfold. It is this 'unknown and indescribable totality' that Bohm called the 'holomovement', as the 'fundamental ground of all matter'.

Bohm's work was challenging some fundamental beliefs underpinning the Western scientific endeavour. His ideas challenged the almost divine status of rationality, found in all substance-driven physics stemming from the Atomists. This belief holds that it is only rationality that can uncover the secrets of the universe. The belief that we just need to keep penetrating further with the sharpened probe of the intellect, expresses a very masculine-dominant metaphor. However, Bohm was saying that the 'implicate order' is utterly inaccessible to the rational mind, because it is only when we put the intellect to one side, in meditative silence, that we can experience this different dimension of Being.

The implicate order is not an idealistic transcendent realm that is beyond human experience; rather it is an immanent one, accessible to any person 'sensitised' through meditation. Bohm encouraged a radically different epistemic path from empirical and rationalistic science. His ideas challenged the deeply rooted dualistic mindset that sees the separation of the observer and the observed, as subject and object. He was challenging ideas embedded in the Western psyche for over two thousand years, and by challenging this conditioning, it is not surprising his colleagues reacted negatively.

Bohm lamented that physics is primarily concerned with prediction and control, rather than with truth. However, because his theories appeared to offer little to enhance 'hard science', many scientists were simply not interested in them. Indeed, Bohm's interpretation of quantum mechanics was criticised because it did not yield results that differ from orthodox quantum theory, which makes it difficult to test against conventional interpretations. In this sense, Bohm's theory was charged with failing to satisfy Popper's falsifiability criterion, in order to be considered a legitimate scientific theory. But, of course, this could equally be said about all interpretations of quantum theory.

In response to the criticism that concepts like the 'holomovement' cannot be observed in the laboratory, Bohm pointed out that a rigid adherence to 'Occam's razor' (or the *law of parsimony* which maintains that, when faced with competing hypotheses, the one with the fewest assumptions should be selected) is over-restrictive, and could obscure a deeper reality that may underlie laboratory observations. To illustrate his point, Bohm used the following example:

> *...a fish in an aquarium that is observed by means of two television cameras at right angles to each other. The observed images on the two television monitors give the appearance*

of distinct, correlated entities, but these observations are not the reality; rather they are merely different aspects of a deeper underlying unity – in this case, the fish itself.

—David Bohm[43]

Bohm's insight was that pure awareness, *prior to thought*, tells us that reality is a single, undivided whole. This insight of course only happens to someone who has gone beyond the conditioning of mind itself. But his challenge was to marry the process of physics and its reductive nature, to explain how apparent separateness and the fragmentation into objects and particles manifests. He was also stepping outside the belief in the primacy of rationality itself in knowing reality, and the assumed separateness of the observer and the observed. This is part of the historical assumption that conditions science where it assumes the fragmentation of reality, as a self-verified part of the process of reduction, in the search for the ultimate constituents of matter. However, as Bohm was aware, just because the majority of physicists adhere to this assumption, and have a strong belief in this reductionist project, does not make it so.

After all, perhaps the principle of Occam's razor argues for, rather than against, Bohm's Pilot-Wave Interpretation – the idea of undivided wholeness and the two kinds of order (explicit and implicate) does exemplify parsimony.

The truth is that Einstein understood the Copenhagen interpretation of quantum mechanics perfectly – he just wasn't happy with its vagueness. His intuition, that a deeper, more precise explanation is possible, has been fully justified. As we have seen, Bohmian mechanics is just such a deeper explanation.

—Thad Roberts[44]

The holographic universe and the 'holomovement'

David Bohm's universe is a seamless whole, with all its parts containing information about the whole universe, just as a hologram does. He theorised that this information is held in the 'implicate level of order', outside space and time. From this it follows that each of us, with our bodies at the quantum level, enfolds information, albeit at an unconscious level, of the whole universe. Each of us is constituted from the dust of exploding super novas containing information about the story of the universe.

In the 1960s Karl Pibram, a Stanford neurophysiologist, proposed a holographic model of how and where memories are stored in the brain. Memories are not only specifically localised in the brain – as continues to be assumed by reductionist theories of brain function – Pibram showed that memory lies in the patterns of nerve impulses that criss-cross the entire brain. This is similar to the interference patterns created by laser light on a piece of film containing a holographic image, with each fragment containing an image of the whole. That is, every piece of information in the brain is cross-correlated with every other piece.

If what we perceive as the phenomenal world, is actually a holographic blur of frequencies of the infinitesimal vibrating quantum world, and the brain – being also holographic in nature – selects only some of these frequencies out of the blur, transforming them into our sensory experience, then the notions of 'objective reality' as being out there, dissolves. And this is precisely what the sages have said all along; that the consensus reality constructed by mind, thought and language, has no 'absolute' basis. The phenomenal has a truth but it is relative. To know the absolute requires a letting go of the thinking that constructs our phenomenal map in order for us to know-experience directly 'the Is-ness of Being'.

> *The eternal order is not properly to be regarded as static, but rather as eternally fresh and new.*
> —David Bohm and David Peat[45]

Bohm's different levels of 'implicate order' are realms invisible to ordinary perception but he considers them as the true structure of reality. The holomovement is the nature of this reality. The implicate order and super-implicate order are its primary structural features, while the explicate order is the surface appearance – the one we detect with our senses and which we can measure and describe. Bohm thought that there was no concrete evidence in science to favour the mainstream fragmented world-view over his unbroken, flowing holomovement; rather it was a matter of individual beliefs and predilections.

These 'implicate orders' may be involved in innumerable physical and natural processes, such as guiding the emergence of all the myriad life forms, informing genetic changes, etc. In this way Bohm's work was analogous to archetypes, or to Rupert Sheldrake's controversial 'morphogenetic fields', as fields of information. The subtle orders in Bohm's metaphysics are hidden to empirical science and therefore difficult to assess, let alone measure, with science being focused only on what is explicate.

Bohm's use of the 'holographic principle' in the form of the 'holomovement' as central to his cosmology preceded its development as a prime candidate in a comprehensive cosmology, and as a theory of everything.

* The holographic principle was first proposed by Gerard 't Hooft in 1975 and reworked with a string theory interpretation by Leonard Susskind as a theory of 'quantum gravity'. It reconciles relativity with quantum mechanics, using the central idea of the 1D strings from string theory, resolving the scales of difference and the forces at play, from galaxies to quarks.

The interior 'universe' projects from the lower-dimensional boundary system like a hologram. Maldacena's discovery of this hologram has given physicists a working example of a quantum theory of gravity. Holography is the idea that the entire universe exists as a hologram projecting from a 2D plane, including what we experience as 3D (volume of space) in our phenomenal reality. Phenomenal reality is mathematically reduced at a more fundamental level to a 2D projection on a surface. This 2D plane houses all the bits of information, encoding all that we see, feel and hear in our 4D world of space and time.

In Stephen Hawkins' last published paper with Professor Thomas Hertog offers a version of the holographic principle, with the inclusion of time (the fourth dimension) into the theory. The holographic principle holds that at the beginning of time, eternal inflation can be reduced to a two-dimensional timeless state, on a spatial surface.

An informed universe: consciousness interpenetrating matter

When Bohm's *Wholeness and the Implicate Order* was published in 1980, the holographic model quickly became a lively topic of discussion among new paradigm thinkers.

> *The actual nature of the information and the way it is carried is not yet entirely clear. Is it really correct, for example, to speak of a 'field' of information, since information does not fall off with distance, neither is it associated with energy in the usual sense. Possibly the notion of field should be widened or, at the quantum level, we should be talking about pre-space structures, or about algebraic relationships that precede the structure of space and time ... Yes, if you say that all matter actually works from information, not merely matter in the nervous system or DNA matter working in the cell, but even the electron is forming from empty space being informed as it were by some unknown source of information which may be all over the space ... there is no sharp division between thought, emotion and matter.*
>
> *I would say that in my scientific and philosophical work, my main concern has been with understanding the nature of reality in general and of consciousness in particular as a coherent whole, which is never static or complete but which is an unending process of movement and unfoldment ...*
> —David Bohm, *Wholeness and the Implicate Order*[46]

Bohm considered consciousness to be enfolded deeply in the generative order and to be present in varying degrees of unfoldment in all matter, including supposedly inanimate matter such as electrons or plasmas. He proposed a 'proto-intelligence' in matter, so that new evolutionary developments do not emerge in a random fashion but creatively, as relatively integrated wholes from implicate levels of reality.

Bohm's term 'soma-significance' represented his insight that matter and informational processes are completely interwoven throughout existence. As he explains:

> *Consciousness is much more of the implicate order than is matter ... Yet at a deeper level [matter and consciousness] are actually inseparable and interwoven, just as in the computer game the player and the screen are united by participation in common loops. In this view, mind and matter are two aspects of one whole and no more separable than are form and content. Deep down the consciousness of mankind is one. This is a virtual certainty because even in the vacuum matter is one; and if we don't see this, it's because we are blinding ourselves to it.*
>
> —David Bohm and David Peat[47]

However, with Bohm's interest in exploring consciousness throughout nature as a kind of 'proto-consciousness', it is always vis a vis 'inert matter', thus expressing a duality. There is still a separate materiality, even if suffused with a conscious knowing property. While this 'panpsychist' view is an important step in the right direction, yet it is still a duality and different from the view offered this book.

Bohm's scientific and philosophical views were inseparable. In 1959 his wife gave him a book by the Indian philosopher Jiddu Krishnamurti, because she saw in the book the similar concern given to the observer and the observed. Bohm was struck by how his own ideas on quantum mechanics meshed with the philosophical ideas of Krishnamurti. From his many dialogues with Krishnamurti, a renowned philosopher/mystic teaching 'non-duality', Bohm came to a deeper understanding of the role and nature of thought, as well as how theoretical models – as maps of reality – were not the territory itself. Only experiential knowing could provide this.

His exploration of the assumed separation of observer and observed (which was an assumption he was reared with as a scientist) and the potential experience of non-duality, captured his attention for the rest of his life, as expressed in his concept of 'undivided wholeness'. In understanding the limitations of thought, Bohm saw that it was vital to go beyond it, with meditation offering a pathway to do so. Bohm had a realisation of the existence of pure awareness beyond thought, wherein lies the source of all true insight, intelligence and creativity.

> *Meditation would even bring us out of all [the difficulties] we've been talking about ... somewhere we've got to leave thought behind, and come to this emptiness of manifest thought altogether ... In other words, meditation actually transforms the mind. It transforms consciousness.*
>
> —David Bohm[48]

What marks Bohm's metaphysics as unique is that it is centrally informed by his experiential insights, with consciousness at the centre, while preserving a degree of empirical, mathematical, and an informed scientific basis.

> **WEBER:** *What you have been saying sounds like mysticism – that we are grounded in something infinite. How does it differ from what the great mystics have said?*
>
> **BOHM:** *I don't know that there's necessarily any difference."*
>
> **WEBER:** *Is the super-implicate order a euphemism for God?*
>
> **BOHM:** *But we can't grasp that in thought. We're not saying that any of this is another word for God. I would put it another way: people had insight in the past about a form of intelligence that had organised the universe and they personalised it and called it God. A similar insight can prevail again today without personalising it and without calling it a personal God.*
>
> —David Bohm, from *The Essential David Bohm*[49]

Bohm's theories challenged accepted epistemologies in his exploration of universal order, which led him to conceive the 'ontological hypothesis' (the holomovement and the implicate order) offering a unique metaphysics. His breadth of vision connected scientific knowledge and spiritual perception. Bohm's conception of the super-implicate order, a universal, spiritual domain of a wave-like information field beyond space and time, is accessible to all. Bohm offers some sage advice for our transformation:

> *What is needed today is a new surge that is similar to the energy generated during the Renaissance but even deeper and more extensive; the essential need is for a 'loosening' of*

rigidly held intellectual content in the tacit infrastructure of consciousness, along with a 'melting' of the 'hardness of the heart' on the side of feeling. The 'melting' on the emotional side could perhaps be called the beginning of genuine love, while the 'loosening' of thought is the beginning of awakening of creative intelligence. The two necessarily go together.
—David Bohm[50]

Bohm's ideas of an enfolded implicate order, and undivided wholeness are only knowable experientially because they are beyond the epistemic range of phenomenal knowing. A domain of knowing beyond the mind, the senses and conventional notions of space and time, points to how each of us enfolds the 'Totality'. Only by facing our ignorance is this 'inner knowing' revealed.

So, to say that consciousness is non-local, and is spread throughout space enfolding everything, and that ultimately there is only consciousness, are philosophical statements about the truth of Being. It is not science, it is purely experiential, but it is not imagined, because imagination is a product of thought. When we takes the 'final step' in experientially exploring consciousness, the separation of knower and known (the primary assumption underpinning all objectivist knowledge) there is a collapse: one experiences consciousness as everything, a conscious universe, or the truth of Being.

Linking quantum theory to consciousness in an essential way is an idea, one that is neither established nor verified in a scientific sense. Many scientists would argue that it is utterly wrong and unwarranted to make this link, but this also indicates that they have not yet fully explored their own epistemic range as *multi-dimensional* sapiens. Rather, it speaks of the natural gulf between the theoretical/conceptual, and the experiential/actual through non-conceptual awareness. It is easy to understand that if a person had no direct experience of the universality of consciousness, it would be hard for them to seriously consider the reality of this.

Direct experience is the only way possible for us to know a noumenal level of reality, while analytical means give us a picture, as an objectivist model. As the wise hominid we can know these two realities: the intimacy of Being which is our natural state, and simultaneously navigate and use the concept-making gifts of the mind that give us our phenomenal world. Ultimately these realities may appear as separate, and in distinguishing them with language 'they' may seem to represent another form of duality created by the mind, but in truth there is just *one all-encompassing reality in experiential knowing*.

CHAPTER 13

PROBLEMS IN PHYSICS AND PHILOSOPHY

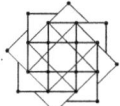

Philosophers, physicists and theologians have perennially grappled with certain problems. Some of these appear unsolvable because they have been conceived in well-trodden dualistic thinking, forming assumptions about: human identity, the mind's capacity, the nature of consciousness in relation to thought, about reality, and about time and existence. Some problems also continue because thought functions within the confines of known models, at times under the illusion of discovering something new, but is merely restating old conclusions, ensuring the problem remains unresolved. In this chapter we explore five time-honoured questions:

Why is there something rather than nothing?
Do we make up our own reality?
What is the nature of consciousness?
What is time?
The anthropic question: is our universe special and are we special?

Why is there something rather than nothing?

In Western civilisation, the Greek philosopher Parmenides first conceived of this question in the fifth century BCE. It was contemplated even earlier in Ancient India, by the authors of the Vedas and later the Upanishads, and we can also find expression of it in Buddhist and Taoist philosophy in Ancient China.

In the early 20th century, the phenomenologist Martin Heidegger suggested that this was the most essential question in philosophy. More recently, physicist Lawrence Krauss tackled this question in his book, *A Universe from Nothing: Why There is Something Rather than Nothing*.

The question begins with an assumption: that 'something' exists in the first place. This something is assumed to be some kind of 'stuff', so in order to address why there is something, we first need to be clear about what meaning is attached to 'something', and whether it is congruent with experience.

Science has its own take on 'something' – it implies the existence of discrete things composed of particles of 'matter' as part of the underlying belief driving science as a form of 'substance philosophy'. However, this becomes problematic because the stories of what constitutes matter from the subatomic particle zoo in the standard model of physics, cannot truly state that there is an 'ultimate something'. Rather it is the forces and fields that give matter its stuff-like property. Stephen Battersby, writing in the November 2008 *New Scientist*, stated that: '*Matter is built on flaky foundations. Physicists have now confirmed that the apparently substantial stuff is actually no more than fluctuations in the quantum vacuum*'. Hence 'matter' as substance is sounding rather hollow.

In astrophysics most of the mass of the universe has not been detected. All we have are the hypothetical substances that are explanations to cover existing mysteries in the way the cosmos behaves, affecting visible matter. Most of the universe is comprised of 'dark matter' (27%), and 'dark energy' (68%), both being hypothesised 'somethings' that affect the visible stuff (stars, galaxies and planets) which is the 5% that we can see.

But consider the small part of the universe that we can see: dive into the atom and we find a nucleus in the centre surrounded by a vast region of space, with 'clouds of electrons' held a considerable distance – relatively speaking – from the nucleus by electrical forces. Pry into the nucleus and there are the protons and neutrons. Delving into the protons and neutrons which are 100,000 times smaller than an atom, reveals quarks of six different varieties. Quarks are point-like particles with no spatial extent. Open up the quarks and at this stage we are at the limits of known reducibility, because the quarks (described in terms of 'flavours' and of being 'up or down') are less like stuff and perhaps more like vibratory signatures.

The protons and neutrons in the nucleus of each atom constitute 99.9% of all the mass around us. Yet the mass of quarks is vanishingly light, compared to a proton or a neutron, which is one thousand times more. So virtually all the mass we perceive is proton or neutron mass, which comes from the 'binding energy' of the quarks produced by the *strong nuclear force*, which is the force that holds the quarks together. A field of virtual particles called gluons, popping into existence and disappearing again, carries the binding property of the strong nuclear force.

Put simply, over 99.9% of all the mass we come into contact with is not the mass of elementary particles, but a mass produced by the strong field. In the standard model, all matter is made of this, and it has every appearance of being something – when particles agglomerate in their trillions to form definable shapes. But it is less of a 'something', and much closer to 'fields of binding energy', than to anything of substance. Does 'something' need redefining? Are fields and energy 'substance'? Can a field constitute 'something'?

These fields of frequency, and the ghostly bits that make up an atom, interact with other atoms through different kinds of 'fields of force', operating across vast regions of space – relatively speaking in the quantum world – to give us a world that does appear stable, solid and substance-like, as 'something'. This 'something' is not really solid though because, as we have seen, it is mostly space with vibrations, and the electromagnetic fields between atoms, which are powerful enough to give the appearance of 'something'. It means that your hand does not just pass through this book, and the book maintains its integrity along with everything else. This is why, when an atom is broken apart in a nuclear explosion, there is a release of tremendous energy – from the binding forces at the atomic level – and these are truly staggering.

Subatomic particles are regularly described as excitations in a field. However, science is still uncomfortable with the concept of 'fields', because it is a concept that calls into question the substantiality of matter. Fields are almost 'something', but never quite. They are detectable, and they exert influence at a distance, and while exerting the influence of being 'something', and things we may regard as 'something', they are not substantial or stuff-like. But it is because fields exert influence on things at a distance, that they too are considered an insubstantial 'something'.

Yet we are left with 'something' being apparent only. In his book *The Particle at the End of the Universe*, Sean Carroll suggests that, despite appearances, there is no separate 'something' in the first place. Of course, it is hard to accept intrinsic nothingness when we bump into a bookcase, when the apparent reality of something-ness sends messages of pain from this collision through our central nervous system. In this instance we are experiencing the interaction of the frequency fields generated by trillions of atoms and their subatomic units comprising our body, its central nervous system, and the furniture, all operating in vast regions of space – sending intelligible messages in our bodies of this collision.

'Matter' is much less something-like or substance-like, the further you look into it. When many of these subatomic 'things' agglomerate, and we perceive an object, it only appears as a tangible something. But when we look deeply into the theoretical map of this domain we have hit the end of the road in our quest for an ultimate substance or 'something'. Because while the bookcase and your body feel and look like 'something', in the story of science, it is a complexity, and much closer to nothing. 'Something' is a mere appearance of.

In an article appearing in the *Scientific American* on 5th March 2019 titled 'Quantum Monism Could Save the Soul of Physics' by Heinrich Pas, outlining the theory of Rutgers University philosopher Jonathan Schaffer – that there is only one substance – a non-separable universe. 'Quantum monism' is a universe expressing a single entangled quantum state as its underlying reality. Here Schaffer echoes the monism of Hegel, and the metaphysics of David Bohm, but it is not substance as conventionally conceived.

In mathematics 'something' is recorded as a number, expressly one. One is something. The West was remarkably slow to pick the mathematical antithesis of something – zero. The first conceptual leap to understand 'nothing' lies in an ancient Indian text, known as the Bakhshali manuscript, in a region near Peshwar in Pakistan. Radiocarbon analysis dates it to as early as the 3rd or 4th century AD. It is inscribed on 70 pieces of birch bark and contains hundreds of zeroes.

But there is a suggestion that it is no accident that zero first finds its place in Ancient India. Here there was already a long developed philosophical tradition, stemming from the Vedas, of contemplating the void, and conceiving of the infinite. In contrast, the Ancient Greeks, with all their sophisticated mathematics, had no symbol for zero. As Hannah Delvin outlines (*The Guardian*, September 14th, 2017): 'The development of zero in mathematics underpins an incredible range of further work, including the notion of infinity, the modern notion of the vacuum in quantum physics, and to some of the deepest questions in cosmology of how the Universe arose, and how it might disappear from existence in some unimaginable future scenario'.

Unsurprisingly, some of the writings of modern physicists read like alchemical texts. For example, physicist Frank Wilczek, (winner of the Nobel Prize for physics in 2004) describes in his book *The Lightness of Being* how matter, as quarks and anti-quarks, bursts out of empty space. A seeming something coming from nothing! We have just asked above, 'How something is the something?' And equally it could be asked, 'How nothing is the nothing, that from which the something, comes?'

Steven Hawking has stated that the Big Bang theoretically could have emerged from nothing. This carried the subtext that the notion of God as a transcendent separate creator is no longer necessary. This is a quite a turnaround because something coming from nothing was regarded as anathema to physics, but not to alchemy. The kind of 'nothing' that is talked about in physics is a world apart from the idealised nothing of Western philosophy or mathematics, which is a completely empty set, or zero.

The 'nothing' of physics is in fact an infinite sea of information and energy, as the 'zero-point energy', or the 'quantum potential', an implicate order, as spoken of by David Bohm. And yet 'nothing' as the universal background field, enfolds all that 'something' could ever be. This appearance of 'something' is the level of reality that we all come to know, because it is intimately tied in to how we come to perceive – using thought and language – a world of 'things' is what becomes our 'something'. In terms of science's model of 'something' this is a paradox of existence. It is 'nothing' but it appears as 'something'. Consciousness expresses itself as a universe.

Like 'something', 'nothing' is easily thought of as being 'thing-like' because as soon as we use thoughts and words to describe 'it', it takes on a substance-like property, simply because it is thought of and named. However, the 'nothing' of current cosmology is informed with the 'zero-point energy' in the intergalactic vacuum of space. Indeed, if the idea of the quantisation of space–time is a useful intuition then there is a structuring of space that informs a dynamic kind of 'nothing'.

Some in the scientific and philosophical community have come to believe that consciousness is ubiquitously placed in the very fabric of space–time. This is known as panpsychism. And it has been since the beginning of this current universe giving us a knowing causality with nothing that is random, as outlined in the 'super-determinism' interpretation of quantum mechanics. This connects to the kind of perfection of reality as articulated by Spinoza.

After we have gradually been conditioned with language from earliest childhood, our conceiving of a world of 'something' becomes truly automatic. 'Everything' becomes a noun and it seems natural to objectify everything, resulting in widespread materialism. Even the religious, in their particular kind of duality, have an underlying belief in materiality. We become skilled at literally 'thinking' our description of the world, which carries with it the embedded assumption that it is made of solid stuff, is unassailably correct. This appearance, we assume, is real; it is our 'common sense'. However, this colonisation of mind is so subtle that it mostly escapes our attention because it is all taken as given.

In our current scientific conceiving of 'nothing' where there may be no particulate matter – as in the great voids of space – these voids are still informed with fields. So, from nothing to almost 'something', or a different kind of 'nothing', seems perfectly viable. In the realm of the phenomenal, the boundaries between 'something' and 'nothing' have become blurred considerably. Now it seems an easier leap to comprehend the viability of an infinite series of universes emerging from this 'no-thingness' with explosive speed and heat to plasma and then into particulate matter, eventually forming stars, planets and galaxies in the evolution of the phenomenal of almost 'something', then only to fade again after a given epoch of time back into the 'no-thing'.

In this model our universe is part of an infinite series, just as the creation myth conceived in Ancient Indian cosmology, with the endless cycle of in-breaths and the out-breaths of 'Brahmin', portrays the image of cyclic creation and destruction. But the continuing ground of reality behind this cyclic process, is consciousness, which is neither born, nor destroyed.

We have discussed musing on a phenomenal world, but how do we apprehend 'something' and 'nothing' experientially? The 'no-thingness' or 'emptiness', spoken of in Buddhist and Taoist philosophy, is quite different from a mathematical zero, because the latter is purely conceptualised, while the former is only accessible experientially. The profundity of 'no-thingness' is an experience of consciousness arising when the mind is free of thought – free of 'something' – because thoughts are analogously the 'somethings' of consciousness. In the absence of thought 'no-thingness' is as the ground of Being. This corresponds with the 'energy-impregnated nothingness' of the quantum vacuum of physics and cosmology.

What is clear is that we can know the universe in a way different from the phenomenal. This only happens by releasing our attachment to the 'something-ness' of thought, which is our 'doing' of the world, the world of phenomena and their objects. But to let this go and to see through a clear lens is to step from the relative to the absolute: the numinous reality of Being and nothingness. In this there is no substance, there is only consciousness, which is incomprehensible to the finite mind.

What is reality?

With what is commonly referred to as reality, we become part of an agreement as we learn a language, and identify everything under the sun. It is a consensually agreed reality-construct that we inherit and then, perhaps, slightly modify. With this we also cultivate certain attachments, emotional qualities and beliefs, which are also constructs made of thought. An objectified reality that is developed in the process of doing science is also a construct, but it is a specifically rational one. It is also consensual, open to revision, and hence progressive. But it is nontheless something that we invent.

Generally, the realities we inhabit are constructed by our conceptualising. All realities that we construct with our thinking are based in a consensus agreement in the language we share. These realities can be rational, or irrational (alternative facts, fake news, conspiracy theories), or based in belief, such as the world was constructed in 7 days. Fabrications like this are a reality for some, but they have no basis in fact and so without truth value. Some realities that people experience may be a result of mental illness, which are also a reality (and can serve a purpose to assuage a fragmented sense of identity), at least to the person experiencing them. And, it may well be therapeutically unhelpful to confront them by forcefully imposing an 'objectified version of reality'.

Realities that are based in facts can be corroborated (that dinosaurs roamed the earth 60 million years ago), or if they are intrinsically unreal this is because they suffer the distortion of belief and are in factual deficit. These conceptual realities, real or unreal, are based in thought and arise from the past, because thought itself is based in the past. Our sensual experience of the phenomenal world is also based in the past. For we receive visual and sound datum travelling respectively at the speed of light, and the speed of sound, both of which take time to be received and then interpreted, via our central nervous system.

But there is a level of reality that is not constructed, not produced by mind or language, not part of the reality of objectivist science and is neither rational or irrational: the numinous reality of Being. To experience this the mind is uninvited, because it only occurs in the eternity of now.

The epistemic status (that it is superior or the only true source of knowledge) given to objectivist models of reality is misplaced. All our objectivist scientific models of reality are subjective because people, not robots, produce them. They are subjective because we have created them, they are our cultural artefacts, and they are our consensual agreements of conceptual constructs. Models of reality are relative, because they are subject to ongoing modifications.

Science is a progressive kind of knowledge – yet this fact seems to be regularly lost; we often see models being regarded as reality itself. Our tendency is to anthropomorphise nature in all our models of reality, yet we fail to recognise that we do it. We cannot escape their anthropocentric nature because they are artefacts of human thought. And because of this they are totally subjective 'models of reality' and they have no more than a relative truth-value. We are living in illusion if we regard them as more than this. Among scientists, what seems to be elusive is the insight that a model of reality is just a model, and a model is not the actual.

This form of reality is a kind of 'agreement' because it is a shared description of what our particular culture deems is real. This agreement collapses only when we deeply suspend our 'doing' in the world, which we create by our thinking. This constructed reality is challenged when the knower no longer believes herself to be separate from the known. Commonly, people experience this as a veil having been lifted, and they have awoken from the slumber of conditioned perception to a numinous state. It is a revolution in perception, experienced by mystics and sages across the ages, yet it is not something transcendent, it is immanent.

Most of us don't experience a reality of awakened consciousness in a seamless universe. Our sense of reality comes from how deeply we do experience consciousness. Most of us, including scientists, believe that thinking is equivalent to consciousness. This belief alone will keep us at the surface expression of consciousness – thought – but without a deeper understanding of what consciousness is. For most of us stay on the surface of consciousness because we identify with heavily ingrained narratives of what reality is. Sometimes we construct 'unique' and troubling narratives, which may be indicative of mental illness. This is symptomatic of a 'disturbed self' attempting to navigate an environment perceived as hostile. Sometimes this hostility may well be true. It is our collective mind-mapping that ensures a very basic form of shared reality constructed by the mind but, like a collective dream, it is only relatively real, and not the deeper truth.

In a mind that knows silence, reality is not a conceptual construct, it is experiencing prior to thought. It is pure awareness or consciousness, where there is no 'making up' of reality because it is not a model. Reality is as it is, and not just what our thinking makes it.

There is no separate consciousness that can verify the separate existence of anything, because nothing in and of itself has independent existence. This is because consciousness is inclusive of everything: there is only one consciousness, not many, as we assume. Consciousness can verify itself, for example, when we are asked if we exist. And, in responding 'yes', we are signifying a response of the One consciousness manifesting as ourself, the particular.

Consciousness is the knowing property of an intelligent universe, but not a universe of 'matter', for this has been a myth of duality. 'Matter' is an interpretation as a process of objectifying the thingness of everything. It is an interpretation arising from conditioned perception.

Our sense of what is real, what we view as reality, is a product of consciousness. There is no reality without consciousness. Consciousness gives rise to reality whether this reality is constructed by thought, or with a numinous reality beyond thought, being a reality arising from direct perception.

Consciousness is our experience of reality. If we are only informed by what we think and believe, we exist only in the surface of consciousness, experienced as phenomenal reality. It is a *conditioned reality* whether it is created by rational scientific thinking, or in structures of belief and the imagination. But to see through a lens unconditioned by thought is to experience from the hidden depths of consciousness, and to know the real.

What is consciousness? Is there a 'consciousness' problem?

Looking for consciousness in the brain is like looking inside a radio for the announcer.

—Nassim Haramein[52]

Before more recent discoveries in the field of neuroscience, it was believed that the brain stopped developing after about eighteen years of age, but researchers have now discovered that the brain itself has plasticity: the brain continues developing throughout life, can continue to grow new cells, and indeed changes itself even at the level of DNA. These changes are stimulated by environmental learning, and are in turn encoded and passed on, by changing the way the DNA works, to the next generation. In this way we each carry the whispers of our ancestors' experience, known as 'transgenerational epigenetic inheritance'. But while this informs us about the brain, DNA and the transmission of information, it does not really tell us anything about the nature of consciousness.

The following question has become one of *the* questions to ask: is consciousness itself some kind of special stuff that is 'separate' from matter? From this one question spring many more: how has consciousness come into existence? Or, has it always been in existence? Does the old split between mind/body and matter/spirit have any reality, or is it a conceptually-driven dead end? Do the physical processes of your brain create consciousness? Does your self-awareness, your thoughts, feelings and experiences - your subjective experience - signify that consciousness is separate?

This last question is a common belief among scientists, and notice how there is an ontological assumption in it: that it is your *brain* that creates consciousness. This is similar to the assumption that the universe creates consciousness (eventually) in biological systems, like us. Many consider this to be *the hard problem* confronting science, because there is nothing about the physical activity of the constituent particles of your brain – cellular, molecular, subatomic, et cetera – from which the qualities of subjective experience can be directly derived.

At a subatomic level, whether it is brain or rock; it is all just quantum particles and fields. The rock is a something in the universal field of consciousness, exhibiting the characteristic unconsciousness found in rocks. We, with our specialised brain and nervous system existing in the universal field of consciousness, characteristically for human beings exhibits, relatively, a 'conscious knowing' quality. Unlike the rock we have a specialised tuning instrument (brain and nervous system) for this knowing quality to potentiate, so we can amplify our knowing and can be aware of being aware.

But the view here is that consciousness does not just magically appear as an emergent property of complex biological nervous systems. Rather it is the complex nervous system that is emergent from consciousness, because in nature there is nowhere consciousness is not, and there was never a time when it was not. However, it is the particular concentration of the quality of consciousness in humans that makes us self-reflective. And the last time I checked, a rock is definitely not as conscious as we are, even though it is part of the ocean of consciousness: the universe as Being.

Below are the three basic theoretical positions about the place of consciousness in the universe: materialism, dualism and idealistic monism (considered the opposite of dualism), and 'experiential non-duality' which is not theoretical.

Materialism

Materialism is a 'substance-driven' philosophy. It has its roots in the philosophers from Thales in Ancient Greece, beginning with Anaxagoras (500–428 BCE) before finding voice in the Atomists, Lucretius and Democritus. It uses the methodology of reductionism, viewing that everything is constituted from tiny, inert constituents: atoms. It also maintains that 'matter' is without organising intelligence. The philosophical ideology that developed from this, as articulated by its most prominent exponent, Daniel Dennett, believes that mind is an illusion, and is reduced to the biochemistry of the brain. So a person's experience of consciousness is an illusion created by the brain's biochemistry. Thinking is just brain activity as the firing of neurons and experience is an illusion. As a result, the subjective 'you' is also an illusion.

Yet materialism happens in a mind, blind to its own knowing. For extreme materialists their ideological position is that there is no consciousness. Consciousness and mind are fantasies. Yet the materialist fails to address what knowing is. This is because it is consciousness that knows, not thought, not sensation, not feeling and not the brain. Consciousness knows thought, knows feeling, knows sensation, knows experience, knows its sense of reality, and in us, knows itself. But to dismiss consciousness as materialists do by reducing it to the brains' biochemistry and equating it with brain patterning and neuronal firing, explains very little.

The materialist stance speaks of ignorance, as a form of cultural blindness, because it fails to recognise that it is itself a cultural artefact with historical roots, and built on a belief in the veracity of an extreme form of objectivism. Despite a belief in its own truth-value, it is a form of ideological conditioning. Yet somehow those who hold this position are often quick to proclaim the experiences of others as illusion or fantasy, because they are blinded to the fantastical nature of their own rigid ideological position.

In materialism the universe is viewed as essentially mechanistic and separate, with an underlying belief in a random ontology of how our universe comes into being. In a universe that is multidimensional it suffers from a poverty of dimensions in being only mono-dimensional. This view leads to an externalised 'sense of identity' because 'you' have become completely objectivised.

Materialism holds that you are a biological system that won't suffer from the illusion of consciousness if you are a materialist. As a materialist your identity is dependent on, and subject to modifications from new studies by a body of experts — scientists, particularly neuroscientists — who are engaged in developing an objectivist explanation of the human being. It is legitimised by a belief in the authority of a certain type of constructed knowledge and anything outside this (such as experiential knowing or knowing beyond thought) being deemed not legitimate. Things experiential do not carry the same truth-value as the sanctioned interpretation of authorised kinds of experts, or data from the laboratory.

In this approach there is only room for a belief in materialist types of thought-constructed models, so much so that there is no longer a capacity to really *see* beyond the limitations of its own framework. Without adherence to belief in its own 'modus operandi' as the only true way that we can have knowledge of ourselves, everything else is considered invalid. In this philosophy 'you' and 'I' are objects, as bodies (the mind or consciousness does not exist) amongst a universe of disconnected objects.

In looking for a reductive, materialist solution, scientists search for physical measurements to account for consciousness being a 'purely physical process'. They do this without any appeal to direct experience because of being unaware of the value of this. And they are conditioned to distrust their own conscious agency. In doing this, materialists have escaped 'consciousness' by accepting as primary evidence that which is, in fact, secondary. That is, they posit that objectivist studies on the brain are primary, confirming that there is no consciousness, just brain chatter as electrical and chemical firing of neurons, et cetera. Experiential knowing is deemed illegitimate and regarded as fantasy. In this they suffer the illusion by regarding their objectivist account as though, by weight of scientific authority, it confers some kind of specially elevated status, enough to dismiss the prospect of direct experience and consciousness altogether.

Without knowing, materialists have trapped themselves in a 'loop of thought' of their own invention. It is an isolated, and dissociative philosophical ideology within a theoretically disconnected universe. Believing in a mechanistic universe leaves a materialist bereft of a 'meaningful living universe'.

In the epistemic of materialism there is no possibility of direct perception of reality, nor a direct knowing of consciousness. Materialism's tight theoretical loop ensures that consciousness is ignored rather than examined, but in doing this it resolves nothing, only maintaining its rigid program. In this way it is similar to rigid loops of belief held by the religious.

When consciousness is seen as an illusion, there can be no true intimacy with anything, be it plant, human, mineral, animal or ourselves. There can only be a theoretical intimacy, removed by thought – *you* as the thinker, thinking about the *object*, which is in fact *our stored knowledge of it*. In this there is no intimacy of Being, because the lens through which we see is 'theory laden'. Everything can only be known through the 'correct theoretical knowledge' using thought in a deductive process, or reasoned argument.

The difficulty in challenging such limiting beliefs lies in their resulting from such a closed theoretical position that prevents experiencing beyond thinking. It stultifies what is viewed as possible by circumscribing what we are 'permitted' to experience. (This is similar to how priestly authorities hold a tight rein on their own minds and those of their congregations, in religious orthodoxies, in order to ensure that it is only they who have sanctioned experiences, and thoughts.) This was well illustrated in a documentary about a materialist scientist doing anthropological research, and taking part in a traditional *Ayahuasca* ceremony in the Amazon basin, under the guidance of a shaman. The experience of this potent psychotropic jolted the scientist's perception to a point where he realised how he had become colonised by a sophisticated structure of thought, which he 'saw' was only culturally relative: nothing more than a belief preventing deeper knowing of a living numinous universe.

I am not advocating the use of psychedelic plant substances, but they can play a role in dislodging rigid attachments to conditioned mindsets. Their therapeutic value in 're-setting' the nervous system, for example in treating chronic depression, is currently being properly researched, as outlined in *New Scientist*, 25th November 2017.

Dualism

In his book, *The Patterning Instinct*, Jeremy Lent outlines how the origins of dualistic thinking about the universe have their roots in Aryan culture. The Proto Indo-European nomadic horsemen (the Achaens) moving southwest into Greece in approximately 1500 BCE brought with them a different mindset from the existing shamanic hunter-gatherers of pre-Ancient Greece, who had a more dynamic, process-oriented view of nature. As Lent outlines, this mindset articulated 'fixed natural law, a binary conception of right and wrong, and a dualistic universe'. These patterns of thinking were to profoundly influence the Greek philosophers. This 'golden age' cultivated a new level of sophistication in thought, with a capacity for abstraction, generalisation, and a cosmology which was a Oneness with the organising intelligence of the Logos governing the impurity of earthly matter and sensory experience. But this dualistic attitude was increased with the advent of Christianity which supplanted the overarching Oneness of the Greeks and the possibility to know the Logos as the Self, with a pernicious form of dualism. It has continued through the Christian era deeply informing Western culture to this day. Its mindset has had significantly damaging consequences for us, and the living systems on this planet.

Dualism, referring to the dichotomy of matter and mind, was also famously articulated by French philosopher Rene Descartes in the 16th century. His theory, known as Cartesian Dualism, states that inert matter can only be known by the senses (*res extensa*) and by the mind by itself (*res cogitans*). On the one hand, the inert matter of materialism is present, with the other is mind (in the sense that Descartes uses mind as being equivalent to thought rather than consciousness in the expanded sense) found particularly in human beings and, to a lesser extent, in other animals.

The belief in dualism generally is that mind (thought/consciousness) is an 'epiphenomenon' of matter, a by-product of brain activity. Thus, human beings are considered to be made of matter (atoms constituting cells, organs and the body) but also having a higher mind or consciousness seen as a mysterious 'event-process'.

The consciousness of dualism is regarded as some kind of emergent 'special stuff' confined to the human brain. Other animals have a more rudimentary repository of this special stuff, but are not capable of self-reflection. Matter is regarded as separate and devoid of consciousness, unless found in the special kind of matter within nervous systems, and especially in the brains of animals like us. The problem is that the atoms of brains are not special, they are the same as in a piece of concrete! It is likely that many more people hold this dualist view than hold the more extreme materialist one above, where consciousness is viewed as an illusion and does not exist.

Here, consciousness as an 'emergent' property is unlike other emergent properties in nature, which are deduced directly from the physical processes from which they emerge; for example, the liquid property of water emerging from the combination of two gases, hydrogen and oxygen. Yes, we can measure the activity of the brain, and we can note the corresponding subjective experiences, but these phenomena are irreconcilable, leading to nagging conceptual difficulties that cannot be reconciled, because there is a serious gap in evidence. The approach of separating mind and matter, the subjective and objective, leads us down a conceptual dead end, a bottomless rabbit hole. Ultimately 'mind' and 'matter' cannot translate to each other because they are mutually exclusive in how they are conceived, with matter being on the shakier ground of the two.

Those seeking dualistic solutions will continue to look for them in the relationship between a physical process and the experiential knowing of consciousness, and then attempt to explain how and why the two are associated. In gambling language, dualists are trying to have a bet each way. But inevitably they stumble upon the same intransigent issue: the belief that the atoms in the brain miraculously generate consciousness. They struggle to make a case for the special experience of *being conscious* that cannot adequately be explained by materialist reduction, yet it somehow magically occurs in so-called 'inert matter'.

The dualistic approach, in a way, is more troubled than the materialist one, which simply denies consciousness. With the dualist position the question of consciousness is essentially unanswerable, because the measurements are not actually measuring consciousness. For instance, looking at a brain scan to detect consciousness can be likened to the difference between looking at a map of a place versus actually being there. The map is not the territory. Science in its objectivist manner, elevates the authority of the map over the territory.

However, we must *be* in the territory to truly *know* the territory. An understanding of the nature of consciousness can only come through the direct experiencing of it. In this we need no instruments of measurement, and no external authority, nor a degree in neuroscience or psychology, because we are all living exponents of consciousness and potentially all experts.

> *Not only is there nothing remotely like a flowchart in some neuroscience textbook, displaying a sequence of discrete material steps or processes, describing a smooth transition from physical processes to you; "the hard problem" is one of the very few problems in science, for which there is not even the beginnings of an inkling, of a clue, of what a progression of causality from meat to self-awareness might look like. Forget theories, forget hypotheses, after over one hundred years of research, attempts to think about and then elucidate explanatory ideas about this progression of causality amount to vague notions that often reveal more about the limitations of language than "the hard problem" itself.*
> —Robert H. Clark[53]

Consider this: rather than consciousness being an emergent phenomenon from matter (the brain and nervous system) what the mind interprets as 'matter' is an emergent – but not separate – phenomenon of consciousness. 'Matter', as we interpret it, is consciousness. And wherever we go, whether we are walking in a city or in a beautiful country landscape, or visiting a distant land, we are ever part of a universal 'field of knowing'. Experiencing consciousness is not driven by ideas, as something transcendental; it is immanent in resting in awareness.

Idealism

There are many different strains of idealism, from transcendental idealism, subjective idealism and objective idealism to absolute idealism. There is a general theme in idealism, whether of Hindu or Greek origin, that runs through both cultural streams – that it is of a transcendent quality. Transcendentalism gives priority to ideals, values, realising a godhead, reaching a lofty realm of pure ideas or standards of perfection. There is a pining for an unreachable elevation.

Idealism is a philosophical view attributing oneness or singleness to existence, where mind or consciousness is a precursor to matter. Unlike materialism and dualism, consciousness is primary. Anaximander, Heraclitus and Parmenides, in the pre-Socratic era, were the first to speak of reality and the cosmos as being undivided. This was further articulated by Plato and later by Plotonis in the 3rd century CE, six centuries after Plato called Neoplatonism, a philosophy where everything is connected in *The One*.

> *For Plotinus, the first principle of reality is 'the One', an utterly simple, ineffable, unknowable subsistence which is both the creative source and the teleological end of all existing things.*
> —Wikipedia

Idealistic monism denies the existence of a duality such as matter and mind. It is the most consistent and theoretically untroubled of the three models. Idealistic monism, as a philosophical position, postulates that all existence is 'one', and is the opposite of dualism, maintaining that everything is 'mind', as a form of absolute idealism, contrasted with the duality of mind and matter in dualism. This philosophical point of view has continued in Western thinking from Parmenides, amongst others, in Pre-Socratic times to, most notably, Spinoza, Hegel and Schopenhauer. It fell out of favour with the rise of the rigid materialistic ideology culminating in the ideological extreme of positivism in the early 20th century.

Idealism regards everything as having some level of rudimentary consciousness and fundamental organising and patterning intelligence, encompassing all that is. It holds that there is no inert, separate stuff called matter; there is only consciousness exhibiting different features. Within this are gradations from the least conscious (inanimate) to the more evolved 'self-knowing' humans. Human thought and emotion are particular manifestations of consciousness. It has been speculated by some that this is implied in quantum theory (most notably in the 'hidden variable' theories of David Bohm and in super-determinism) and in the 'quantum monism' of Jonathan Schaffer, with a universe of a single patterning, self-organising substance, similar to the infinite substance of Spinoza, pointing to the universe being pan-psychic in nature.

Monistic idealism is not a position that could be backed by science. Empirically, there are no experiments that can definitively demonstrate that consciousness is in everything, and that everything is in consciousness. The idea that consciousness creates the universe is not a falsifiable theory (super-determinism is in the same boat). So there can be no claim for it having scientific status, but this does not alter the potential for it having status in truth. Falsifiability in science does not automatically confer truth, it simply adds confirmation to theory, but it can never prove anything. Intuitively it makes sense and corresponds to a particular experiential understanding of consciousness. It also solves some of the seemingly insolvable problems that dualist models of the 'emergence' of consciousness face.

In the *non-materialist* solution, consciousness is seen as non-physical and non-measurable, even if it may appear to be closely, but not always, associated with physical processes. Furthermore, in a *non-reductive* solution, consciousness is used as a basic part of the explanation. The monist view can overcome the so-called 'hard problem' of consciousness, which is to explain why the same electrons and quarks that make up a piece of concrete, can experience feeling, thinking and insight in another form – the human body.

> *I propose that the obvious thing to do is to take consciousness itself as the ontological primitive ... explain every other aspect of reality in terms of excitations of consciousness, which obey certain patterns and regularities amenable to modelling. Under this view, the ground of all reality is an impersonal flow of subjective experiences that I metaphorically describe as a stream, while our personal awareness is simply a localization of this flow – a whirlpool in the stream. It is this localization that leads to the illusion of personal identity. Moreover, it is your body–brain system that is in consciousness, not consciousness in your body–brain system. Furthermore, the body–brain system is merely the image of that process of localisation in the stream of consciousness, like a whirlpool is the image of a process of localisation in a stream of water. For exactly the same reason that a whirlpool doesn't generate water, your brain doesn't generate consciousness. Yet, because the image of a process carries valid information about the process – just*

like the colours of flames carry valid information about the microscopic view of combustion – brain activity correlates tightly with subjective experience.
—Bernado Kastrup[54]

The hard problem really is an impossible one for dualists, because it is implicitly tied to the assumption that there is something called mind and something called matter and they are separate – that the brain generates consciousness. (Or for the materialists, that consciousness is an illusion.) But as Kastrup explains 'it is consciousness that generates your brain and the entire universe'.

Research in neuroscience must continue because there is so much to discover about the brain and the nervous system. But the theoretical modelling and mapping of these phenomena will never reveal the actual nature of consciousness. Only we can do that by *living a deeply examined life*. Robert Clarke gives us a useful piece of advice in regard to the assumptions conflating 'consciousness as thought activity and the brain' and the status we might give it:

> *That is the impossible gap that materialist scientists and philosophers must fill, in order to explain how your brain and you can be the same thing. I urge you to remember this the next time you read about the latest experiment purporting to show how scientists are 'unravelling the mystery of consciousness' or other such public relations hyperbole.*
> —Robert H. Clark[55]

A vibrational theory of consciousness

* Panpsychism is an ancient view gaining currency in philosophical and scientific circles. It recognises that there is an intelligent aspect to matter from all scales. From the subatomic scale through to the scale of complex biosystems such as humans. The *Scientific American* posted

on December 5th 2018 an article entitled, 'The Hippies Were Right: It's All About Vibrations, Man!' by Tam Hunt, a lawyer and philosopher explaining a new theory of consciousness, developed with his colleague, psychologist Jonathan Schooler, at the University of California.

The oscillatory frequencies of all matter particles and their associated fields has always been a sticking point for substance-oriented physics and philosophy. Yet it is the functioning of these fields that gives matter, on its macroscopic scale, its sense of solidity and phenomenological integrity. Frequencies are generated in everything, from the tiniest subatomic to the largest and residing, in the nature and structure of these waveforms, is information. The microwave background radiation, for example, is a patterned vibration encoding the origins of the universe.

The idea is that all matter has frequencies that enfold information and that, when scaled up through organisational complexity, molecularly and cellularly, there is a higher order of consciousness that manifests, such as in primates. In varying degrees this is across all biological systems and, to a certain degree, in non-biological systems, which exhibit self-organisation and an ability to sync up. This self-organising ability of moving in sync occurs, for example, in flocks of birds in flight, bee and ant behaviour, schools of fish, in humans, and even in trees. Thermodynamic systems also produce collective behaviour; for example, during crystallisation the components will simply 'organise themselves', creating specific order. All these examples demonstrate matter acting intelligently and collectively, with an easily perceived higher intelligent functioning.

In humans, synching phenomena occurs in brain-wave frequencies detected by an EEG machine. Brain-waves carry information signifying a correlation with particular states of consciousness. For instance, pronounced excitations of the brain trigger EEG waves in the gamma domain, a frequency range of up to 100 hertz. The everyday world appears in the beta range, which is between 12 and 30 hertz. In the lower frequency alpha range of 7.5 to 12 hertz, are the more deeply relaxed and meditative states of consciousness. More mystical experiences seem to occur mainly in the even lower band of theta, between 4 and 7 hertz. Deeper still is the delta range 0.1 to 3hz resting in unattached awareness, healing and sleep.

But x-ray frequencies pass right through the seeming solidity of our bodies. There are frequency changes in our brains detectable by an EEG machine as the brain starts syncing at an alpha rhythm, for example, a rhythm associated with non-attachment to thought, bringing a deeper state of calm. Conversely, states of excitation or emotional worry exhibit signature frequencies. When these frequencies are maintained through regular mindfulness practice there are changes to brain structures (increased synaptic networking, et cetera) that would indicate that the brain is regenerating, exercising its neuro-plastic abilities. Indicating that we are potentially getting smarter and younger.

Tam Hunt's 'vibrational consciousness theory' maintains that consciousness is ubiquitous throughout nature – panpsychism. Consciousness manifesting in vibrational frequency is a challenge to the standard substance-oriented approach in science. It does however, offer new avenues for investigation in neuroscience, and in therapeutic approaches for mental disequilibrium and trauma (neurofeedback, mindfulness) with devices to enhance synchrony in order to access and heal deep stresses in a vibrational manner, rather than using 'top down' 'thought-based' cognitive therapies.

Anyone who has seriously engaged in meditative practice will intuitively understand the vibrational view of consciousness. A vibrational view is a window into a world that can remain undetected by those engaged purely in the busy cognitive functioning of the brain, analytical thinking, and the process of identifying with their thoughts and assuming that it is only thought that signifies consciousness.

Experiential non-duality

Note that with panpsychism there is still a duality – matter with interpenetrating consciousness. The philosophical position of idealism stands opposite to the confused thinking of dualism, and is diametric to the rigid denial of consciousness seen in materialism: there is only one way to understand consciousness beyond the theoretical. Materialism is a purely theoretical position; dualism is significantly more experiential; idealism is mostly experiential, but because they are all in varying degrees theoretical, they can be accepted or rejected intellectually, and believed or disbelieved.

There is nothing that can be completely resolved through clever argument or belief, in relation to consciousness, nor in the process of identifying with a particular philosophical ideology, because our assessing, through this particular lens, is constructed by thought, with all its biases and assumptions. Theoretical positions are all arguments, and thus are subject to the scrutiny of thought as the arbiter of truth. Our judgments in this matter, as in all matters, result from whether we are still informed by any conditioning that we remain unaware of.

The reality is that consciousness poses no problem at all – there is no 'hard problem' – unless we have already bought into the assumption that we, the observers, are separate from the observed. The only way out is through 'bootstrapping' ourselves with an epistemic that is beyond the dualistic nature of thought, with no assumptions, and hence beyond the theoretical.

The term 'experiential non-duality' it is not offered as another philosophical ideology, but as a way of directly experiencing non-separate Being. Consciousness is the origin of everything; it is everywhere, every-when, and everything. The universe is self-organised consciousness-Being. Consciousness is Being. But while consciousness is the basis of everything, only certain beings can knowingly experience this. A rock cannot. A sloth can experience, but it cannot know that it knows. Humans can know that they know, and in the process of awakening experientially, the knower and the known are experienced as one.

Perceiving unity cannot be achieved through thought, clever argument, or science. Knowing this is to know our identity prior to thought. This understanding is across all cultures; in fact it is not cultural at all. It is the source of the various mystical traditions, and the animism of Indigenous cultures. While any idea can be held as a belief, and this includes 'non-duality', because just believing in it as a concept, means there is no actual experience of oneness.

When consciousness is understood as the ground of Being, there is no hard problem. While it is a problem for some conceptual schemes, particularly materialism and dualism, experientially, it is rather *the universal solution* to problems, because it is our level of understanding of the nature of consciousness which informs our experience of reality and how we live in the world.

Science and the nature of time

Below is a standard definition of what we commonly refer to as time:

> *Time is the indefinite continued progress of existence and events that occur in apparently irreversible succession from the past through the present to the future. Time is a component quantity of various measurements used to sequence events, to compare the duration of events or the intervals between them, and to quantify rates of change of quantities in material reality or in the conscious experience. Time is often referred to as the fourth dimension, along with the three spatial dimensions.*
>
> —Wikipedia[56]

The invention and construction of time using the mind, exemplifies thinking as a 'tool-making function' for Sapiens. Time is a product of thought, and thus its truth is relative. It has a particular kind of reality – to ensure that we run to catch the bus – but one that is not absolute. Few of us really experience the absolute or timeless but we may have episodic glimpses of it. Yet on the other hand, all of us know about time because it is a consensus agreement and, as a product of thought, we have to conceive of it, measure it, and think about it.

We are 'hard-wired' in our consciousness to experience a world, through all our senses, of both form and movement. And it is this movement that we can measure which creates the existence of time. Through our empirical checking, we locate the origin of sounds in the environment. The colour and shape of objects and phenomena are detected as photons of light travel from the environment to reach our corneas. Sound vibrations and particles of light take different times to reach our sense organs, according to their different velocities, for us to experience them.

Along with this interaction with the environment, is the functioning of memory, and the further ability to predict. For instance, we can predict, and hopefully dodge the trajectory of a falling branch, alerted by the loud cracking above us, before it hits us on the head. Hearing is a necessary part of our survival equipment. Our memory function will also remind us to be wary the next time it is very windy when we are near the same or other trees. Memory is essential to our knowledge of time, and for survival.

Time is our way of measuring: we witness the body change through time. We remember and mark natural events by the movement of stars, moon and planets, cycles of seasons, the tracking the movement of herds and the migration of birds. We give names to time's units of measurement: years, months, weeks, days, hours, minutes, seconds and nanoseconds. And, compared with other animals, our notion of time is a conscious, abstract, consensually-agreed measuring process; one that has developed with ever-precise instrumentation. It is an essential part of an objectivist description of nature.

Today we can measure deep time with the passage of light from distant galaxies registering through the lens of a space observatory, or the evolving epochs of our solar system; or, in micro-time, the fairly exact length of a second, using the great precision of an atomic caesium clock calibrated at the quantum level.

Time is essential to science as it is probably the quantity that is measured most; for example, the ring growth in trees, the extinction of species in palaeontology, the atomic signatures found in the structure of rocks and crystals indicating magnetic history of the earth, and the carbon dated remnants of lost civilisations. All these signatures provide evidence of previous geological events, animal and plant species and the migratory history of our ancestors.

The caesium clock, as mentioned above, measures a natural vibration inside a caesium atom. Within the clock, lasers push together a ball of ten million caesium atoms and cool them to near absolute zero (which helps reduce noise). This ball of caesium atoms is tossed up in a three-foot chamber, passing through a microwave beam. The microwave beam kicks some of the caesium atoms up into a higher energy state, which causes them to emit light. In 1967, scientists defined one second as equivalent to the time it takes a caesium atom to move 9,192,631,770 times between two particular energy levels. It is not perfectly accurate because caesium atoms actually experience time differently at the top of the three-foot chamber and at the bottom, due to the minutely different gravitational effects of the massive object (our earth) on which the clock is sitting. As an extremely precise measuring device it records this slight difference, making its time-keeping ever so slightly inaccurate. Nevertheless, it is accurate to one second in 300 million years.

In 2018 the most accurate clock to date was found in a laboratory at the University of Colorado, Boulder, with physics professor Jun Ye using a metaphorical strontium 87 pendulum. Strontium 87's atoms tick at femtoseconds, which is 1 million billion times per second. This version of atomic clock has thousands of supercooled strontium atoms arranged in a three-dimensional lattice. A red laser tuned to strontium's frequency prods the strontium atoms to start vibrating and then, using an optical frequency comb, reads out that vibration. It has such precision that its accuracy would be just one second discrepancy over 13.7 billion years – the life of our current universe.

By checking hundreds of thousands of temperature measurements across the planet over the years, we have compelling evidence of climate change caused by human activity over the last three hundred years. This evidence is now so compelling as to be unequivocal, and is clearly enough to inform government policies that would, through immediate action, mitigate further human-made emissions.

In the deeper time of the earth, from the analysis of the north–south alignment of ferrous ions embedded in rocks in the earth's crust, we can read the history of the magnetic poles' shifting throughout the earth's history. This can help us to uncover the pattern of these shifts and plan how humans might adapt to meet these profound changes when they happen.

In physics we can speculate about the first three seconds after the super dynamic beginning expansion of the universe (conjectured to have happened at trillions of times the speed of light). And we can further detect the reverberation of the background microwave radiation left over from the inception of the current universe. In fact, to look at the distant galaxy clusters through a light telescope is to look far back in time, as we calculate how long the photons from these distant objects took to reach us. The furthest object so far measured took 13.2 billion years to reach us – which is far older than our solar system (the sun and earth being about 5 and 4.5 billion years old respectively).

Despite these impressive measurements, we should bear in mind that all of this information is secondary evidence, inferred by using some exceptionally clever thinking, using mathematics and very sophisticated equipment (such as telescopes and sophisticated computers). It is part of our objectivist modelling of the universe.

From this perspective, in the journey of science every square cubit of space in nature is potentially a memory code, storing information for a scientist to analyse and decipher. But while this is rational and empirical, none of this information is *directly known*. This does not downgrade its importance. It merely places it in the epistemological sense, as what we can know and what kind of knowledge it is. Is it empirical or intuitive? And how do we know it? Is it through thought (rational) and the senses (empirical) or through perceiving directly.

Importantly empirical knowing is the only way time can be known. Our sense of time is dependent on consensus assumptions: that the 'time keeper' is separate from the 'act of measuring' (a clock, the turning of the earth, the vibration of strontium atoms); that there is an independent time that exists; and of how time is quantified, so that it has a workable place in all scientific activity and our experience of phenomenal reality. Time is not a thing or a substance, nor even an energy. Rather it is abstract, as a frame of reference associated with movement, particularly of light, and is an essential feature of our objectivist modelling.

In science there is a conception of time known as the 'block universe', in which time is seen with past, present and future all viewed as being equally real. Doug Evans, writing for *New Scientist*, stated that this notion of the 'block universe' is the most widely held view of time amongst scientists today. The block universe holds that all of space–time is contained within an unchanging, four-dimensional block. To consider time, we are asked to adopt an abstract vantage point outside of the block and to imagine that if 'now' was marked in the block it would be conceptually equivalent to any other spot. In the block universe, there is no special status given to 'now', and no possible objective definition of 'now' either. However, this is just one definition of time amongst many in science.

One physicist who articulates a deeper understanding of 'now' in his understanding of time is Julian Barbour. In his book, *The End of Time*, Barbour postulates that the block universe idea is wrong, and that, in actuality, time does not exist. Rather it is an illusion, just as motion is: 'Time is not a linear story but is an artefact of how nature works.' The Newtonian and popular 'common sense' notion of 'the river of time' presupposes time as some kind of 'absolute substance' extending evenly and infinitely from the past through the present into the future. Einstein's theory of relativity was to show that, in conceiving of time, it is more accurate to consider it as relative, rather than absolute as Newton did.

But the 'now', as Barbour maintains, in fact has no duration, nothing to measure, and nothing that changes, for there is essentially 'no-thing' to it. If nothing changes, then you cannot say that time has passed. The 'now' is truly instantaneous and these instants are really eternal because, in a deeper sense, nothing ever changes, because the very concept of 'change' implies duration.

In theoretical models of the universe the second law of thermodynamics is enlisted to explain the 'one-way arrow of time', where things move from a state of higher order, to one of disorder. Barbour has proposed that, rather than enlisting a law, the arrow of time can be explained by an already existing force – gravity.

Whether through Newton's gravitation, Maxwell's electrodynamics, Einstein's special and general relativity or quantum mechanics, all the equations that best describe our

> *universe work perfectly if time flows forward or backward. Of course, the world we experience is entirely different. The universe is expanding, not contracting…*
>
> *…work from Julian Barbour of the University of Oxford, Tim Koslowski of the University of New Brunswick and Flavio Mercati of the Perimeter Institute for Theoretical Physics suggests that perhaps the arrow of time doesn't really require a fine-tuned, low-entropy initial state at all but is instead the inevitable product of the fundamental laws of physics. Barbour and his colleagues argue that it is gravity, rather than thermodynamics, that draws the bowstring to let time's arrow fly.*
>
> —Lee Billings[59]

Time is also local, with every atom and subatomic particle in your body, for example, each carrying different records of time with different histories tracing back to exploding supernovas. This is expressed in the explicitly deterministic Pilot Wave Theory, and the super-determinism of quantum theory. Paradoxically, the 'non-local wave' of the PWT instantaneously connects, in a universal now, across the vastness of space, connecting local ensembles of matter (galaxies) where distance is irrelevant and yet, paradoxically, in the PWT all particles have a defined history.

We live here on earth in a particular shared space–time that is 'local', one that has emerged from a deeper reality, subsuming large-scale space–time phenomena. As space–time spreads into different regions across the vastness, direct linkage has the appearance of being diminished, with photons taking many light years to traverse such distances. Yet these 'distant' patches across the universe are fundamentally linked through the 'non-local connectedness of the quantum potential, and entanglement. It is conceived that this entanglement happened at the genesis of our current universe. So, while particles such as photons or neutrinos may take time to get around, there is a non-local connectedness that is independent of time.

Einstein made it clear that when talking about time in science we must also talk about space. He envisioned space and time like a smooth fabric extending continuously throughout the universe, warping under the weight of the matter it contains. The smoothness of this stretchy 'space–time' fabric assumed no underlying structure. This was even at infinitesimal scales, making it irreconcilable with quantum mechanics. General relativity works perfectly well on the grand scale, explaining gravitational interactions between planets, stars, and galaxies. But it cannot account for the quirky movement of photons or electrons on a fabric with no (apparent) elemental structure, in which the equations become nonsense, signifying the impasse between relativity and the quantum world.

Quantised space–time: In reconciling quantum theory with relativity, a way ahead, perhaps, is to conceive of space and time as granular or quantised. The size of electrons, photons and quarks is 10^{-18}, which is many orders of magnitude greater than the Planck length (equivalent to a billionth of a billionth of the diameter of an electron) and so small that they cannot be detected directly.

The predicted scale of 'space–time foam', an idea introduced by John Wheeler in 1955, is this Planck length 1.61×10^{-35} m. This hypothesis that space–time is quantised at the Planck length for the space coordinates, and for the time dimension it has 5.4×10^{-44} seconds as the Planck time. This is the time it takes light to travel one Planck length. At this Planck scale the 'vacuum' is portrayed as a 'quantised foam' of tiny black holes. Each black hole is hypothesised to be the size of a Planck length, each one forming and evaporating in the duration of a Planck time. This conjecture is in a realm that is currently impossible to test.

It is hypothesised that photons can scoot through the vast distances in the geometry of a quantised space–time without losing energy. This was recorded experimentally when photons were measured arriving within an instant of each other, after billions of years of their travel at the speed of light. It is hypothesised that 'quantised fabric/foam of space–time', rather than offering a resistance, is conceived to act more like a 'superfluid', offering no resistance at all to their passage.

However, the main reason why physicists have struggled with developing a theory of quantum gravity, is a complete lack of experimental evidence at such an inaccessibly tiny scale. In fact, 'Plank time' is so brief that no experiment has ever come close to examining it directly, with the most precise tests accessing a time interval to roughly 10^{-17} seconds, which is many orders of magnitude greater in duration.

Despite Einstein's objections, entanglement might be the basis of a geometric theory of quantum gravity. The geometry of space–time rather determines how quantum particles are entangled. Entanglement is the process knitting particulate life (particles and, most importantly, the fields that generate these particles, which can be in vastly separate regions of space yet still connected) in a quantised space–time into a smooth whole, whether in wormholes or black holes or anywhere.

Physicist Leonard Susskind thinks the pathway to quantum gravity is through the wormhole, which demonstrates the unity of the two theories of quantum and relativity. Maldacena and Susskind conjectured that, if any two particles are connected by entanglement, then they are effectively joined by a wormhole. And vice versa – the connection that physicists call a wormhole is *equivalent* to entanglement. They are different ways of describing the same underlying reality.

Scientists have also suggested that any proposed changes to the basic equations of quantum mechanics, would modify the definition of time. If time is discrete (quantised) it would suggest that the commonly held perception of time, as something that is flowing, is an illusion. (However, if one is deeply embedded in experiencing presence-awareness – the now – this is certainly not an illusion one holds). A superfluid quantised space–time universe is analogous to how we experience a movie, in which a series of still images projected on to a screen creates the illusion of continuity; yet quantised space–time has a hidden discrete underlying mathematical structure. Naturally this awaits experimental testing.

The resolution of the problem between quantum theory and relativity could well be found in how each of these theories treats time. As Barbour describes, time in relativity theory is viewed as extremely flexible, relative to different observers' motion, whereas quantum theory uses a Newtonian, fixed absolutist conception of time, in which quantum phenomena occur. The fact that the two major successful theories of reality have diametrically opposed notions of time is a glaring discrepancy. However, this impasse could possibly be resolved if theorists adopted Bohm's Pilot Wave Theory in quantum mechanics, as some have suggested.

In finding a resolution to the long-debated question of whether time is continuous or discrete, with quantised space–time proposing the discrete hypothesis, as Carlo Rivelli suggests, it is a promising candidate for 'the theory of everything'. This will reveal itself in the fullness of time.

> *I believe Einstein was on the right track. His idea was to generate subatomic physics via geometry.*
> —Michio Kiku

In the eternity of an experiential now, time has no existence at all. Time may be something of a problem in our modelling of the universe, but in a numinous experience of reality, it has no reality beyond the mind that conceives it.

The anthropic principle: is our universe special? Are we special?

'I would say that I lean toward the God of Einstein and Spinoza; that is, a God of harmony, simplicity and elegance, rather than a personal God who interferes in human affairs', Kaku muses. *'The universe is gorgeous, and it did not have to be that way. It could have been random, lifeless, ugly; but instead, is full of rich complexity and diversity.'*
—Michio Kaku[60]

Mathematician Brandon Carter coined the term 'anthropic principle' (anthropic meaning 'human') to describe the way the universe has been 'finely-tuned' to produce human beings. This fine-tuning is seen in the universal constants such as the mass of the proton, the gravitational constant and the age of the universe. These things must be as they are, for even if fractionally different, they would make for radically different outcomes, and the evolution of human life would not have been possible. This evidence is used as the reasoning behind this idea.

Carter unveiled his anthropic principle in 1973 at a conference celebrating Copernicus' 500th birthday. The irony here is that it was Copernicus who challenged the long-accepted view that the Earth was the centre of the solar system. Instead, he posited that it was orbiting around the sun. Carter conjectured that the universe had taken nearly fourteen billion years to formulate the 'right conditions' to produce a conscious species that could contemplate its origins. He also believed that homo sapiens has a projected span of ten million years or so on the planet, signifying a gross 'inequality' between the enormous time taken to set the stage for humans, and their fleeting presence and eventual departure.

Since Carter, many different shades of the anthropic principle have developed: the 'cosmological anthropic principle', the 'strong anthropic principle', the 'weak anthropic principle', the 'modified anthropic principle', the 'participatory anthropic principle', and the 'final anthropic principle'. Scientists regard more highly the weak anthropic principle, which maintains that the universe, because of its fine-tuning, provides the right conditions for conscious life to occur without it being compelled to do so. However, it is also seen as a hypothesis that offers no possibility of falsification or scientific testing.

> *An example is the fine structure constant, a number that Nobel laureate and world-renowned physicist Richard Feynman puzzled over. 'It has been a mystery ever since it was discovered ... and all good theoretical physicists put*

> *this number up on their wall and worry about it ... It's one of the greatest damn mysteries of physics: a magic number that comes to us with no understanding by man ... We know what kind of dance to do experimentally to measure this number very accurately, but we don't know what kind of dance to do on the computer to make this number come out, without putting it in secretly!'*
>
> *Feynman realised that if the fine structure constant was somehow even a tiny bit different, the universe we experience would not be the same. Certainly, human life would not have evolved.*
>
> —Andrew Boyd[61]

It is assumed that these constants, like the fine structure constant (1/137) appear designed to support the kind of life that evolves into human beings with the capacity to ask such questions, implying that these constants of nature 'must' have values that support human life. In this case it is not surprising that they are what they are. This argument has generated a great deal of debate within scientific and philosophical circles. Some have accused this argument of being proof by lack of imagination, with an ending that silences enquiry. The argument has been likened to an impatient adult saying, 'just because it is so', when a child asks annoying questions.

> *But in reality, the weak anthropic principle embodies a logical explanation for the Constants of Nature. In doing so, it provides a candidate scientific explanation for why the universe supports human life, even as physicists continue their search for that Holy Grail.*
>
> —Andrew Boyd[62]

Meanwhile, the strong anthropic principle maintains that the universe is compelled to produce conscious life; a view that is generally criticised as a flight of imagination, although there is nothing inherently wrong with this, because flights of imagination are essential in science.

Some physicists are very uncomfortable with the idea of the anthropic principle, possibly because it echoes the religious idea that human beings are special and chosen, with everything centring around them: with the planet earth having been specially created, within a special galaxy, in a special universe amongst all possible universes. In fact, many religious people hold the belief that an external creator made the universe purposely *for* human beings.

Although human beings currently occupy a unique position on our planet, it is sobering to consider the great epochs of the Earth: the tearing apart of the supercontinent Pangea, the formation of Laurasia and Gondwana, and then the forming of today's continents. During these great epochs many species have come and gone, with each holding a unique position. The dinosaurs roamed successfully for 100 million years. We might be special, but are we more so than a worm, an amoeba, or a dinosaur? Only from our own point of view, perhaps, but this is profoundly in error. The 'anthropic principle' seems directly connected to a self-aggrandising self-image.

This planet is of course special to us because it is our home, but it is no more special than our near companion, Mars. Neither is it more special than the exo-planet 16Cygni Bb in the Cygnus constellation, nor the potentially billions of other planets that exist throughout the Milky Way, and the trillions that most surely exist throughout the universe.

Our universe, as a unified field of Consciousness, is special for the kinds of life it makes possible. But we do not know how many other kinds of biological life there are in this universe. And each of these would be uniquely special, and this is just biological life within a living universe.

The anthropic principle is our form of human ego projection, invented to bolster us against nagging feelings of isolation and powerlessness. This is similar to the religious view, where people within a religious community view themselves as a 'chosen people', and hence entitled to 'God's special treatment, both here and in an after-life. The idea of the universe having been specially designed just for human beings to morally develop, with the goal of redemption by entering a transcendental spiritual paradise with a transcendent God, is the product of a mind caught in its own dualism of separation, fear and self-projected grandeur. Yes it is a universe for us to learn in, but it was neither designed especially for us to do this, nor are we the focus of the Logos, because like everything *we are the Logos*. And it is the resistance in us, as the illusion of self, to experiencing our true identity as, the Self. Realising the Self sees the dissolution of a reincarnating ego wherein all learnings, and the need for rebirths to resolve the unresolved, comes to an end.

What is clear is that the universe is finely tuned to evolve biological life, as we know it, because it does, but that is all. Any thoughts that it is designed especially for us are in error. If we experience the universe as living and intelligent, this question does not arise, because life is absolutely ubiquitous. The anthropic principle is just another symptom of humans' collective self-importance. And it is this very self-importance that makes us insensitive to the life around us, and is placing the health of the planet in peril as we head further into the 'Anthropocene'.

The anthropic question can never be resolved in any kind of modelling of reality, for there is no definitive proof either for or against an anthropic principle. The proof that is definitive is that the universe is finely tuned for all biological life only. But it is not definitive for the 'human-centred' bit. However, anthropic proponents of any persuasion, whether scientific or religious, will believe what they will. And, while belief may have self-comfort value, it has zero truth-value.

The finite cannot comprehend the infinite. Thought cannot know what is beyond itself as consciousness. Only being-ness as consciousness can know consciousness. Conversely, the infinite – consciousness – can recognise the illusion of the finite. Such knowing is the province of anyone, because anyone who is curious can become spiritually wise in this way.

Awareness of Being is not a matter of privilege. This knowing is beyond empiricism and rationality, which is why there is a disconnection between those who enter a non-dual experience of Being, and those who are still looking in the realm of the conceptual mind with models, reasons, and explanations, for the answers to existence. Developing models of reality is an essential function, and indeed part of fulfilling our potential as humans, but it falls hopelessly short in addressing what is fundamental to human existence.

To understand consciousness, the truth of Being and our identity, the models and reasons we may construct are not fit to the task. For unless we go beyond the mind in experiencing reality directly, in the expanse of a living universe, we may have a distorted sense of place in it – an anthropic one. With this ignorance we will be nature's unfinished business.

Time, personal history and identity

Time is only an idea. There is only Reality. Whatever you think it is, it appears to be. If you call it time, it is time. If you call it existence, it is existence, and so on. After calling it time, you divide it into days and nights, months, years, hours, minutes, etc.

—Ramana Maharshi[64]

Time is also used to create an identity from a pastiche of memories that we can recall in rough chronological order. But memory is never completely reliable, because it undergoes constant modification as we continue to layer information and experiences in and around previous memories. Then we do something unnecessary, we create an entity, as a separate keeper of our memories, that we believe signifies identity. This entity may well modify, shift, embellish, fabricate, repress, suppress and distort memories – all the things a virulent ego-entity might do.

We measure how this narrative of 'me' changes through time, transforming this into our collection of images of who we think we are. We mark the progress of a psychological self, saying things like, 'I am making progress', 'I am going downhill, 'I am falling apart', or 'I am getting better every day'. It is a game of constant modifications overseen by an independent 'time-keeper', itself another fragment of thought. We seek improvements for this self over time, convincing ourselves that it has independent reality over time, and some kind of permanence. Yet the only aspect that is changeless from birth to death is awareness, which is the screen on which the drama of our living takes place – appearing as modulations on the screen – with the screen (our awareness), unmoved by whatever is taking place.

As is the case with many things that thought creates, we can become slaves to the offspring of our imagination. But we speak, think and act as though time is fundamental, and much more than the concept that it is. In identifying ourselves as a time-based entity with a unique personal history, this ground is always shaky because, while we may be informed by past experiences, we are not reducible to the stories of the past. Further still we can be haunted, and even enslaved by our response to these memories making us anxious and fearful.

However, we can never completely live in the past, despite the self's best effort to do just this. The self may search nostalgically, or attempt to recreate similar patterns of events, complete with a cast of characters. Yet it is impossible to relive even one moment ago, because in actuality we can only ever be living in the present. It is only the mind that would have it otherwise. But we can, in a very real sense, get stuck in the past as we attempt to construct things now as they used to be or, conversely, become lost in our projections of the future.

Thought itself is of the past. For even as we use language, naming and labelling the world of things, we create a contextual mind map that becomes recognisable. We do this in order to see a world that is familiar, and objectified, so that it is a continuation of the past and *known*. This is useful and necessary for our survival and functioning in the world. But if we attach to this mapping that thought creates, it profoundly limits our capacity for living in the present, living creatively, and experiencing the freedom we already have – a freedom found in experiencing the absence of time because in time's absence is a sense of the numinous.

Without a 'time-keeper', we are free of procrastinating, rushing, getting bored, and restlessly waiting for anything. There is also freedom from measuring changes in the self, because there is no longer the desire for mental or emotional modifications. Instead we are naturally 'present' in a now that is eternal. With no self to mark time, there is no sense of duration. One simply is. There is no duration between different 'now's' – there is only *now*.

Beyond the mind is the timeless that is ever-fresh. By entering this experience, we discover our fountain of youth. It is our birthright to know this timelessness, and through this experience, we discover the universality of love. Love, not as emotion, but as consciousness, the Intelligence that generates, enfolds and moves the universe.

> *It was taught by the Buddha, oh Monks, that ... the past,*
> *The future, physical space ... and individuals are nothing*
> *But names, forms of thought, words of common usage,*
> *Merely superficial realities.*
> —Madhyamika Karika Vrtti[65]

Does time heal all wounds? Why it can be difficult to live in the now

It is commonly said that time heals all wounds. However, can time heal when it is not fundamentally real? Memories of insults or traumas fade just like scars on the skin, but this fading is not really healing, it is just fading. We may no longer appear to be so concerned about what happened, having buried the pain from a hurtful incident so deeply that it becomes somatised, in the unconscious of the body. But in this case we live in denial, with the body itself manifesting various disturbed symptoms, such as rashes, swelling, pain or other disturbances. We can remain unconscious to the somatic origins, yet respond dramatically to 'triggers' like sounds, situations, people and events that can activate the original memory of the incident.

A trauma can be buried completely, or just subliminally conscious, as we endeavour to get on with our lives. Yet can still be profoundly impacted as we are informed - often unconsciously - and then strategise to prevent similar injuries in the future. Some may attempt re-enacting a similar situation with a cast of real characters (for example, adopting roles such as tyrant, victim, bully, rescuer) in the living situation, ready to play it out again. Here we seek comfort in the known by repeating patterns of the past, as the ego tries to relive the past.

But ever at hand is an undiscovered potential to break the spell of these habitual dramas and resolve the original wounding. It is not a given that we awaken and move on, unless we examine our living. For those of us so imprisoned by the fear we have created, we may instead suppress our responses as a strategy to maintain the status quo, because healing does involve risk. There will be disturbance, there will be change and things will get chaotic in the process of releasing stored stresses. It takes both curiosity and courage to invite this healing, and then insight in resolving it.

Unless these traumas of the past are emptied of their 'emotional-energetic residue', the ego structure will maintain its protective shell, replete with emotional scars and the festering wounds underneath. The buried memories of perceived negative experience can be trapped at a cellular level in the various tissues of the body – the visceral organs, nervous and other bodily systems – profoundly affecting the healthy functioning of the body, possibly until the grave.

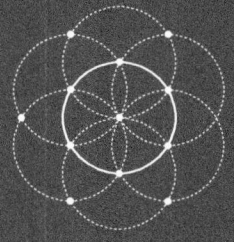

PART FOUR

SPIRITUALITY – THE PATHLESS WAY

In which we explore the nature of spirituality, and how it is particularly present in certain traditions, places and cultures. At the core of these traditions is the understanding that 'no-mind' is the gateway to reality.

CHAPTER 14

THE PARADOX OF TIME

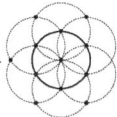

And likewise time cannot itself exist,
But from the flight of things we get a sense of time...
No man, we must confess, feels time itself,
But only knows of time from flight or rest of things.
—Lucretius, Roman poet, from *De Rerum Natura*[63]

It is a relatively new phenomenon for a person to own another's time as we do in the field of employment, as per hours a day, or over a week. Owning another's time necessarily brings a power dynamic. And we have become a culture that is time obsessed, by regarding time as a commodity where someone's time can be bought and sold.

With Indigenous cultures, which have a shared economy, everyone is provided for, with all tribal members contributing, and no-one owns anyone else's time. However, with the developing of agricultural societies wealth was accumulated and stored, and labour organised to such ends, and their time was owned as slave or serf: often for life, with their family and succeeding generations shackled to the same time and power dynamic.

Today, a corporation, a business, a department, a boss, might own our time, and then we have 'time off'. We have free time. When we are un-owned economically it confers a different order of personal sovereignty, and a different ownership of time. This freedom creates a different set of social norms and power relations, than what we currently experience in our economically driven world. The emergence, over the last few hundred years, of private property and profit-motivated commodity production, has changed the power relations between us, with the owning, sharing, buying and trading of time.

However, if in our daily living we have an experience that is beyond time, all our relationships including our work relationships cannot be construed in a power dynamic, nor can our time ever be wasted. Having time off makes no sense at all, because at a deeper level there is the understanding that there is no time. While we may attend work on time, and for a set duration, we have dispossessed ourselves of time in the freedom of Being. Here we can live a regular existence, doing regular things such as showing up for work on time, working set hours, and having leisure time, yet experience the timeless nature of Being. In actuality, anchoring in the absolute, as the truth of Being, also enables us to navigate effortlessly in the relative, as the world of time, work, and relationships.

If unhealed, these insults affect our living and our relationships by limiting and conditioning us, making us fearful, angry, guilt-ridden, self-pitying, vengeful, depressed or even paralysed.

Holding painful memories subliminally requires an enormous amount of energy. Commonly, drug strategies (legal or illegal) are employed as a way of maintaining the fragile stability of the self, which can lead to another 'illness layer' of substance-dependent addiction. With our mental health suffering, we can become increasingly diminished energetically, and sometimes our efforts to maintain a semblance of conscious order and control may become bizarre. The stress involved ensures that the body ages ahead of time. By carrying such psychological baggage and spending much of our available energy to keep this form of unconsciousness going, we are far from experiencing life in the 'now'.

These insults from the past can contaminate consciousness, fuelling attitudes of self-pity, victimisation, guilt, defensiveness or aggression. They are the things that entrap us as a time-based entity. Without these thoughts, emotions and attitudes being cleared, it is not possible to experience being present. It requires forgiveness to release the toxicity that these emotional conflicts involve. These issues are the storm clouds eclipsing ever-present awareness. Forgiveness is an essential pathway to the now, healing this particular kind of clinging to the past.

The unresolved events from our personal history become the weight that makes living in the present painful and difficult. Ekhart Tolle refers to this in *The Power of Now*, perhaps more metaphorically, with his concept of the 'pain body'. Rather than an idea of a separate 'pain body', it is useful to think of the body as having more subtle domains as an 'inner energetic landscape'. This is the domain of an energy/information field in the body-mind which holds the accumulated insults and traumas that continue to resonate as unresolved issues, thereby distorting our experience of living. And unless these insults from the past are healed at an energetic level, we continue to be caught in a loop with the past.

Traumas may form part of an extended narrative intergenerationally, where they can be passed on trans-generationally from parent to child. In this way we can experience the 'insults' going back even further to previous generations. We can further identify with our suffering when we believe that the pain we carry defines who we are, and this attachment creates further resistance to resolving it, because having the pain can become an important part of our identity.

Intergenerational or 'tribal pain' can become an essential part of how we develop identity. We may seek to dull this pain with drugs, or even thoughts of suicide, which can gather momentum and may indeed be acted upon. Here, in the felt desperation the isolated self, identified with its 'situation' and its pain, seeks its own demise. Yet, this is not a successful resolution because consciousness continues after death, as the fragment of ego continues with its unresolved pain. It is just a different aspect of consciousness – the body aspect of consciousness – that dies. But even the consciousness that was the body transforms in the process of decay, feeding other microbial forms of life, so consciousness continues.

It is only if we believe time and self are independent realities that we become convinced that our past and our pain are in fact us, and hence feel stuck in our situation, thereby seeing ourselves as victims. In this way we *become* our emotional baggage because we have identified with it. And it is the thought of letting go of this kind of distorted self-knowing that can engender great fear of the unknown – of letting go of the pain we know. Who would we be without this weight that we carry? Too often the egoic mind prefers itself, its pain and the known.

Letting go of this knowledge of ourselves, even though it causes pain and is essential to maintaining the dream-sleep of ego, profoundly challenges our identity. However, the energy cost of maintaining things as they are is a significant stressor, ensuring that we age much faster than our biological years. The way to heal and clear this stress is to forgive, and in forgiving we empty ourselves of the continued suffering.

When we realise we are not fully present in the now, the mind may then 'try' to be more present. But we cannot be *more* present when now is already at hand. The now always is, and always has been here. Our inability to experience the now may have been obscured by our trauma, ruminations on issues or memories that remain unresolved, and attaching to passing thoughts, moods, and emotions.

It is only love that heals, as a universal, existent dimension of Being. It manifests in us as forgiveness and compassion as a deep acceptance of the confused struggles and traumas of the self. This brings an emptying of the stored pain or trauma, which sees a diminishing of the self. Being able to accept and articulate our narratives of the past, including that of our ancestral lines, is an essential step in a healing process that enables us to be more experientially present.

Our stories are essential and important, but they are not the deeper source of our identity. With the emptying of the past there is a feeling of peace and unity with all that is, signalling the end of believing in thought as the primary narrative of living. What is left when the detritus of mind is in abeyance, is the be-wonderment of presence-awareness.

> *Let us forget the lapse of time,*
> *let us forget the conflict of opinions.*
> *Let us make our appeal to the infinite,*
> *and take up our positions there.*
> —Chuang Tzu[66]

Resolving the past: the body is a reservoir of consciousness

In forgiveness we free ourselves by 'resolving' the emotional charge of our 'baggage', letting go of habits, of regret, guilt, and worry, by not clinging to the content of the mind. There are some useful therapies that can help those who have experienced trauma of one sort or another.

Talking therapies using cognitive approaches are important for accessing the 'story level' where information may have barely been accessed by conscious awareness. But to more deeply heal, rather than talking, 'feeling into' the unconscious of the body is the way to completely release the residual trapped energy-memory (because it is unconscious) that continuously hijacks our experience of the present, to the past.

Therapies such as 'somatic experiencing' as pioneered by Peter Levine (who gave a comprehensive lecture to the Jungian Society on 'Spirituality, Archetypes and Trauma') give a clear outline and demonstration of this simple yet profound way of working with the 'unconscious of the body'. As well if we research the available material, there is enough to coach you do some basic self-regulation with body-stored trauma.

But for serious deep-seated trauma it is better always to find a qualified and skilled therapist. EMDR (Eye Movement Desensitisation Reprocessing) as well as 'Thought Field Therapy', both appear to get results where cognitive approaches are less than adequate. Other body-oriented movement therapies such as yoga, tai chi, qi gong and dance (particularly Butoh) can also be useful.

In the mix are also the important re-syncing of the brain hemispheres through re-establishing harmonious brain-wave patterns to replace the reverberating of stressed patterns established habitually from earlier trauma. This can be done using neurofeedback and mindfulness meditation.

Somatic meditation: Old wounds, held in the unconscious of the body, can be located directly with what I call 'somatic meditation'. It operates by bringing bring forth into awareness any issues or stories that have caused deep inner disturbance, and simultaneously scanning the field of inner consciousness. This enables locating where in the body sensations of disturbance are experienced, such as the throat, heart, stomach, lower abdomen, head, face, limbs, etc. At this point, usually there emerges a palpable sensation. Here we leave the story and any associated memories, and now focus only on the areas of energy disturbance, attending purely to the sensations in the body to see if there is particular colour, shape, feeling and density to these sensations. There may also be disturbing emotional energy (feeling panicky, great fear, dread, anger, rage or sadness). But by staying present purely in the experience of it – not analysing, judging or trying to change it – but just accepting it as it is, there is usually a period where the sensations may amplify in intensity expressing as heat, cold, a colour, density, shape, vibrating, or a shift in in size or area. All of these features may change as undivided attention is applied. But in staying present the intensity and sensations we thought could be there forever, eventually (it may well take more than one session) dissipate by themselves. There is no willing for this to happen; a healing has taken place that is intuitively understood, and with this, a palpable sense of release – and a feeling of peace.

Here we are embarking on a journey into the '*energy landscape of the body*', because these areas of disturbance are where we are 'unconsciously absent'. Now, through the light of awareness, beyond the story level of the mind, a healing process takes place. By 'getting out of the way', by putting the mind and its stories to the side, deep healing can happen.

Therapeutic approaches like this can access the unconscious store of trauma in the body from the 'bottom up', in ways that more conventional talking therapies with their cognitive 'top-down' approaches, cannot. These approaches reveal a hidden order of the body's inner energy landscape, making the unconscious conscious.

Separating from thought by *resting in awareness* is the gateway to the freedom – from time, from the mind, and from the known. So, we should not be fooled into believing that a very busy mind is natural for us, when it is really a default state driven by what is unresolved in us.

It can still be difficult to live in the now because, even after we may have resolved the issues that pulled us into ruminating on the past, we may still identify with our thoughts as though we *are* them. We might imagine that a truly quiet mind is impossible, or of no significance. Yet inner quiet is a natural state that happens by itself by *letting go, by being*. We cannot stop thinking, nor should we; however, thinking is only really healthy when it is not sovereign over us – when consciousness rules, not its progeny.

The challenge of being aware is always now, choice-less. With undivided attention to 'what is', we experience first hand the immensity of timeless Being. It is the buried treasure within us all, bringing a profound sense of peace. And whether we are monks, gardener,s or biochemists, we all have equal access to Being.

With this understanding we can still engage in the world of time, wear a watch, catch the bus and be punctual at work. We can still know whether our menstrual cycle is in or out of phase. We can still know when the best time is to sow seeds, or have insight into our circadian rhythms, or intuit the right moment to ask someone out on a date. But in the treasure that is Being, we are no longer victims to time as the psychological self.

When asked about what surprises him most, the 14th Dalai Lama responded with,

> *What surprised me most about humanity.*
> *Because he sacrifices his health in order to make money.*
> *Then he sacrifices money to recuperate his health.*
> *And then he is so anxious about the future that*
> *he does not enjoy the present;*
> *the result being that he does not live in the present*
> *or the future;*
> *he lives as if he is never going to die, and then*
> *dies having never really lived.*
>
> —lifeadvancer.com

Living for the moment

Am I advocating a philosophy of 'live for the moment'? Living for the moment is a distorted interpretation of hedonism. Hedonism was articulated by Epicurus in the third century BCE in Ancient Greece. He advised the 'savouring' of experience and enjoying the delight and beauty of the senses. In order to do this, he advised not indulgence, which he thought dulled the senses, but rather a tempering of desires and a natural modesty.

Hedonism was not the relentless pursuit of pleasure by an insatiable self, a kind of license to indulge, as it has come to be in the current era. It was a calmly joyous celebration of aliveness, equanimity and friendship, inspiring the establishment of an estimated 400 Epicurean centres (gardens) that spread throughout the Mediterranean during this time.

Living for the moment is something quite apart from being in the eternity of now. It implies a 'seeker of pleasure' attaching to experiences and restlessly searching for new ones, whether what is sought is gourmet food, wine, other drugs, or sexual pleasure - Hedonia. With relentless seeking, more exotic sensations are sought to satisfy the bottomless search for sensual highs. Corresponding with this is a decaying inside, as the mind becomes jaded, requiring evermore extreme experiences. Yet with this craving for 'new sensate experience', there is no awareness of the ever-fresh in each moment. This was a different philosophy advised by Heraclitus and also by the Stoics, for our challenge is not to live for the moment (for experiences) but to be completely present *in* (experiencing) the moment.

The craving for new and heightened sensations is as prevalent today as it has ever been. It is indicative of mental fragmentation, a disconnected culture of materialism, and excessive clinging to the body. This was portrayed in the story of the earlier years of Gautama the Buddha. As a younger man his search for pleasure became jaded, his body having lost its vitality, and the possibility of truly living in the 'now' only seemed more remote. He was to discover after a period of mortifying his body with ascetic practices, that this form of extremism was also a form of attachment to the body, driven by a search for pleasure and avoidance of pain. This drew him to articulate the 'middle path' between indulgence and the ascetic life. Upon realising that the self did not exist, there was an end to his seeking and craving.

However, when desire is deeply listened to and understood as the natural voice of a healthy body, there is no struggle, for struggle is the interference of mind attempting to control. By resting in awareness, we break the *attachment* to desire. It is this attachment (which is a form of unconsciousness) rather than desire, that is the source of suffering.

The danger of 'short-cuts' to the now

To see a world in a grain of sand
And a heaven in a wild flower,
Hold infinity in the palm of your hand
And eternity in an hour.
—William Blake (1757–1827)[67]

What is it that experiences the flow of time? If we examine this carefully, it is a sense of a self, marking the passage of time as if it is a flow of duration. And so, time can be said to flow slowly or quickly, depending on the mood-state of the 'time-keeper'. We may have expectations that something will happen at a given time, and when it does not, there is frustration. Time seems to flow too slowly, and frustration and then anger will arise as a measure of our level of attachment to expectant happenings. But this experience of the flow of time is only conceptual. It does not exist now, because moment to moment there is no duration, as now is all there is. Now does not flow through to another now. *There is only now.*

When people take mind-expanding drugs, particularly the plant hallucinogens, they may get a glimpse of this heightened sense of 'now'. Their normal experience of time flowing, which is how they locate themselves in space and time, becomes altered. It is an expansion of consciousness but because it is induced, it is only temporary. During the hallucinogenic journey, there can be an acute reduction of the internal dialogue, a self-medicated experience of 'no-mind'. This inner silence is perhaps one of the primary reasons why the mind-expanding hallucinogenic drugs are so attractive, and have been used in shamanic cultures across the globe.

The thought structure sees the defining of space and time, but in attaching to this structure, it is also our confinement. The finite mind develops a prison in what is essentially, infinite. The objectivist description we carry as the regular internal monologue that gives us a sense of normality (including the framing of space and time) is suspended during the course of the drug experience. The plant hallucinogens used in shamanic traditions are a 'fast track' to release the novice from this constriction, along with other spiritual purposes. (Drugs of addiction are a different matter and are more commonly used as escape routes from facing psychological pain.)

Since the 1960s, the New Age movement has catalysed interest in drugs for consciousness expansion. Drugs such as the potent plant hallucinogen *ayahuasca*, used by the South American forest shamans are now used across Europe, America and Australia. The active molecule – isolated in chemical analysis from the plant – is DMT, also referred to as the 'spirit molecule'.

> *N,N-DIMETHYLTRYPTAMINE is an N-methylated indoleamine derivative and serotonergic hallucinogen which occurs naturally and ubiquitously in several plant species including Psychotria veridis. It also occurs in trace amounts in mammalian brain, blood, and urine, and is known to act as an agonist or antagonist of certain SEROTONIN RECEPTORS."*
> —National Centre for Biotechnology Information[68]

Such short cuts are not encouraged here, for there are many dangers in taking both plant-based and synthetic hallucinogens. They can powerfully shift our sense of normality and, in someone already struggling with a fragmentary experience of life, tip them over the edge into mental illness. This can include heightened paranoia, delusions, and psychosis, which can lead to permanent mental health issues, and even death.

Moreover, taking hallucinogens only gives a temporary state of heightened awareness; a glimpse. What I am encouraging is exploring awareness and being alert to restless desires for immediate solutions. And rather than searching the external plant pharmacopeia for consciousness accelerants, better to investigate consciousness, which will orchestrate the naturally sees the natural releasing of our endogenous supply of these substances already existing in the body.

We are discovering in laboratories around the world that the active alkaloids in these plants are remarkably close to the biochemicals already existing in the human brain and nervous system. This is true for the DMT of ayahuasca, the THC in cannabis, psilicibin from 'magic' mushrooms, and mescalin from peyote.

It is an under-recognised feature of our neuro-endocrine system that it has a rich internal pharmacy, producing its own supply of DMT, amongst other consciousness enhancing substances. And it is suggested that endogenous DMT is potentiated by meditative practices. How do we create the right conditions to maximise the production and circulation of our natural internal pharmacy? The right conditions are the deconditioning of the mind of that which binds us, and the resting in awareness.

The search for a 'consciousness accelerant', regarded as some kind of 'philosopher's stone', is a furphy as much as a distraction from what is already at hand as the 'natural state'. *It is only by immersion in a present that is eternal, with the complete attentiveness that effortlessly brings a deep quietening of the mind, that there is a transformation of consciousness.* No substances are required.

In living an examined life, exploring moment-to-moment existence we realise the inherent power in being 'present', and notice simultaneously the spontaneous silence of the internal dialogue. We may also notice the effortless shift in the perception of space and time – space expands, and time disappears. And an uncaused feeling of happiness may also arise. This is not dependent on a drug, and there is no 'coming down'. It is our ever-present birthright.

Time is of your own making,
Its clock ticks in your head.
The moment you stop thought
Time too stops dead.

—Angelis Silesius[69]

Destiny

The word *destiny* can be defined as a sense of organising intelligence, immanent throughout nature, including us, that is beyond the intellect or reason (note the similarity to super-determinism). There is a growing realisation that the universe is indeed 'intelligent' and 'alive', and much more highly organised than previously imagined. To accept destiny is to recognise that there is a deeper, organising, intelligent energy making for a meaningfully connected universe.

The meaning of destiny challenges the materialist notions of chance, coincidence and randomness, because all these notions are informed by the assumption that there is no 'connecting, patterning, intelligent energy' in the universe. Instead this view maintains that the universe is disconnected, chaotic, meaningless, and unintelligent.

We explored earlier the meaning of 'choice-less awareness', and embedded in this term is a sense of destiny. Awareness is consciousness, and consciousness is the organising and patterning intelligence, manifesting as all that is, as the universe itself. Destiny refers to the unfolding of consciousness as an organising intelligence.

It could be said that Hitler was destined to potentiate existing collective forces in Germany and Europe in the first part of the 20th century. Hitler did not arise by chance; Hitler was rather a catalyst to an already existing negative mindset and extreme prejudices, a form of toxic dualism. We could say it was destined that someone like Hitler would manifest from the collective psyche in Germany and Europe, acting as a catalyst to fomenting prejudices in a collective psycho-pathology. He was the madman we were destined to have, which it is not a question of being right or ethical. It was not something evil, in an archaic struggle of evil against transcendental good, but rather, a virulent form of unconsciousness, or ignorance to what is humanity's true nature.

We could say that everything that happens is destined. Yet we become confused about this when we think of ourselves as separate and independent decision-makers and having 'free-will', as if we are in some way independent from the organising intelligence of consciousness. Our destiny is that which is called up in our lives regardless of any ego-driven desired outcomes, for it includes everything that happens to us. This includes what we may regard as negative events, like having a car accident, or losing a loved one. Of course, no sane person would want to get injured by having a car accident! But by not resisting 'whatever is', we can accept all that is, including the so-called negative events. By resting in awareness, we can be at peace with whatever happens.

Destiny is not a scientific concept and cannot be proved like a hypothesis in a theoretical argument. Rather, destiny is what is revealed from within. But even in the core of science this occurs with the notion of super-determinism, held by a tiny minority of quantum theorists. Super-determinism holds that 'free-will' is an illusion, and the destiny of every subatomic particle is, and has been known, from the primordial genesis of the current universe.

Destiny also carries an implied meaning of there being a journey through time to some 'pre-ordained' event or end. However, as we have already explored, time itself is not ultimately real and, like all concepts, destiny is merely a way of talking about the certain way things happen in a world, that is more intimately connected than the objectifying intellect can appreciate. But through understanding intuitively there is a letting go, wherein there is no longer a separate 'you' who are on a journey, rather *you are the journey*.

In fulfilling our destiny, in doing what we are 'meant' to be doing, we are realising something that has been a potential within us. This holds true at the individual as well as the collective level. And while we can only know a sense of destiny experientially, simultaneously there is a freedom and creativity in living. This is the paradox: we are at once destined and yet also free in Being, filled with creative potential.

Freedom is to consciously actualise our destiny: harmonising in Being. You could say I was destined to write this book, not as a superficial mental act of making a choice; rather, I was free to follow this destiny, to reveal the book that was within. And the organising intelligence, makes way for this to happen, if it is to be.

In destiny there is an impersonal sense of participating in, and being guided. Here the existence of the self or ego is a form of interference. The important questions here are: do we experience a sense of destiny in how we live, and know the freedom that comes from this? Do we experience a deeper domain beyond choice? And is it possible to be a master of our own destiny, as some people suggest?

Being a master implies some kind of absolute degree of control and domination. It is misguided to think that we can do this, for only a 'self' seeks notions of mastery or power over something. The psychological self may cultivate a self-image of mastery, and may become successful at this delusion both with itself, and others. Notions of mastery are a perennial form of self-inflation that only humans seem to suffer. We can experience the freedom of fulfilling our destiny, rather than harbouring illusions of control. So better to be engaged in service in life, rather than cultivate notions of mastery.

Many live under a fatalist notion where destiny is a passive form of unconsciousness, as an expression of the separation from Being. From this separation comes praise or blame on an outside transcendental agency, or a conspiring 'destiny'. Awareness of the infinite is knowing that *we are universal consciousness,* so our understanding of 'destiny' becomes completely participatory because it is conscious. It does not suffer from the ignorance of egocentric self. When this happens, 'destiny' is something we understand as within us and encompassing all that is, beyond choice, and beyond the sovereignty of the mind.

> *The absolute tranquillity is the present moment.*
> *Though it is at this moment, there is no limit to this moment,*
> *and herein is eternal delight.*
> —Hui-neng, quoted in *The Way of Zen*[70]

Freedom from time is a conduit to 'free energy'

For many of us, time has become a prison of our own making because it is our belief in the reality of time that oppresses, not time itself. Time is a useful concept; it is not an enemy. However, time is thought's progeny and identifying with thought as the self, time is then regarded as being absolutely real. We feel pressured and struggle with time, or race against it which furthers an experience of separation.

What is it that sees itself in a struggle against time? The self perceives that it is in a battle with time, fuelling the attempt to achieve some permanence and imagined control over our lives. Of course, it does not help that the surrounding landscape of human societies are addicted to time being an actuality, and are engaging in the same struggle. But this is the way of the human world, and need not be an obstacle, because if we are curious, time is not a problem: the body can age gracefully and we can live unbounded, outside of time.

Being unbound by time is a liberation. In engineering, the 'Holy Grail' is to create a 'free energy device'; that is, a 'perpetual motion device' that draws energy from the ubiquitous magnetic and gravitational field, so that it essentially runs endlessly by itself. In the realm of physics, the possibility of this is presently unconfirmed, and despite a multitude of claims by inventors that this has already been achieved, there is nothing as yet substantiated.

Each of us is like a free energy device. We do need a regular supply of food, water and air, but if we are aware of the 'subtle energetic body' we exchange energy with the environment in ways hidden from the objectivist knowing of science. It is a hidden order of Being known to the sensitive: meditators, mystics, shamans, Sufis, Taoists, Tibetan Buddhists and Yogis. However, this is really accessible to anyone. It is possible to experience a different property of 'energy-consciousness' that is both in and around us, and that is transformative to our living. But how can we experience this? It automatically sensitises the body, aligning us harmoniously with the intelligent energy that is the deeper functioning of the universe.

We experience this 'free energy' in no-mind, wherein there is no grasping, and no expectations, when the mind is spontaneously quiet. Inner silence aligns us harmoniously in Being, enabling the body to conduct a 'subtle energy' from the environment, in a way as yet unknown to science. It is analogous to how a superconductor transfers energy without resistance; we too can conduct a subtle form of universal energy-consciousness, aligning ourselves with the Logos.

Many complicated esoteric practices lay claim to being *the* special practice that will bring liberation. But not one of these claims is true. Practices such as yoga, Tai Chi, prayer, meditation techniques, qi gong, breathing practices, or meditative dance, can enhance the conduction and circulation of energy, quieten the mind, improve our health and retard biological ageing, each giving unique experiences and insights. With all practices we can experience the circulation of *subtle energy* through engaging in them.

But it is only pure observation itself that brings us into presence. Resting in awareness, is *the* only non-practice that truly liberates 'free energy', specifically because it does not involve thought and is neither a technique nor a practice. In the 'no-thing-ness' of awareness there is an abundance of free energy because there is no 'thought entity' existing as resistance.

Awareness needs no practices or special experiences, 'it is', regardless of what we do. And by relaxing into awareness transformation occurs. If we engage in practices without attachment, they become more beneficial because they are done with *an aware presence as an absence of self.* When we are present we are not outcome driven and we let be.

Letting be brings a flow of free energy, engulfing the whole body-mind enabling us to experience a different order of 'subtle energy-consciousness' moving through every cell. While not a substance it is a dimensional energy, part of the spectrum of consciousness itself, and is experienced as a subtle force of life.

Experiencing Being is the end of time, a primary signature of spirituality.

CHAPTER 15

SYNCHRONICITY AND OUR PERCEPTION OF REALITY

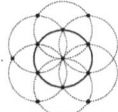

It may come as no surprise that there is a connection between the worlds of quantum theory and depth psychology. Carl Gustav Jung (1875–1961), a prominent student of Sigmund Freud and pioneer psychiatrist, stated in a letter to a colleague that Einstein's General Theory of Relativity was the inspiration for his concept of synchronicity. He said it had stimulated his thinking about the relativity of time and space, and what he called their 'psychic conditionality'. Jung intuited that physicists' understanding of the atomic world would provide a mechanism to explain the connection between mind and matter. In collaboration with Nobel laureate physicist Wolfgang Pauli, Jung sought to find this mechanism in the quantum world, which could account for what he was experiencing and seeing in his research.

Basically, Jung coined the term 'synchronicity' to signify a meaningful interaction between three aspects: the psychic state of a person, an external event, and space and time. A psychic state for Jung meant a state that is not part of a normal consensus reality, which can appear as a dream, a vision or sudden intuition, whereas an objective, external event is part of the consensus reality of space and time.

In our everyday world, most of us have experienced connections and events that seem highly unlikely according to the standard axioms of probability, such as suddenly thinking of someone you have not seen for years, and then meeting them in a most unusual place. (And this has happened to me numerous times – one occasion while travelling after having had a dream about meeting this particular person that night – and the next day in the back streets of a foreign country, as I was recounting the dream to my wife, literally bumping in to them, having not had any contact for many years.) For Jung, synchronicity was this connection between the inner and outer worlds that demonstrated an essential connectedness. It was the direct experiential evidence of an underlying unity. And while there are 'apparent' inner and outer worlds, there is, in actuality, only one world, one consciousness.

Synchronicity challenges the consensual dualistic mindset separating inner from outer, objective from subjective, and also space from time. Curiously, quantum theory has done something of this as well, because its experiments have been interpreted by some as suggesting that the long-held notion of duality – that mind (consciousness) and matter are separate types of stuff. Quantum theory also challenges the notion that the subject can separate herself from the object studied, because at the quantum level, the experimenter is by necessity, a factor influencing the experimental outcome. Theorists like David Bohm suggest that the mind of the observer is indissolubly linked in the one totality, eradicating the gulf between inner and outer, observer and observed.

Collective unconscious

The concept of synchronicity developed as a natural consequence of Jung's overarching theory of the 'collective unconscious', which is defined as a psychic domain shared by all human beings across space and time. It is a domain of collective memory and knowledge. Freud, on the other hand, believing in his dualistic conditioning, developed the more reductive, separate individualistic concept of a 'personal unconscious' – a repository of repressed memories, instincts and urges.

Freud, fearful of where his younger colleague Jung was going with his ideas of a mystical collective unconscious, instead looked to the rationality of pre-quantum classical physics as the source to validate his theories. This was in contradistinction to Jung's research into quantum theory in his collaboration with physicist Wolfgang Pauli.

The conflict between them came to a head in 1909 in Vienna when Jung asked Freud what he made of precognition and parapsychology. Freud replied that the occult phenomena were to him a 'black tide of mud' and as they were sitting in the office together, Jung's diaphragm began to feel hot. Suddenly, a bookcase in the room cracked loudly and they both jumped up. 'There, that is an example of a so-called catalytic exteriorisation phenomenon', Jung retorted, referring to his theory of an uncanny 'action at a distance' where physical events could be projections of inner states of conflict. 'Bosh!' Freud responded, but as he was about to leave, Jung predicted that there would be another crack which, to Freud's astonishment, there was.

Despite Freud's criticism that Jung's theories were unscientific, the same could equally be said of his. In fact, both theories were viewed by the scientific community as being seriously less than rational. In Freud's case this was not simply because of the question as to whether his cases were fabricated, but because with both theories of the unconscious – whether 'personal' in Freud's, or 'collective' in Jung's – neither were falsifiable or testable. And therefore, neither met the essential criteria of the methods and practice of science. But while meeting falsifiability criteria may well be important for validation in an objectivist account of nature in the phenomenal domain, it is not, nor can it ever be, the litmus test of truth.

Jung differed from Freud with his more expansive, mystical concept of the collective unconscious and his attitude to the spiritual. He understood that the human quest for spiritual truth, expressed in the core values of different religions, was both real, and important. He regarded that it as an expression of a collective desire of human beings to find a deeper meaning in living, and for people to experience wholeness, integration and individuation.

> *In general, it [individuation] is the process by which individual beings are formed and differentiated [from other human beings]; in particular, it is the development of the psychological individual as a being distinct from the general, collective psychology.*
>
> —Carl Jung[71]

Jung's expanded view of memory to a collective unconscious, which is greater than the experiences of our present life, is a radical departure from Western psychology's belief that humans are born with a blank slate, or 'tabula rasa'. Hence Jung understood that human consciousness is at times beyond the grasp of empirical evidence, and certainly beyond rationality.

Jung's curiosity led him to investigate far beyond the confines of rationality into cross–cultural religious experience, pointing to a universal desire of humans for spiritual truth. He had a different, more experiential view of 'God' from conventional belief, which in the major monotheistic faiths is of an externalised, transcendental, patriarchal figure.

Jung expressed this in a television interview in 1959. When asked if he believed in God, he replied, after a pregnant pause, 'I don't need to believe, I know.' His retort caused some controversy at the time and has continued to, since then. It was quoted by Richard Dawkins, in his book *The God Delusion*[72], being cited as an example of blind faith, in support of Dawkins' central argument that having a 'belief in God being delusional'. Jung, however, was referring to something of a completely different order from what Dawkins had superficially accused him of. Jung's reference to 'God' was pointing to a different kind of experiential knowing rather than representing the 'blindness of belief'. 'God' for Jung was impersonal as a Universal Consciousness. It was not a belief in an imagined 'transcendent super-being in the sky' that exists separate from human beings, but rather in consciousness, something immanent and experiential.

> *One of the main functions of organised religion is to protect people against a direct experience of God.*
> —Carl Jung[73]

The archetypes

Jung's theory of a 'collective unconscious' holds that all humans have automatic access to a collective, cross-cultural memory. (We find the same concept in Yogic and Buddhist theory, where it is called the 'Akasha'.) Jung understood that humans having knowing access to this was unique to our species. Certainly, consciousness is collective to all species, but the way in which humans have access to it, is unique amongst living beings.

Within this memory were the archetypes: collective repositories of universal archaic patterns. In Jung's theory of the psyche, these archetypes or universal, mythic character aspects of the human personality exist within the collective unconscious the world over. As humans evolved, they came to represent and enfold fundamental human motifs of our experience. Consequentially these 'archetypal motifs' evoke deep emotions and meaning across cultures. Each archetype has its own set of attributes, characteristics, values, and meanings with both positive and negative (shadow) traits.

In a more biological sense they could be viewed as inborn tendencies that shape human behaviour. (Genes were discovered toward the end of Jung's life, whereupon he stated that the archetypes were most likely transmitted through them.) Some of the archetypes in the collective unconscious that we all have access to are: the crone/sage, the trickster, the warrior, the priest/priestess, the clown, the fool, the artist, the mother/father, the hero, the healer, the investigator/detective, the mystic, the prostitute, the pioneer, the monk/nun, the student, the saboteur, the magician, the hermit, just to name a few. Jung isolated twelve as the core representative patterns symbolising basic human motivations in the psyche: hero, creator, explorer, outlaw, jester, lover, caregiver, everyman/woman, innocent, ruler, sage and magician.

The archetype is not merely a psychic entity but Jung regarded them more fundamentally as a bridge between matter and consciousness. Jung used the term *unus mundus*, which is Latin for 'one world', signifying an underlying unified reality from which everything emerges, and to which everything returns, thereby organising not only ideas in the psyche, but also the fundamental principles of matter and energy in the physical world. Jung believed the *unus mundus* is immanent in all manifest phenomena, and he considered the archetypes to be the mediators of this *unus mundus*.

All human beings carry the archetypes as part of specific patterns of information in the collective consciousness. However, while every human being is informed by the full composite of these aspects of the human psyche, there is a specific constellation of key archetypes which act like the *modus operandi* of how each of us functions in life. This manifests in what kind of vocation we are drawn to, our passionate interests, as well what kinds of people we are attracted to. The archetypes we connect to most strongly draw us to vocations, such as a life in the sphere of economics, martial arts, scientific research, spirituality, inventing, farming, acting, philosophy, writing or art. The archetypes also inform what attracts us to other people, and significantly, what we look for in a romantic partner.

Examining our life will reveal the types of archetypes that are at play in us and others, especially loved ones, friends and co-workers. Understanding at this archetypal level can provide useful insights into how behaviours and motivations are informed from the deeper levels of our collective psyche and how we function in relationships and the world.

Jung maintained that the archetypes shared both psychic and material properties; this dual quality he called 'psychoid' (psychic-like). Wolfgang Pauli embraced Jung's concept of psychoid archetypes because it bridged the outside world and the inner world. In doing this it offered a way of explaining some quantum mysteries. Nearly four centuries before Pauli, the German astronomer Johannes Kepler also held this position, intuiting that there is a deeper level of order, an objective order (similar to the 'implicate order' of David Bohm) transcending both the human mind and the external world.

Collaboration between the physicist and the psychoanalyst

In both quantum and chaos theories, quite unintentionally there was a bridging of the traditional dualistic split between matter and mind. Intellectually, the conceptual map that these theories point to is suggestive of a dynamic, intelligent and integrated universe. Theorists like David Bohm have argued that the 'matter' of the new physics is both alive and suffused with consciousness. This is quite unlike the inert and unknowing matter of the classical era of mechanistic physics, and materialist philosophy, wherein nature is viewed as being blind, random, and without consciousness.

It is no accident that the concept of synchronicity emerged in the first half the twentieth century, at the same time as quantum theory. By studying ancient cultures alongside his own and his patients' experiences, Jung observed that synchronicity is a universal phenomenon. Nonetheless, he sought a form of confirmation in science. In the early days of quantum theory, most physicists did not take synchronicity seriously. Jung found a collaborator in key quantum theorist Wolfgang Pauli, with whom he co-authored a book on the subject of synchronicity, titled *The Interpretation and Nature of the Psyche*[74].

Pauli, inspired by Jung's insights, discovered the 'Pauli Exclusion Principle', which he saw as the juncture in the physics of matter, in which synchronicity occurred. The Pauli exclusion principle is mysterious to physicists because it describes how subatomic particles seem to 'know' how to maintain their own 'energy space', behaving in an orderly manner instead of collapsing into a chaotic mess. How do they know this? The three quantum forces (electromagnetism, and the strong and weak nuclear forces) cannot account for this knowing. This, it was conjectured, appeared to indicate some kind of *proto-consciousness*, a knowing property, at the subatomic level, in the particles themselves and/or, the space they inhabit.

> *The Pauli exclusion principle is one of the most important principles in quantum physics, largely because the three types of particles from which ordinary matter is made (electrons, protons and neutrons) are all subject to it, so that all material particles exhibit space-occupying behaviour. Interestingly, though, the principle is not enforced by any physical force understood by mainstream science. When an electron enters an ion, it somehow mysteriously seems to 'know' the quantum numbers of the electrons which are already there, and therefore which atomic orbitals it may enter, and which it may not.*
>
> —Luke Mastin[75]

Pauli and Jung viewed the exclusion principle as a way to account for the acausal connecting phenomenon in human experience, calling it *synchronicity*. Synchronicity connects consciousness and matter, further indicating the essential place of meaning as a primary aspect in the consciousness/matter/energy triad.

Synchronicity and non-locality

The Pauli exclusion principle is not the only candidate in quantum theory to explain acausal knowing and synchronicity. There is also the principle of non-locality, as described earlier. With the advent of non-locality and the idea that the universe is 'entangled' right from its very origins, there has been more interest in the concept of synchronicity amongst the more philosophically minded physicists.

While some people experience synchronistic events regularly, not everyone does (materialists regard the synchronicity as a fabrication) and there are particular reasons for this. People who are 'open', tend to experience synchronicity. By open, I mean that they do not have a strong mindset of belief and opinions (religious or philosophical) or view themselves as isolated separate beings in a disconnected universe. Being open is experiencing that we are connected to everything, in an undivided universe, a universe with patterning intelligence-energy as the primary essential nature of reality. This openness is *energetic* rather than conceptual – it is *presence*. And in this there is an understanding of the meaning, and the exquisite timing of all interactions. In the openness of 'no-mind', we become a receiving and transmitting antenna of consciousness, alive and receptive.

Synchronicity, as expressed in the Taoist philosophy from ancient China, in the writings of Lao Tzu and Chang Tzu, is a philosophy of connectedness in a living universe. Understanding the Tao is to be consciously congruent with the deeper, patterning energy Intelligence present in all there is. This intuitive perception of Being enables us to see how events are connecting inner and outer worlds as the 'one reality', in a meaningful slipstream.

The significance of this is inaccessible to those with a mind burdened with excessive thinking (rational or otherwise) and unchallenged dualistic or materialistic mindsets. Such people commonly experience a vacuum of both meaning and connective significance, because the universe they inhabit is interpreted through mindsets that are closed, relegating their experience of living as fragmented and disconnected.

A natural inner quiet is the gateway to experiencing synchronicity.

> *Do you have the patience to wait*
> *Till the mud settles and the water is clear?*
> *Can you remain unmoving*
> *Till the right action arises by itself?*
> —Lao Tzu, from *Tao Te Ching*

> *A good traveller has no fixed plans*
> *And is not intent upon arriving.*
> *A good artist lets his intuition*
> *Lead him wherever it wants.*
> *A good scientist has freed himself of concepts*
> *And keeps his mind open to what is.*
> —Ibid.

Below is one of Jung's favourite parables, a Taoist folk story illustrating the principle of synchronicity. It signifies a universe connected as a web of consciousness, unifying matter and mind, and the potential for human beings to align harmoniously with the universe. This too was explicit in the philosophy of the Stoics.

During a time of great drought, a Taoist master was asked by members of a village if he could help bring rain to their dry fields. They confessed trying many other approaches before reaching out to him, but with no success. The master agreed to come and asked for a small hut with a garden that he could tend. For three days, he tended the garden, performing no special rituals or asking anything further from the villagers. On the fourth day, rain began to fall on the parched earth. When asked how he had achieved such a miracle, the master answered that he was not responsible for the rain. However, he explained, when he came to the village, he had sensed disharmony within himself. Each day, as he tended the garden, he returned a little more to himself. When he returned to balance, the rain came naturally.

—Alan Briskin[76]

No-mind is the matrix of synchronicity

If we experience the non-duality of Being we become aware of the synchronistic nature of things, as a function of deep inner listening. The thinking functions of the mind, such as rationality, deductive reasoning, imaginative and creative faculties, engage us in the conceptual mapping of reality necessary for our practical, social artistic and scientific functioning, but they have no access to synchronicity. With inner listening, an underlying, connected order is revealed to us, independent of the different kinds of thought activity.

The word 'matrix' (a term hijacked by the sci-fi movies of the same name) actually means 'an enclosure in which something originates' and in Latin, means 'womb'. The state of consciousness of a person is like a matrix. It sets the particular conditions regarding how we perceive things and how we engage with people, situations and the world. Conditioned thinking, beliefs, living in habituated patterns of behaviour and thinking, significantly diminish our ability to experience connectedness. In this way we are in the dream-sleep, and do not feel particularly connected to anything, except in an attached way: with people, with the habitual pursuit of pleasures, and looking for happiness in unhelpful places.

Some people's experience of living becomes 'closed', because it is only informed by their conditioning, and their accumulated knowledge, beliefs and assumptions about what is, and is not, possible. People with this mind-set will experience a universe that is without synchronicity, that neither feels connected nor living. Always below the surface in this experience is a nagging loneliness as a feature of the 'trance'.

Living the examined life is to question the folly of trying to control by imposing the 'thinker's' will over ourselves, others, or events, and we can begin to know a different universe. Questioning the authority of thought destroys its illusion of control and sovereignty. We surrender and let be. Dropping the illusory need to be in control, opens the way to experience an order beyond the will of mind, and phenomenal appearance. In this kind of *unknowing* we experience the truth of Being. Rationality and reason are still there, but simply in abeyance to enable us to experience this kind of intimacy in living. It is an intimacy to which thought is not invited. In silence we witness rather than analyse and explain, with awe, the numinous.

Jung and alchemy

Grounded in the natural philosophy of the Middle Ages, alchemy formed the bridge on the one hand into the past, to Gnosticism, and on the other into the future, to the modern psychology of the unconscious ... Only after I had familiarised myself with alchemy did I realise that the unconscious is a process, and that the psyche is transformed or developed by the relationship of the ego to the contents of the unconscious.

—Carl Jung[77]

In the alchemy of Yoga and tantric Buddhism, there is a subtle non-physical energy-consciousness current known as the *kundalini*. It has been imaged in ancient esoteric texts and in folk art as a sleeping snake coiled at the base of the spine. In the unawakened state this small reservoir of 'consciousness' lies dormant at the tip of the coccyx. When it awakens through the process of yoga and meditative practice, it moves from the coccyx at the base of the spine, and travels upward along the spine, through the 'nadis' (psychic nerve channels which conduct the kundalini energy) passing through the energy centres (chakras) up into the brain, and finally to the crown of the head. It thus passes through the five chakras along the spine and the two centres in the head – the forehead and the crown chakras. Jung wrote of the kundalini process:

...when you succeed in the awakening of Kundalini, so that she starts to move out of her mere potentiality, you necessarily start a world that is totally different from our world: it is a world of eternity.

—Carl Jung[78]

This process is considered an 'awakening' of the subtle energy-consciousness (prana) and even with arduous years of various meditative practices, it occurs spontaneously. It is life-changing to those who experience it, and because it is not physical and phenomenal, it is not subject to regular empirical processes of measurement, detection and analysis. It is not part of the objectivist description of the biological processes of the body. Hence, it can only be verified through experience, which once kundalini awakening occurs, reveals a dimension of consciousness previously hidden to the experiencer.

Jung presented a seminar on kundalini yoga to the Psychological Club in Zurich in 1932. This presentation was considered significant because it outlined the symbolic language and imagery of kundalini (the sleeping snake with its awakening and ascending through the chakras to the crown) as a developmental model of 'phases of awakening into higher consciousness'. The experiential nature of this personal awakening, with the impersonal force of kundalini, Jung interpreted as the process of *individuation*.

The root meaning of 'yoga', 'yuj' in Sanskrit, means to yoke, or bind together. Yoga's path to liberation is by balancing opposites, and in uniting them to create a harmonious being. For Jung, yoga was the embodiment of internal alchemy, achieved by joining the female polarity at the base of the spine (Shakti) with male at the crown (Shiva). This energy, once aroused, was conducted via the passage of the 'shushumna' (psychic nerve channel – 'nadi') along the central channel, with the kundalini energy-consciousness ascending to the crown.

This is foreign to Westerners, who elevate the rational intellect, and will classify, measure and explain things to support the process of empirical knowledge. And this is part of a prevailing concern with an epistemic governed by the dualism separating body and mind. Yet totally relying on, and believing in, this objectivist view, has led to an inner fragmentation, and an experience of separateness. In the spiritual tradition of yoga, verification comes through experience, with the understanding that the experience of separation is a form of delusion created by mind. The proof of union is in the pudding, a union arrived at through the practice of yoga.

The Western view of life is more structured in terms of staying sane, rational and stable, valuing going to work and being a productive member of society. Commonly, the Western approach is to split the conscious mind from the unconscious, with the latter represented in our experiential intimacy of feeling, the body, and nature. Jung suggested that this split happens as a result of an overly dominant rational and controlling mind, suppressing what becomes unconscious and then somatised in the body. And this, Jung believed, potentially led to psychosis.

Jung thought that Westerners would be healthier if they valued contemplation and self-reflection. But in the West deeper self-understanding is judged worthless, whereas objectivist and empirical knowledge is prized. Jung saw that Yoga could connect Westerners back to their intuitive spiritual side, but eventually he believed that the most appropriate route to the unconscious, for Westerners, was to use the imagination, instead of practising the meditative science of yoga.

Jung understood that yogis develop a heightened sense of awareness – where we are less rooted in conscious material, and more rooted in the unconscious, which transforms to a 'supra-personal consciousness'. He believed that types of energetic experiences like the arousal of kundalini, were evidence of a form of internal alchemy; thus, he borrowed alchemical concepts from both the West and the East.

> *In 1928 the eminent German Sinologist, Richard Wilhelm, recently returned after a long period of residence in China, sent Jung a manuscript of a translation of an alchemical treatise of Taoist origin and requested that Jung might write a psychological commentary on the text. This work, subsequently known as 'The Secret of the Golden Flower' catapulted C.G. Jung into the very midst of alchemical themes and interests. His studies disclosed that Chinese alchemy, just like the alchemy of the West, deals primarily with the transformational symbolism of the human soul. Although the ancient Taoists postulated that the quest for immortality was the central work of alchemy, their 'Golden Flower' of immortality is not substantially different from the 'Stone of the Philosophers', which is the supreme objective of Western practitioners of the Great Art.*
>
> —Stephen Hoeller, from *C.G. Jung and the Alchemical Renewal*[79]

Richard Wilhelm, the translator of *The Secret of the Golden Flower*, offered the following:

> *Chinese wisdom and Dr. Jung have both descended independently of one another into the depths of man's collective psyche and have there come upon realities which look so alike because they are equally anchored in truth. This would prove that the truth can be reached from any standpoint if only one digs deep enough for it, and the congruity between the Swiss scientist and the old Chinese sages only goes to show that both are right because both have found the truth.*
>
> —R Wilhelm, quoted in *C.G. Jung and the Alchemical Renewal*[80]

For Jung, the alchemy and its symbolism were pointers to realms of experiential knowing and transformation, which connect a person both within, as a process of individuation, and spiritually, with the living Cosmos. Rather than just analysis, Jung emphasised the primacy of direct experience in building self-understanding. Jung's curiosity led him beyond the thought of his contemporaries and, combined with his rigour and introspection, enabled him to develop a vision of human psychology expanding beyond the limitations of empirical science to a deeper understanding of the evolution of consciousness in human beings.

Awakening consciousness: the kundalini

Theories and explanations of kundalini made by those who have no experienced are done in ignorance. As a consequence, they invariably struggle to understand its meaning, what it signifies, and its relevance in the human exploration of consciousness. An issue that arises with the kundalini is that because it is not phenomenal, the type of language it is traditionally expressed in does not connect with a rationalist and empirical culture. Hence the esoteric description of this experience using the traditional yogic terminology and symbols, means that it can be sidelined as a system of obscure belief, with those experiencing it captive to a fabricated 'esoteric secret'.

For people with an 'objectivist' mindset there is a tendency to portray those experiencing these 'energetic phenomena' as true believers, and to judge such experiences as an indulgent fantasy. And it can easily be regarded as fantasy, as there is no corroborating evidence that can be investigated, unless it is experienced.

So, its very 'other-worldliness', when conveyed to someone with an empirical-cum-rational mindset, would probably invite instant dismissal.

Jung believed that once we have awakened the kundalini, which is an awakening of our unconscious, it is critical not to identify with it. Rather, we should just *observe* what takes place and rigorously *not identify with it* – the danger being that this identifying could lead to madness. Jung advised that the way to handle these experiences was to regard them as if they were outside the human realm. Jung states, in his lecture on the repercussions of identifying with the kundalini experience,

> ... *Otherwise you get an inflation, and inflation is just a minor form of lunacy, a mitigated term for it. And if you get so absolutely inflated that you burst, it is schizophrenia.*
>
> —Carl Jung[81]

Those who experience this powerful 'energetic type' awakening can be drawn into the pitfall of attaching to such experiences and believing that by experiencing this, it confers 'enlightenment'. Those succumbing to this soon engage in the same old pattern of grandiose entitlement. The 'new self-declared guru' develops a cult with its own theology and a hierarchy of authority, with some invited to become initiated into the fold. There are three problems with this illusion: the guru is not enlightened; the followers have allowed themselves to be duped; and another separatist enclave is formed.

Esoteric terminology is another form of labelling, and as such becomes a subjectivist description, albeit esoteric, of a hidden dimensional reality in the human being. It exemplifies the epistemic difficulty in conveying something that cannot be readily verified empirically. We cannot just go and measure an activated kundalini with its current moving up the spine and into the brain with an electronic scanning device. And what are termed 'chakras' – experienced as the energetic 'power stations' along the spine – can only be truly validated by direct experience. Reading about chakras and kundalini, or looking at drawings of chakras, and hearing stories about others' experience of them, is only ever secondhand, and completely unsatisfying to the curious mind. And because the kundalini is a 'numinous' experience, it can only be verified directly.

To someone educated in the empirical mapping of the body with anatomy and physiology, or to a rationalist, kundalini and chakras may sound delusional. After all, there is no physical evidence, and they are not part of empirical science. Such a person might point out that chakras are certainly not found in *Grey's Anatomy;* nor if they performed a dissection into the localities of the chakras, they would not find any evidence of them. This kind of epistemology, as we have discussed earlier, is driven by philosophical assumptions central to the practice of objectivist science, which for all its merits is singularly lacking in dimensionality. But this 'subtle' dimension of consciousness within the body requires a different approach, and a different level of curiosity that entails leaving empirical mapping behind.

Jung was also concerned about this epistemic issue, and questioned the way in which modern psychology positions itself as an empirical science. He did not believe that the multi-dimensional nature of human psychology could be completely understood with empirical evidence, because he himself had experienced events that were beyond empirical facts. These were experiences that were explicitly in the outer realms of the spiritual.

Jung admired yoga as a science because it was grounded in experientially-based evidence, and it corroborated his own spiritual experiences, but it demonstrated the inadequacy in science to examine and to understand the multidimensional nature of the human being.

Experiencing kundalini

If you experience the energy of the kundalini moving through the central channel (shushumna) into the head and the crown (sahasrara chakra) it can be powerful to the point of overwhelming, as I can attest. The force of this experience is of an order that captures our attention more dramatically than simply feeling your toes, being tickled or having a stomach ache. And we know intuitively that we have moved into a dimension of experience of a completely different kind. The energy of kundalini is dimensionally different from any energy experienced before this. We at once know that we are entering unknown territory in the core of ourselves, and alone. We also understand that it is not part of a consensually constructed reality, even though it is recorded in the esoteric literature, particularly of Indian and Tibetan yoga.

Yet kundalini is not something just for the privileged few, because it is a natural unfolding of energy that is usually unconscious but existing in everyone. However, only relatively few do experience its awakening. Few undergo the kind of meditative training that is commonly a precursor to experiencing kundalini. But even with this training there is no guarantee that it will happen. Analogous to this, in the study of sophisticated mathematics undertaken as a pre-requisite for grasping advanced physics, there is similarly no guarantee that that the student will really understand the physics at hand, despite having done the required training.

There are many reports of the transformative experience of kundalini, such as from philosopher Jiddu Krishnamurti who carefully avoided any reference to esoteric terminology (like the term 'kundalini') instead describing his experience of the mysterious 'process' as a psycho-energetic event in his body. This had a profoundly transforming effect on Krishnamurti's consciousness and revolutionised his experience of reality. Also, the spiritual teacher U.G. Krishnamurti (no relation) speaks of the inner alchemy of his inner experience, which he referred to as 'the calamity'. This was because it was at once bewildering, painful, and completely destructive to any kind of mooring in a habitually normal consciousness or identity:

> *Every gland in my body, every cell in my body, has undergone a radical mutation. Why do I use the word mutation? Because I can't think of a more appropriate word. Every gland has undergone a transformation because it seems to be functioning in a different way. The brain waves are incredible, and I would very much like to have the opportunity to use a brain wave machine. The electricity that goes out of my body is tremendous since there is no point inside of me. There is no space for me at all. Then it expands. The electricity that is generated in this body goes to the end of the universe, affecting the whole thing. When I come out of this state, whatever you call it, the whole body is filled with peace. It's some kind of a substance like a white substance. The whole body is filled with this white substance. You can look at it and it shines like a phosphoresce. It's the whole body.*
>
> — U.G. Krishnamurti (1918–2007)[82]

While unusual, these experiences do happen and I experienced a similar event in my early twenties. I had been meditating – resting in awareness – for over two years with a daily practice of an hour or two. I noticed that there was an intensifying of inner silence for about a week before the kundalini event, and the steady building of subtle 'vibrational-humming' sensations throughout the body. At the base of the spine a palpable sensation of energy was gathering. One evening it began in earnest with a powerful electric-like charge at the base of the spine. This went on for a few days and concomitantly with this, my mind was particularly quiet with a feeling of deep calm. I felt exceptionally clear and focused.

Suddenly, as I was sitting quietly in my usual meditative posture, a tremendous surge of internal energy-consciousness travelled from the area of intensity at the base of my spine, moving upwards along the spine, and finally engulfing the whole of my head. The head, and soon my whole body, became flooded with luminosity. At the same time as energy was flooding the brain, there was a roaring sound like an avalanche in my ears. I felt both a sense of awe and some fear at the sheer power of what was occurring right in the center of my being. It was a magnificent power unto itself. At the same time there was a profound sense of connectedness to everything. After what must have been an hour or two, it subsided, to a pleasant glowing throughout the body. I was able to fall asleep in a comfortable feeling of bliss.

During that same night I was awoken with an intense light in the center of my head and the roaring had returned, only magnified. It was truly overwhelming, like a rocket launching in the center of my spine and head. I became anxious as to whether my nervous system was strong enough to handle the immensity of what I was experiencing. I found myself asking if the volume of this energy could be turned down. To my complete surprise it responded. Almost immediately it diminished, which was such a relief, because of its sheer power. It reduced again to a blissful glow and I was able to return to sleep.

Over the next days, weeks and months this energetic experience subsided to a gentle glow, being accompanied by an oceanic feeling of bliss, and a deeply felt connectedness to everything. This was particularly so with the natural world, plants, animals and people. All seemed to be 'glowing with a luminosity'. I experienced an intimacy of being surrounded in love, in a numinous living universe.

Later it crossed my mind that the last person I would mention this to would be a psychiatrist: besides, I was not at all unwell. On the contrary I felt profoundly well, and in a state of heightened lucidity with barely a thought in mind. I did feel the need to exercise care regarding to whom, and how I communicated this experience, if at all. Generally, my attitude was to embrace this new window into the nature of consciousness. For some time, however, I found myself attaching to this experience, as the ego always finds ways to add new experiences in its quest for self-importance, and further structuring identity. It took a while to understand that awareness is primary, and experiences, however elevated and blissful, including kundalini, or those perceived as negative, will all come and, just as surely, go.

I was also aware that these types of experiential noumena would not surrender themselves to any kind of scientific probing, whether by scalpel or scanning device. The devices we have can only measure what they are designed to measure. And the kundalini, with its circulating energy/consciousness of 'prana' or 'chi', is dimensionally different, and not part of phenomenal reality.

Kundalini is mysterious; and why it occurs in some and not others, even with the same training, is perhaps best understood as matter of *grace*. It is not uncommon for it to occur in those who discover a degree of inner mental stillness. But it should not be regarded as 'necessary' or a 'precursor' to enlightenment, that a grasping 'self' may then use an indicator of its spiritual elevation. This only leads to the inflation that Jung spoke of, and the megalomania seen in some gurus and spiritual teachers.

However, in some who experience the kundalini awakening things can go awry and when this does happen it is sometimes considered a curse. Gopi Krishna's account of his experience documented how things for some time went rather badly, until he sought some advice from a guru who could tell him that he could redirect the flow of energy through the 'correct' channel. And this made all the difference.

Sometimes, because it is such a powerful core experience, there is a breakdown, where any psychological mooring in what we thought we knew about life and about our identity is profoundly challenged. The breakdown occurs in the abyss of the unknown in the face of an inner force, wherein everything we have experienced before pales in comparison. When there is overwhelming difficulty in managing and integrating the experience, it can lead into depression and mental illness.

Some have an easier time than others, and this depends to some degree on the general health of the body; whether there are existing unresolved issues (and a tendency for mental illness); whether there has been some inner meditative preparation, particularly of the pure observational kind, which will lessen both resistance and attachment; and how fiercely there is ego resistance to what is happening. Some will sail through on a wave of bliss. In my experience, the profound change to identity was felt immediately, for the kundalini was, and continues to be, a blessing.

The person who has had a mystical experience knows that all the symbolic expressions of it are faulty. The symbols don't render the experience, they suggest it. If you haven't had the experience, how can you know what it is?

—Joseph Campbell[83]

CHAPTER 16

HOW LANGUAGE AND CULTURE INFLUENCE OUR PERCEPTION OF REALITY

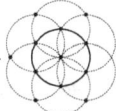

The diversity of human languages is a testament to our creative ingenuity, an expression of the remarkable intelligence expressed in how we move, act, think and speak. There are nearly 7,000 languages currently spoken by human beings, though many of these are heading for extinction. Of these languages none are identical in sound, syntax, lexicon or grammar. We could ask to what extent our perception of reality is shaped by the language we grow up with.

In the halls of university linguistic departments debates have raged between those who believe in a universal grammar and those who hold that languages are relative. Linguist Noam Chomsky maintains that languages have a minimal effect on world view, because they have so much in common at a fundamental level. This Universalist idea was in opposition to the earlier work of the pioneering linguist Benjamin Whorf (1897–1941). In his book, *Language, Thought and Reality: How Language Can Shape Our*

Innermost Thoughts, Whorf outlines the concept of 'linguistic relativity' – that our perception of the world and our ways of thinking are deeply influenced by the structure of the language we speak.

This idea was well portrayed in the 2016 film *Arrival* with the central figure a linguist attempting to decipher alien communication. What is clear is that the language we speak affects how we know, and how we find meaning in life. This is an influence, but it is not strictly determined. We can change things, and we do this through becoming aware beyond the content of where linguistic norms we have been enculturated with – and their implied meanings – may lead us. But, particularly if we are unaware, there is a tendency to be shaped by the cultural root metaphors. For example, the dualistic mindset in the Anglo–European culture that we inherit frames how we perceive things by separating the 'knower' from the 'known', giving rise to an objectified sense of reality. But by being aware of this conditioning, we can be free of it.

Lera Boroditsky, an associate professor of cognitive science at the University of California, and her colleagues, have shown that language – from verb tenses, to gender, to metaphors – can shape the most fundamental dimensions of human knowledge. This includes space, time, causality and our relationships with others. Different languages will have markedly different influences on our perception of reality:

> *English is unusual in that English speakers don't very strongly distinguish between accidental events and intentional events, while other languages do distinguish more strongly. Spanish and Japanese are languages that make that distinction more clearly. If someone intentionally breaks the cup, you'll say, 'She broke the cup' but if someone accidentally does it, then a description is more likely something like, 'The cup broke' or 'The cup broke itself'.*

What I mean by that is that we all intuitively believe that the world is the way that it appears to us, that we perceive reality. And so when you find that someone else thinks differently, the first natural thing to assume is that they are wrong, that they just haven't perceived the world the right way, or they haven't been exposed to the right facts, or they are biased by something. Those are the only explanations, because you believe that you see things the way they are.

The next step in understanding a difference is to say, 'Well, wait a second. None of us see the world the way it really is.' We're all doing a lot of constructing and construing in order to make sense of the information that we get. And so, I see it this way because I've been exposed to these patterns of language, these patterns of culture and this is my history of experience. Based on that history, this is my interpretation, but based on a different history, you might come to a different interpretation. I think that's the hardest thing to learn. It's very easy to note other people elsewhere think differently. It's much harder to then turn the mirror on yourself and say, 'Well, that tells me something about how I think also'.

—Lera Boroditsky[84]

As illustrated by the above example, this research indicates that our language draws our attention to specific types of information, which then in turn influences how we experience events. For speakers of another language there will be a different emphasis, and so they will see and describe the world differently; hence, experience is relative.

And since such habits of speech are cultivated from the earliest age, it is only natural that they can settle into habits of mind that go beyond language itself, affecting your experiences, perceptions, associations, feelings, memories and orientation in the world.

—Guy Deutscher[85]

Collectivist and individualist cultures

When we travel to other cultures, we broaden our minds. So long as we are not insulating ourselves in five-star accommodation, we only need to listen and observe to realise there are many different ways of thinking and acting. Within any country there will be certain mind-sets, beliefs and philosophical ideologies, along with certain ways of processing information, approaching problems and interacting with others, and all these variations will in turn be shaped, reinforced and expressed by the language.

Broadly speaking, most countries in the world can be categorised as either 'collectivist' or 'individualistic' cultures. Individualistic cultures, such as those in Western Europe and in English-speaking nations around the world, tend to have a more analytic and cognitive orientation, with details considered to be more important than context. Collectivistic cultures, such as those generally found throughout Asian and Indigenous cultures, tend to value context more, and to be more holistic in their style of thinking. Indigenous cultures universally demonstrate the collectivistic tendency to think holistically by looking for patterns and connections between events, and between pieces of knowledge or information.

Individualistic societies elevate the individual over the group, emphasising independence, competition and individual achievement in their education systems. Identity is more ego-based and is sought independently from the group. In contrast, collectivist societies place greater value on the harmony and wellbeing of the group over the individual, and on social cohesion and collaboration. People in collectivist societies see themselves fitting into a larger structure with strongly coded mores, obligations and ways of behaving.

> *Where the Euro–American mind will decontextualise information for analysis, the Native mind contextualises for synthesis, with the view that nothing exists in a vacuum, and that there is more to every situation than the event itself. Work by Morris & Peng (1994) provides an example of this, and also the dichotomy of agency; individualistic Euro–Americans view agency as residing within the individual, whereas collectivistic Indians look to the situation and greater context first.*
>
> —Doe Hain-Jamall[86]

Both of these ways of thinking become embedded in our outlook through our particular cultural conditioning, though it is worth remembering that the human mind can show great plasticity, and is capable of using both modes; that is, so long as the mind itself has not already become ossified.

Cultural views of 'matter'

Our use of the term 'matter' perpetuates a myth. It is used to signify some form of separate, unknowing substance without intelligence. This is precisely what the materialist philosophers and most scientists would have us believe. Yet, in Indigenous cultures, there is a more intimate relationship with the earth and the universe at large. People from these cultures know experientially the aliveness of 'matter'. They experience this in their bodies, the rocks, the animals, insects, trees, mountains and rivers. This way of perceiving is known as 'animism', coming from the Latin root 'anima', meaning 'soul'. Animists view nature as intelligent and spiritual, with spiritual forces that orchestrate natural events such as weather patterns, natural flora, human and animal behaviour. Indigenous peoples universally hold this animistic view of nature, from the Kalahari bushman in Africa, to the Aborigines of Australia.

> *When I once asked my colleagues, then students, Drs. Nancy Maryboy (Cherokee–Navajo) and David Begay (Navajo), if there was anything that MUST be referred to as inanimate in Navajo, they talked with each other and elders, finally reporting back months later that there was nothing, except maybe plastic – but that was only because they didn't know what it was made of!*
>
> —Dan Moonhawk Alford[87]

> *The punch line to an old anecdote in anthropology has an anthropologist informing his old Native friend that the outside world labels his people as animists; asked for clarification, he explains that an animist would say that (sweeping his arm around) 'all these trees are alive, with spirits in them'. The Native doubles over laughing*

hysterically, and on recovering says it's the funniest thing he's ever heard! Of COURSE he didn't think every tree there had spirit: 'But that one does, and that one does, and that one over there does!'

—Ibid.[88]

The philosophy and spirituality of Indigenous people have commonly been viewed through a lens of ignorance and disparagingly called 'primitive' and 'superstitious' by urban, post-industrial peoples. Indigenous peoples and their ways are often seen as outmoded, even irrelevant, to the 'march of progress'.

Before the industrial revolution occurred during the 18th century in Europe, people generally viewed nature as sacred, but with the rise of mechanisation, the philosophical ideology of materialism, and the socio-economic agenda of capitalism, people began to objectify nature, as well as themselves. It is not surprising that during this era there was an increase in colonisation of the 'third world' around the globe, as Anglo–Europeans were hungry for new resources and wealth. Consequently, nature's resources, animals, and human beings were reframed as economic units. The European colonisers had great difficulty in understanding Indigenous peoples and vice versa; their very different world views find expression in their use and type of language, and these divisions continue today.

Animate languages

We attempt to communicate our perception of reality in our language, and in communicating it, reinforce our perception as real. It was reported that Aboriginal people in Australia could not see the tall ships of the Europeans when they first arrived, because the ships were so strange and unrecognisable that there was no word to name them. It was only when Captain Cook's men rowed ashore in smaller boats that the Aborigines reacted to the invaders. In this way, humans confronted with radically new experiences or perceptions may not be able to see or comprehend what is happening, nor have the language to map this. Likewise, people who have dramatic inner experiences are often bewildered, even fearful, as their sense of reality is expanded by experiences that can be difficult or impossible to convey in language.

Our language speaks volumes about the level of intimacy we experience in relationship with others and with nature. Certain people, for example, have referred to the pristine wilderness of the Tarkine forest of the north-western part of the island of Tasmania, south of the Australian mainland, as a 'field of tin'. But this comes from people in the corporate mining companies, who want to exploit it for its resources. This is their perceived reality of the wilderness, but is it *real*? Rather than perceiving directly *what is there* – the native flora and fauna, the abundance of life and the deeper significance of this wilderness and its beauty – their minds are conditioned by the conceptual world of economic interest and market value, with a view to the profit they will make.

People with conditioned minds insulate themselves in the reality constructed by their own thinking. This then makes it possible to be dismissive of the actual reality of a living environment. Their chosen use of language serves as a conditioning filter determining their particular 'veiled experience' of what reality is. The emphasis is not on directly experiencing what is there, but on an agenda of objectifying and then accumulating what is there. In Western culture, even the way we view knowledge is seen as a process of accumulation of facts, as part of a drive for acquisition, whereas Indigenous societies have a common tendency to view knowledge quite differently:

> 'Knowledge, to a native person, cannot be accumulated like money stored in a bank; rather, it is an ongoing process better represented by the activity of coming-to-knowing than by a static noun.'
> —David F. Peat[89]

In the American Indian culture, the perception of the 'aliveness' and 'sacredness' of nature is reflected in the language, and human beings are viewed as essentially embedded in nature, not as separate from it. This is indicated by their naming of a person, using animals and natural elements as part of that name. Their languages express narratives of direct experiential connections with nature, and the interrelationships between people. This is different from the subject–object differentiation of a language like English, with its emphasis on ownership and separateness.

As a language, English is 'inanimist'. English speakers must re-animate a world made inanimate by virtue of its pronoun system. For example, we define a plant, an animal, an insect, a star or a spirit as 'it'. In English, if we want to convey a sense of life and respect to a treasured object such as a car or a ship, we tend to use the female pronoun 'she'. But when a ship is divested of its serving life and decommissioned, it becomes objectified as 'it'.

Generally speaking, Indigenous people's languages reflect their experiential realities as dynamically alive environments. For example, in the Algonquin languages of native America, the distinction between animate and inanimate occurs without sexual gender, and defines animate things as 'breathers', and inanimate things as 'non-breathers'.

Verb-based languages: events and processes rather than entities

In European languages, and perhaps most particularly English, we have a great propensity for noun creation because we are focussed on the separation and objectification of things and subsequently, on possession. For example, we call a tree a 'tree' and not something else; we all agree on this. We might further define the tree by its species; e.g. a 'birch tree'. Scientific nomenclature then defines the tree as being of the genus *Betula* in the family *Betulacea*. Our obsession with labelling is evidenced in the extensive cataloguing of flora and fauna. For English speakers, being able to name something is to possess knowledge, and this in turn reflects our de-spiritualised view of nature and the universe.

> *Native American languages are described as verb based, and it is thought that this reflects a cultural focus on action, on connections between a beginning and an end. On the other hand, young English-speaking children learn nouns before verbs and develop labeling and categorisation skills at a much earlier age than do children in collectivist cultures.*
>
> —Doe Hain-Jamall[90]

In Native American and Australian Aboriginal culture, people view things less as material objects and more as events. The emphasis, therefore, is more on the use of verbs in their languages rather than on nouns. Nature is seen as interconnected, alive and energetic. Verbs are dynamic, and signify a relationship of processing and engaging with, rather than ownership or quantification thereof. Native American Dan Moonhawk Alford explains how his people conduct conversations using few nouns. This is something which English speakers find hard to comprehend. He notes the dependence on nouns that can be found in the Western thought systems:

> ...*the logic of classical science demands these same noun phrases, and falls apart completely without them; science glossaries and dictionaries have almost nothing but nouns. We not only can't write or speak without them – we can't even truly imagine doing so! But talking day in and day out without using nouns is no big deal, nuthin' special, for speakers of many indigenous American languages. They have to slow down when talking to Westerners.*
>
> —Dan Moonhawk Alford[91]

In English we use the word 'eddy' to describe the circular movement of flowing water. Eddy, although a noun (a thing) is really an event as it has a fleeting lifespan in the fluid dynamics of moving water. The word, therefore, does not adequately reflect the reality. Likewise, what we define as trees or atoms are also processes or events, and do not exist as 'things' by themselves. This supports the process-oriented philosophers from Lao Tzu to Heraclitus.

> ...*our language works in terms of nouns, so what we tend to see is a world of objects and interactions. And because we have a noun-based language we also tend to see categories*

and concepts, and to put things in categories. So a certain way of thinking, a certain logic, follows from the languages that we speak. But some Native American groups don't have those sorts of languages, as a result of which they don't have the idea of categories to put things in, and they don't come up with the sorts of problems that we do. There's a kind of liberation in that, you see: by looking at their world and coming back to mine, I see my experience of the world as culturally conditioned rather than inevitable; I see that there could be other ways of looking at it.

—F. David Peat[92]

In Chinese, many words function as both verbs and nouns so that, for someone who is thinking in Chinese, it is easier to see that objects are at once events or processes. Even the Chinese characters/word for physics is 'wu li', which can have a range of meanings. Author Gary Zukav, in his book *The Dancing Wu Li Masters*[93], outlines the various meanings of 'wu li':

* patterns of organic energy (where 'wu' means matter/energy)
* my way (where 'wu' means 'my' or 'self')
* nonsense (where 'wu' means void or non-being)
* I clutch my ideas (where 'wu' means to make a fist)
* enlightenment (where 'wu' means enlightenment, or my heart/mind)

For a Chinese speaker, 'wu li' (as 'physics') translates as 'patterns of organic energy' ('wu' meaning matter/energy) and 'universal order/organic patterns' ('li'). The Chinese language more accurately captures the dynamic quantum world, rather than the static classical world that is captured in English or other Indo-European languages. And note, in the quote below, the struggles a native Chinese speaker has with learning English as a second language.

> *The fundamental problem with English for me was that there is no direct connection between words and meanings. In Chinese, most characters are drawn and composed from images. Calligraphy is one of the foundations of the written language. When you write the Chinese for sun, it is 太阳 or 日, which means 'an extreme manifestation of Yang energy'. Yang signifies things with strong, bright and hot energy. So 'extreme yang' can only mean the sun. But in English, sun is written with three letters, s, u and n, and none of them suggests any greater or deeper meaning. Nor does the word look anything like the sun! Visual imagination and philosophical understandings were useless when it came to European languages.*
>
> —Xiaolu Guo[94]

With this is in mind, it is little wonder that misunderstandings occur between people of different languages. Consider the battle between Europeans, who believed in a God (a noun) that could be objectified and owned by 'chosen' believers, compared with Indigenous people, who saw 'God' as a universal event/process that is connected, fluid and dynamic, and equally experienced by all members of the tribe.

Language and time

In Anglo–European cultures, time is considered to be moving in a linear, direct way – we look back in time, we are moving forward to a bright or bleak future and, if we are sage enough, we maintain a realisation of being here and now. This linear notion of time is considered to be universal, but it is far from it; it is in fact completely cultural. In some cultures, spatial metaphors of time are used which create timelines that can even be conceived as running through the body, as reported in *New Scientist*:

> ...Over the past decade, encounters with various remote tribal societies have revealed a rich diversity of the ways in which humans relate to time. The latest, coming from the Yupno people of Papua New Guinea, is perhaps the most remarkable. Time for the Yupno flows uphill and is not even linear...

> Núñez and his colleagues noticed that the tribespeople made spontaneous gestures when speaking about the past, present and future. They filmed and analysed the gestures and found that for the Yupno the past is always downhill, in the direction of the mouth of the local river. The future, meanwhile, is towards the river's source, which lies uphill from Gua.

> This was true regardless of the direction they were facing. For instance, if they were facing downhill when talking about the future, a person would gesture backwards up the slope. But when they turned around to face uphill, they pointed forwards

> If they were facing downhill and talking about the future, the person would gesture backwards.

Núñez thinks the explanation is historical. The Yupno's ancestors arrived by sea and climbed up the 2500-metre-high mountain valley, so lowlands may represent the past, and time flows uphill.

'But the most unusual aspect of the Yupno timeline is its shape. The village of Gua, the river's source and its mouth do not lie in a straight line, so the timeline is kinked. This is the first time ever that a culture has been documented to have everyday notions of time anchored in topographic properties,' says Núñez.

Within the dark confines of their homes, geographical landmarks disappear and the timeline appears to straighten out somewhat. The Yupno always point towards the doorway when talking about the past, and away from the door to indicate the future, regardless of their home's orientation. 'That could be because entrances are always raised', says Núñez. 'You have to climb down – towards the past – to leave the house, so each home has its own timeline.'

'This study is an important landmark,' says Pierre Dasen, an anthropologist at the University of Geneva in Switzerland who was not involved in the work. 'It demonstrates both universality of cognitive processes and a fascinating cultural difference'.

Lera Boroditsky of Stanford University in California agrees. 'Each one of these discoveries isn't just telling us something about other people, it's telling us something about us,' she says. 'A lot of English speakers think that it's natural to think of time as a straight line. But that's an illusion. It doesn't have to be that way'.

—Anil Ananthaswamy[95]

Timelines come in all shapes and directions. For example, for the Aymara people of the Andes, time flows from front to back; the future is behind, as the unknown and unseen, while the past is in front, as the known or the seen. Mandarin speakers in China sometimes represent the past as above and the future below, on a vertical axis. The Pormpuraaw, a remote Australian Aboriginal community in Northern Queensland, use geographical markers of an east-west axis, with the past being east. Descriptions of time must consider the direction the person is facing: when facing south, time flows from east to west (left to right); when facing north, it flows from west to east (right to left); when facing west, it flows away from the body, towards the east.

The Pirahã people living in the rainforest along the Maici River, a tributary of the Amazon, exhibit a language that is very present-focussed, speaking mainly of the present, or the most recent past. Daniel Everett, a linguist, spent years studying their language. He initially attempted to convert them to Christianity but failed dismally because the Pirahã, as they stated to him, had no first-hand experience of this Jesus person nor did they know anyone who had. Therefore, they considered it was irrelevant to them, thus reflecting the importance they placed on present time experiences. Everett was inspired by the philosophical outlook of the Pirahã people and eventually left his faith. He wrote:

> *The Pirahã, who in some ways are the ultimate empiricists – they need evidence for every claim you make – helped me realise that I hadn't been thinking very scientifically about my own beliefs ... I sat with a Pirahã once and he said, 'What does your god do? What does he do?' And I said, 'Well, he made the stars, and he made the earth'. And I asked, 'What do you say?' He said, 'Well, you know, nobody made these things, they just always were here'. They have*

no concept of God. They have individual spirits, but they believe that they have seen these spirits, and they believe they see them regularly. In fact, when you look into it, these aren't sort of half-invisible spirits that they're seeing, they just take on the shape of things in the environment. They'll call a jaguar a spirit, or a tree a spirit, depending on the kinds of properties that it has. 'Spirit' doesn't really mean for them what it means for us, and everything they say they have to evaluate empirically. This is what I hadn't been doing, and this challenged the faith that I thought I had, to the extent that I realised that it wasn't honest for me to continue to claim to believe these things when I realised how little investigation I had done into the nature of the things I claimed to believe.

—Daniel Everett[96]

Language and space

Perhaps the most profound example of the influence of language on thought is the language of space. Like time, it is often assumed that the language of space – how we describe our orientation in relation to the world around us – is universal, but this is not so. In Anglo–European cultures, we use *egocentric* coordinates that relate the position of something to the person; for example, we would say, 'Take the second turn to the right and as you face the blue house; it is the third house to your left.' These directions relate to our body, with the axis based on our immediate visual field. Only in hiking do we use geographical determinants for our orientation. However, in many Indigenous cultures, the geographical directions (which stay fixed regardless of how we turn) are used.

> ... *a remote Australian aboriginal tongue, Guugu Yimithirr, from north Queensland, turned up, and with it came the astounding realisation that not all languages conform to what we have always taken as simply 'natural'. In fact, Guugu Yimithirr doesn't make any use of egocentric coordinates at all. The anthropologist John Haviland and later the linguist Stephen Levinson, have shown that Guugu Yimithirr does not use words like 'left' or 'right', 'in front of' or 'behind', to describe the position of objects. Whenever we would use the egocentric system, the Guugu Yimithirr rely on cardinal directions. If they want you to move over on the car seat to make room, they'll say, 'Move a bit to the east'. To tell you where exactly they left something in your house, they'll say, 'I left it on the southern edge of the western table'. Or they would warn you to 'look out for that big ant just north of your foot'. Even when shown a film on television, they gave descriptions of it based on the orientation of the screen. If the television was facing north, and a man on the screen was approaching, they said that he was 'coming northward'.*
>
> —Guy Deutscher, *New York Times*[97]

This study stimulated further research and it was found that Guugu Yimithirr is not an isolated example. There are many languages around the globe that rely primarily on geographical coordinates. What is remarkable about these languages is that, as a child learns this 'program' from birth, she develops a highly sophisticated and precise 'knowing' of directional orientation, regardless of surrounding conditions that might affect visibility, such as weather, terrain or being indoors.

> *They simply feel where north, south, west and east are, just as people with perfect pitch feel what each note is without having to calculate intervals. There is a wealth of stories about what to us may seem like incredible feats of orientation but for speakers of geographic languages are just a matter of course. One report relates how a speaker of Tzeltal from southern Mexico was blindfolded and spun around more than 20 times in a darkened house. Still blindfolded and dizzy, he pointed without hesitation at the geographic directions.*
>
> *Societies start using geographic directions as early as age two and fully master the system by seven or eight. With such an early and intense drilling, the habit soon becomes second nature, effortless and unconscious. When Guugu Yimithirr speakers were asked how they knew where north is, they couldn't explain it any more than you can explain how you know where 'behind' is. Nor is it easy to speculate about how geographic languages affect areas of experience other than spatial orientation – whether they influence the speaker's sense of identity, for instance, or bring about a less-egocentric outlook on life. But one piece of evidence is telling: if you saw a Guugu Yimithirr speaker pointing at himself, you would naturally assume he meant to draw attention to himself. In fact, he is pointing at a cardinal direction that happens to be behind his back. While we are always at the center of the world, and it would never occur to us that pointing in the direction of our chest could*

mean anything other than to draw attention to ourselves, a Guugu Yimithirr speaker points through himself, as if he were thin air and his own existence were irrelevant.
—Ibid.[98]

It is clear that people of different cultures use thought in creatively different ways, and some of these ways, as expressed in their systems of language, communicate radically different types of perceptions of reality. And it would be misguided to construct a belief which elevates abstract reasoning above all else, for a human being's life is guided by so much more: intuitions, emotional responses, unconscious bias and gut feelings and, even deeper, non-rational ways of knowing. It is the latter which can extend a different order of knowing in people who are not culturally constrained by the limiting belief that afflicts the West – that only rationalised knowledge is valid.

The 'rheomode': David Bohm's new language system

Our research into language, mind and reality would not be complete without looking at how the challenging frontier of the quantum world presented problems in the adequacy of language to convey the bizarre reality of its domain. Neils Bohr, the quantum theorist best known as the principal architect of the Copenhagen Interpretation of quantum theory, and for his Complementarity Principle, found Indo-European languages inadequate to the task of conveying the dynamic and ephemeral nature of the quantum world and its interactions. This was an ongoing feature of Bohr's dialogues with both Einstein and Heisenberg:

> *One of the key problems with quantum mechanics, as Niels Bohr pointed out, is that the Indo-European languages, which we use, deal with concepts and interactions between static objects, and because of that they just cannot seem to deal with the quantum world. We seem to be cut off from it by virtue of our language.*
> —F. David Peat[99]

While not agreeing with Bohr on some key issues about an ontology for quantum theory, Bohm agreed that Indo-European languages, being highly noun-oriented. He thought they were better suited to describing categories and concepts, while the events, processes and constant transformations of the quantum world were difficult to represent accurately.

From his insight into the inadequacy of English to convey quantum interactions, Bohm developed a new language system that he called the *rheomode*, which gives the verb a primary role ('rheo' from the Greek root, meaning 'to flow'). In *Wholeness and the Implicate Order*, Bohm proposed to 'experiment with changes in the structure of the common language'. It was an experiment that was very different from those previously undertaken in linguistics, cognitive psychology, cognitive science and philosophy. In a way he was also heralding the dynamic interconnectedness of things, as it was to be expressed in chaos theory.

Bohm maintained that, in order to deeply understand how language contributes to the way thought is constructed, he considered that it is necessary to actively interfere with its function. In the verb-based rheomode system, flow and movement are emphasised and therefore the language is more able to convey quantum processes and represent the dynamic and ephemeral nature of reality:

> *We may say 'one elementary particle acts on another' but each particle is only an abstraction of a relatively invariant form of movement in the whole field of the universe. So it would be more appropriate to say 'elementary particles are on-going movements that are mutually dependent because ultimately they merge and interpenetrate'.*
>
> —David Bohm[101]

In this way, the rheomode language captures the dynamic nature of events without the nouns that imply stasis and separation. The manner of description Bohm encouraged was mindful of the essential dynamic, seamless connectedness to the whole. When speaking of a thing such as an ocean current, which is not separate from the ocean, it is meaningful to articulate its relative autonomy, while also describing its connection to the oceanic body. In the same way, we can be relatively autonomous as individuated beings, yet mindful of our connection in undivided Being.

It remains unclear whether Bohm ever considered the rheomode to have any practical applications, and whether he wanted people to end up speaking it. However, he does appear to have encouraged staff and students at the Brockwood Park School in England (founded by J. Krishnamurti) to experiment with its use. Towards the end of his life, Bohm met with Blackfoot and Ojibwaj speakers and discovered that their family of languages, as well as their process-driven world views, had much in common with the rheomode as we have discussed above.

Parallels between Indigenous people's world views and new physics

In the 20th century, quantum theory and chaos theory both emerged as challenges to the mechanistic theory of the universe, and its accompanying attitude that humans are separate from nature. Quantum theory, as we have seen, introduced a view of a connected and dynamic universe, along with a mysterious uncertainty, that opened the door, conceptually at least, to a universe that is alive, creative and intelligent. Some quantum theorists have found that, in some important ways, this quantum view of the universe is more akin to the philosophies of Indigenous peoples. At the same time, mechanistic theories are virtually impossible for Indigenous people to understand, so removed are these classical theories from their experience of living.

In the 1980s, quantum theorist F. David Peat was invited as guest speaker to an Indigenous gathering called the Blackfoot Sun Dance Ceremony, in Alberta, Canada. Peat had written extensively on the connection between synchronicity and quantum theory, chaos theory and the nature of creativity, and he recognised that Indigenous cultures have an appreciation of the connectedness of natural systems. After the conference he was inspired to write *Blackfoot Physics*, a comparison of the philosophy of Indigenous peoples and quantum theory. Likewise, physicists Fred Alan Wolf (author of *The Eagle's Quest*) and Arnold Mindell (author of *Quantum Mind: The Edge between Physics and Psychology*) wrote specifically of these parallels. It is no accident that the Blackfoot people, who essentially have a holistic philosophy of living, felt an affinity with the new rather than old mechanistic physics. Their understanding of the connection between their inner life and outer events, the cycles of nature and, most importantly, their process-oriented perception of nature as dynamic, exhibiting the constancy of change, meant that they could see that their philosophy had much in common with these scientific theories.

Although there are significant differences between the many different Indigenous cultures across the globe, there are also important common features, such as: the intimacy of their contact with nature; their experience of the sacredness of place; that nature itself is spiritual; that humans are totally connected to this living environment; their use of non-rational ways of knowing; and the primacy of their experiential perception of reality.

Thus there is much to be learned from these cultures. In 2008 Ecuador became the first country to legally protect Pachamama (Mother Nature). The Bolivian government, being the only Indigenous government on the planet, has recognised the earth as a living entity, equivalent to a human or an animal, and therefore equally entitled to rights. Elevating the status of 'Earth-rights' is now happening in other places across the globe, with legislation now in Papua and New Guinea.

Perception beyond the influence of language

There is truth in the saying that 'when a language dies, so does a whole view of the world and of reality'. Human language is a marvellous invention and each language has its own beauty.

It behoves us to explore the intimacy between thought and language, and to recognise that language and thought are expressions of Consciousness, but should not be conflated with it.

From the perspective that Consciousness is everything, the space between the words, and from whence thought arises – the source of ultimate meaning and identity. For those grounded in the experience of no-mind, there is a deeper reality, beyond the word, beyond language and beyond mind. To express insights of this deeper reality is certainly a challenge for language, particularly a language like English, with its emphasis on noun, possession, and the separation into duality with subject and object. The difficulty is the finite expressing the infinite. How can one express 'that which passeth all understanding'?

When we become aware of the relationship between language, culture, and thought, and that these are all manifestations of Consciousness, we also become aware of how different languages can shape our thinking and perception of reality from birth. But this is not strictly determined, because awareness can shine a light on attitudes enfolded in language.

Our birth language encourages us to think about the world in certain ways, different from those of the speaker of another language and, importantly, this influence is not necessarily permanent. Language unconsciously influences us in the way we identify with 'what we own', 'what we are worth', 'what our status is', 'what our place is in life', how we go about relating to everything and, more fundamentally, 'what reality is'. Essential to any kind of spiritual awakening is being conscious of this.

To find a true sense of universality, we must go beyond thought and language to the source of Consciousness as Being. Some languages, like English, engender a more disconnected view of the universe while others, such as Indigenous people's languages, indicate the dynamic nature of reality. But all language, despite its beauty, is relative and limited, because the map language provides in describing reality, is not the territory.

In Indigenous cultures, it is the shaman who journeys beyond the mind to the spiritual. And in the landscape of our digital age, with the dangers posed by big data, and the inappropriate use of objectivist knowledge, particularly with human beings, it is imperative for us to journey into the unknown regions beyond mind and language, as the shamans do, but we need not go to the forest to do this.

The thirst to know and to communicate is fundamental in human beings. But do we want to stop at the kind of knowledge constructed by thought and limited by language, or do we want to know directly, beyond thought? The different ways of knowing are neither incompatible nor mutually exclusive. Of all the animals on the planet we are exquisitely evolved to be a 'master thinker', a 'master communicator' and, by stepping beyond the known, 'a sage'. Yet we cannot realise our full potential, particularly as a sage, while we are imprisoned by thought. Awakening to the silence of Being transforms this limitation. We can know the unknowable directly beyond mind; in anyone's life, this is an awakening of utmost significance.

I think I could turn and live with animals,
They're so placid and self-contained,
I stand and look at them long and long.
They do not sweat and whine about their condition,
They do not lie awake in the dark and weep for their sins,
They do not make me sick discussing their duty to God,
Not one is dissatisfied,

Not one is demented with the mania of owning things,
Not one kneels to another,
Nor to his kind that lived thousands of years ago.
Not one is respectable or unhappy over the whole earth.
—Walt Whitman (1819–1892)[103]

CHAPTER 17

TRADITIONS OF NON-DUALITY

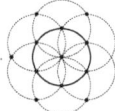

Beyond the concept-making mind, common in religions, is spirituality, which is a direct experience of what is unknown to the mind. 'Non-duality' is essentially the experiential result of awakening. Experiencing the non-dual nature of existence is a cornerstone of the spiritual. To know non-duality conceptually, at the distance of the intellect, is not to 'know' it at all.

But religions have struggled with this, sometimes fiercely. The difficulty in translating spiritual knowledge is exacerbated in cultures where attachment, with the drive to believe and the clinging to form, is the order of the day. For example, this is apparent in religious Buddhism when teachings become doctrines, doctrines become beliefs, teachers become deified, scriptures are revered, endless ritualis are practised, with the pomp of special initiations and the formation of hierarchical monastic cultures, along with the particular deification of the founder.

Rather than acting as agents of awakening, these things serve as props in maintaining a collective trance. Following a religion is a form of dream-sleep that furthers us from standing alone and experiencing direct perception. The wisdom and insights in religious teachings may point to 'that' which is beyond the known, but inevitably the interpretive mind steps in and, in so doing, misses the spirit but finds religion. And so, the mind invariably finds ways to confine that which is not confinable, and measure what is immeasurable.

The idea of following a 'correct path' to a distant spiritual goal has ancient roots stretching back to the Aryan culture as it influenced both Greece and India. Each of these cultures took on transcendentalism from the Aryan invaders. But while sharing the common goal of a transcendent realm, the means and the pathway to get there was similar for some of Greek philosophers, such as Plato who regarded the ultimate quest in our living was to know the Self as the universal Logos – a divine rationality; to the authors of the Vedas in India their journey was also experiential from realising the Self (Brahmin) through meditation.

In India two particular spiritual movements emerged that took a different view from the transcendentalist ideology of Brahmanic culture – Advaita Vedanta and Buddhism. Some regard Buddhism as a reformist movement within Vedic culture. In Ancient China, rather than the transcendentalism of the Greek and Indian experience, a form of spirituality was to develop that connected primarily to nature. It developed an understanding that there was 'a way' that we could cultivate, wherein we exist in a deep harmony with others and the cosmos. And this harmony itself was an expression of the Tao. In Ancient Greece a different manifestation of spirituality emerged with the Stoics, and like the

Taoists, signifying Nature as a divine. With the Stoics, humans were invited to experience being in harmony with the Logos or consciousness interpenetrating all existence.

An ideology of transcendentalism is a duality. The duality exists to provide certainty, and the comfort of an illusory escape from a perceived physical existence, where the 'soul' or 'atman' is regarded as entombed in defiled matter and the senses, for the time-bound ego. This transcendental escape can be the pursuit of a hallowed state of enlightenment in this or a future life. Or it can be a pining for an idealised being of perfection, a transcendental 'God', and a special place for the ego in a heavenly afterlife. It is not surprising that religious followers are bound to miss the central message of the 'spiritually wise', who point out the folly of a belief in the transcendental, as being no substitute for direct experience. *It is only understanding, rather than practices, beliefs and rituals, that can truly liberate.* By leaving the known we embrace a profound uncertainty and unknowing, which requires courage, a point expressed by the Stoics.

'Resting in awareness' or 'presence' is not a technique, nor can it be practised. There has never been a technique that can truly awaken consciousness because, even when some techniques (like Ramana Maharshi's enquiry of 'who am I?') may initially have their use, at some point this too must be discarded. A practice, by definition, is something that the thinking mind has learnt in the past, and repeats in order to refine and improve. This is more relevant to becoming accomplished in playing the guitar or improving our game at table tennis. Presence-awareness goes to the heart of experiencing non-duality, found in the philosophies of Taoism, in the philosophy of Buddhism, in Advaita Vedanta in India, and, to a degree in the Stoics.

The four traditions outlined below (and with the possible inclusion of Sufism) stand out because they emphasise at their core the experience of non-duality. The three traditions from the East explicitly encourage the spontaneous cessation of the internal dialogue, to abide in the 'natural mind'. What they all share is an absence of theology (that usually manifests as transcendentalism and belief in a separate God). Instead, they promote a direct experience of consciousness that is immanent and universal.

Non-duality sees no separation between an imagined 'higher' and 'lower' self, a dualism commonly found in all religions, and esoteric/occult circles, including the New Age movement. There is no admonition to 'believe' in anything, and because of this, they are spiritual philosophies rather than religious theologies.

At their core they speak with a single voice, even though informed in some cases by different languages and cultural settings. And like a chorus they point to an immensity of Being that is immanent, here and now, and accessible by us all. Rather than believe, follow and join, they ask us to enquire and individuate through our own experience, to find our 'inner sage'. To be sage is to know that there has never been a self that has discovered enlightenment. Being is already enlightened.

Spontaneous insight: the 'Jnanis' of Advaita

Brahmanism, a transcendental religion, holds that the individual soul, Atman, aspires to reach the Godhead Brahmin, a 'universal consciousness' achieved through religious observance and practice. Two break-away approaches expressing non-duality developed: Kashmir Shaivanism and Advaita Vedanta.

Advaita Vedanta emerged as a philosophy of non-duality (advaita means 'not two' or 'oneness') from Ancient India. The first clear expression of this was by the famous philosopher Adi Sankara, who lived in the 8th century CE. As the first recorded spokesman of Advaita, Sankara encouraged the importance of the monastic life as outlined in the Upanishads and Brahma Sutra. He stated that, without the qualities outlined below, there can be no realisation of the Truth. These qualities are:

* discrimination between the real and the unreal;
* disinclination to enjoy the fruits of our actions;
* the six virtues of tranquility, self-control, withdrawal, forbearance, faith, and concentration of the 'Self' (universal consciousness); and
* intense yearning for liberation.

Moving into its more modern era the Vedantic traditional aspect was de-emphasised. With emerging new teachers like Ramana Maharshi and Nisaghadarta, inviting seekers, particularly from the West, to participate in the experience of non-duality, the (Vedantic) traditional aspects were put to the side.

Non-duality in Advaita teaching is often expressed as 'one without a second', reminding us that if there is only 'one', there is no 'two', or no 'other'. This 'one' is traditionally referred to as Brahmin, or the 'Self' as impersonal consciousness. The phrase 'I am That', uttered by Advaita philosophers, is a profound epistemic leap from the position of duality – the duality of being a spiritual seeker with an idealised spiritual liberation at the end. In Advaita, awaken now, as you are, as there is no-one to get enlightened. To truly understand non-duality, it must be experienced; otherwise it is just an empty concept, just as a description of the sunset is not the actuality.

Jnana literally means 'wisdom by experience', which is among the eight traditional branches of Indian yoga. Famous Advaita *jnanis* or 'wise seers' of the past hundred years or so are: Ramana Maharshi, Nisagadhatta Maharaj, Jean Klein, U.G Krishnamurti, J. Krishnamurti and Poonjaji. Ramana Maharshi holds a significant place, because he was the first Advaita teacher to emphasise Advaita, without the 'Vedanta' component and its traditional practices of a monastic culture and ideology.

There are also a number of more recent Advaita teachers from Anglo-European cultures. For example, 'Sailor Bob' (Bob Adamson, a disciple of Nisagadhatta), Francis Lucille, Rupert Spira, Unmani, Suzanne Mari, and Adyashanti.

> *Your duty is to be: and not to be this or that. 'I AM that I AM' sums up the whole truth. The method is summed up in 'BE STILL'. What does 'stillness' mean? It means to 'destroy yourself'. Because any form or shape is the cause for trouble. Give up the notion that 'I am so and so'. Our sastras say aham iti sphurati (it shines as 'I').*
>
> —Ramana Maharshi[104]

Jnanis make vital contributions to our understanding of the nature of Being, and in addressing the nature of human identity. They offer their 'non-teaching' with clarity, refreshing directness and, generally, in plain language. They challenge us to discover the 'original mind' beyond conditioning, belief or conceptualising. They maintain that there is no moment in time in which this direct knowing of who we are can be achieved. How can we achieve that which already is, and has always been? We are in a perennial state of distraction, and just not used to resting in awareness.

Most importantly, they offer nothing in the way of practices to achieve what already is. There is no promotion of an ideology of enlightenment, won through hard work and struggle by a 'me', that is itself a fabrication. The mental effort we experience, including the pining for God or realisation, is all part of the actual resistance to being fully present in moment-to-moment living.

> *Reality is simply the loss of ego. Destroy the ego by seeking its identity. Because ego is no entity it will automatically vanish and reality will shine forth by itself. This is the direct method, whereas all other methods are done, only retaining the ego... No sadhanas (spiritual practices) are necessary for engaging in this quest. There is no greater mystery than this – that being the reality we seek to gain reality. We think that there is something hiding our reality and that it must be destroyed before the reality is gained. It is ridiculous. A day will dawn when you will yourself laugh at your past efforts. That which will be on the day you laugh is also here and now.*
>
> —Ramana Maharshi

Jnanis can be at once ruthless and humorous in pointing to the follies of mind that obscure what is already here and now. They expose the cleverness of the mind that insists on playing with notions such as a separate thinker and doer, time-based spiritual cultivation of the 'seeker', notions of a separate God, and seeking comfort in the shadow of the guru – the culture of transcendentalism common in the religious. The jnanis suggest that the key is in 'non-doing' – the realisation that there really is no 'doer'.

> *By being free from all desire and fear, from the very idea of being a person. To nourish the ideas 'I am a sinner', 'I am not a sinner' is sin. To identify with the particular is all the sin there is. The impersonal is real, the personal appears and disappears. 'I am' is the impersonal Being. I am this is the person. The person is relative and the pure Being – fundamental.*
>
> —Nisargadatta Maharaj[105]

They emphasise that 'the way' of liberation is all-inclusive, because there is no particular lifestyle required to be who we already are. We are no closer to Truth if we are celibate or in a relationship, with, or without children. There is no hierarchy in the no-thingness of Being. The great liberation is in letting go the striving for attainment, the search. That there is 'no one' on the search, nor to give up the search. With no other time than now, there is nothing to achieve, and there are no special conditions for awakening. This provides a challenge to the traditional paths, often part of monastic culture, such as taking vows, of being 'chosen', or needing a 'special birth'.

A criticism of the Advaita teachers is that they offer a 'lazy person's approach to enlightenment' because gone is the effortful struggle through time, the arduous practice of spiritual cultivation with its trials, tribulations and many sacrifices with a promise of just reward at the end. In contrast, the jnanis of Advaita challenge the mind's sense of attachment to personal history, to striving, to the identity of being a 'spiritual seeker', and personal authorship – the doer. With no striving and no psychological self to do it, and no special initiations needed, we are ripe to realise that freedom is already at hand. But importantly, as Nisagadatta advises with his ripening fruit metaphor, there is a period of intensity as we deepen in abiding in awareness, and just as the fruit ripens on the tree, at a certain point it will drop suddenly – awakening.

The key is abiding in awareness:

> *Reality is simply the loss of ego. Destroy the ego by seeking its identity. Because the ego is no entity it will automatically vanish and reality will shine forth by itself.*
>
> —Ramana Maharshi[106]

The 'effortless way' of Taoist philosophers

The philosophy of Taoism originated before the arrival of Buddhism in China over 2,500 years ago. Story has it that an elderly royal archivist, Lao Tzu, disillusioned with court life, set off on an ox towards the western mountains. Legend says that Lao Tzu was stopped at the Chinese frontier by a guard who would not let him pass until he had transcribed what he knew, in what became the Tao Te Ching (which translates as 'The Classic of the Way's Virtues'). The emphasis here is on accepting the constancy of change in Becoming and, just as a fist cannot grab water, the mind through thinking, cannot know *reality*.

> *The 'this' is also 'that'. The 'that' is also 'this'…*
> *That the 'that' and the 'this'*
> *Cease to be opposites, is the very essence of Tao.*
> *Only this essence, an axis as it were,*
> *Is the centre of the circle responding to the endless changes.*
> —Yu-lan Fung[107]

The Tao is the ultimate Ground of Being, but cannot be grasped with the mind. It is purely experiential. From the absolute primordial void or emptiness (parallel to Nagajuna's Emptiness) arise things as they appear. Everything is viewed as consciousness-energy as imbued with *chi* (life force). *Chi* is not a separate essence but it manifests experientially and energetically, exhibiting the relative polarity of yin (receptive, electro-negative, cold, moist, yielding, internal, female, feeling) and yang (outgoing, electro-positive, hot, dry, assertive, external, male, thinking). Experiencing the universal subtle energy '*chi*' directly (the equivalent is 'prana' in the Indian cosmology) is a matter of intuitive perception through meditative practices, signifying a developing awareness that consciousness is much more than thought.

The forced actions of human beings resulting from the separation of mind, in relation to Tao, is explored in a dialogue between Ch'an masters Nan-ch'uan and Chao-chou:

> *Chao-chou asked, 'What is Tao?'*
> *The master (Nan-ch'uan) replied, 'Your ordinary consciousness is the Tao.'*
> *'How can one return into accord with it?'*
> *'By intending to accord you immediately deviate.'*
> *'But without intention, how can one know the Tao?'*
> *'The Tao', said the master, 'belongs neither to knowing nor to not knowing. Knowing is false understanding; not knowing is blind ignorance. If you really understand the Tao beyond doubt, it's like the empty Sky. Why drag in right and wrong?'*
> —Nan-ch'uan[108]

And this from Chang-Tzu:

> *The Tao has reality and evidence, but no action and no form. It may be transmitted but cannot be received. It may be attained but cannot be seen. It exists by and through itself. It existed before heaven and earth, and indeed for all eternity. It caused the gods to be divine and the world to be produced. It is above the zenith, but is not high. It is beneath the nadir, but is not low. Though prior to heaven and earth, it is not ancient. Though older than the most ancient, it is not old.*
> —Chang-Tzu[109]

The *Tao Te Ching* approaches life from an experience of '*wu ji*', meaning 'nothingness', and '*wu wei*', meaning 'effortless doing without the doer'. Nothingness is the essence of all form, and awareness of this primordial void allows for the unimpeded flow of '*chi*', or life force. In the forms, shapes and energetic dance of manifestation, the polarity of 'yin' and 'yang' is an energetic description of the landscape of Consciousness as Being.

Taoism, in developing its 'ism', became religious with the development of different sects with their own philosophical differences, each presided over by a priestly hierarchy, sacred writings, and the godly status of Lao Tzu and other 'immortals', along with the development of ceremonial and religious rituals. There is also esoteric Taoism (Hsien Taoism), specialising in its quest for immortality. With this comes attachment to endless practices in the culture of practising 'internal alchemy'. This is a different kind of transcendentalism in its one-pointed quest for enlightenment and immortality, similar to the Sadhus of India. Yet this approach, with its attachment to practices, only confuses the mind by strengthening a transcendentalist ideology of the 'special path of the aspirant', and subsequently preventing a deeper understanding of 'the Way'.

Lao Tzu was keenly observant of universal patterns, the impermanence of existence, the follies of the human mind, and the eternal immanent dimension beyond mind. His philosophy is compassionate, all-encompassing, and grounded in the depth of Being. He offered no specific practices to achieve the Tao, or 'the way', because it simply is, cognisant that any attempt of the mind to grasp it is futile, leading only to error. The experience of the Truth of Being as beyond the mind is in resonance with Advaita, the non-dualistic strains of Buddhism and the Stoics, all being philosophies of the numinous.

> *Confucius said, 'Unify your will and don't listen with your ears but listen with your mind. No, don't listen with your mind, but listen with your qi. Listening stops with the ears, the mind stops with matching (perception), but qi is empty and waits on all things. Tao gathers in emptiness alone. Emptiness is the fasting of the mind'.*
> —Confucius Daoism[110]

The Tao explains that all phenomena are changing and impermanent, and that the timeless nature of the Tao is ungraspable through reason. We are encouraged to experience and flow with the currents of universal life, as 'awakened' yet ordinary members of society. In this Taoist approach, the ethical compass is informed by the silence of Being. True virtue is not idealism but is found beyond mind and the rigid adherence to codes born from the duality of good and evil. This is a matter of realisation rather than a belief.

> *Those who follow the natural order flow in the current of the Tao.*
> —Lao Tzu[111]

The *Tao Te Ching* is essentially 'a-religious' while being deeply spiritual. Like Advaita, there are no specific beliefs, practices or special conditions. The opening stanza of the *Tao Te Ching* sets the tone:

> *Tao, if articulable, is not the eternal Tao.*
> *The name, if can be named, is not the eternal name.*
> *Heaven and earth start with no name,*
> *The named is the mother of everything under the sun.*
> *Thus, with a detached mind, you see the secret,*
> *With an interested mind, you see the appearances.*
> *These two grow out of the same,*
> *But they are named differently,*

*They are both mysterious.
Mysterious and ineffable,
They are the essence of all secrets.*
—Lao Tzu[112]

Whereas Lao Tzu was the epitome of the gentle knowing sage, his pupil Chang Tzu was an irreverent, unconventional, wild-man sage. Through his stories and teachings he challenges us to deconstruct any ego self-importance, and calls us to travel lightly, effortlessly and with humour. Chang Tzu's style is confronting and provocative, designed to upset complacency, religiosity, systematised belief, pomp and hierarchy. His humour and penetrating insight expose the folly of self-importance and point to the heart as a refuge, and origin of the ethical living. Chang Tzu, ever playful, symbolises a different kind of internal alchemy, one not self-obsessed with esoteric practices to physically achieve an idealised immortality (transcendentalism), but as lived in the hermetically sealed vessel of conscious human awareness. It is transforming to the natural state, the primordial innocence of the *original mind*, leaving behind the inauthentic and the false.

*The most extensive knowledge does not necessarily know it;
Reasoning will not make men wise in it.
The sages have decided against both these methods.*
—Chang Tzu[113]

No-mind of Gautama and Zen

Siddhārtha Gautama, born into a noble family in Northern India sometime between the 6th and 4th centuries BCE, was driven by an abiding curiosity to discover the truth of Being. Awakening to this under the Bodhi tree, he spent the rest of his life in compassionate service, teaching his realisations. Gautama did not approve of the title 'Buddha', which in Sanskrit means 'awakened one'. Instead he referred to himself, as outlined in the Pali Cannon, as 'Tathagata', signifying, more modestly, that he was 'beyond all coming and going', and by this, meaning that he had escaped the cycle of rebirths. Gautama may well have been aware of the pitfalls in carrying the more elevated title of 'The Buddha', because this deification emphasises him as transcendent being, an elevation favoured by those with a religious mindset (often he is referred to as 'Lord Buddha') bent on constructing and following a 'saviour', rather than a person who is sage.

Generally, the Buddhist view emphasises:

* understanding the nature of reality: this is done through meditation.
* that there is no separate self. 'The foolish man conceives his idea of Self; the wise man sees there is no ground on which to build the Self. Thus, the wise man has a right conception of the world. He will conclude that all component things will be dissolved again, but the Truth will always remain.'
* non-duality: the Buddha is recorded in the Pali canon, speaking of the practice of 'non-abiding', which is to perceive the rejection of the separation of the objective

and subjective: '*You will not be able to find yourself either in the world of this [subject] or in the world of that [object] or anywhere between the two.*'

* the 'middle way' between asceticism and hedonism;
* that the path to freedom from unease (not self) is through ethical action (the eight-fold path and the Four Noble Truths);
* compassion for all sentient beings caught in samsara or ignorance;
* 'emptiness' for Nāgārjuna (and Gautama before him), means that all things are 'selfless' or non-substantial; all phenomena are without 'self-nature', or 'inherent existence', and thus without any underlying unique separate essences or souls. As Nargajuna said, '*One who is in harmony with emptiness is in harmony with all things*'.
* the non-duality of form and emptiness as famously expressed in the Heart Sutra:

Oh, Sariputra, form does not differ from the void,
and the void does not differ from form.
Form is void and void is form;
the same is true for feelings,
perceptions, volitions and consciousness.
—Bodhisatva Avalokiteshvara[114]

* the impermanence of all forms. The phenomenal world, with its appearance of separate things and beings, including thought itself is eternally changing.
* that following the Dharma is to understand the truth, or the ultimate reality of 'the way that things really are'.

Gautama taught that mind is not the source of identity, and that we are in error by attaching to it. He advocated all-encompassing attentiveness in mindful meditation as the foundation for living. Practising this would break the illusions that lead us to identify with the mind and the body – this ignorance leads to suffering. The term 'mindful' does not refer to a mind full of thoughts but rather to awareness itself which, in the process of observing, brings non-attachment to thinking and sensation. It thus encourages a spontaneous quietness of mind as 'no-mind'.

In Pali, 'dukka' means 'suffering, dissatisfaction, and stress'. When the Buddha said that 'the five aggregates subject to clinging are dukka' he did not mean that life was suffering, as it has been mistakenly interpreted. But, more wisely, when we cling to, or are attached to the five aggregates: form, sensation, perception, volition, and consciousness, that suffering arises. Freed from clinging, we automatically live the middle way, the way of equanimity, and it is this understanding that brings the end of suffering.

Zen has its origins in the passage of Buddhism from India to Japan via China in 200 BCE. The Buddhist Bodhi Dharma, who had travelled from India to China, founded Chan (Zen) Buddhism in China. There, Buddhism was influenced by Taoist philosophy, which transmuted to Chan Buddhism, and then into Zen as it moved across to Japan.

Dogen Zenji (AD1200–1253), a monk disillusioned with the Buddhism he practised in Japan, journeyed to China where he gained inspiration and returned to Japan bringing a more essential form of Buddhist teachings. The emphasis in Dogen's way is sitting meditation or zazen.

To study the Way is to study the Self. To study the Self is to forget the self. To forget the self is to be enlightened by all things of the universe. To be enlightened by all things of the universe is to cast off the body and mind of the self as well as those of others. Even the traces of enlightenment are wiped out, and life with traceless enlightenment goes on forever and ever.

—Kim, Hee-jin, *Eihei Dogen, Mystical Realist,* Wisdom Publications, 2004 p. 125.

Like the Taoist philosophers, genuine Zen masters hold no stock in the theorising or interpretation of the mind. In this they differ from a number of other Buddhist schools. In Zen, for example, no importance is given to the more religious idea of taking 'refuge' – in the Sangha (Buddhist community), the Buddha, and the Dharma (the way). A famous saying in Zen circles is that 'if you see the Buddha on the road kill him' – a metaphor referring to the perils of any form of attachment. Deifying a teacher is an impediment to awakened seeing, and the Dharma.

Zen also differs, in emphasising that enlightenment comes to a person instantaneously, in a flash, like the spontaneous seeing of the jnanis, rather than gradually. In Zen, the mind and reasoning is regarded as an obstacle to the immediacy of a direct experience of Truth.

Another 'direct path' Buddhist school, the Zogchen tradition from Tibet, also shares some similarity with Zen. In Zogchen it is said that the primacy of an all-inclusive awareness is expressed thus: *'non-conceptual, ever fresh presence – awareness, thou art this and only this'*.

To a mind attached to the consensual reality created by mind, the poetry and teachings of Zen may appear incomprehensible and baffling, but they are specifically designed to awaken the seeker from the slumber of their conditioned rationalistic and empirical conclusions about living. Questions that seem like nonsense are deliberately posed, such as, 'What is the sound of one hand clapping?'. But while the simplicity and austerity of Zen seems otherworldly, the sitting practice of zazen is essentially meditation without technique, as pure observation, to awaken the 'beginner's mind' – a mind free of concepts and interpretations, dissolving separateness and any kind of mental fixity.

> *A special transmission outside the scriptures,*
> *Not founded upon words or letters,*
> *Pointing directly to the human mind,*
> *Seeing into one's nature and attaining Buddhahood.*
> —Albert Welter[115]

The essence of Zen is that no-mind can neither be practised nor forced; rather, it just happens. The Zen master is indistinguishable from the ordinary person. After enlightenment, we are still seen sweeping the path, just as before. All that is different is a profound sense of undivided presence. Awakened consciousness alongside the ordinary and day-to-day is a recurrent theme in Zen teaching. The Zen way to see truth is 'through your everyday eyes', but with a lens cleared of interpretations. It is only the relentless resistance of life-as-it-is that ties a person in knots. Zen teaches that we do not need an answer in order to find peace; we need to surrender, to cease the needless, empty questioning. To a Zen master, the secret of awakening is: 'when you are hungry, eat, and when you are tired, sleep'.

> *One day the great Master Huang-po and a monk were walking along, talking and laughing together like old friends. When they came to a swollen river, the monk tried to take the master across but Huang-po said, 'Please cross over yourself'.*
>
> *The monk walked across the waves as though walking on a field. Once on the other side he called, 'Come across! Come across!'*

The master scolded him: 'You self-perfected fellow! If I had known you were going to perform a miracle, I would have broken your legs!'

The monk sighed with admiration and said, 'You are a true Master of the Great Vehicle'.

—*The Little Zen Companion*[116]

In the 'doings' of life, whether assisting others or doing menial tasks, the Zen sage is 'doer-less', acting without self: without identification as 'doer' is 'non-doing'. The essence of this state is transmitted from the Zen master to disciple in a nonverbal transmission of understanding. In a flash, the student understands immediately and effortlessly in no-mindedness.

Does a monastic culture exemplify a 'middle way'?

Being a renunciate, adopting the trappings of a 'spiritual life: robes, name changing, taking vows and living an idealised monastic life – rather than affording an unattached life from materialism, pleasure seeking and ego desires, the monastic way may instead encourage other forms of laziness. Just by renouncing the conventions of the world in the formal lifestyle and ideology of being a monk or a nun means nothing in terms of addressing the root of the problem we face, attaching to the sense of agency in all our doings – ego. In fact, it can create the illusion that the ego is further along a spiritual path towards enlightenment.

Monasticism is a form of extremism and can hardly be regarded as exemplifying a 'middle way'. If the middle way is a course between a life of self-indulgence and ascetic denial, monasticism obviously puts it towards the ascetic end. Monasticism in Buddhism has its origins in the particular life of Siddharta after he left his family and wandered as a sadhu in his search for truth.

He lived the life of a wandering renunciate amongst the community of spiritual seekers as a sadhu for years, finally engaging in more extreme bodily mortification indulgences. As story has it, he was saved by a passing woman who kindly fed him, and he realised his error. In this realisation he discovered the 'middle way' between extremes, yet failed to understand that the 'monastic path' does not really address the nature of what a middle way is, nor the primary issue of how we become enmeshed in attaching to things.

But the life of a renunciate, a wandering spiritual seeker who must forebear physical hardship, was the only kind of 'spiritual life' he knew. After his awakening the renunciate's life was enshrined as the way. The move from spirituality to religiosity thus ensued, as Buddhism came to flourish as a religion, with its emphasis on belief, rituals, dogma and attachments. And, as commonly happens after the death of a religious leader, the factions started to emerge and his closing wish, that he should not be followed, went unheeded.

Beneath the surface there is, from the outset, an unexamined fear in the monk's or nun's path; as though living in relationship as a sexually differentiated animal, with natural desires to eat and socially engage, will in some way distract us from focussing on discovering truth. Rather, the monk's or nun's path speaks of a dualistic mindset, embedded in Brahmanic and Buddhist culture, of an idealistic life and identity, as a sannyasin, for fear of the uncontrolled and unavowed.

The rigorous restriction of the monk's life, is an attempt to control both thought and behaviour, through the sheer willing of it, as an idealistic pursuit. This only perpetuates ignorance, by maintaining a life of rigid imitation and habitual, unquestioned attachments under the illusion of following a spiritual path. It encourages all the functions of a striving 'self', ever fearful of its fall from 'grace', with its issues of control, frustration, and ambition. All of this necessarily sees an unhealthy cultivation of a shadow energy (resulting from vows of restriction) that may manifest in destructive patterns of behaviour. Monastics are not immune from committing or encouraging violence, grasping for wealth or status, and in seeking promiscuous, predatory and sometimes violent sexual adventure.

However, the idea that relationship is not regarded as an essential part of a committed spiritual life, is fundamentally wrong. Also, the belief that the necessary preconditions for awakening are compromised by relationship, desire and sexuality is an imposed religious dictum, rather than arising from the truth of Being. Attachment to the body and to the mind, and a belief in separate agency is a universal affliction of humans. But the 'original mind' spoken of in Zen and Zogchen is ever available, regardless of whether we are monastic or not. But it is not accessible to those who are struggling with fear and desire in the guise of vows of control, for most surely their minds are full of ego-centric struggle.

Stoicism: the individuating sage in harmony with Being

Similar to the three Eastern traditions of enlightenment, Stoicism is the sage experiencing eudamonia (a state of blessedness). During the Hellenistic philosophical flourishing in Ancient Greece, Zeno of Citium (Cypress) founded his school of philosophy in Athens from about 300 BCE. As the story goes, Zeno, a wealthy merchant, was sailing with all his goods from Phoenicia to Peiraeus. He survived being shipwrecked in a storm, having lost everything but his life. Later, in Athens, while visiting a bookseller he read Xenophon's *Memorabilia,* and was inspired by stories of Socrates. He asked the bookseller where he could find men like this. Then, in a moment of synchronicity, the bookseller pointed out Crates of Thebes, a famous Cynic, who at that moment happened to be walking by.

Zeno became Crates' pupil, studying the Cynic (dog-like) philosophy. The Cynics flouted convention, advocating a radical ascetic approach to living in accordance with nature, maintaining that living a life of virtue was singularly enough, and that the essence of living a good life lies in self-control, independence and shunning worldly materialism.

In the story of Zeno, we see some parallels with the story of Gautama the Buddha. Both were wealthy men losing all worldly goods (in Gautama's case by choice) and, in their search for spiritual wisdom, both becoming ascetics, only to reject this (Zeno left the Cynic way) with both going on to develop a 'middle path': one between sensual indulgence and its opposite, ascetic denial.

Zeno distanced himself from the cynics, holding that they were too extreme in their rejection of the basics of living (food, clothing, housing, education) while maintaining that the essence of a 'good life' was living a virtuous and moral one (in this way similar to Kantian 'virtue ethics') for its own sake. He wrote a response to Plato's *Republic*, challenging Plato's idealised society, and proposing a more egalitarian one.

The term 'stoic' comes from the Greek 'stoikos', meaning 'of the stoa' (porch). The painted stoa in Athens is where Zeno and his followers would meet. It was an open space where learning was encouraged without the adherence that occurs in a formalised school.

The physics of the Stoics was based on the process philosophy of Heraclitus: a cyclic universe, with the matter of the universe suffused with logos (consciousness). The logos or God was nature (as with Spinoza) and here we could equally use 'Being'. The human being was a fragment of this universal intelligence, and hence could actively align with it by living harmoniously in accord with nature and knowing the Self. The Stoic view is sometimes described as pantheism, in equating God with nature.

The Stoics differed epistemically from the Universalists (Plato, Aristotle and Socrates) in holding experience (rather than abstract theory) as primary to our knowing, and indeed as the only way we can have certainty. To the Stoics, nature is divinely intelligent, ordered and self-organising, from the particular things to the whole, with nothing happening by chance. The Stoics, unlike the Epicureans and the Atomists, held that the entire universe is strictly determined, intelligent, living, and connected. The cosmic order of things, exactly as they are, is an expression of divine will, and by accepting things exactly as they are, we can be in alignment, harmonising with the living universe.

Being in harmony with existence is a primary concern; for example, if a Stoic is pursuing a particular goal in life or in business, of greater importance is alignment with the will of the universe from moment to moment. This awareness makes for a more valued connection to being present, and with being unattached to outcome.

In the vision of the good life the pre-eminent Stoic philosopher becomes a sage. That is, people of impeccable moral character and a true cosmopolitan. With their 'polis' being the cosmos, they are at home wherever they are. And this is possible whatever their circumstances, whether as the most powerful man in the world as the Emperor of the Roman Empire (Marcus Aurelius) or as a slave (Epictetus) – both prominent Stoic philosophers during the Roman period. However, Aurelius's support for the persecution of the Christians was more barbaric than sage-like.

For the Stoic, self-control, achieved through attentiveness/mindfulness and fortitude, rather than an effort of will, is primary to overcoming destructive emotions in order to be free from anger, envy and jealousy. This de-conditioning allows us to become clear and unbiased in our thinking. We can then understand the 'universal reason' (logos) through both intuition and reason. The foundation of ethical wellbeing is in aligning our will in agreement with the 'Divine Will of Nature'. Agreement with nature also applies to our interpersonal relationships, as outlined in the Stoic adage to accept even slaves as 'equals of other men, because all men alike are products of nature'. This was a radical proposition in the slave culture of Ancient Greece.

The key idea is that the human condition is full of troubles and worries, but to the Stoic it is a matter of working out what is, and is not, in our control. What is not in our control is left in the hands of nature, the logos. But we can control all of our responses to things – people, events, situations – which include our behaviour, our actions, our beliefs, our interactions, our emotions, our thinking and our attitudes. And by taking full responsibility we are free, and can live a virtuous, blessed and happy life known as 'eudamonia' – a state of awakened consciousness or blessedness perhaps similar to enlightenment.

This requires rigorous attention or mindfulness to our inner world. In this way, which is very similar to Buddhism, we root out ignorance, which manifests by being a slave – to our conditioning, to passions, or by being pushed about by emotions, and to all forms of unconsciousness, as the automatic and conditioned responses to situations. Everything is exposed to the light of awareness, and this brings a capacity to think rationally and develop serenity in all matters, including extreme adversity. To the Stoic if we want to be fully human it means being fully free (through deconditioning), rational, and living harmoniously in Being.

The Stoic, by being in harmony with nature and following the four virtues of wisdom, justice, courage and temperance, appeals to the logos of nature in all ethical action, through awareness, and the right use of reason. In this way, rather than engaging in group-think or unconsciously following the mores of popular belief or opinion, but instead through conscious awareness, a person individuates. Our freedom lies in conscious awareness, freeing us to respond spontaneously and creatively to situations and living in the present: knowing the Self.

Stoicism excels as a very practical set of philosophical insights serving as guidance for right action. Each of us gets the opportunity through the inevitable 'curve-balls' that any life presents, to define in ourselves the invisible etchings of character, in living a virtuous life, by openly facing life's difficulties. Any obstacle is transformed to instead 'become the way', as Marcus Aurelius states, echoing the Taoist teachings of being in harmony with the current of life and following the water-course way. The Stoics also advised having a 'plan B', to encourage flexibility and unattachment.

Living the good life is not dependent on health, wealth or education, because the natural state is one of happiness when we are freed of attachment to that which is inessential. The Stoics held the category of 'preferred indifference' for things like health, wealth and education, and 'non-preferred indifference' for sickness, poverty and no education.

The sage embraces challenges as they present themselves, by addressing injustices that happen to us as social beings. We are encouraged to accept with equanimity the reality of ignorance in the human world, but not its sovereignty; and to accept that, while wrong-doing is a part of life, it is not part of our common bond in the universality of Being. Our challenge is to align with the logos in nature, and sometimes this may involve speaking out at injustice. In doing this, the Stoic sage harmonises with nature, dynamically engaging in the social milieu with the signature stoic equanimity.

PART FIVE

PILGRIMAGE WITHOUT A DESTINATION

(but make sure that your camel is tethered)

*The power of presence brings constant renewal
– the innocence of the natural mind.*
—Lao Tzu

CHAPTER 18

A NEW AGE BESET BY OLD PATTERNS

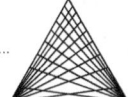

After the Second World War the search for spiritual immanence, rather than the transcendence of theistic religions was found in the 'beat generation', captured in the writings of Alan Ginsberg and Jack Kerouac. Soon the books containing the teachings that inspired them were found on bookshelves from the suburbs to the airports. Teachers and gurus filled auditoriums to which people (including myself) flocked in the late 60s and 70s. We were hungry to hear some kind of illumination that was beyond the formulaic rigidity of religious orthodoxies, the shallowness of intellectual materialism, the rampant commercialism afflicting the world, and the various political conflicts that were then part of one's backyard. And we not only wanted to hear it, there was an imperative to experience it.

And so, the era of the New Age was ushered in. 'New Age' is a term that covers a different stance towards religion, which is captured in the term 'perennial philosophy':

> *The Perennial philosophy (Latin: philosophia perennis) also referred to as Perennialism and perennial wisdom, is a perspective in modern spirituality which views each of the world's religious traditions as sharing a single, metaphysical truth or origin from which all esoteric and exoteric knowledge and doctrine has grown.*
>
> —Wikipedia[117]

Growing up in this era I observed and experienced some of the adventures and excesses that characterised it, with its new frontiers of social bonding and an emphasis on the *integration* of body, mind, and spirit. As a young catholic boy, I was indoctrinated with the distorted attitude to the body as being a 'playground of the devil', with the senses not to be trusted. The soul was thought to be trapped in corruptible flesh, a type of dualism creating inner conflict, even torment.

Along with a new interest in spirituality came the development of such disciplines as sociology, anthropology, psychology, body-oriented psychotherapy, and psychoanalysis. This resulted in a corresponding surge in popular self-help psychology and philosophy. There was a smorgasbord on offer, from shamanistic practices to neo-Reichian therapy, and I tried several practices from the many that were available.

The New Age has continued, and now in any bookshop there are many rows of self-help books by a plethora of teachers, psychologists, gurus and life-coaches. It has become a burgeoning industry. Yet only a very few can genuinely point to awakened living. Many of these books have become part of the problem because they reinforce a belief in the reality of a separate self. And with this comes the further belief that this 'self' always needs improving. In this way, people who may be feeling, depressed, lonely, anxious, bored, stuck, restless or unfulfilled in their living, and looking for some kind of escape from their situation are ripe pickings for the many forms offering 'techniques to transcend'. Yet what is offered cannot fulfil these claims, nor are they grounded truth.

On offer in this personal growth industry are generally partial solutions. The root of the problems - a belief in the permanence of a separate permanent self, and its associated culture of dualism with a longing for transcendence - is not understood. People become entrapped in a cycle of modifying a psychological self that is not real in the first place, and chasing new ways to transcend. With this is the felt need to consume further workshops, intensives and books to get there. Armed with the belief is 'I cannot be free until I've done this workshop, read this book, seen this guru, taken this initiation, or learnt this special new (or ancient) practice'.

This restless modifying of self can at once become a craving and a form of addiction. But establishing the veracity and substantiality of this self rests on nothing more than a chorus of voices. It seems true because everyone is writing about this self, working on it, modifying it, having therapy for it, and trying to transcend it. But, in reality, it exists purely as a belief.

Fool's gold: the New Age spiritual marketplace

Part of the 'fool's gold' is the phenomenon of the hoax, where we are duped into believing, only to discover that the book we are reading and assume to be factual, in actuality is fiction (fiction is a perfectly legitimate form of writing and is only lacking in merit when passed off as fact). We find that the shaman we were following was more of a sham, or that the guru we idealised was found not to be a shining light but instead a much more shadowy figure pursuing a very ego-based, selfish or toxic agenda, than we projected.

For example, as a young man, I was an avid reader of the Carlos Castenada books about the author's supposed apprenticeship with Don Juan, a *Yaqui Man of Knowledge*. I found these books compelling and transformative (even fiction posing as fact can have a transformative effect) discovering much later that they were a clever fabrication (for this go to www.salon.com and find *Dark Legacy of Carlos Castenada*). Yet to this day the publisher keeps selling them in the non-fiction category. It was another sober awakening amongst many for the author!

There are genuine shamans and spiritual teachers; however an essential part of an examined life is discriminating the true from the false in people and situations. We achieve this by looking carefully, listening deeply, and questioning to see what is really there. If we approach anything or anyone expecting to believe and follow, we only invite being duped by what the mind wants to see, because we have become blindly guided by our own projections.

New Age culture has been described as the 'spiritual marketplace' where spirituality entangles with a market-driven consumerism. For example, some forms of yoga in the West have been fashioned into money-driven franchises. A particular style of 'Hot Yoga', originating from Mumbai, markets a package of a patented, formulaic series of *asanas* (poses) to be practised in artificially-heated rooms (to mimic the climate in Mumbai) to induce excessive sweating, with scant regard for the carbon footprint of such practices. It should rather be called 'hot stretching class', for traditional yoga involves ethics, et cetera, with the asanas being only one of Patanjali's eight limbs of Yoga. Is this living in harmonic alignment with nature? Practices like this are the very antithesis of Yoga, which is a culture of realising inner and outer connectedness, and bearing in mind that the meaning of the word 'Yoga' is 'connection' and 'union'.

How can this ancient art, which seeks to connect us to our spiritual roots, retain its integrity and yet be commoditised by being 'patented', franchised, marketed and then consumed? The obsession with the modern cult of gymnastic exercise found in the physically strenuous systems calling themselves yoga, is a distortion of this ancient practice. Do people attending or teaching classes like this genuinely believe that they are engaged in something of genuine depth, and that it is in some way spiritual? An essential part of living a spiritual life is questioning and challenging unconscious structures of belief, and avoiding fads and cults. Essential to the spiritual life is experiencing the oneness of Being which is the source of our ethical compass. It can involve engaging in practices authentically, rather than being entranced in group-think.

Fast tracking to nowhere

In its process of marketing, the 'self-improvement' culture is full of inflated promises. Advertising hype, promising an enlightened state or instant realisation from a workshop, is instead engaging in some 'unreality spin'. What is real is that people just make stuff up. There are fast-track meditation programs promising that you can meditate like a Zen monk in a few minutes, but how does this compare to a lifetime of committed practice? In taking this short-cut, will you have the same understanding of Being?

Likewise, Neuro Linguistic Programming (NLP) techniques offer to 'reprogram your brain for success' by 'hacking in' to your subconscious mind. Success, it is assumed, will come from imprinting the 'correct program'; but again, what kind of success? Of course, no one could argue with the benefit of releasing ourselves from self-limiting, negative beliefs and conditioning. Some of the NLP techniques are useful for altering these negative, sub-conscious beliefs (such as 'I'm essentially unlovable, so I cannot form long-term, loving relationships') but is the imprinting of new narratives necessary? And at a deeper level, who is it that needs these new narratives?

In NLP the imparted messages may be helpful, offering a short-term, partial solution to emotional pain, depression, having an eating disorder, or being 'financially strapped'. As the spin goes, for the price of a seminar, we are 'baited' to get a lot more: we will receive a restructured self and, with this, a new 'we' will have a 're-conditioned self-image'. But what is not challenged is the universally common process of constructing and identifying with self-images as an authentic way to know of our true identity.

Focusing on just the reprogramming of thought shows a complete unawareness that what is required is a complete revolution of the mind, to bring human transformation. But this is something that is un-programmable. In fact, it involves a completed de-programming by removing the veil of ignorance. For in order to discover our full epistemic potential as human beings we have to realise that thought, as a narrative of self, is the source of our limitation, rather than the limitless nature of consciousness.

The shortcomings of these approaches are that the focus is too narrow with their modifications of thought, and they are time obsessed. Of course, true insight can be experienced now, but it is not arrived at through grasping, nor through programming.

In fact, if we are in a rush or trying so hard with our mind, we will miss what is already at hand – that we are free now. Fast food of the spiritual kind invariably leads to a different type of indigestion!

Unless we address the source of our suffering – the ignorance of our living trance as a separate self – there can be no meaningful conversation about issues of social justice. These issues arise from collective ignorance that results from a belief in separateness. Genuine awakening connects us to community, to nature, compassion for human beings, and the dire situation our planetary home is facing.

The salvation offered is limited to a type of personal transcendence, but only as an isolated individual who is still caught in duality. On offer is a reconditioned ego embedded in a consumerist individualistic culture. The real gold of spirituality can neither be sold nor consumed, and is anathema to the fast food of individualism.

Do you have the patience to wait for the mud to settle?
—Lao Tzu

The vacuum of individualism

The philosophical ideology underpinning modern psychology and psychotherapy is *individualism* (as opposed to individuation which, as the reader may recall, comes from the depth psychology of C.G. Jung) as the cultivation of the private self. The self is in constant need of esteem-boosting, feeding an industry that fills a complete section of the local bookshop. Modern psychology fails to address the deeper human malaise by not investigating the basic reality of whether there is a self at all. If it were investigated, then it would be clear that the 'self' is only a belief and, further, that it is *the* source of our experience of isolation and troubled mental health. Human beings are unique amongst living species in the troubled mental malaise we have, manifesting as alienation, selfishness, prejudice, violence and a disconnection from nature.

Psychology uses the understanding of the self, with its insecurities, vanities, and restless desires, to inform the media and advertising that drives the consumerist ethic. In doing this it maintains a broader social control, and hence we are constantly appealed to act in our 'self-interest'. In the commercial world with its pandering to the vanities and insecurities of the 'self', we are portrayed as never good enough, eternally dissatisfied, and always searching for new experience, hungry for better goods or more luxurious services. It is all part of our championing of individual freedom, because it is our right, regardless of how it might affect others, or the planet. As political citizens we are ruthlessly enticed to act in 'self-interest', to narrow our focus to the 'hip-pocket' and to pamper our New Age selves with endless products and therapeutic services.

The ego receives special attention in the New Age, as we are told we need to know a special secret, find the pathway to esoteric knowledge, be invited to an initiation into higher knowledge, experience a short-cut to mythical enlightenment, or discover the key to achieving longevity. And always present is the sure path to abundance, with the promise of great financial reward and getting whatever the ego wants. All these offerings manufacture an expectant state of belief based on unreal promises. But why do we want to believe so easily? What is at the base of all this restlessness? What is the source of this unhappiness? An examined life asks difficult questions.

More important is living in a simple manner within one's own nature and keeping the well-being of others at heart. Living an unpretentious life with compassion and keeping your desires tempered is to live in your own true nature.

—Lao Tzu[118]

Appropriation of ancient practices

Another trend in the New Age is to adopt an ancient principle or practice from the culture of Indigenous peoples, repackage it with extra hyperbole, and then market it. A well-known example is *Mutant Message from Down Underour* (published by Harper Collins) written by Marlo Morgan, an American woman, and purportedly based on real encounters and teachings from the Indigenous peoples of Australia. It was insulting to Australian Aboriginal people because, while it was promoted as a work of fiction, it was supposedly based on the fact of the author's time with Aboriginal people. Instead, it was badly researched and a complete fabrication, with the Aboriginal people in question knowing nothing of her.

We see this occurring regularly with the spiritual practices of the Orient, which are artfully packaged and re-sold commercially, with the accompanying spin that they are life-transforming. This is also done with shamanic cultures. For example, the appropriation of the ancient Hawaiian healing practice of Ho'oponopono is illustrative of this. Ho'oponopono is a practice of apology, forgiveness, love, extended responsibility, and gratitude.

Ho'oponopono means to make right. Essentially, it means to make it right with the ancestors, or to make right with the people with whom you have relationships. We believe that the original purpose of Ho'oponopono was to correct the wrongs that had occurred in someone's life including Hala (to miss the thing aimed for, or to err, to disobey) and Hewa (to go overboard or to do something to excess) which were illusions, and even 'Ino (to do harm, implying to do harm to someone with hate in mind), even if accidental."

—Ancienthuna.com[119]

Similar practices of reconciliation and forgiveness were performed on islands throughout the South Pacific, including Samoa, Tahiti and New Zealand. Usually Ho'oponopono is practised by healing priests or *kahuna lapa'au*, and performed among the family members of a person who is physically ill. It is inspiring and worthy of great respect, and we could all do well to adopt something of these practices and qualities. However, when books appropriate these practices, we soon becomes aware of the blatant adverting and marketing. In the very process of becoming commercialised, practices like these lose their contextual cultural connection, and essential spirituality. Because of our consumerist conditioning, we buy all the merchandise – the books, CDs and DVDs, we attend the workshops and seminars, and get the T-shirts and affirmation cards, thinking perhaps that we are investing in our spirituality. But this is not what spirituality is. I suspect that it is not what the originators and those who humbly practise Ho'oponopono had in mind either.

In manifestation circles, which foster individualism in the central concern of generating private wealth, is there any real sense of community, or the compassion that resonates as spiritual awakening? What is offered is limited because it is still informed by the capitalist ethos of promoting the individualistic culture of 'me'. Spirituality, in essence, looks at living in harmony with all living systems, and this is not the main priority of the individualistic culture of manifestation.

The New Age started full of promise with its exploration of new insights challenging the narrowness of religious orthodoxies, embracing ancient knowledge, its deconstruction of dogma, and its adoption of a more universal view of life. (For the interested reader, a talk entitled 'How You Scale Empathy and Change The World', by Taylor Conroy, co-founder of WeJourney.co, speaking at MindValley's 2017 A-Fest, exemplifies a positivity of spirit that can still be found in things New Age.)

Openness is an essential part of curiosity, but openness is not gullibility. It is an error to put aside the active intelligence that helps us to discern the true from the false. This discrimination impels us to ask important and sometimes difficult questions. If our priority is other than to see clearly, we are instead well-placed to naively believe, and to blindly follow. In this, we may fail to recognise that a new type of dogma is in the making, or a new sham spiritual teacher is looking for followers, or that the 'spiritual spin' and hyperbole is only serving self-aggrandising for consumerist ends and profit margins.

Being aware demands our curiosity and discrimination, informed by the intelligence-energy that is the basis of life. It behoves us to know the reality behind proclamations, practices, teachers and their behaviours.

Gurus: the 'god–man/woman' complex and its 'shadow'

A healthy curiosity asks questions without fear, and this is invited by any genuine sage. What have emerged, however, over the last 60 years, are many accounts of fraud and abuse by so-called spiritual gurus after exposure by their followers acting as whistleblowers. Once exposed, the sermonising rants of pious, unexamined and confused teachings are shown to be in conflict with their actual behaviour.

Teachers claiming that they are 'enlightened' in the public arena, is a proclamation of elevated spiritual status. We could ask, is this congruent with truly 'enlightened' behaviour? Self-claims of this kind may or may not be true, but how are we to know? There is nothing in particular that identifies enlightenment from the outside. As the Buddha is said to have stated, when asked this question, that in order to tell if someone is enlightened we must spent time with them to see how they function and meet the many different challenges that any life presents. Certainly, we can be wise and kind but not necessarily enlightened. And enlightenment is not the exclusive domain of spiritual teachers – probably only a few are enlightened. The absence of self – a key indicator of an awakened mind – can manifest in the most surprising places, and is not necessarily found front and central in a 'guru' in the public eye.

Something well recognised in Buddhist circles is 'zen fever', which is paralleled in Advaita circles by 'advaita fever' (classically exhibited in the Neo-Advaita teachers). These 'fevers' signify the same thing – a premature phase of intoxication from experiencing the absolute. The rush to go out and be a 'spiritual teacher' ignores the value of a 'tempering process' which sees the integration of the relative phenomenal reality with the Absolute – the Truth of Being. Unfortunately, the energetic intensity of any inner transformation of consciousness does not necessarily provide wisdom, which is why it is essential to just sit with it for a while (some people recommend 10 years) to allow the 'process' to integrate and mature.

When untempered, the excursion into premature teaching results in the 'god–man/woman complex'. This is a type of 'self-inflationary syndrome' because, rather than an absence of self, there may now be a 'mega self'. And despite the claim to enlightenment, superiority is practised toward others, and an authoritarian exercise of control, placing the teacher in a state of contradiction because the fact remains that, if a person has truly found liberation, they automatically encourage others to be free. These types of 'god–men/women' may still offer some insights, and certainly instructive lessons, although this may be as embodiments of the myth of Icarus, who flew too close to the sun.

Public 'self-claims' of enlightenment are particularly problematic in our age of celebrity. The aphorism below can be interpreted as a warning to be aware of potential gullibility, and the New Age has been ripe for this kind of phenomenon:

He who knows, does not speak,
and he who says he knows, does not know.
—Lao Tzu, from *Tao Te Ching*

This mysterious saying from Lao Tzu alludes to a person who truly experientially knows the non-dual nature of Being as a unique kind of knowing beyond mind and language. But to speak of what is known as a form of achievement – enlightenment – is not possible because there is no longer a self to attain anything, or to recognise it. To draw attention to ourselves by saying 'I am enlightened' can muddy the waters. Is it a statement of truth, or in saying this, are we inciting others to regard us as elevated, with the potential for adulation? Whatever our motivations are, do we understand the truth of Being? When the ignorance of 'self' is banished there is humility without artifice, which precludes 'self-claims'. Public proclamations of ultimate states like enlightenment are, rather, an indication of its opposite.

In Neo-Advaita the propensity for self-delusory inflation and contradiction shows itself in public forums like Quora. For example, when teachers extol themselves as having come 'full circle' to enlightenment, and then go further to postulate how rare and special this achievement is – all stated, of course, with a complete absence of ego because after all they are just stating the 'truth' – so that we can rest assured that only they are the 'real deal'. Yet if they proceed to egotistically engage in defensive and offensive internet chatter, we can ask whether their 'enlightenment' and 'self-absence' claims, have any real credibility. Remember, 'he who speaks does not know'. Another more extreme example is a teacher, in a fit of unbridled ego enthusiasm, asserting that theirs is a rare case of 'authentic' enlightenment (most others are fakes and he is the only genuine one) and then engages in confused, unhinged, and self-absorbed ranting, And, by being cleverly obscure and provocative, he attempts to impress the gullible. Is it a naked drive to collect followers? These examples behove us to be aware, to be discriminating and, particularly in relation to spiritual matters, to keep a pinch of salt ever at hand.

> *Yield and overcome, empty and be full.*
> *Have little and gain, have much and be confused.*
> *Not putting on a display, not justifying,*
> *not boasting, not bragging.*
> *Be really whole and all things come to you.*
>
> —Lao Tzu

But does a realisation of the 'truth of Being' mean not speaking? Rather, it means to speak without the ignorance of self-claims that are both unwise and unenlightened. Perhaps essential to the definition of a 'genuine spiritual teacher' is one who does not make self-claims, and hence does not suffer the 'god/goddess complex'. With freedom from ignorance comes the insight of how destructive it is to have power over anyone else. Conversely, it is essential not to give this kind of power to a guru. A power relationship is only possible if we are still trapped in a 'believed-in' duality. Facing ignorance of this duality alone is the way to understand. Genuine gurus can be really helpful spiritual guides, but it is essential not to give power to them. If they ask for or demand it – walk away, for it is also not necessary to have a guru to find truth.

The shadow is ignorance

While espousing peace, love and harmony and the monkish life, some teachers, through their ignorance, are in a state of contradiction because their psyche is plainly unbalanced. This imbalance is expressed in the duality of their idealism, espousing all as 'light and love', while simultaneously feeding the repressed energy of the 'shadow', resulting in a multitude of distorted behaviours. For example, some gurus, like many members of religious priesthoods, have been discovered to have sexually abused disciples, including children. Generally, it is much later that we hear of the events that go on behind the scenes – orgies, child molestation, harems, et cetera. And then there are the grotesque power plays within the organisational hierarchies, violence, and naked profiteering.

This lack of congruence between the private and the public face only occurs because what is preached to the world does not really come from a place of direct experience. Instead, it offers the transcendental, which is an idealisation, with teachings based in the dualism of 'should' and 'should not', rather than in actuality.

The conditioned morality of dualism is expressed in an idealistic good, with evil as its opposite. In this kind of morality there is guilt, blame, revenge, punishment, and salvation in following and believing in an afterlife, whether it be a better incarnation, or heaven. Teachers engaged in the duality of an idealised higher self/soul, feeding the fomenting shadow of a lower self, are only furthering existing confusion with this kind of conditioned ignorance.

Many seekers idealise teachers, imagining how an enlightened person should be, and then placing them in some hallowed realm beyond that of mere mortals. In the film *The Life of Brian*, from the Monty Python team, Brian is inadvertently thrust into a series of comic situations as a Messiah, closely paralleling the Jesus story. It stands as an irreverent send-up of the dangers of belief, of blindly following, and the absurdity of religious celebrity, standing as a great exposure of cultish behaviour. Another is the 2012 documentary film, *Kumaré*, about a man who impersonates a wise Indian guru, and builds a following in Arizona, USA. Among the instructive lessons in these films are how our projections can obscure the lens through which we perceive, disabling any discriminating intelligence.

As we have already touched on, the darker side of self-inflation is abuse. Joel Kramer and Diana Alstead wrote a much needed and sobering treatise about guru abuses in *The Guru Papers*[120], released in the 1990s in the wake of the rising flood of teachers coming from the East into Western culture. Abuses can happen as a result of the authoritarian relationship encouraged by many of these spiritual teachers, who demand blind obedience from the seeker, with the expressed intention of dismantling the ego. If the student questions such a guru, it is viewed as an example of the student's swollen ego, when instead this questioning may just be active and discerning intelligence.

Yet, in genuine spiritual teachers the opposite is the case, because they encourage curiosity, and questioning is regarded as essential to the spirit of enquiry. The 'god' complex is singularly unhelpful in furthering any kind of awakening because it encourages bondage, in a form of 'spiritual lobotomy'. It does this by keeping people in a holding pattern as 'seekers' complete with 'rose coloured' glasses, endlessly searching for authority and validation.

However, the pressure is off when you realise that you are nobody and alone. At once we are freed from the restless and self-limiting struggle, of imaging ourselves on a path, and being a disciple, to be 'somebody'significant. Instead, to live in truth is to take refuge in nothing, yet in all that is. In the 'experience of nobody', or Nargajun's no-thingness, is to let go in a knowing universe. Thus, liberated from the need to be special, making self-claims makes no sense at all, it is an irrelevance. You travel in the lightness of Being. What is special is that like everybody, even though so many do not know it, we all already have the liberating treasure of awareness inside.

> *Knowing others is intelligence;*
> *knowing yourself is true wisdom.*
> *Mastering others is strength;*
> *mastering yourself is true power.*
> *If you realise that you have enough, you are truly rich.*
> —Lao Tzu, from *Tao Te Ching*

Can we be masters of Being?

There is no one there to tell you, 'you are enlightened'.
— U.G. Krishnamurti

In the truth of Being, the term 'master' is a misappropriation of the word. Because in Being there is no hierarchy. We can cultivate certain skills and talents, such as developing mastery in a skill like playing a musical instrument, or as a chef, but we can never be more, in the truth of Being, than we already are now. Techniques can be learnt and practised, but our understanding of Being is not intellectual and cannot be measured. Unlike a skill that we can learn, or even improve on, Being is horizontal and ever now: nothing can be added, nothing can be taken away.

But assuming the title 'master' can be an instant road to recognition and money, and mostly this title is far too easily proclaimed and given. In the area of Being, however, it is of no relevance. Doing a few weekend intensives and then receiving a title such as 'Master', regardless of what, only feeds an ego grasping for instant gratification and the desire for short cuts, found in the 'fast enlightenment intensives'. This need for instant gratification signifies a poverty of true understanding.

By disregarding authoritarian ways, with their titles, structured hierarchies, and attachment to pomp and ceremony, that only serve to maintain a form of unconsciousness. And in one who truly 'sees' there is no opposition to anyone, nor an engaging in the various forms of separation, implicit in all hierarchies. Living in the truth of Being exposes dishonesty, arrogance and power plays in all their guises, while having compassion for those engaged in this kind of folly.

So, in reality no one can be a 'master' of Being, but anyone can live in the truth of Being. Those attached to the title of 'master' are, instead, still suffering from a self-image problem, as evidenced by the fact that they have, or want a title, and then to go further, in trying to establish their superiority in the minds of others.

Is a guru necessary?

Three gurus emerged in the latter 20th century who were not specifically attached to any religious tradition, and took centre Stage and were all spiritual luminaries. First, Jiddu Krishnamurti presented an austere persona offering insightful non-dualist teachings (observer and the observed are one). However, his anti-guru teaching was dissonant with his authoritarian and, at times, intimidating presentation. And this was precisely because he was just that – a guru on a rostrum, in every sense of the word, and one who brooked no serious personal questioning. Second, there was Osho (formerly Rajneesh) who was originally a philosophy teacher who, having gathered a marvellous eclectic mysticism, engaged in a playful form of non-duality. However, he indulged in all the 'god-man' pomp and ceremony of a conventional guru, while mocking religion and conventions. Moreover, his wealth and status as a 'celebrity guru' was every bit conventional. Third, the iconoclastic U.G. Krishnamurti who, before his 'calamity' or 'awakening', had slavishly followed J. Krishnamurti and then later rejected him without acknowledgement. He seemed to take a mischievous delight in turning spirituality on its head, in a stubbornly contrarian manner, ostensibly to differentiate himself as the 'anti–anti–guru'. And while he purposefully did not do the celebrity speaking circuit, as his guru colleague J. Krishnamurti did, nor partake in guru-pomp like Osho, his penchant for provocative Nietzschean-style statements belied a similar 'alpha' ambition.

U.G. Krishnamurti (not related to J. Krishnamurti) appeared as a cranky iconoclast, lampooning his contemporaries (namely J. Krishnamurti, Osho and Ramana Maharshi). In the early days of his spiritual search he gained an audience with Ramana Maharshi. U.G., as he was commonly called, asked about 'moshka' (a Sanskrit word meaning spiritual liberation, where one is freed from the cycles of birth and rebirth):

> *'Is there anything like moksha?'*
> *The sage answered in the affirmative.*
> *'Can one be free sometimes and not free sometimes?'*
> *'Either you are free, or you are not free at all.'*
> *'Are there any levels to it?'*
> *'No, no levels are possible, it is all one thing. Either you are there or not there at all.'*
> *And then U.G. shot his final question. 'This thing called*

> *moksha, can you give it to me?'*
> *Ramana answered with a counter-question: 'I can give it, but can you take it?'*
> *No guru before had given such an answer. They had only advised him to do more of sadhana, more of what he had already done and finished with. But here was a guru, who was supposed to be an enlightened man, asking, 'Can you take it?'*
>
> —Mukunda Rao, from *U.G Krishnamurti Reader*[121]

U.G. went on to spend a number of years studying with J. Krishnamurti, eventually leaving disgruntled and frustrated with what he described as J. Krishnamurti's abstractions. U.G would regularly berate the chicanery of mainstream gurus. And, in order to short-circuit the celebrity circus that tends to develop around gurus, U.G. refused to give talks to large gatherings, branding such activity as 'poppycock'. Instead he preferred to have smaller discussions with anyone who sought him out. In this regard U.G. Krishnamurti offered some sage advice:

> *'Man cannot become man so long as he follows somebody. What is responsible for man remaining an animal is 'that' culture – the top dog, following somebody – that has not helped you at all. You want to be a cheap imitation of Sankara or Buddha; you don't want to be yourself. What for? I tell you, you are far more unique and extraordinary than all those saints and saviours of mankind put together. Why do you want to be a cheap imitation of that fellow? That is one of the myths. Forget it."*
>
> —Ibid.[122]

Celebrity is anathema to spirituality. However, celebrity is central to cults and to the spiritual lobotomising that often takes place in people, who will follow blindly in the shadow of a self-promoting master, with the latter often so keen on developing a magnified ego. Celebrity is certainly not a criterion for enlightenment, nor is it relevant to those only interested in abiding in reality.

In the 21st century 'guru celebrity' continues, with similar patterns repeating, where spirituality is commoditised with naked commercial marketing. This is driven by the economic imperative to sell; the strident ambition to achieve guru status; the self-claims of enlightenment, and the simplistic and individualistic solutions offered to solve all the ills of humankind. And, in varying degrees, some celebrity teachers exhibit genuine wisdom. This wisdom however, can be marred by an apparent lack of reflectivity, with their 'enlightened vision' impaired by their shadow – the vestiges of the unexamined, and a still present and virulent ego-centre.

These celebrities also show us, by providing an example of the opposite, that in Being, there is no elevated status, there is no desire to be 'somebody', or to imitate someone else. *Spirituality is to experience the luminous sovereignty of the original mind*, rather than the trance of ego. Thus, there is a singular lack in ambition with regard to the world, in celebrity, nor to garner an adoring following. To the discerning, the noise that falsity, hypocrisy and contradictions create are detectable as patterns of dis-harmony which are plainly obvious.

A teacher of Being, rather than a master, is empty of self, a 'nobody'. And in reality, underneath any of our struggles to be somebody, we are all really nobodies. The 'human condition' is that we want to be important, individualistic somebodies. When Jiddu Krishnamurti, in response to the question 'who I am?', stated that it is meaningless … 'because firstly, who I am, is nobody'. Claiming the celebrity status of enlightenment indicates a need for importance that is useful if you have the agenda of starting a religious movement!

Is a guru necessary to discover the truth of Being? No, but it is a matter of destiny unique to each person, because finding truth can involve studying directly with a guru, or without. However, great care needs to be taken in finding a genuine teacher, and the student also needs to question their own fitness and readiness to the task. The story of Sri M stands as a fine example of someone who had the good fortune and destiny of finding a genuine teacher, a journey which he has (with some trepidation) shared with the world in his *Apprenticed to a Himalayan Master*. Sri M's guru sagely advised him, as part of his learning process, to seek out the 'anti-guru' in Jiddu Krishnamurti contributed to his spiritual education.

A genuine guru embraces the essential individuation of the 'student' from the outset. But everyone has sources of inspiration, whether there is a formalised discipleship or not, and the question is whether one is attached to those sources. Certainly, in awakening to Truth, while gratitude remains, attachment to the 'guru' as the source, inevitably drops away. A lack of respectful gratitude on the part of 'followers', however, does happen, as was pointed out by Osho in commenting on how this respect was tellingly absent in UG's acerbic attitude towards Jiddu Krishnamurti after his 'awakening'.

Spiritual teachers are generally not likely to be celebrities. In the world, they could be doing anything – they could be monks and equally bread-makers. They might be recognised teachers, but not necessarily. However, in their 'non-doing', whatever they do, they are more like a 'holy fool'. 'Holy' indicating wholeness and naturalness, rather than any artful piety; 'fool' signifying a playful unconventional nature imbued with spontaneous wisdom. They offer no transcendence, beliefs, vows, idealistic notions, special practices, or initiations that must be undertaken as the formulaic paths, because attaching like this only furthers the trance of duality.

Illusion and Reality

What is seen is not the Truth
What is cannot be said
Trust comes not without seeing
Nor understanding without words
The wise comprehends with knowledge
To the ignorant it is but a wonder
Some worship the formless God
Some worship His various forms
In what way is He beyond these attributes?
Only the Knower knows
The music cannot be written
How can then be the notes?
Says Kabir, awareness alone will overcome illusion.

—Kabir (1398–1448)

CHAPTER 19

FREED FROM ILLUSIONS

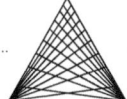

Evolutionary ideas about consciousness have explanatory power as a model of reality, just like models about phenomenal reality. Their model of consciousness gives rise to an intelligent universe as an unfolding narrative, with an increasing display of patterning energy in the early universe. Gradually emerging forms, from plasma to particulate matter (different emergent forms of consciousness) these slowly coalesce to become the stars, planets and galaxies. Earth evolves in an emerging evolution of the universe in the journey from intelligent unconscious 'inanimate matter' to intelligent conscious 'animate matter'. Finally, Sapiens sit at the apex (on this planet) in terms of the capacity for 'knowing' (but not in anthropocentric importance) where consciousness contemplates itself. But while we may sit at the apex of knowing, nature is not designed for us, it is designed for itself, as a single reflexively knowing Being.

Is spirituality an evolutionary process?

This 'knowing that it knows' in us, uniquely places us amongst other species. By contemplating consciousness, being aware of being aware, prior to thought, signifies a form of completion in the circle of knowing. Spiritual evolutionary models of consciousness are quite popular, as seen in the teaching of Gopi Krishna, an Indian public servant, whose disturbingly traumatic story of his kundalini experience is documented in his book *Kundalini: The Evolutionary Energy in Man*[123]. In his book, Krishna suggests that the awakening of this cosmic energy-consciousness is behind all spiritual awakenings, Eastern or Western. He regards the awakening of kundalini as the drive towards personal and collective enlightenment in our species. This idea is similarly developed in the work of the Christian mystic, Teilhard de Chardin, and in the prolific writings of philosopher Ken Wilbur.

All these models have merit, but can we come to know Being in a gradual manner, through time? Does it take a lifetime (or lifetimes) of struggle, effort, or practice to know Being – 'that' which is ever-present? Is this kind of knowing cumulative, like learning to play a musical instrument, practising karate, or studying algebra? Knowing Being, rather than needing endless practices, instead requires the immediacy of awareness prior to thinking about it.

Evolutionary 'models' of consciousness and reality can be believed or disbelieved and argued about because, as with all models, they are theoretical and subject to opinion. But to engage in the non-theoretical direct approach to understanding the nature of consciousness requires moving beyond all models that naturally arouse disputation. For this we need a mixture of courage and curiosity in leaving the comfort of the theoretical to experience directly Being as it is.

> *Disputation is a proof of not seeing clearly.*
> —Chang Tzu[124]

Being is timeless. When we speak of gradual awakening, we invite the confusion of an evolutionary historical 'me' proceeding to a goal in linear time. Yet, in deeply experiencing 'presence', the self and its history is absent. Genuine awakening is never evolutionary, because moving beyond the conceptual mind only happens in an experiential now. But realising the futility of the struggle of chasing knowledge, states of consciousness and experiences, does not involve a kind of spiritual or psychological lobotomy. For the treasure of Being is already here, where it will always be. We cannot evolve into this realisation because it is spontaneous. Nevertheless, in an appeal to memory, we may recall that there was a person who had a sense of struggle before awakening, and that this too was just a necessary part of it all. In our particular destiny of Being 'the fruit gradually ripens, but the fall is sudden'.

> *There is nothing but water at the holy bathing places;*
> *And I know that they are useless, for I have bathed in them.*
> *The images are all lifeless, they cannot speak;*
> *I know, for I have cried aloud to them.*
> *The Purana and the Koran are mere words;*
> *Lifting up the curtain, I have seen.*
> *Kabir gives utterance to the words of experience;*
> *And he knows very well that all other things are untrue.*
> *I laugh when I hear that the fish in the water is thirsty;*
> *You do not see that the real is in your home,*

And you wander from forest to forest listlessly!
Here is the truth!
Go where you will, to Banaras or Mathura;
If you do not find your soul, the world is unreal to you.
—Kabir[125]

Spirituality: 'a way without a path'

A famous parable the Buddha used, is that he likened his teachings to a raft, used for crossing from danger to the security of the other side, over a fast-flowing river. The raft is for crossing and then put aside, not for seizing hold of. These words seem to have gone unheeded. And this is not unique to Buddhism, because all religions function in a similar way: in the process of following and believing, people seem to love carrying rafts!

Religions specialise in developing the duality that creates the transcendental by: living in the known while pining for an 'otherness'; attachment to an ideology; idealising unachievable perfection in the belief that practices, rituals, ceremonies, or reading sacred texts will bring the salvation of enlightenment. But the ego that pines for this can never be enlightened, because it is the very resistance to awakening. Only Being is enlightened, and this can only be known in the absence of self. In spirituality the formlessness of direct experience is apprehended, while the form of phenomenal world, rather than being dismissed as illusion, is subsumed in an experience of 'complete reality'.

The way of spirituality is a transformation of all dualities. These are expressed in the dichotomies of: higher and lower selves; a culturally conditioned morality of good and evil; the grasping for idealisation and perfection; fear of desire and the reciprocal reach for transcendence – all of which are signatures of religion. Spirituality is the way of non-duality born of simplicity as a result of abiding in awareness.

So, can one walk a spiritual path? Following a path is invariably the way of religion. It is governed by rules, practices and vows, often under the guidance of a religious authority, leading towards a particular goal. The language it speaks is one of conformity and inauthenticity, serving to further its followers in a culture of the known. In the East, the goal is enlightenment, self-realisation or liberation; in the West, it is union with God, saintliness, or piety.

Life becomes scripted as to what we 'should' do in order to progress in the religious life; for example, meditate, or pray every day, perform certain rituals, attend the temple or church, attend retreats or satsangs, or undertake certain other recommended practices that are seen to be leading the 'higher self' towards the projected goal. This kind of transcendentalism creates an 'everyday' that becomes separated as mundane, where the practicalities of living are viewed as lesser aspects of a lower self. In spirituality, everything is elevated in numinous Being; there is no higher and lower.

In Eastern traditions changing names, or being given 'spiritual' names by the guru, represents a spiritual rebirth, signifying the seeker (chela) is on the spiritual path, and has become part of the special 'sangha'. The person 'dies' to the 'old me' and gives birth to the 'new spiritual me', yet the drive to be 'somebody', regardless of new or old names, is just another kind of prison in the self's restless search for identity in form: to be special – now a spiritual somebody. New or old names are irrelevant in the ever-newness of Being. In this, we only take refuge in reality.

*'Do **not believe** in anything simply because you have heard it. ... Do **not believe** in anything merely on the authority of your **teachers** and elders. Do **not believe** in traditions because they have been handed down for many generations.'*
—Buddha

'Non-doing' with practices

In the early tradition of Advaita Vedanta there was a lot made of the prerequisites on the part of the 'student': asceticism or tapas (a culture of practices such as formal meditation) – things regarded as essential to being on the path. The tendency for Neo-Advaita teachers now, in speaking to general audiences in the West, is to give the impression that we can practise Advaita along with an affluent lifestyle and, with little modification of our personal behaviour, in a materialistic world. That we can go about being materialistic but just add on attending satsangs, using 'Advaita speak' ('call off the search'; 'we are all already enlightened'; 'with nothing happening, anything goes) and the odd workshop as a 'spiritual veneer' on top.

But it is the *attachment to* things, to activities, and to the body in a materialistic lifestyle that is the obstacle, rather than the things or activities themselves. A materialistic lifestyle is a form of spiritual suffocation where we slowly die spiritually from the excesses of comfort, immediate gratification, and a feeling of entitlement to everything. The 'doing' of certain practices or attending talks or spiritual gatherings, does not, in any way at all, signify that we are on a hallowed path to anywhere special at all. The key is the 'non-doing' in all that we do: doing without self.

* ***The right approach*** is to understand at the outset that if we: meditate, chant, pray, do labyrinth walking, go for sound healing, practise yoga, zazen, Tai Chi, Qigong, or do Sufi dancing, simply as goals to be achieved, we are short-changing ourselves, because in Being there is nowhere to go, nothing to do. All striving and ambition only strengthens our sense of self. Understanding this enables us to enjoy the beauty of practices innocently and use them wisely. These practices can globally sensitise the body, activate 'subtle energy', and have a calming effect on the mind. But in doing them, like anything else – going to work, cooking a meal – it is the *presence* we bring to bear in this 'doing' that invites the noumenal. And 'presence' in this way happens in the absence of any ambition of self.

* ***The wrong approach*** is to be goal driven. That is, to start under the false premise that if we do these practices they will eventually give us a payoff in the future, as part of the self's need for acquiring certain experiences, states of consciousness, psychic accomplishments, or enlightenment. Then we are attached to these doings, as 'the devotee', 'the meditator', the yogi/yogini', 'the adept', or 'the Sannyasin' on a special spiritual path. In this we becomes heavy, burdened with self, caught in ambition and time.

Spirituality is understanding from the outset that everything we do *is* spiritual practice, when there is no doer. It is the *presence* we bring to each moment, regardless of our doings. In the conversation below, Nisagadatta outlines the apparent paradoxical nature of the relative and the absolute with regard to practice.

Nisargadatta: 'To go beyond the mind, you must have your mind in perfect order. You cannot leave a mess behind and go beyond. He who seeks Liberation must examine his mind by his own efforts, and once the mind is purified by such introspection Liberation is obtained and appears obvious and natural.'

Q: 'Then why are sadhanas prescribed?'

Nisargadatta: 'Freedom to do what one likes is really bondage, while being free to do what one must, what is right, is real freedom.'

Q: 'How can the absolute be the result of a process?'

Nisargadatta: 'You are right, the relative cannot result in the absolute. But the relative can block the absolute, just as the non-churning of the cream may prevent butter from separating. It is the real that creates the urge; the inner prompts the outer and the outer responds in interest and effort." "You seem to want instant insight, forgetting that the instant is always preceded by a long preparation. The fruit falls suddenly, but the ripening takes time.

The way to truth lies through the destruction of the false. To destroy the false, you must question your most inveterate beliefs.'

—Sri Nisargadatta Maharaj[126]

Residing in awareness: 'presence' – the only spiritual practice

As mentioned, practices such as yoga, meditation, et cetera can be beneficial but, as with all practices, anything becomes an obstacle if we attach to it, or seek our identity in it, particularly if we fall prey to the illusion that the doing of practices will make us enlightened. Being is already enlightened and we are Being. Nothing in and of itself can give us the truth of Being. It is rather that we need to get out of the way. While our guitar playing improves mostly with practice, spiritually there is nothing to become, nothing to gain and nothing that requires improving. Awakening is the ever now, regardless of what we may be doing.

Changing a nappy on a child, rearing a family, showing up for work on time, listening to a friend, are as much of a spiritual practice as sitting cross-legged on the floor with your eyes closed. 'Spiritual practice' is an undivided attention to whatever is happening in the ever-present moment. *The only spiritual practice is being present* in all that you do. *Presence* is a non-doing, a resting in reality.

There is nothing to cure in Being. In Being there is ultimately no healing journey through time, because Being is only now, without duration. And yet, paradoxically, we all know that recovering from ill health, with the aspect of consciousness we call the body, does take time. Whether it is consciousness expressing as the mind, or as the body, we can experience a meaningful sense of a 'healing journey' in overcoming adversity, to experience a renewed sense of wellness. With the body it is easy to see this healing process, but with things mental and emotional it is no less real, only more hidden. Equally, a healing process can occur mentally, because traumas, emotional disorders, personality disorders, psychosis, phobias and neuroses can and do heal, each with different degrees of difficulty.

Healing journeys can also happen at a cultural and social level, with the healing of injustices, the liberation of those who have been persecuted, the prosecution of crimes against humanity, and the public acknowledgment of wrongful actions by governments and individuals against the wellbeing of their citizens. These events are always important and the process of restitution, forgiveness and compensation, can be likened to a form of currency feeding into the 'spiritual bank account' in the collective consciousness of human beings. And this is an account that can always do with extra funds.

Emotional–psychological healing really involves a lessening of the self, rather than a reinforcement of it. The psychological entity, the self in crisis, seems as real as we think it is, as was discussed in chapter 2. Psychotherapy works on what appears like an emotional/thought entity – and with the connectedness of mind and body – hence affecting the body. Ultimately therapy, in the sense that I am using it, is complete when there is 'no one' to be healed.

The myth of enlightenment

Enlightenment is the currency of the spiritual world, promoted as the final state of attainment of the self. But the self can never attain enlightenment. Enlightenment is not a something, it is not an attainment, it is revealed only in an absence of self.

So much is attached to the term 'enlightenment', and so often it is used for self-inflation, even to justify a lacking of ethical compass with an 'anything goes' mentality. This occurs when absolutist-style teachers maintain that everything is an illusion, and hence nothing matters, and because nothing is happening, then anything goes. This kind of nihilism leads to a moral vacuum.

In the list below, those engaging in Neo-Advaita (which is a shadow of a true experiencing of non-duality) are particularly prey to a number of these hindrances, such as: attachment to the absolute – 'everything is an illusion', self-importance, a moral vacuum, and a crisis of authenticity, with parroted lines freely circulating in this unreflective culture. Below are some recognisable patterns challenging the authenticity of a spiritual teacher; and perhaps, dear reader, you have already witnessed some of these:

* Speak *only* in absolutist terms. Those engaging in Neo-Advaita are particularly prey to this, whereas genuine teacher embraces the totality, the absolute and the relative, bringing compassion, empathy and kindness.
* Do not tolerate questions well. Someone who is insecure in understanding will use strategies such as:
    * obfuscation – bewilder with platitudes;
    * getting cranky and bullying the questioner;
    » belittling the questioner by saying they are 'stupid', or the question is stupid.
    * Behaving in an imperious and arrogant manner above other mere mortals.
* Deep listening on the other hand, brings confidence born of humility, and an ability to genuinely address questions.

* As mentioned above, lacking an ethical compass, signifying an 'anything goes' moral vacuum because you are enlightened in the absolute. This kind of self-inflation confers a 'license' to do anything. Liberation is not license to indulge, it is the freedom to know and do what is right.
* Clearly, they have other motivations, such as elevation of status, sexual gratification, or filling the coffers.
* Inauthentic people like to put other people down, rather than the behaviour. They will name names (talk disparagingly about other teachers), as part of their own insecurity in order to elevate a preciously-held image of self.

Why is it that the Neo-Advaita teachers seem to be unreflective with themselves? It would appear that they have assumed teaching authority too quickly. Discovering the absolute is not the end of the awakening process, because there is a necessary phase of tempering, which sees the integration of the absolute with the relative, ensuring a re-grounding in the human domain. Otherwise there can be a form of spiritual psychosis. Sagacity happens with the complete integration of the absolute truth with the relative: Truth with Love.

A spiritual teacher may or may not be a sage, and a sage may or may not be a spiritual teacher. What is of central importance is awareness, which we ignore by habitually identifying with the mind and the body. *Ignoring awareness is a form of Self-sabotage, and is the conduit in which we create unconscious patterns of habit. An examined life is confronting our ignorance, short-circuiting any tendencies that sabotage our Self-knowing.* With the ideology of enlightenment promoted as a 'final state' for an ambitiously restless self to fixate on, it becomes yet another distraction for the ego to strive to acquire.

The mythology that surrounds different sages, and the whole culture of enlightenment as an attainment, along with endless opinions about who is enlightened, and who is not, all become distractions from what is essential about living: awareness in daily living.

I cannot translate Pali or Sanskrit, but I found the conversation piece below of particular interest, and pertinent to what is discussed above:

> *The two words, Awakened and Enlightened, are both translations of the same term, the root 'Budh-', which is the same in both Pali and Sanskrit. The correct translation is Awakened. Buddha is one who is Awake, one who has his eyes open, one who is aware, one who sees things as they are.*
>
> *The term Enlightened did not enter into the Buddhist tradition for centuries after the lifetime of the Buddha. It was a result of two different mis-translations. The first was accidental. 'Island' as in 'Be an island unto yourself' from the Buddha's final sermon, was mistranslated as 'light' because the two words are homonyms in Sanskrit. We can confirm that the Buddha said 'island' and not 'light' by looking at earlier Pali sources.*
>
> *The second mis-translation was less innocent. British scholars and explorers, wanting to promote their own Western idea of Enlightenment, projected it onto Buddha and Buddhism, creating a lot of misunderstanding that persists to this day.*
>
> *We do not need light to Awaken. The light is already here. We just need to open our eyes. When we do this, we are on the Way to being a Buddha.*
>
> —Sid Kemp, Zen practitioner, Qora.com 2016

Paradoxically, in order to know undivided wholeness – which is our connection with everything – we must experience aloneness. And it is through surrendering in this aloneness that we experience nothingness as the ground of Being. In aloneness we are also individuating, separating from all illusory forms of group-think. Alone and individuated, we connect with the collective mind of human beings, and consciousness as the immensity of the universe.

Individuating immunises us from the need to join any cults or organisations (as well as the need to form any new ones) and to live in the shadow of anyone else. If we cultivate self-images and also project images on to others, we chain ourselves to the illusory duality of power dynamics.

The map is not the territory, and identity is not the image. In a fundamental way we become esentially unknowable to the finite grasping mind. For 'you' are no longer on a 'journey', which implies separateness but, as Lao Tzu states, *'you are the journey'*.

A Fisherman

Studying texts and stiff meditation can
make you lose your Original Mind.
A solitary tune by a fisherman,
though, can be an invaluable treasure.
Dusk rain on the river, the moon
peeking in and out of the clouds;
Elegant beyond words,
he chants his songs night after night.

—Ikkyu Sojun (1394–1481)[127]

Signatures of spirituality

A central element setting spirituality apart from religion is the experience of non-separate Being, because experiencing this renders belief irrelevant. Seeing the emptiness within forms, rather than attachment to 'so-called' trappings of the religious (rituals, ceremonies, beliefs, sacred texts, et cetera) is to experience the absolute. Attachment to form is the domain of the religious. In Being, non-attachment to the absolute is essential, because complete awakening involves love that is all-inclusive – the relative and the absolute in Being. Love brings humility and a grounding in human awakening.

In spirituality no practice or activity, in itself, is either more or less spiritual than another, yet in religious circles the opposite is true. In the *direct way* there is a steadfast laziness about carrying the rafts! We may read a teaching, or listen to a spiritual teacher, but in deep listening (which is the opposite of a desire to believe) teachings, if understood (as with all rafts) are put to the side.

This is because the mind uses the language of time and separation, along with the habituated belief that regards all journeys as having a known destination – but these are just the fixities of thought. In Being there is no journey in time, for we are already at the destination in each moment. Journeying language describes the ego treading a 'religious path with its fixed transcendental destination'. In contrast, *spirituality is a pilgrimage without a destination, and we are the journey, now, beyond what is possible for thought to know, in unfathomable Being.*

Validation in spirituality lies in the 'intimacy' we experience in Being. It is in the texture of our relationships with our human companions (fellow travellers, colleagues, friends and family, plants, animals, the earth and the stars). The very movement of life, in and around us, informs who we are and how to conduct our lives. There is no need of any illusory external validation, because we receive real validation by abiding in awareness with *life as the teacher*.

> *The waters of life are thundering over the rocks of objects –*
> *desirable or hateful.*
> *Remove the rocks by insight and detachment*
> *and the same waters will flow deep and silent and swift,*
> *in greater volume and with greater power.*
> —Sri Nisargadatta Maharaj[128]

CHAPTER 20

ABIDING IN THE REAL

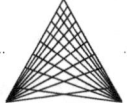

Grace

Between the far-off mountain
And the journey you never start

Between the latest headlines
And the secret of every heart
Between the burning night time
And the darkest day

Between the hands of the clock
And the things you didn't say

You will fall you will fall
You will fall into grace

Between the name of the beloved
And voices in the street

Between the dew on the bud
And a branch on the barest tree

Between the rush of river water
And your stumbling gait

Between the face in the mirror
And the loss that leaves no trace

You will fall you will fall
You will fall into grace

Between the beauty of her laughter
And what is right or wrong

Between the crowd outside waiting
And the band's last song

Between the first raindrop
And the hours that go to waste

Between the sound of sirens
And the only hiding place

You will fall you will fall
You will fall into grace

—Max Ryan

In the objectivist quest to understand the universe, the great void of 'nothingness' may hold the key to a deeper understanding of the cosmos. Historically, the emphasis has been placed on 'substance' and, in the modern era, subatomic particles holding the key to nature's secrets. In the history of science, space and time were regarded as providing an 'absolute back-drop', a largely irrelevant 'great void'. Of prominence are the subatomic zoo of matter particles, all of which constitute all visible structures in the universe. Yet this detectable matter constitutes roughly 5 per cent of the universe itself. In re-examining the nothingness of space and time, there is a new horizon, wherein matter's subatomic particles are entangled in the ground-bed of a void that is 'informed', in a universe that is non-separate as an entity unto itself.

Nothingness, the conception of a structuring of space and time at an infinitesimally small scale, heralds a new order in quantum cosmology. Naturally, with things at this scale, it could be some time before there is any – if at all – confirmation of this hypothesis coming from experimentalists. But the void exists, with the potential to resolve the division seen to exist between the micro realm of the quantum and the macro world of galaxies, into a holographic quantum gravity. This is because the nothingness of the void is not zero; rather, it is informed, holding the connectedness of an entangled universe. Already, a number of physicists, including Paul Davies, have the view that 'the vacuum holds the key to the full understanding of nature'. And, as outlined in quantum monism, it is a universe in which there is no division, with a single underlying reality.

Parallel to the central role nothingness may hold in the drive for a complete theory of phenomenal reality, there is also an experiential key to what 'nothingness' holds for any of us. Experiencing nothingness is not a negation; rather, we realise the following: the non-dual nature of our existence; the non-existence of 'self'; that there is no time – all are aspects of the hidden order of Being. In experiencing nothingness is the dimension of a knowing consciousness.

Inner stillness moves us beyond the narrative of objectification, that sees the constructing of the separate self, and the phenomenal world, as observer and observed. Experiential knowing reveals a 'deeper order', our universal birthright, not a subjectivist one created by thought, imagination, or conjecture. The intimacy of this knowing sees the collapse of the knower and the known and reveals an experience of oneness. And with this kind of epistemic no academic training is required, only the intense curiosity to look deeper than the mind's surface murmurings.

Many do not experience the numinous nature of our existence. The reason for this is that the sensitivity of their 'tuning system' has been dulled by cultural conditioning, particularly self-limiting mind-sets, primary being the noise of ego. We develop busy self-absorbed minds, colonised mostly by consensus driven, dualistic narratives, full of personal troubles, clouding the lens through which we perceive. Hence, we are able to ignore the deeper truth we carry, conscious only of a phenomenal reality; the numinous escapes us. However, this sabotaging of our own truth is not necessarily forever, because it is so readily broken with curiosity and courage.

In the theoretical world of constructing models of reality, a particular well-honed sensitivity and curiosity is also necessary. When looking deeply into the heavens or the subatomic world we require remarkably sensitive instruments and well-developed skills in observation, combined with the patience and appropriate theoretical background, to interpret the data from these observations.

And rather than needing special instrumentation that amplifies our senses into areas normally undetectable, *in our direct experience of reality it is our ability to purely observe without the interpretive mind, that enhances our experience of the numinous.* The senses are not primary to this mode of knowing as they are with empirical knowledge, but the senses are refreshed and enhanced by inner silence. When we are mentally silent and attentively present heightened sensitivity occurs.

We do not need to search in order to find True Being. We already are it. And the mind which searches for it is the very reason we cannot find it.

—Nisargadatta Maharaj

Living authentically

Be yourself; everyone else is already taken.

—Oscar Wilde

People in wealthier countries, having financial opportunity, will often enjoy their leisure-time in nature. Yet, on returning to their jobs they will commonly say, 'now it's back to reality', suggesting that a particular place, experience, or time is more real than another. However, 'reality' is our experience of consciousness and can only be apprehended in the moment we are present, wherever we are.

Perhaps this attitude arises from being engaging in some kind of drudgery at work, and resistance to this particular 'unpleasant' reality. Out of this we create an ideal of what real living 'should be'. That is, being on holidays is the ideal, but it is not considered reality. So there is a feeling of being trapped between an 'ideal reality' we can only glimpse occasionally on holidays, and the day-to-day one we seem forced to endure. In this we have created a duality, and it is in the inherent nature of dualities – they are never real – that we can never be completely present in, or find, happiness.

And while being on a holiday in nature brings the intimacy of a deeper experienced communion of ourselves as Being, it does not completely solve the division. Only enquiry can do this. Reality can only be known in the *now* of our existence, regardless of when and where that is, because the division between what may be interpreted as humdrum and what may be seen as ideal are all interpretive fabrications of the mind. If we want to abide in reality as it is, there is no room for ideals and divisions. Complete presence – experiencing the now – is the one authentic reality. It is our avenue to authenticity.

So, what is living authentically? The key to authenticity is to live beyond programmed narratives. By resting in awareness and living in the now a seamless experience of reality is revealed. By being present – not living in regret, not living in ideals, not worrying about what has not happened, not wishing that things were otherwise – we have escaped the confusing complexities of the duality driven 'self'. These dualities are all the 'doings' of the erroneous use of mind. And *in non-doing we are keeping it real.*

There are, however, other pertinent questions that might arise: is the work that we are doing a true expression of our inner nature? Is our work meaningful and of service to the world? Is our work congruent with the deeper reality of Being? Is it connected and aligned with the living systems on this planet, including ourselves? If these questions are difficult for us to answer, then we could further ask: is the habitual 'default arbiter' that we use in defining our reality – the mind – actually fit for this task?

One thing that is sure about minds is that they have been, and continue to be, successfully conditioned. By adopting limiting beliefs such as the consumerist mind-set to own the right stuff, to compare with others and to get materially ahead; to have a certain self-image; and we may also believe that we have a particular status according to our gender, our sexuality or our skin colour; or we may believe that the purpose of existence is to make more money in jobs that are not really of service to the planet or anything except our bank balance or share portfolio.

In the above we are heading further into hedonia, and sabotaging our ability to know the Self, only to experience a form of spiritual bankruptcy. And, in comparison with our animal friends, it is our unique form of fragility. Within this inner impoverishment there is a misplaced search for love and happiness in directions that only seem to take us further away from actually experiencing them. Our inauthenticity is signified by a lack of intimacy.

Abiding in awareness loosens our attachment to things, and shifts us from believing in attitudes and behaviours that are conditioned. We can then see that we are just following the beliefs and scripts that we have been colonised with. When we are colonised like this we develop the 'pseudo-identity' or the inauthenticity of the 'self'. These narratives tell us what we 'should' believe, what we 'should' do, how we 'should' behave, what is important in life, what our perceived sense of duty is, or lack thereof, and even what we 'should' be thinking and doing at the various stages in our lives. Conversely, we may be in a state of rebellion, reacting to this conditioning. But in rebelling and rejecting those scripts we are still entrapped by them, in a pattern of reactivity.

By simply following our conditioning and imitating others, whether they are parents, friends, mentors, or gurus, we are not genuinely living authentically. Who or what is authoring our lives, our decisions, motivations and behaviour? To live authentically requires first becoming aware of what our conditioning is. Ironically, in the midst of all this conditioning, there is the belief that we have free will, and that we are free to choose. But clearly we are not free if we are conditioned. Part of the illusion that comes with the conditioned mind, is the belief that the choices we make are an expression of this freedom.

The moment we become aware that we are conditioned is the moment we stop believing in it, and this commences the letting go of it. This falling away comes as a relief, and we realise that there is the deeper freedom of Being that has been there all along. But it is not the free will created by thought as the ego-centre, nor just expressed as an ability to choose. Freedom is not achieved as an act of mind, but rather with the releasing of attachment to mind. *Freedom is in Being, not in willing.*

Living authentically does not come from imitating, comparing or following, because these are all things of the mind, that might be useful in doing things other than creatively living. In the timeless silence of Being we are in the ever-new, not following in the known. *Authenticity comes from un-attaching to all the myriad voices of the world, wherein we can experience our innermost, and this is the way to truly individuate and authenticate.*

The silence of Being is the matrix of authentic living. In this matrix, truth is revealed as a 'non-teaching', because there is nothing to believe, no set of rules, and no script for how things should be. Our moral compass is informed by the experience of being connected to everything rather than by the dualities of cultural conditioning. Authenticity, then, is not a mental choice from a range of options decided by another aspect of the mind, because ultimately it comes from 'seeing' the non-dual nature of existence.

A saying well known in the Zen community is: 'before enlightenment chopping wood carrying water, after enlightenment chopping wood carrying water'. This signifies the integration of the absolute and the relative. Few will cognise the shift in the Zen Master's consciousness, or sense their inner silence, a silence that enfolds the mystery of existence. However, there is no one there. The phantom entity, self, has dissolved into the nothingness from whence it came. From the inside there is no longer the 'sweeper' sweeping as the 'doer', nor is there any engagement in the illusion of chasing some distant experience to become enlightened. Only Being is present.

Deep listening

We excel in the type of listening focused purely in the phenomenal. In this we enhance our objectivist description of reality with devices designed to exponentially extend our senses, by apprehending extremely subtle perturbations of sound as vibration. We can now listen into the far reaches of the universe, extending our 'listening capacity' with the Laser Interferometer Gravitational-Wave Observatory (LIGO). This led to the discovery of gravity waves in 2015, waves very subtly stretching and compressing all the atoms constituting our bodies.

These specific waves were generated by the cataclysmic collision and fusion of two mammoth black holes 1.3 billion light-years away, sending ripples through the fabric of space–time. No one would have noticed, but each time these absolutely minuscule gravitational waves pass through our bodies, we are stretched and squashed by less than the nucleus of an atom. The signal from this event travelling at the speed of light, reached the outer regions of our galaxy over 200,000 years ago, just as we, as a species, may have been emerging from Africa. (Homo sapiens could well have emerged much earlier than this, as paleontology keeps rewriting the place and time of human origins.)

Yet while we can admire how clever we are in this conceptual construction of reality, and the extraordinary skill we have in extending our empirical capacity with highly sophisticated technology, we are much less cultivated in deep listening into Being. This is simply because our attention is captured by the concept-making of the mind. We are captivated by the image or conception of reality, unaware of a non-conceptual reality. Deep listening is not just empirically listening with the ears.

Stilling the mind is the conduit enabling deep listening. And in discovering life beyond the conceptual, is where our success as a species ultimately rests. Our global environmental issues, our challenge to live sustainably, and our ongoing conflicts, all exist because we have stunted our capacity to listen, because in order to deeply listen, we must be mentally completely quiet. And in this quietness, we experience reality as it is, undivided.

Look at any parliament across the globe and you will notice the extent to which men, in particular, are incapable of deep listening, so busy are they arguing about how right they are. Listen to the shrill sound rising from the chests of these self-important ideologues, so often full of high-sounding principle, but so lacking in virtue, because this quality only comes from the space of deep listening. Their incapacity to listen does not have to be so, because they all already have the necessary equipment. Each of us does, for our body–mind is like a great tuning system and it is free, but of course, we must have the necessary curiosity to explore this.

Unify your will and don't listen with your ears but listen with your mind. No, don't listen with your mind, but listen with you qi (energy). Listening stops with the ears, the mind stops with matching (perception,) but qi is empty and waits on all things. Tao gathers in emptiness alone. Emptiness is mind-fasting.

—Taoist philosopher

Children and adults introduced to 'deep listening' to the body and the mind (mindfulness) and walking in nature, discover a refreshingly ever-new universe, the dynamic one that Heraclitus spoke of. And by listening to others' stories, listening deeply to different cultural ways, listening to politicians, to the religious, and listening to the animals and plants as well as the stars; in fact, by listening deeply to the very movement of your life, we can experience the mysterious connection between everything. The 'world' we currently know through the filter of the conceptual mind, in this type of listening disappears, in its place a numinous wonder.

'Deep listening' is referred to as 'daddirri' by Indigenous Australians and is central to their spirituality. From deep listening comes the experience of 'patterned thinking' which, as expressed by Aboriginal elder David Mowaljarli, is a 'seeing' of the connectedness of all things, between nature and the human being. But these 'gifts' Aboriginal peoples offered to the colonisers – deep listening and 'patterned thinking' – have yet to be taken in, because we can neither 'listen', nor 'see the connectedness of things', because our conditioning to analyse and think scientifically keeps our minds filled with too many thoughts.

Deep listening is the basis of our intimacy with nature, with animals, with the trees, the waterways and the land, and is the key to an empathic relationship with each other. Deep listening is the 'feeling in' with all of life. 'Feeling in' is the nature of empathy, because we are not thinking or making judgments; it is not emotional sentimentality. Rather, empathy is essential to compassion.

The origin of the word 'empathy' appears to have come from the German word *Einfuhling*, which means 'feeling into', and in a subsequent search for an English equivalent, the term 'empathy' was derived from the Greek word *empatheia*, meaning 'in' plus 'suffering'. With deep listening we 'feel into' the being of another person and hence become empathic. 'Feeling in' gives an appreciation of the lives of animals and their suffering, and an intimacy with the earth itself in a living universe *as a listening from the spiritual heart*, wherein arises compassion. Deep listening magnifies our capacity for empathy, essential to us as the cooperative hominid, which moves us from the phenomenal, to experience the noumenal.

Strengthening the 'awareness muscle'

Events don't cause stress.
What causes stress are the views you take of events.
—Epictetus (CE 55–135)

To be confused is not a birthright. Inevitably, as the adults around them have done, young people become skilled in developing a fragility of self, and in having a moral compass that is conditioned. And across a spectrum of the many things the young can identify with, from consumerist brand names, to the more extreme kinds of ideologies that can be toxically destructive, they find a path that is limited in the known. It is this restless search for identity, with the many tribal sub-groups, that is the primary way of the world. And this very lack of adult leadership creates a vacuum vulnerable to negative influence.

With overly busy minds young people can become just like the adults around them; internally divided, individualistic, selfish, acquisitive and fragmented. And, like adults, they engage in a constant search to boost self-esteem, to be happy, ever fearful of loneliness. The 'connectivity' that young people and the world currently engages in belies a resistance to real intimacy in ourselves, with others, and with nature. This lack of intimacy is the root of alienation, isolation and loneliness.

Rather than supporting young people to discover their birthrights of 'how to know' and 'how to be', formal education tends to focus instead on 'what to know', 'how to fit in', and 'how to do'. These are also important, but their heads are being crammed with information, only some of which is necessary and useful. And there is no space to allow their curiosity to really explore nor to discover the nature of deep listening.

This happens in formalised education because we are ignorant as the real significance of the human capacity to know, and the understanding that we share in the living systems here on Earth. Education teaches models of reality and belief, designed to maintain the status quo. By unquestioningly engaging in this conditioning process we are discouraging young people from finding the truth of who they really are, and actualising their potential.

If we offer a way for children that encourages in them an understanding of the nature of awareness and a deep inner listening, inevitably they discover a domain of silence that is always there. This imparts an equanimity to navigate through life's difficulties and experience a true intimacy with life itself. This, combined with curiosity fosters their individuation, immunizing them to colonisation by any form of ideology or commercialism, and thus equipped, experience the freedom of Being.

Mindfulness, as advised by sages over the millennia and, most notably, by Gautama the Buddha, is the natural way to deepen our knowing of the universe. While not the originator of mindfulness the Buddha gave it a central position as a way to awakening. And this was unique. The culture of Yoga amongst the sadhus he was mixing with were engaged in mindfulness amongst various other concentration and kundalini meditations, including austerities. Buddha realised that such practices and concentration techniques were 'doings' that were ultimately 'ineffective' to deeper awakening. Simply paying attention strengthens, metaphorically, the 'awareness muscle'. This is the opposite to identifying with thoughts and images as a conditioning process, in the 'self's' restless search for identity. Observing brings a dis-identifying or un-attaching to the content of consciousness; thoughts, feelings, urges, perceptions and sensations. It is the foundation of an experiential apprehension of reality as distinct to a conceptual one.

The significance of this connectedness (rather than 'connectivity') is that it reveals both the meaning of living, and a capacity for empathy with all things: humans, animals, plants and the earth. By developing their 'awareness muscle' young people come to know that their identity is infinitely more – and, paradoxically, less – than the mind can ever construct. Resting in awareness enables us to think clearly, productively and creatively. In the space of awareness children and adults alike experience a connectedness with all life without mind as an intermediary.

If education includes mindfulness, open philosophical enquiry, understanding the nature of the Sapien virtues, and social connectedness – then it offers the essential ingredients for young people to fulfil their potential as 'global citizens'. If education does not include some appreciation of Being, and a sense of communion with existence as it is, and instead focuses only on the inculcation of conceptual knowledge and belief systems, then we have severely short-changed our young people. By encouraging them to know the birthrights of Being, then education will be much more than a furthering of the process of conditioning, and will instead become a vehicle for awakening.

Already, in a number of schools from the junior to the senior levels across the globe, mindfulness is being taught as part of the curriculum, and the results are encouraging – in awareness, behaviour, social connectedness, attitude, learning and stress reduction.

Living harmoniously is the ending of stress

Disharmony is like discordant ripples through the infinite fabric of consciousness as Being. You can feel this in your nervous system when you are stressed. This agitation can be measured by recording brain-waves patterns in an EEG. The discovery of our inner harmonic through presence-awareness, simultaneously brings harmony in our nervous system and with our living environment, and this emanates to subtly affect others. Currently there is more interest in this now than perhaps at any other time, with the spread of curiosity into spirituality, the questioning of old beliefs, and the challenging of habitual disharmonies and ways of living, all of which are symptomatic of living unconsciously.

Knowing ourselves as Being does not involve seeking some ever-elusive state of enlightenment in a projected future. Neither does it involve living in imitation of spiritual teachers, present or past, and using their words and concepts as our own. Living in truth is to be authentically ourselves, alone and without artifice.

There is a growing understanding that the mind cannot provide the answers to the perennial questions like 'What is reality?', 'How do we live in real intimacy and harmony with each other and all life on earth?', and 'What is the truth of our identity?'. There is also a growing number of people realising there is more to life than the promises of materialistic comfort, the solutions offered by objectivist conceptual understandings of the universe, or the beliefs of traditional religious culture. And, despite all the marvellous things that science can do, and is doing, science itself cannot answer these most fundament questions, although many scientists are under the illusion that it can. Consider the passage below:

> *Why are you worried about clothing? Consider the lilies of the field, how they grow; they do not toil nor do they spin. Yet I say to you that not even Solomon in all his glory clothed himself like one of these. But if God so clothes the grass of the field, which is alive today and tomorrow is thrown into the furnace, will He not much more clothe you?*
>
> —Jesus of Nazareth, *King James Bible*, (Matthew 6:28–30)

In these words, we are directed to step away from the morass of mind, with its worrying attachments and self-concern. By 'seeing' the lilies of the field, as the man called Jesus is said to have asked us to do, we will know Being. And in this we will simultaneously intimately know the depths of ourselves in the 'natural mind', where being clothed will happen, but without all the struggle that comes from agitated self-concern. It is a call for a different level of understanding and action, like the 'non-doing' advocated by the Lao Tzu, advising us that *'the sage does nothing, yet leaves nothing undone'*.

The 'lilies' and the 'field' as Being will be our teacher, just as the Bodhi tree was the silent witness for Gautama, who experienced his awakening while sitting under it. And when asked how he could prove he was enlightened, he did not call upon transcendent heavenly beings, or validation from other people, instead gesturing to the Earth with his hand, indicating that the earth itself bore witness to his spiritual awakening. It is not a person who gets enlightened; Being already is.

A life of meaning

In a television program *'Grand Design: The Meaning of Life'*, physicist and author Stephen Hawking suggested that, in order to find the meaning of life, we must ask whether there is an independent or 'objective' reality. The program explained that we get meaning from the kinds of models of reality that we create with our thinking. Indeed, we all engage in constructing a shared objectified reality, as a function of social, linguistic, cultural, economic and intellectual discourse. An objectified reality created through thought and language can be relatively meaningful, but there is a level beyond this, as I have articulated, which is actually *the* source of meaning.

The highly sophisticated objectified reality of science is one that is sanctioned by the broader community of scientists, and it has a relative level of meaning because its knowledge is relative. And in this context, meaninglessness would imply constructing irrational, contradictory, belief-driven and potentially destructive models, leading to toxic human narratives. Some of these distorted 'models of reality' may result in suicide, murderous outcomes, and war, or wreak havoc upon the Earth and, as a species, we already engage in some of these.

Meaninglessness can be seen in the distorted cultural narratives such as: a belief that we can and should conquer nature; a belief that inequalities amongst humans are justified and that meritocracy is in the natural order of things; a belief that 'might is right' and that colonisers are both 'right and just' in conquering and exploiting those they colonise. We may have a belief in the commodification of everything, including spirituality; that everything is marketable and for sale; or the belief that an objectivist account of reality *is* the only reality; or a belief that we live in a materialist, disconnected universe which occurred randomly; or a belief in the dualistic nature of existence in which we are essentially separate from each other; or that we are dominant over nature, giving us the right to exploit as we do. All these narratives arise from ignorance each creating further disharmonies. Of pressing need is to develop a narrative for human beings enbaling us to be cooperative in consciously living harmoniously amongst ourselves and with all life on Earth.

But science does not have the last word on meaning, despite some of its eminent spokesmen's proclamations. Meaning is universally derived from experiencing some kind of connectedness.

While we do get meaning from understanding a mathematical formula, reading a poem, listening to a story or attending a funeral, this meaning lies more in our lived experience in doing these things, because of our unique connections to them. But not everyone can understand the meaning of a given poem or mathematical formula, or by knowing a particular person who has died. But we can all (unless we are conditioned otherwise, with a narcissistic narrative, for example) get meaning from giving, or being of service to the world, whether as an artist, a volunteer, a friend, a scientist, a philosopher, a parent, a social worker, or a chef. Meaning comes from experiencing connectedness in a universe that is intrinsically connected as one.

Connectedness is expressed in whatever service we offer the world, in our vocation, relationships, family, culture, art, music, science. Meaning and connectedness are not dependent on the mind or on rational knowing, because these cannot give us an experience of intimacy and communion with life. Deeper meaning is gained experientially through our sense of wholeness, not just the intellect – it is spiritual in nature.

Neuroscience can help us map brain patterning and see the correlation – but not causation – between thought and brain activity. It can further develop an understanding of the essential neuroplasticity of the brain itself. But while it can give us very useful objectified knowledge, it can only ever be an image or conception of the actual. It offers nothing for us in the ultimate quest to truly know ourselves, as consciousness, and to know reality. It is somewhat bizarre that this externalised knowledge is often promoted as giving us a deeper wisdom about our identity. And while I have a keen interest in neuroscience and the developing field of neuroplasticity, this is not for its insight or wisdom, but for its knowledge.

The 'Big Kahuna' of meaning lies in awakening from the conditioned trances we may be living to experience the unconditioned non-duality. Taking refuge in reality beyond the conceptual is a journey without duration, right now, to the very source of the meaning in our existence. The meaning of living is this awakening, rather than a formula, theory or model or an attainment. No one can give us this meaning because it is revealed in our direct experience. In our unrestrained curiosity it is a journey alone; yet being in communion with other humans, the animals, trees and the stars signifies spirituality. And unlike the ceremonies, rituals and practices of religion, spirituality is hidden, as the inner silence and life of Being.

The absolute and relative resolve in experiential knowing

Nature, as conceptually conceived in the quantum world, with the guiding wave (quantum potential) guiding the particle (as in pilot wave theory) portrays a historical universe that is simultaneously connected non-locally to the Totality. This concept was developed further by Bohm, with the 'implicate' and 'explicate' orders' as different 'orders of reality', in his metaphysics. Bohm's model of reality of the phenomenal universe exists in parallel with experiencing a numinous reality.

Buddhist philosophy, draws reference to the 'form and the formless' (relative and absolute) as expressed in the Heart Sutra, and Nargajuna's insight on Emptiness, both signifying non-Being as the foundation of Being. The 'relative' is the conceptual, historical, phenomenal, and particulate universe, and the 'absolute' is the oneness of Being apprehended experientially in a timeless now.

Both these realities are experiential: the relative is experiential-conceptual (a tree is known as a tree), while the absolute is completely experiential and non-conceptual (the unknowing of the tree experienced as Being). The relative cannot comprehend the absolute, which is why scientists are generally flummoxed by the potential of knowing without thought.

Yet when there is complete identification with the absolute, there is a failure to appreciate the truth value of the relative, even to the point of appreciating the great beauty of the phenomenal world. We see this in those who enter a form of 'spiritual psychosis' where there is a complete identification with the absolute; for example, some spiritual teachers who regard the phenomenal world as valueless, and nothing but an illusion. However, what is illusory is the attachment to the phenomenal, as if this is all there is to reality. But if we identify only with the absolute it is still a function of ego.

Attaching to the absolute, and seeking identity solely therein, is misguided and is another form of 'transcendentalism', in its dismissal of the relative. From this lofty spiritual height kindness, respect for others and their beliefs (with all their errors), the beauty of the phenomenal world, and the truth in relationship itself are all relegated to being illusions. We can only know our identity in the eternity of now, the truth of which is naturally tested in our connection with phenomenal reality, and especially in our most intimate relationships. Actually, friends and family provide an opportunity to check that we are not stuck in the absolute of non-duality; so that *we can enjoy the 'play' of apparent duality.*

Nargajuna, after outlining his thesis on Emptiness, went on to articulate the 'Two Truths' (relative and absolute) developing on what was originally articulated by the Buddha. The Two Truths bring awareness to the fact that there is truth in the relative which needs to be respected and honoured, and that the absolute is also a truth, but not the only truth, as some in spiritual circles would have it.

Are there really two realities as well as two truths? Does this framing of reality as phenomenal/relative and noumenal/absolute only ensnare us further in duality as though it is really real? We only have to look at the dogma schisms that have plagued Buddhist philosophy over the centuries to see how people get bogged down in conceptual bottlenecks of their own creation. But this only signifies that reality is multidimensional pointing to different orders of truth.

The middle way occurs for us through experience, wherein simultaneously we see the tree, and beyond the concept, in Being, the not tree – no-thing. This encapsulates a wisdom that springs from a deeper unknowing, because we have to let go of the mind to knowingly 'be' in this experience. In experiencing non-duality, we also embrace the phenomenal – the beauty of the tree, or it could be a friend, or a spotted pardalote as it alights from the nearby branch – and the absolute, Being and nothingness.

In lived experience there is no complication: no division, no schism, no duality, no non-duality, no ultimate truth, and no two truths, no concept, no mind: there is only taking refuge in the real, wherein Love meets Truth.

> *Wisdom is knowing I am nothing,*
> *Love is knowing I am everything,*
> *and between the two my life moves.*
> —Nisargadatta

Experiencing beyond the known liberates us from the world of human knowledge, with all its intricacy and magnificence, in the understanding that this knowledge, while useful and holding truth-value, is relative and limiting. Any map of reality is ever limiting, because we see no further than our mind's reflection. Marcel Proust echoes this:

> *The voyage of discovery lies not in seeking new horizons,*
> *but in seeing with new eyes.*
> —Marcel Proust, French novelist (1871–1927)[129]

Each of us enfolds the mysteries of life and our identity, suffused in us as the truth of Being. With deepened curiosity we listen, no more keenly to a friend, a poet, a politician, a guru, a scientist, than to the ignorant and prejudiced, as they are all equally expressions of Being. As such, they, along with the very movement of life, are all our teachers. How could it be otherwise?

An examined life also brings a specific leaning into difficulty, and a letting go of whatever arises, whereby any areas of the mind that may remain hidden receive the healing light of awareness. Essential in a journey into awareness is to discover 'what is', rather than ideals created by thought and its search for transcendence, and to take refuge in reality. In this, our understanding is commensurate with letting go of the unnecessary; assumptions, beliefs and conclusions. Letting go just happens by itself as we rest in the real, because in any journey, particularly one into the 'now', it is imperative to travel lightly!

Experiencing what is unknowable to thought is to discover an intimacy that we are lived by *the immensity of a numinous universe.*

> *Invisible, indivisible, unspeakable radiance we hold.*
> —Kavisha Mazzella

REFERENCES

1. F Caplow, and S Moon. *The Hidden Lamp: Stories from Twenty-five Centuries of Awakened Women.* Wisdom Publications, 2013

2. Clarke, David, and Eric Clarke eds. *Music and Consciousness: Philosophical, Psychological, and Cultural Perspectives.* Oxford University Press, 2011

3. Blake, William. *The Marriage of Heaven and Hell. Vol. 321.* Oxford University Press, USA, 1975.

4. Thich, Nhat Hanh. *The Heart of the Buddha's Teaching.* Parallax Press, 1998, p124

5. Lee, Bruce and Žarko Modrić. *Tao of Jeet Kune Do.* Texas: Ohara Publications, 1975

6. Pascal, Blaise and Ernest Havet, *Pensées.* Dezobry et E. Magdeleine, 1852

7. Whitehead, Alfred North, David Ray Griffin, and Donald W. Sherburne. *Process and Reality: An Essay in Cosmology.* Cambridge: University Press, 1929

8. Pine, Red, and Mike O'Connor, eds. *The clouds should know me by now: Buddhist poet monks of China.* Simon and Schuster, 1999

9. Ashtavakra, and Nalin N. Nyas. *Ashtavakra Gita: Sakshibhanum* satya. Pravin, 2000

10. Frankl, Viktor E. *Man's Search for Meaning.* Simon and Schuster, 1985

11. *Abide as the Self – The Essential Teachings.* Directed by Salzman, Bertram W. Inner Directions, 1998

12. Maharaj, Nisargadatta. *I Am That, Volume I.* Bombay: Chetana, 1978

13. Ashtavakra, and Nalin N. Nyas. *Ashtavakra Gita: Sakshibhanum satya.* Pravin, 2000

14. Clarke, Richard B. *Hsin Hsin Ming: Verses on the Faith Mind.* Eric Putkonen, 1974

15. Sutta Nipata is a Buddhist scripture in the Khuddaka " Nikaya, part of the Pali Canon of Theravada Buddhism.

16. Kierkegaard, Søren. *Kierkegaard's Writings, VII: Philosophical Fragments, or a Fragment of Philosophy/Johannes Climacus, or De omnibus dubitandum est.* Vol. 7. Princeton University Press, 2013

17. Leitch, Donovan. *There is a Mountain* from album *Sand and Foam.* USA: CBS Studios, 1967

18. *Açvaghosha's Discourse on the Awakening of Faith in the Mahâyâna.* Jain Publishing Company, 2001.

19. Ashtavakra, and Nalin N. Nyas. *Ashtavakra Gita: Sakshibhanum satya.* Pravin, 2000

20. Beauregard, Mario, Gary E. Schwartz, Lisa Miller, Larry Dossey, Alexander Moreira-Almeida, Marilyn Schlitz, Rupert Sheldrake, and Charles Tart. "Manifesto for a post-materialist science." Explore: The Journal of Science and Healing 10, no. 5, 2014: 272-274.

21. Whitman, Walt. *Song of Myself.* Routledge, 2013

22. Davies, Paul, and John Gribbin. *The Matter Myth: Dramatic discoveries that challenge our understanding of physical reality.* Simon & Schuster, 1991

23. Musser, George. "Einstein's assertion that God does not play dice with the universe has been misinterpreted" Scientific American September, 2015. Accessed 1st June, 2017. http://web.mit.edu/asf/www/Press/Musser_Scientific_American_2015.pdf

24. Quoted in Musser, George, "Einstein's assertion that God does not play dice with the universe has been misinterpreted" *Scientific American* September, 2015. Accessed 1st June, 2017. http://web.mit.edu/asf/www/Press/Musser_Scientific_American_2015.pdf

25. Crichton, Michael. *Jurassic Park*. Vol 1. Alfred A Knopf, 1990

26. Quoted in T. R. V. Murti. *The Central Philosophy of Buddhism*. Munshiram Manoharlal Publishers, 2003: p138

27. Rumi, Jalaluddin. *The Essential Rumi, translated by Coleman Barks*. Harper, San Francisco,1995

28. Conger, George. *Whitehead lecture notes: Seminary in Logic: Logical and Metaphysical Problems*. Manuscripts and Archives, Yale University, New Haven, Connecticut, 1927

29. Einstein, Albert, Boris Podolsky, and Nathan Rosen. "Can quantum-mechanical description of physical reality be considered complete?" *Physical Review* 47, no. 10, 1935: p777

30. Wolchover, Natalie. "Time's Arrow Traced to Quantum Source." *Quanta Magazine*, June 24, 2014

31. Hardesty, L. "Fluid mechanics suggests alternative to quantum orthodoxy." September 12, 2014. Accessed September 19, 2015, from http://news.mit.edu/2014/fluid-systems-quantum-mechanics-0912

32. Rovelli, Carlo. *Reality is not what it seems: The journey to quantum gravity*. Penguin, 2017: p 118

33. Herbert, Nick. *Quantum reality: Beyond the new physics*. Anchor Books, 1987: p 194

34. Trimmer, John D. "The present situation in quantum mechanics: A translation of Schrödinger's" Cat Paradox" paper." *Proceedings of the American Philosophical Society*, 1980: pp 323-338

35. Keepin, Will. "Lifework of David Bohm – A River of Truth". *ReVision*, Summer 1993

36. Wigner, Eugene P. "Remarks on the mind-body problem." (1961). Quoted in Wheeler, John Archibald, and Wojciech Hubert Zurek, eds. Quantum Theory and Measurement, Princeton University Press, 1983 p.169

37. Wilber, Ken. "The holographic paradigm and other paradoxes: Exploring the leading edge of science. Shambala, 1982: p 217-218

38. Schrodinger, W. Moore, and P. K. Hoch. "Life and thought." 1994: p 173

39. Oberhaus, Daniel. "Dalai Lama: Religion Without Quantum Physics Is an Incomplete Picture of Reality". *Motherboard*, 17th November, 2015. Accessed 2nd August 2017. https://motherboard.vice.com/en_us/article/8q89x4/dalai-lama-religion-without-quantum-physics-is-an-incomplete-picture-of-reality

40. Quoted in Brown, David Jay. *Mavericks of the Mind and Voices from the Edge*, November 15th, 2011. Accessed 2nd December, 2017. http://mavericksofthemind.com/nick-herbert

41. Brooks, M. "Seven Wonders of the Quantum World". New Scientist, May 5th, 2010. Retrieved from https://www.newscientist.com/article/mg20627596-000-seven-wonders-of-the-quantum-world/

42. Peat, David and Briggs, John. "Exclusive Interview: David Bohm". *Omni*, January 1987. Accessed 1st June, 2017. http://www.fdavidpeat.com/interviews/bohm.htm

43. Keepin, Will. "Lifework of David Bohm – A River of Truth." *ReVision*. Summer 1993

44. Roberts, Thad, quoted in "Why don't more physicists subscribe to pilot wave theory?" *Quora*, March 15, 2017. Accessed 1st June, 2017 https://www.quora.com/Why-dont-more-physicists-subscribe-to-pilot-wave-theory

45. Bohm, David, and F. David Peat. "Science, order, and creativity: A dramatic new look at the creative roots of science and life." New York: Bantam, 1987

46. Bohm, David. Wholeness and the implicate order. London: Routledge, 1981

47. Bohm, David, and F. David Peat. "Science, order, and creativity: A dramatic new look at the creative roots of science and life." New York: Bantam, 1987

48. Agarwal, M. K. *From Bharata to India: Chrysee the Golden*. iUniverse, 2012

49. Nichol, Lee. *The Essential David Bohm*. London: Routledge, 2003

50. Keepin, Will. "Lifework of David Bohm – A River of Truth." *ReVision*. Summer 1993

51. Carroll, Sean. *The Particle at the End of the Universe*. Oneworld Publications, 2012

52. Haramein, Nassim. Comment on Twitter, 7:30 p.m., 10th May, 2014. Accessed 1st June, 2017. https://twitter.com/nassimharamein/status/465317900509667328

53. Clarke, Robert H. Quoted in "Bernardo Kastrup's Metaphysical Speculations: Grokking the Hard Problem of Consciousness." *Bernardo Kastrup's Metaphysical Speculations*. Last modified July 27, 2014. http://www.bernardokastrup.com/2014/07/grokking-hard-problem-of-consciousness.html.

54. Bernardo, Kastrup. "Bernardo Kastrup's Metaphysical Speculations: The Magic Trick of Disappearing Consciousness." *Bernardo Kastrup's Metaphysical Speculations*. Last modified September 15, 2014. http://www.bernardokastrup.com/2014/09/the-magical-trick-of-disappearing.html.

55. Clarke, Robert H. Cited in "Bernardo Kastrup's Metaphysical Speculations: Grokking the Hard Problem of Consciousness." *Bernardo Kastrup's Metaphysical Speculations*. Last modified July 27, 2014. http://www.bernardokastrup.com/2014/07/grokking-hard-problem-of-consciousness.html.

56. Wikipedia. Accessed December 2, 2017. https://en.wikipedia.org/wiki/Time

57. Evans, Doug. "Solving the eternal mystery that is time". *New Scientist*, issue 2941, November 2013: p 35

58. Barbour, Julian. *The End of Time: The Next Revolution in Physics*. Oxford University Press, 1999

59. Billings, Lee. "Two Futures Can Explain Time's Mysterious Past," *Scientific American*, December 8, 2014. Accessed June 6, 2017, https://www.scientificamerican.com/article/2-futures-can-explain-time-s-mysterious-past/

60. Cited by Finkel, Elizabeth. "Interview with a Physicist". *Cosmos*, Feb 12th 2013

61. Cited in Leinhard, John H. "Engines of Our Ingenuity". Podcast: Episode 1952. *Constants of Nature*. Accessed October 8. http://www.uh.edu/engines/epi1952.htm.

62. Ibid

63. Lucretius. First century BC. *De Rerum Natura*. Set in English verse by A. D. Winspear. Harbor Press, New York, 1956, p. 22

64. Ramana Maharshi, cited in Osborne, Arthur. *The teachings of Ramana Maharshi*. Random House, 2014

65. Madhyamika Karika Vrtti, cited in T.R. V. Murti. *The Central Philosophy of Buddhism*. Routledge 2008, p 158

66. Legge, James. "The texts of Taoism: Two volumes" The T'ao Shong Tractate, 1891

67. Blake, William, Lillian Frost, James Guthrie, and S. J. Housley. *Auguries of Innocence*. Taurus Press, 1970

68. National Centre for Biotechnology Information. "N,N-Dimethyltryptamine" Accessed June 7, 2017, https://www.ncbi.nlm.nih.gov/mesh/68004130

69. Bedrij, Orest. *Living Your Divine Life: Experience God's Glory, Absolute Happiness, and Great Prosperity*. Xlibris Corporation, 2009

70. Watts, Alan. *The Way of Zen*. Pantheon Books, 1957

71. Jung, Carl Gustav. *Collected Works of CG Jung. Volume 6: Psychological Types*. Princeton University Press, 2014: par.757

72. Dawkins, Richard. *The God Delusion*. London: Bantam, 2006. p 51

73. Case, Zenko. *Despite Fear: A Visceral Plight*. Ebook Edition. Lulu Publishing Services, 2016

74. Jung, Carl, R. F. C. Hull, and W. Pauli. "The Interpretation of Nature and the Psyche: Synchronicity an Acausal Connecting Principle." 1959

75. Mastin, Luke. "Spin and the Pauli Exclusion Principle". *The Physics of the Universe*. Accessed June 7, 2017. http://www.physicsoftheuniverse.com/topics_quantum_spin.html

76. Briskin, Alan. "Translating Meaning into Life: A Taoist Parable". *Huffington Post*, May 18, 2016. Accessed August 2, 2017. http://www.huffingtonpost.com/alan-briskin/a-taoist-parable_b_10007270.html

77. Jung, Carl Gustav. "Psychology and alchemy. Collected works of CG Jung." Volume 12, 1968

78. Jung, Carl Gustav. "The Psychology of Kundalini Yoga, Lecture 2, 19 October 1932". *Notes of the Seminar*, Princeton University Press, USA, 1996

79. Hoeller, Stephen. "C. G. Jung and the Alchemical Renewal." *Gnosis: A Journal of Western Inner Traditions*. Vol. 8, Summer 1988

80. Ibid

81. Jung, Carl Gustav. "The Psychology of Kundalini Yoga, Lecture 2, 19 October 1932" Notes of the Seminar, Princeton University Press, USA, 1996, p 27

82. Brawley, Louis. *No More Questions: The Final Travels of UG Krishnamurti*. Penguin UK, 2012

83. Campbell, Joseph. *The Power of Myth*. New York, Doubleday, 1991: p 73

84. Volckmann, Russ. "6/26 Language and Thought: An Interview with Lera Boroditsky". Integral Publishers, April-June, 2014. Accessed August 2, 2017. http://integralleadershipreview.com/11523-language-thought-interview-lera-boroditsky/

85. Deutscher, Guy. "Does Your Language Shape How You Think?" New York Times, August 2, 2010. Accessed August 2, 2017. http://www.nytimes.com/2010/08/29/magazine/29language-t.html

86. Jain-Hamall, Doe. "Native American and Euro-American Cultures: A Comparative Look at the Interaction Between Language and Worldview." *Multicultural Education 21, no. 1*, December 2013: pp 13-19.

87. Alford, Dan Moonhawk. "Nurturing a faint call in the blood: a linguist encounters languages of ancient America." *ReVision 25, no. 2*, 2002: pp 23-34

88. Ibid

89. Peat, F. David. *Blackfoot Physics*. Weiser Books, Boston, 2002

90. Hain-Jamall, Doe. "Native-American & Euro-American cultures: A comparative look at the intersection between language & worldview." *Multicultural Education 21, no. 1*, December 2013: p 13

91. Alford, Dan Moonhawk. "Nurturing a faint call in the blood: a linguist encounters languages of ancient America." *ReVision 25, no. 2*, 2002: pp 23-34

92. Peat, F. David, and Simon Alev. "Look for Truth - No Matter Where It Takes You." *What is Enlightenment?* Spring 1997. Accessed at http://www.fdavidpeat.com/interviews/wie.htm

93. Zukav, Gary. *The Dancing Wu Li Masters*. London: Fontana, 1979

94. Xiaolu Guo, "Is this what the west is really like? How it felt to leave China for Britain". *The Guardian*, January 10, 2017. Accessed June 8, 2017 https://www.theguardian.com/world/2017/jan/10/xiaolu-guo-why-i-moved-from-beijing-to-london

95. Ananthaswamy, Anil. "Time flows uphill for remote Papua New Guinea tribe". *The Guardian*, May 30, 2012. Accessed June 8, 2017. https://www.newscientist.com/article/mg21428675.400-time-flows-uphill-for-remote-papua-new-guinea-tribe/

96. Everett, Daniel L. "Recursion and human thought: Why the Pirahã don't have numbers." *Edge: The third culture* 213, 2007

97. Deutscher, Guy. "Does your language shape what you think?" *New York Times*, August 29, 2010

98. Ibid

99. Peat, F. David, and Simon Alev. "Look for Truth - No Matter Where It Takes You." *"What is Enlightenment?"* Spring 1997. Accessed at http://www.fdavidpeat.com/interviews/wie.htm

100. Bohm, David. *Wholeness and the Implicate Order*. London, 1980: p 27

101. Ibid

102 Peat, F. David. *Blackfoot Physics*. Weiser Books, Boston, 2002

103. Whitman, Walt. *Song of myself*. Courier Corporation, 2001

104. Cited in Oddie, Geoffrey A. *Religious Traditions in South Asia: Interaction and Change*. Psychology Press, 1998

105. Maharaj, Sri Nisargadatta. *I Am That: Talks with Sri Nisargadata Maharaj (1973)*. Trans. Maurice Frydman. Ed. Sudhakar S. Dikshit. Durham, North Carolina: The Acorn Press, 1988: p 71

106. Maharshi, Ramana. Be as You Are: *The teachings of Sri Ramana Maharshi*. Edited by Godman, David. Arkana Press, 1985

107. Fung, Yu-lan. *A Short History of Chinese Philosophy*. Simon and Schuster, 1997

108. Cited in Watts, Alan (with Al Chung-Liang Huang). *Tao: The Watercourse Way*, 1975. p 38

109. Cited in ibid, p 41

110. Walsh, Roger, ed. *The World's Great Wisdom: Timeless Teachings from Religions and Philosophies*. SUNY Press, 2014

111. Cited in Needham, *Joseph. Science and Civilization in China. Vol. 1: Introductory Orientations*. 1954

112. Cited in Liping, Yang. *The Tao Inspiration: Essence of Lao Zi's Wisdom*. Asiapac Books, 2005

113. Cited in Legge, James. *The Texts of Taoism. Vol. 1*. Courier Corporation, 1962

114. Schoeberl, Ansgar. *The Gift of Abhyasa*, Books on Demand: Norderstedt, Germany, 2013

115. Welter, Albert. "The Disputed Place of 'A Special Transmission' Outside the Scriptures in Ch'an". Ch'an Meditation Center, Institute of Chung-Hwa Buddhist Culture, 1996. Accessed December 2, 2017 http://www.thezensite.com/ZenEssays/HistoricalZen/A_Special_Transmission.htm

116. Schiller, David. *The Little Zen Companion*. Workman Publishing Company, 1994

117. Wikipedia. Accessed December 2, 2017 https://en.wikipedia.org/wiki/Perennial_philosophy

118. Cited in Waller, Dennis. *Tao Te Ching: Lao Tzu, A Translation*. CreateSpace Independent Publishing Platform, 2012. Accessed February 1, 2016 http://www.returnofkings.com/15711/24-pieces-of-wisdom-from-lao-tzu. .

119. Ancient Huna. "What is Huna? Basic Huna Ho'oponopono". Accessed June 23, 2017 http://www.ancienthuna.com/ho-oponopono.htm

120. Kramer, Joel, and Diana Alstad. *The Guru Papers: Masks of Authoritarian Power*. Frog Books, 1993

121. Rao, Mukunda. "The Search, the Calamity and the Birth of a New Human Being: A Life Sketch of U.G. Krishnamurti". An extract from *The Penguin U.G.Krishnamurti Reader*, edited by Mukunda Rao. Penguin Books India, 2007. Accessed from http://www.ugkrishnamurti.org/ug/mukund-rao/ p 8.

122. Ibid, p 76

123. Krishna, Gopi. *Kundalini: The Evolutionary Energy in Man*. 1967

124. Ibid

125. Cited in Tagore, Rabindranath. *One hundred poems of Kabir*. Orient Blackswan, 2004

126. Cited in Dikshit, Sudhakar S., ed. *I Am That: Talks with Sri Nisargadatta Maharaj*. Acorn Press, 2009

127. Sojun, Ikkyu. *Wild Ways: Zen Poems of Ikkyu (Companions for the Journey)*. Poem translated by John Stevens. White Wine Press, 2007

128. Maharaj, Sri Nisargadatta. *I Am That*. Acorn Press, 2008: p. 250

129. Cited in Papacostas, Savvas. "Madness and Leadership: From Antiquity to the New Common Era." Edward Elgar Publishing, 2015

www.ingramcontent.com/pod-product-compliance
Lightning Source LLC
Chambersburg PA
CBHW082102250426
43661CB00079B/2561